Narrative and the Politics of Identity

Narrative and the Politics of Identity

The Cultural Psychology of Israeli and Palestinian Youth

PHILLIP L. HAMMACK

OXFORD

UNIVERSITY PRESS

2011

OXFORD
UNIVERSITY PRESS

Oxford University Press, Inc., publishes works that further
Oxford University's objective of excellence
in research, scholarship, and education.

Oxford New York
Auckland   Cape Town   Dar es Salaam   Hong Kong   Karachi
Kuala Lumpur   Madrid   Melbourne   Mexico City   Nairobi
New Delhi   Shanghai   Taipei   Toronto

With offices in
Argentina   Austria   Brazil   Chile   Czech Republic   France   Greece
Guatemala   Hungary   Italy   Japan   Poland   Portugal   Singapore
South Korea   Switzerland   Thailand   Turkey   Ukraine   Vietnam

Copyright © 2011 by Oxford University Press, Inc.

Published by Oxford University Press, Inc.
198 Madison Avenue, New York, New York 10016
www.oup.com

Oxford is a registered trademark of Oxford University Press, Inc.

Library of Congress Cataloging-in-Publication Data

Hammack, Phillip L.
Narrative and the politics of identity : the cultural psychology of Israeli
and Palestinian youth / Phillip L. Hammack.
   p. cm.
Includes bibliographical references and index.
ISBN 978-0-19-539446-7
1. Youth—Israel—Attitudes.   2. Youth—Palestine—Attitudes.
3. Identity (Psychology)—Israel.   4. Identity (Psychology)—Palestine.   I. Title.
HQ799.I75H36 2010
305.235095694—dc22   2010009155

9 8 7 6 5 4 3 2 1
Printed in the United States of America
on acid-free paper

To the memory of my father, P. Larry Hammack
(1942–2009), for modeling generativity

Preface

Writing a book about the Israeli–Palestinian conflict is a complex endeavor for any number of reasons. First, one must acknowledge the purely *physical* challenges of travel in a war zone: the logistical complexities of navigating a place of highly polarized identity politics, a place at which one is interrogated at almost every moment, along with the financial cost of this complex navigation. For making my travels to Israel and Palestine all too easy, I must acknowledge the generous guidance of my Israeli and Palestinian colleagues: Amal Eqeiq, Abigail Jacobson, Rami Mehdawi, and Razan Makhlouf, among others. There are, of course, numerous Israeli and Palestinian families to also thank for their generous hospitality to a "stranger." The customs of research ethics require that these families and my interviewees all remain unnamed. While it is painful not to acknowledge them by name, I recognize the need to keep their true identities a mystery, for they shared so many of their innermost thoughts and feelings with me on history, politics, and identity. For making me feel so safe and welcome, my "second families" in Israel and Palestine deserve special recognition.

A study of Israeli and Palestinian youth of such an intimate design also necessitates considerable financial support, and I am most grateful for the funding provided by the United States Institute of Peace and the Spencer Foundation for the research. I also acknowledge the support of the Alfred P. Sloan Foundation for their support during my time at the National Opinion Research Center (NORC) at the University of Chicago. The Division of the Social Sciences at the University of Chicago and the Committee on Research at the University of California, Santa Cruz, also provided essential financial support for the study at various stages. At Seeds of Peace, I acknowledge the support of the Evaluation Committee, especially Bill Taylor and Marieke von Woerkom, to conduct the research. Finally, I acknowledge the generosity of Gretchen Grad and the Steering Committee of Hands of Peace, for not only supporting the research in word but also supporting much of my travel to the region.

A book on Israeli and Palestinian youth by a young scholar could be considered a great risk, not solely for the politics of the academy but also for the intellectual complexity of the issue. I conducted the research described in this book because I firmly believe in the need for a psychological approach to young Israeli and Palestinian lives that can provide a context for *transformative voice* (Sampson, 1993)—an opportunity to listen to youth narrate their tragedies and triumphs as they muddle through the murky waters of war. Rather than make assumptions about historical and cultural forces that maintain conflict—forces like *narrative*—I was determined to query the process of youth identity development through a lens that could facilitate both *individual psychological* and *social structural* analysis. In so doing, I develop an audacious argument about culture, identity, and peace. For me, the risk is worthwhile if it facilitates our confrontation with challenging new knowledge—knowledge generated from the voices of young Palestinians and Israelis. I can hope for nothing more than a conversation about peace, social justice, and the politics of identity as a consequence of this book. Immodestly, I believe that the analysis I present in this book has the potential to open up new conversations across disciplines in the social sciences—conversations that might help us move toward a more transformative model of knowledge production.

I could not have developed the arguments I make in the book were it not for some major architects of my intellect. For their unconditional intellectual guidance and support, as well as their critical commentary, I am particularly indebted to Bert Cohler, Rick Shweder, Dan P. McAdams, Barbara Schneider, and friends and colleagues in the Department of Comparative Human Development at the University of Chicago. Much of my thinking evolved in conversations at Chicago with friends, teachers, and colleagues, including Matthew Bird, Lara Braff, Julia Cassaniti, Bambi Chapin, Jennifer Cole, Amy Cooper, Bianca Dahl, John Davy, Johanne Eliacin, Bill Goldstein, Drew Guest,

Cage Hall, Jen Hanis-Martin, Pinky Hota, Jason Ingersoll, Mike Kaufman, Rashid Khalidi, John Lucy, Tanya Luhrmann, Neely Myers, Christine Nutter, Shira Offer, Lara Perez-Felkner, Barnaby Riedel, Lilah Shapiro, Ben Smith, Gabe Smith, Ronald Suny, Richard Taub, Greg Thompson, Linda Waite, Bernard Wasserstein, Jason Yee, and others whom I have likely neglected to mention.

At the University of California, Santa Cruz, I must acknowledge the numerous colleagues who have contributed to the development of my thinking on this project as it has continued to evolve: Margarita Azmitia, Catherine Cooper, Per Gjerde, Craig Haney, Aída Hurtado, Regina Langhout, Andrew Pilecki, Barbara Rogoff, M. Brewster Smith, Avril Thorne, and members of the Narrative Identity Research Group (NIRG). Many other colleagues at Santa Cruz deserve recognition for their friendship, support, and guidance: Nameera Akhtar, Mark Anderson, Heather Bullock, Maureen Callanan, Marty Chemers, Faye Crosby, Ray Gibbs, Shelly Grabe, Cam Leaper, Dean Mathiowetz, Marcia Ochoa, Tom Pettigrew, Travis Seymour, Megan Thomas, Su-hua Wang, Aaronette White, Meg Wilson, and Eileen Zurbriggen.

The book has also benefited greatly from the counsel of other scholars beyond the neo-Gothic quadrangles of Chicago and the redwoods of Santa Cruz: Glenn Adams, Jeff Arnett, Danny Bar-Tal, Brian Barber, Zvi Bekerman, Julia Chaitin, Michelle Fine, Tony Gallagher, Eran Halperin, Jennifer Hammer, Lene Jensen, Ruthellen Josselson, Herbert Kelman, Jim Lamiell, Ned Lazarus, Ifat Maoz, Hazel Markus, Claire McGlynn, Kate McLean, Fathali Moghaddam, Nimrod Rosler, T. S. Saraswathi, Elli Schachter, Brian Schiff, Michalinos Zembylas, and many other valuable friends and colleagues.

I had the good fortune to present the ideas developed in this book in a number of stimulating professional settings over the years. In addition to several presentations at the University of Chicago and the University of California, Santa Cruz, responses to presentations at several other universities (including Georgetown University, Northwestern University, Stanford University, Queen's University Belfast, University of Notre Dame, and the Graduate Center at the City University of New York) and at several professional meetings across the globe (including in the United States, Israel, Bosnia-Herzegovina, Ireland, Germany, France, and Turkey), have provided me with valuable opportunities to clarify and refine my arguments. Audiences at these various venues typically transcended both national and disciplinary boundaries, which afforded me the rare chance to engage with colleagues from a diversity of paradigms, theories, methods, and political and intellectual worldviews.

Modified versions of some of the chapters in this book have appeared in scholarly articles and book chapters. An earlier version of Chapter 3 was published in *Peace and Conflict: Journal of Peace Psychology* in 2009. An earlier version of Chapter 4 was published in *Culture & Psychology* in 2010. Finally, an earlier version of Chapter 5 was published in the *International Journal of Intercultural Relations* in 2010. Some material contained in Chapter 7 was published in 2006 in the *Journal of Adolescent Research*, and an earlier form of the arguments I develop in Chapters 7 and 8 was published in a book chapter in the volume *Peace Education in Conflict and Post-Conflict Societies: Comparative Perspectives* (Palgrave Macmillan, 2009). Though some of the material from the book has been published in a number of outlets, the book represents a new synthesis of my ideas and an integrative approach to the analysis of my narrative data. I recognize and greatly value the feedback I have received from editors and anonymous reviewers of these outlets over the years.

Some of my closest colleagues in group facilitation deserve special recognition, for our many conversations have greatly contributed to my analysis and interpretation of Israeli–Palestinian contact: Manal Al Tamimi, Abigail Jacobson, Liz Shulman, Scott Silk, Husam Jubran, Hatem Darawashi, and Bill Taylor. Liz Shulman also carefully read a final version of the book and provided me with extremely useful comments, for which I am most grateful.

This book would have been impossible were it not for the support of several research assistants who transcribed my interviews: Brian Lobel, Alex Strauss, Michael Singh, Yaser Eid, Jerri Skog, Julian Farzan-Kashani, and Aaron Dewey. I am grateful to Andrew Pilecki for his supervision of this important process. Other research assistants who were not directly involved in this particular project have contributed greatly to my thinking on the subject of young Israeli and Palestinian lives, including Neta Caspi, Nicol Ruber, Elena Ricks, and Eric Windell.

It is something of a cliché to deliver magnanimous praise to one's editor and editorial team, but in this case the praise is very much deserved. My editor at Oxford, Lori Handelman, has been incredibly supportive of the book since its origins. She and her thoughtful team have given an author just the right level of guidance and support. I am privileged to work with such a professional editorial team.

I must recognize the support of my family and friends, who did not allow their anxiety for my safety to preclude my ambitions. For his love, trust, and faith in the possibility of my contribution, I owe my gratitude (and much, much more) to Brendan Smith. The inspiration for this work emerged in the context of our relationship, and he can undoubtedly be credited for awakening within me a passion for international politics. In addition to his constant support and encouragement, Brendan provided me with a valuable early education on the Israeli–Palestinian conflict and continues to inform me on political and economic issues related to the region. He also carefully read the final version of the book and offered essential critical feedback. I regret that, despite his great interest in the region, Brendan did not accompany me during any of my field trips.

Other family and friends deserve recognition for their emotional support during my years of fieldwork, particularly Joe Radtke, Liz Shulman, Tim Bechtel, Scott Everett, Abigail Jacobson, Brian Lobel, Aparna Sharma, Rachel Frailich, Safa Hamed, Hussein Zaghal, Nicole and Ted Foley, Josephine and Greg Firehock, Meagan Coleman, Angelica Hammack Meade, Don and Ruth Smith, Aimee and Michael Munnelly, Dan Smith, Sherman and Paula Hammack, Michelle Smith, John and Lina Linarelli, Dave Frech, Deborah Friedman, Ethan McKittrick, Rebecca Bronheim, Jason Yee, Greg Carroll, Beth Marco, Emily Edlynn, Charlotte Ford, Katy Jacob, Gabe Steritt, and others. Members of my more recent community in San Francisco deserve recognition for keeping my life in balance during the writing of this book, including Christian Holden, Dominic Levasseur, Malcolm McQuirter, Mark Mendenhall, Vik Singh, Peter and Andrea Hendricks, Austin Phillips, Mike Hastings, Petrus Phoa, Mark Wiesen, David Johnson, Jonathan McNarry, J.D. Thomas, Rob Raasch, Jim Romer, and Salvador Flores, among many others.

Finally, the unconditional support of my parents, Larry and Cathy Hammack, deserves recognition. Their encouragement and pride in my accomplishments have always been a source of great satisfaction for me, and I am indebted to them for making this project possible by ensuring, throughout my life, the nurturing of my intellect. I believe that I acquired, through their mutual influence, a unique interest in fusing science and artistry, philosophical idealism and practical realism. I deeply regret that my father did not live to see this book in print, but his influence is central to the project, for it is his model of compassion, generosity, and pragmatism that has informed my practice as a social scientist and my own moral code. The legacy of his moral education for me lives through the pages of this text, and I trust that he died knowing of the merits of his investment in me.

Contents

"We ought not to create new distinctions between people; we ought not to raise fresh barriers, we should rather make the old disappear.... Universal brotherhood is not even a beautiful dream. Conflict is essential to man's highest efforts."
—Theodore Herzl (1896/1997), *The Jewish State*, p. 223

"In the social jungle of human existence, there is no feeling of being alive without a sense of identity."
—Erik Erikson (1968), *Identity: Youth and Crisis*, p. 130

PART I

Orientations

A Note on Geographic Terminology

Upon meeting most Palestinians for the first time, many Americans may be surprised by their response to a very basic question: "Where are you from?" The response is invariably "Palestine." I have heard a number of my Palestinian colleagues and research participants indicate that the response of the American—assuming he or she is neither Jewish nor Arab—is typically one of two possibilities. Either the American asks genuinely, as if having simply misheard, "Pakistan?" Or, alternatively, rather quizzically, the American may reply, "Where is Palestine?", recognizing that the geographic term sounds quite familiar and must be *near* Israel, yet somehow still uncertain of its precise location in world geography.

As I will discuss in greater depth throughout this book, the naming of Palestine as a geographic locale is a far more complex issue, particularly when Israelis and Palestinians enter into situations of contact, than may at first appear. The question of the naïve American—"Where is Palestine?"— perhaps offers a precise summary statement of the Israeli– Palestinian conflict itself, as the establishment of actual borders for these two states (one as yet emerging) represents the crux of the problem.

Throughout this book, I have chosen to use the term "Palestine," as opposed to "the Palestinian territories" or more specifically the territories "West Bank" or "East Jerusalem" (whose status as a "Palestinian territory" remains contested in some circles), to refer to those regions internationally recognized as under Israeli military occupation since the Six Day War of 1967, thus falling inside of what is considered the "Green Line." (Territorially, this does indeed include East Jerusalem, the West Bank, and the Gaza Strip.) The use of the word *Palestine* is deliberate in that it legitimizes the Palestinian aspiration of national statehood in these territories (and the recognition by the United Nations and other international bodies that such desire for sovereignty is justified, legitimate, and ultimately necessary for a sustainable peace in the Middle East), the borders of which remain undetermined as of the writing of this book. It is worth noting also that a Palestinian Declaration of Independence was formally proclaimed in November of 1988 (with implied borders that recognized the State of Israel in its pre-1967 form) and that the State of Palestine, though not formally recognized by the United Nations or the United States, is recognized by a significant number of countries, including India, Russia, China, Turkey, and nearly all countries in Africa and the Middle East. (Palestine does indeed have "observer status" at the United Nations, represented by the Palestine Liberation Organization [PLO].)

My use of this geographic term is thus meant to accord equal legitimacy to the two narrative perspectives on the region—that there are indeed "nations" called "Israel" and "Palestine." In my use of this terminology, I refer *very concretely* to the occupied territories *and not to any part of what is internationally recognized by the United Nations as the State of Israel.* I do acknowledge, however, that when Palestinians refer to Palestine they often refer to the British Mandate of Palestine, which includes present-day Israel, to describe the entirety of what *was* Palestine. I will refer to that territory when speaking in historical terms as "Mandate Palestine."

I hope that my decision to use such terminology accords an adequate measure of recognition without the suggestion that I myself am aligned with the ideology of one group over another. In fact, it is my conviction that the use of such terminology ought to possess the opposite effect, securing my status as a legitimate "stranger" in the Holy Land, possessing no aspirations for political expression and simply a documenter of a basic empirical reality: the reality of conflict and its impact on the course of individual lives. It should be clear from this brief note on terminology that I believe my own role in telling this particular story and in selecting a particular lexicon with which to tell it must be transparent. A responsible cultural psychologist is *reflexive* about his own identity in conducting his research. For this reason, I devote considerable attention in Chapter 2 to the issue of reflexivity about my role as a social scientist in a contentious zone of conflict for which I, in fact, possessed remarkably few preconceptions, but to which I, of course, came to feel deeply connected.

Prologue

I awake to the sounds of roosters and cows rising above the remote-controlled air conditioning unit somehow affixed in the top corner of the wall in Daniel's[1] room. As is the case in almost all of the families who graciously host me, Daniel has given up his room for me. Even in situations where a bedroom has two beds, as is the case in Mohammed's room in East Jerusalem, I am typically given my own room with complete privacy. Such is the common custom of both Israelis and Palestinians in the realm of hospitality. "Hospitality is part of our culture," as many Palestinians have said to me, as if, to my horror, I have failed to cloak my surprise as the stereotypes I have of Palestinians disintegrate, and my Palestinian friend, subject, or colleague feels obligated to suggest that perhaps the image of "Palestinian as terrorist" is not completely authentic.

This morning, though, I am in Israel, in the home of a Jewish-Israeli family living on a *moshav*, a cooperative farming community in which, unlike the socialist *kibbutz*, families retain their own income and children are not reared apart from the family. As I arrived in their home on a prior trip 6 months earlier, it was the eve of the Palestinian election in the wake of

---

1 The names of all individuals (research participants, their family members, and most of my colleagues) appear as pseudonyms.

Yasser Arafat's unexpected death, and I had only just arrived from a week deep in the heart of the West Bank. Daniel's father, a sharp and foreboding man, exceedingly masculine in the fashion of the Israeli "warrior"—the face of a new Jewish identity as Fighter—asked me the requisite probing questions I receive as I traverse between these two entirely disparate worlds with the speed of a rat furiously trying to find his way out of the maze. He was sizing me up, of course, trying to get a picture of me and where I stand on the conflict, in not-so-indirect ways. Over time, I realize I have satisfied his need for trust and security in whatever of my own identity I have communicated through my somewhat cautious replies to his queries. It is an experience I have come to expect, and it is the source of considerable exhaustion as I visit with families at the end of sometimes excruciatingly long days of travel throughout the region.

This morning I am too cold, having unsuccessfully tried to maneuver the air conditioner in the middle of the night. But I am also haunted by a horrible dream that I recorded immediately into my field diary, beside me in bed, the ink on yesterday's notes still fresh:

> I am standing at a checkpoint. Suddenly I see a young man I didn't recognize, bearded, wrapped in a *kafiya*[2], running toward us. He is strapped with explosives and detonates them as he arrives. In a moment of terrible panic, I run from the checkpoint but can get no more than a few steps. He detonates, but nothing happens. We are all suddenly frozen in space and time.

It is my third trip to the region, and the *intifada* continues. But my dream is primed not by my everyday experience, during which I allow denial and rationalization to overpower the fear and anxiety I might experience spending any time at all in this region. (The use of these defense mechanisms suggests there is a part of me that has adopted the preferred coping method of most Israelis during this latest rise of violence.) My dream, rather, is primed by the last evening I spent with Gal, one of my research participants, and his father, Eli, on their nearby kibbutz.

In narrating his life story the night before my dream, Gal, a 15-year-old Jewish boy with a tall, lanky frame and somewhat absent-minded disposition, referred to the day he and his father witnessed a suicide bombing on a bus they were traveling just behind. His method of "casual insertion" of the incident into his life story nearly caused me to leap out of my seat, as few of the youths

---

2 The *kafiya* is the black and white head covering symbolic of Palestinian nationalism. It resided famously on Yasser Arafat's head throughout his life. Though it is almost never worn by young Palestinian men in this same fashion, it is typically worn around the shoulders or, in smaller form, as a scarf.

I have come to interview have flirted so closely with disaster. Yet, for now, I retained my composure and prompted Gal to tell me about his experience in detail. To hear him tell the story, no matter how deeply I probed, was to absorb some thickly repressed experiential collage, in which he recalled almost nothing except the nearby restaurant where his father instructed him to take refuge as he went to the aid of victims. No doubt such a recollection was tied to a posttraumatic reaction in which Gal had "stored" parts of the memory out of his immediate consciousness. I had the good fortune of spending the evening with Gal and his father, Eli, an amiable, intelligent, and pragmatic chainsmoker whose face itself narrated a particular story, with its deeply cut lines. In the typical light Israeli dinner, Eli prepared a salad of tomatoes, cucumbers, and onions with olive oil, bread, and omelets for each of us.

"So how was Gal in the interview?" he asked, as virtually all parents ask of me following an interview, wanting to ensure that their child has proven himself or herself a worthy repository of interesting data. I was generally disappointed with the interview, mainly because Gal was the kind of adolescent boy who seemed to have minimal desire to integrate his life experiences into a coherent narrative, as if he were not quite ready for the emotional and cognitive challenge that such an act entails. Thus, our interview was not as rich as I would like, but, of course, I could not share this impression with his father and instead practiced the skill of "protective fabrication" that my work in this part of the world has come to command—out of a need for safety more than mere politeness.

"He told you the story of the suicide bombing, right?"

I assured him he had, though of course I was curious to hear Eli's version of the same event. Fortunately, I did not even need to ask for it.

We were driving in our car in front of a bus when suddenly the explosion happened. We thought it was a flat tire or something. I got out of the car and saw the shrapnel. Then I realized what had happened. It was like a scene out of hell. There were bodies everywhere. I had Gal run to a nearby restaurant, to get out of the place. I went on the bus and saw what happened. I couldn't resist. It's strange, I guess, but I had to see. I now know what it looks like in hell. I'll never forget that experience.

Eli's description and Gal's posttraumatic memory lapse replay in my mind as I lay in bed that cold morning on the moshav, the sound of cows and chickens clearly audible as they awaken from their own slumbers. Having wandered safely and without significant concern throughout the region, and having interviewed few Jewish-Israeli youths whose life stories contained such close encounters as Gal's, I suppose I had become a bit complacent psychologically.

All of that had changed by this morning, and the vivid imagery of my night-mare at the checkpoint haunted me as I prepared to face my host family on this, my final morning with them.

After Daniel's mother prepares me a miniature version of the Israeli breakfast—an omelet, a light salad of tomato and cucumber, delicious yogurt and cheese made on the moshav, bread, and a cup of Nescafé—we head to the bus station where I am to take a coach bus to Netanya to meet a colleague. Our goodbyes are not filled with strong sentiments. Unlike with Daniel's father, I feel I have failed to win the approval of his mother. Her constant quizzing of my research and its intentions reveals a level of anxiety in her, perhaps enhanced by my "outsider," non-Jewish identity. But I despise emotional good-byes anyway, and so am perfectly comfortable with our icy parting.

I generally avoid the inner-city buses of Tel Aviv, Haifa, and Jerusalem, which have been the main targets of suicide bombers during the second Palestinian *intifada*. But coach buses, I rationalize, have never been a target, and Daniel's mother insists this bus is the best means of transit to Netanya. But this morning I feel particularly ill at ease to make the trip. I disguise my reluctance, though, and make my way into the station.

I enter the bus station through a makeshift metal detector, monitored by a security guard who looks the part. I undergo a highly cursory search, even though I have multiple pieces of luggage. The guard has detected my American accent, and therefore I fail to fit the right "profile" for a would-be bomber. After a 30-minute wait for the right bus, I board, choosing to sit near the front. As each person boards, I look at each carefully, sizing them up one by one, trying to discern whether they have the potential to be a bomber. I feel relieved as we leave the station, having decided that none of the passengers seem suf-ficiently "sketchy" to blow themselves up. To my horror, the bus stops 10 min-utes out of the station to pick up more passengers. Another 10 people to size up, and this time they do not all meet my criteria for benign threat. Needless to say, I spend the next hour, including several more unanticipated roadside pick-ups, on the brink of a full-fledged panic attack. It is not a feeling I am used to, but it gives me a clear sense of the experiential possibilities of daily life in Israel—the real dangers of basic existence in a state under constant threat.

Six months earlier, I am in Ramallah, the cosmopolitan Palestinian capital city. I meet up with Khalid at his office. Khalid has become a good friend and colleague of mine, having agreed to host me sight unseen the first time I had come to Ramallah. Though he is in fact my age, he has the appearance of an older, more experienced man, with his stocky build, great height, dark goatee, and receding hairline. We meet at his office just off of the famous Rukab Street, a major thoroughfare in downtown Ramallah named for a celebrated homemade ice cream shop. Walking down the streets of Ramallah with Khalid typically takes about triple the amount of time it would take me walking alone, as he seems to know pretty much every other person on this bustling boulevard and, in Palestinian custom, stops to greet each one of them. He takes me that evening to an engagement party for a friend. Again consistent with custom, the sexes are separated, and only men are present at this party. I spend a good deal of time conversing with Khalid's many friends and acquaintances, including Ibrahim, who I quickly learn is from Jenin.

Though I had never been there, the image of Jenin weighs heavily in my consciousness, as it was the site of a major Israeli incursion during this *intifada* and the subject of a very powerful film called *Arna's Children*. The film chronicles the lives of several young Palestinian boys, from their childhood days in a theater in the refugee camp to their gradual ascendance into the ranks of the Palestinian resistance movement in Jenin. Ultimately, all but two die as "martyrs." It was the first time I really understood the genesis of what some would label a "terrorist," and others, a "freedom fighter."

I ask Ibrahim whether he was in Jenin at the time of the invasion (referred to by Palestinians as "the massacre"). He confesses that he was, and as he does, his eyes water and his whole face grows tense. I realize I should let sleeping dogs lie, and I stop the conversation with an expression of empathy and genuine concern for his family.

As the night comes to an end, Khalid and I seek a ride to his nearby village. It is a cold winter night, bone chilling and very dark. We make our way down the bumpy, poorly maintained road, until we are forced to come to an abrupt stop behind a truck that has suddenly stopped in the middle of the road. I ask Khalid what is happening, as scores of Israeli soldiers come running from the truck, flashing lights into our car, pointing their guns at us, and shouting. "It's a traveling checkpoint," he says. "They just decide they want to set up a checkpoint, and they do it." It is 10:30 at night, the road is quiet, the night is calm. But no longer for me.

I have certainly experienced checkpoints before, time and time again, as I travel throughout Palestine and between Palestine and Israel; they were ubiquitous during the period of my field research. The frustrations of waiting at these checkpoints and dealing with the harsh words of a young Israeli soldier relishing a moment of power have somewhat desensitized me to the experience of the checkpoint. Yet I am not fully prepared for the range of emotions that are about to engulf me.

Khalid tells me in a quiet but confident voice, "They want us to get out of the car." Naturally, we comply, as anyone would do when a gun and bright light are staring them down. Waiting on the sidewalk, I am shaking with a mixture of cold and fear of our unknown fate. I am, after all, in the middle of a war zone—albeit a "low-grade" war that has gone on in some varying degree since long before 1948.

I hear dogs howling in the distance. I look around to the many hills, and the bright lights of the nearby Jewish settlement perched on top of one of them. The sidewalk is accompanied by a major cliff, so there is no escape if we need to. The soldiers will not look me in the eyes. I try to make eye contact. I want to know what they think and feel about all of this, and I want them to see the fear in my eyes, to know I have never been through something like this before. But their eyes never venture anywhere near ours, even when Khalid asks them permission to smoke a cigarette. The eyes will reveal too much of their own stories, I think to myself.

We stand in the cold, in solidarity with others, for an entire hour. My fear subsides, and feelings of helplessness—they could do anything they want to me—and powerlessness emerge. These feelings naturally beget frustration and anger. After an hour, the soldiers return, throw all of our IDs to the ground, again without eye contact, and give us permission to leave. The whole experience leaves me with a great deal of anger and disgust. I can only imagine what kind of impression this leads to among Palestinians over time. At one point as we stood on the sidewalk, Khalid turns to me and says, "Don't worry, this happens all the time."

If indeed Palestinians endure with relative consistency the misery of this experience at the hands of soldiers—in many cases perhaps the only Jews or Israelis that they come into contact with at all—how might the emotional response I had develop in them over time? Despite his reassurance that this kind of thing happens "all the time," and his attempts to display a kind of desensitization and resilience, Khalid tosses and turns throughout the night in the bed next to mine. At one point, he wakes screaming. The next morning, he is off to work as usual, one of the most known, respected, and admired men on the streets of downtown Ramallah, the previous night's experience just one of many encounters with Israeli soldiers that infuse his life story.

These two stories, brief excerpts in the narrative of my encounter with Israel and Palestine, painfully demonstrate the emotional and experiential impact of the conflict on individual lives. A pure "stranger" to the conflict is forced to empathize deeply with both experiences, while readily discerning the stalemate that both kinds of encounters establish. The fear of attack motivates a system of symbolic interactions, rooted in the power imbalance inherent in prolonged military occupation of the "defeated" by the "victor," which serves to instill the frustration, anger, and powerlessness that motivate a desire for "revenge," a need to reverse the relationship. The most educated and insightful among the populace of both groups will readily acknowledge the dynamics of cyclical antagonism these encounters naturally foster, but many continue to justify maintenance of the status quo through a regression to the foolish issue of who made the first move, as if the pernicious conflict could be reduced to a game of chess.

To return for a moment to my own empathy, my inevitable identification—experientially if not always ideologically—with both Israelis and Palestinians, how exactly are these experiences so comparable? To travel on a road or on a bus, unencumbered by the fear of imminent death—is this not a basic existential "right"? And yet, the feeling is only subtly different on the "other" side. Is it not also fear of imminent death—at the hands of a soldier, the only Jew a Palestinian has ever known—that frames the symbolic encounter of the checkpoint? On the bus, it is the Israeli citizen who is powerless, a slave to the possibility of attack. At the checkpoint, and throughout Palestine on the roads and in homes, Palestinians are subject to the same unpredictability—the same overwhelming sense of vulnerability—in their life stories. Will their home be invaded by Israeli soldiers in search of "militants"? Will they witness the death of a loved one, carelessly throwing stones at a tank, at the gun of a soldier? Will the image of the cruel soldier, who refuses to look them in the eyes, forever frame the picture of a Jew in their own life stories?

To experience the reality of the conflict and to open oneself up to its painful possibilities is to witness firsthand the "narrative stalemate" that the two groups have entered into, with its clear potential for infinite cycles of escalation. This stalemate is not unique to the particular phase of the conflict during which I conducted my research—the second Palestinian *intifada*. The conflict itself is rooted in a competition between two clashing national narratives that emerged out of the uncertainty and contestation of Palestine following the collapse of the Ottoman Empire and during the British Mandate.

In this book, I develop an argument about conflict, culture, and identity that places the concept of *narrative* at the forefront. In providing these illustrations from my fieldwork, I mean to introduce the reader to the *experience* of life in Israel and Palestine. Throughout the book, I argue that it is through the integration of experience into a coherent life story that Israelis and Palestinians come to reproduce a status quo of conflict. That is, as they interpret their daily experiences—often raw experiences of fear, anger, and frustration—they craft personal narratives of identity that make meaning of these experiences. But going beyond the concept of *personal* identity, I want to illustrate the development of *social* identity through the integration of not just individual experience but also the *stories of collective experience* that comprise what I call a *master narrative* of identity. In fusing a master narrative of identity into the personal narrative, young Israelis and Palestinians contribute to the cycle of conflict.

My vision of culture and identity, however, is far from static or monolithic. Identity, I argue, must be viewed as a *process* rather than a *product* of human development. Thus, social scientists, peace activists, and practitioners of conflict resolution must consider young Israeli and Palestinian lives as *stories in process*. Such a view has powerful implications for conceptualizing and analyzing interaction between Israeli and Palestinian youth—a subject that concerns me greatly as a "scholar-practitioner" who has devoted several years of my life to facilitating such interactions.

While I myself have been intimately involved in these "people-to-people" projects, whose primary goal is most often that all-too-appealing attempt to provide a context for mutual humanization, I have come to look at these efforts in a most critical light. It is not so much that I lack hope, though it is easy to see how so many peace activists and practitioners become hopeless as they devote their careers to Israeli–Palestinian reconciliation. Rather, it is that I have come to view most of these projects as *ideologically* and *conceptually* problematic, for they often demand too much psychologically of the young people whose lives they so desperately want to enhance. They often fail to take into account—in a truly meaningful way—the *structural violence* (Galtung, 1969, 1971) that frames the experience of Israeli and Palestinian youth and hence influences the course of their life stories.

If Israeli and Palestinian youth inhabit this space of structural injustice, this context of cruel and uncontrollable polarization, how then might we, as social scientists, peace advocates and practitioners, and individuals passionate about the security and sustenance of these two fragile identities, envision the possibility of peace? This book, perhaps audaciously and at times reluctantly, seeks to address these challenging questions about youth, peace, and justice. That it might contribute to the conversation on these issues is all I can ask, even as I think it might take our thoughts and our actions on these topics— topics of considerable social and political relevance—to a new intellectual and pragmatic place, a place from which a different set of stories, and a different type of encounter, might flourish and prevail. Such is my own audacity as a passionate scholar of identity and social justice.

I

Culture, Identity, and Story: A Framework for the Study of Lives

Preliminary Provocations

In 1948, a nation emerged from the ashes of the Holocaust.
The sandy shores, fertile soil, and mountainous beauty of their
original homeland once again welcomed them. There was at last
a beacon of light at the end of the darkest of nights. This brave
group of men and women—survivors of perhaps the single
greatest tragedy in human history—took an underdeveloped
land to new heights in the twentieth century, becoming a model
for democracy and economic ascendance in a region known for
exotic habits, the ways of an old world, and tired cultural
institutions impervious to social and economic evolution.

In 1948, the dreams of a people for freedom and independence were thwarted by the will of another. Having welcomed
with open arms the victims of a terrible tragedy in a distant land,
this people shared their land, their food, their customs. But these
newcomers were determined to create a nation all for themselves,
unwilling to share political authority. Resisting foreign attempts
to split their homeland in two, these people chose their only
remaining option: They turned to their neighbors, who shared a
language and a way of life, and collectively met aggression with
aggression. The struggle against the show of dominance imposed

upon them has resulted in interminable loss and suffering for this simple, peaceful people, who continue to vie for recognition of their national identity.

The reader with a close connection to the Israeli–Palestinian conflict will no doubt respond to these divergent interpretations of 1948 with a mixture of emotions, depending on one's own identity. And while these interpretations are themselves subject to heated debates *within* Israeli and Palestinian societies, narratives like these proliferate in both societies, contributing to the reproduction of conflict.

The central premise of this book, which is related to a growing movement across the social sciences, is that (a) we make sense of our lives through developing a coherent life story that possesses *credibility* (or, as Erikson might have called it, *fidelity*) within some cultural surround, and (b) our individual life stories reflect *master narratives* of the groups to which we feel a sense of belonging. In other words, our ability to make meaning of life experience through a process of *storying* it—telling ourselves and others a coherent account—represents a fundamental process of human development. Yet, to the extent that we are, of course, animals of context, subjects of time and place, this is not a process for which we have complete agency. Rather, our ability to craft life stories is inherently bound to the context of story making we inhabit, and I want to suggest that certain contexts are perhaps more constraining than others.

The context of conflict is, indeed, one of these constraining contexts. Perhaps, though, thinking of context as a *constraint* is itself problematic, for it reveals the intellectual bias that so many scholars (particularly scholars in the United States) have toward the individual and toward a notion of free will we inherited from the Enlightenment. As a scholar who can claim neither the identity of a historian nor a philosopher, I will set this debate aside and simply suggest that we ought not to think of adherence to a *collective* narrative as problematic for the individual, for social identity represents a rather positive force for human development, collective action, and mobilization against social injustice (e.g., Hurtado, 2003; Tajfel & Turner, 1979). This critical perspective on the meaning of identity—and on the way in which individuals who inhabit conflict settings navigate the politics of identity—underlies the arguments about peace and coexistence that I develop in this book.

In this book, I present an exploration of this central question of the relationship between master narratives—interpretations of historical events and collective experience, such as the stories of 1948 that introduced this chapter—and the personal narrative of an individual. I want to query the notion that a received master narrative of identity is, indeed, so easily reproduced. I want to probe the extent to which youth contest and grapple with the polarizing content of such discourse—the discourse that proliferates in societies at war and bears some responsibility for maintaining (and exacerbating) a conflict. I want to explicitly interrogate this potential process of social reproduction as it unfolds, in my view, through the identity development of youth.

The concept of *narrative* as an anchoring idea for the book, and for my work with young Israelis and Palestinians in general, is extremely useful for its ability to link a number of strands of thought, which, owing to the fragmentary nature of contemporary knowledge production, have developed somewhat independently. Historians and political scientists, for example, have increasingly talked about and written about issues like narrative and identity when it comes to conflict and international relations (e.g., Khalidi, 1997; Suny, 2001). And yet such scholars are not so interested in the manifestations of identity in individual voices; such is not really the nature of their intellectual craft.

At the same time, a prodigious intellectual movement within psychology has taken shape, beginning in the 1980s with landmark works such as Bert Cohler's (1982) essay on personal narrative and the life course, Ted Sarbin's (1986) volume on narrative psychology, Donald Polkinghorne's (1988) call for a narrative approach to understanding human experience, and Dan McAdams' (1988) early articulation of what would become a major integrative theory (e.g., McAdams, 1996, 2001; McAdams & Pals, 2006). These formulations paved the way for the explosion of the field of narrative psychology in the 1990s and today, in a way as a response to the "coldness" of the cognitive revolution (Bruner, 1990), with its mechanistic metaphor for human consciousness, and to the waning school of humanistic psychology that so captivated earlier students of psychology in the twentieth century.

Yet, owing to the distinct disciplinary foci within the social sciences, psychologists naturally have tended to think about narrative in rather "individualistic" ways, with many nods to issues like culture or social identity but little in the way of specific studies. The unit of analysis for the psychologist—even among social psychologists—continues to be the individual.

In this book, I want to suggest that the concept of narrative represents a natural bridge among the social sciences, not only because scholars from diverse disciplines find the concept of interest, but also for its actual utility at specifying an *integrative*, if more complex, framework for the study of lives in context *and* the study of groups, societies, and cultures. I will privilege the concept of story making through narrative because I believe in the universality of *language* as a "leading activity" of thought. For this, I am intellectually indebted to Soviet psychologist Lev Vygotsky and French social philosopher Michel Foucault. But these intellectual giants are not my sole influences as I develop a framework for the study of young Israeli and Palestinian lives. My aim in this chapter is to present this framework, so that the pages that follow, pages that contain the words of Israeli and Palestinian youth *and my interpretations of those words,* will be comprehensible. To understand my message in this book, the reader needs to understand *me*, my story, my identity, and the way in which I think about conflict, culture, and identity.

This book, however, represents more than an exercise in intellectual exploration, for the existential security of *actual* lives is very much at stake in Israel and Palestine. Being primarily a scholar, I naturally approach Israeli and Palestinian lives with scholarly motivations—a desire to contribute to larger conversations within the institutions of knowledge production of which I am a part. Yet my identity as a *practitioner* and as an *advocate*, also influences the kind of knowledge I want to produce—knowledge that can be of use in application, knowledge that might, in fact, transform practice with and for young Israelis and Palestinians.

Thus, the second major focus of the book is the experience of *contact* between Israelis and Palestinians, and in fact, most of the Israelis and Palestinians with whom I have worked for the past 7 years have been motivated to pursue contact with one another in some way. They are participants in what are interchangeably called "coexistence" programs by practitioners and educators and "intergroup contact" programs by social psychologists. I discuss in Chapter 2 the diverse motivations that youth actually endorse to engage in contact, just to suggest that this is by no means a monolithic group of "peaceniks" who have informed my thinking on young Israeli and Palestinian lives.

The argument I try to develop about Israeli–Palestinian contact stems directly from the findings of my longitudinal research with youth, though I must confess that it did not take long for the ideas to develop simply based on my practice with Israeli and Palestinian youth over the years. This second argument of the book, which will be perhaps obvious or intuitive to some while devastating to others, is that efforts to work for peace and coexistence with young Israelis and Palestinians have little, if any, role in the cycle of conflict. And if they do assume a major role, I suspect it is in the *reproduction*, rather than the *repudiation*, of conflict. This argument is, once again, audacious and risky for me to make, for I have invested several of the last years precisely in such efforts. Yet I mean to provide evidence—through the narratives of youth collected up to several years after contact—that at the very least the philosophical underpinnings of such efforts must be carefully and critically acknowledged and, perhaps, reformulated. In fact, the programs I studied seemed to most often serve the interests of those who organized them—providing them a sense of meaning and purpose and contributing to the fidelity of their own (American) life stories. In other words, such efforts might neglect the psychological needs of Israeli and Palestinian youth in order to meet the needs of, in the case of my field research, the American organizers of such efforts.

My interpretation of the American-based coexistence programs, while deeply unsettling in some ways, might, I hope, contribute to a difficult conversation among liberal Americans motivated to work for peace and social justice beyond (and maybe even within) our borders. I believe we have too often failed to fully hear the voices of the oppressed, the victims of cultural and structural violence (Galtung, 1990), in our society as in other societies, too often relying on a rather *hegemonic* view of intergroup relations, currently going by names like "multiculturalism" and "cosmopolitanism" (see Appiah, 2006; Hollinger, 2006; Moghaddam, 2007). These political, social, and intellectual movements are, in my view, cultural artifacts of a distinct worldview—a worldview deeply entrenched in a "United Statesian" (Moghaddam, 1987) view of social psychology. I will develop a counterview to these perspectives, arguing for the significance of a less individualistic and a more structural approach to the transformation of intergroup (and intercultural) relations.

My critique of what social psychologists call *intergroup contact* will not, however, take a destructive form, for I aim to contribute to difficult conversations in social psychology, conflict resolution, and coexistence education. Through this evidence-based critique, I will call for a *critical psychology* (e.g., Parker, 2007) of intergroup relations to understand the way in which a curriculum that works clearly and unequivocally for social justice and conflict amelioration for Israelis and Palestinians might be adopted.

Having hopefully captured the attention of the reader through these preliminary provocations, I will now outline my larger intellectual framework for the study of lives, which has its genesis in many schools of thought that have come before me. In the pages that follow, I sketch a framework as I see it at this point in my career as a scholar, advocate, and practitioner.

Capturing Culture

The first major intellectual "problem" with which I need to contend is my reliance on a concept of culture. The reader unfamiliar with seemingly esoteric conversations among scholars will no doubt find this notion odd, much as I did early in my training when I discovered that the idea of culture was actually contested. I will try to make this debate, or discussion, within the social sciences (unfortunately, a discussion which many psychologists have yet to discover) comprehensible and accessible, while also acknowledging that my own contribution to this discussion is really only beginning. In many ways, it is far beyond the scope of this book to summarize the vast amount of scholarship on the culture concept. In place of such a summary, I will instead clarify what *I* mean by "culture" and why I continue to think that such a concept has utility.

Like most social scientists, my introduction to the concept of culture came from anthropology. Thanks to the concerted efforts of early anthropologists like Franz Boas (1928), Ruth Benedict (1934), and Margaret Mead (1928), we were introduced to the concept of *cultural relativism* as a much-needed antidote to intellectual movements like eugenics and "social Darwinism" (e.g., Galton, 1909/2004; Spencer, 1884/1969), which presented hierarchical models of identity that, perhaps not coincidentally, legitimized colonialism as a "civilizing project" (Shweder, 2003). In spite of continued language about "primitive" and "savage" societies, anthropologists like Boas, Benedict, and Mead were trying to argue *against* the notion of a hierarchy of human civilizations, thus contesting the very language we had developed to categorize human groups.

Early formulations of the culture concept tended to view (or at least to talk about) culture as a static object—a "thing" to be furiously detailed in field notes and through informants. French structuralism, well represented by the work of Claude Lévi-Strauss (1962, 1963), contributed substantially to this conceptualization. This view of culture became increasingly problematic over the course of the twentieth century as the massive social changes that took place radically transformed those idyllic contexts early anthropologists had romanticized in their ethnographies. And still other anthropologists critically evaluated the unwitting role that they had perhaps taken in the colonial project (e.g., Neiburg & Goldman, 1998).

For our purposes, a proper, more complete history of the culture concept is best left aside, save for one important point. Just as anthropologists were coming to critique the very concept they had introduced into the popular lexicon, this little piece of the lexicon was finally "working" to achieve some important social ends in American society. I refer, of course, to the multiculturalism movement in countries like Canada, Australia, and the United States, which used the culture concept to argue for equal rights across ethnic groups (Hollinger, 2006). In addition, a concept that had so eluded psychological science for much of the twentieth century—with its penchant for producing *decontextualized* knowledge in a laboratory setting—was finally gaining ground. Psychologists had at last come to culture, perhaps best symbolized by the massively successful article published in 1991 by Hazel Markus and Shinobu Kitayama in *The Psychological Review*. This article on culture and the self, with a focus on the contrast between self-construals in the United States and Japan, has proven to be one of the most cited in the entire history of psychology—in just a span of two decades.

What is most problematic about the adoption of the culture concept both within the mainstream American public and American psychology is that it has failed to take an historical view of the concept of culture. In other words, the very idea that "cultures" exist—once again, largely as static "things" such as "patterns" of behavior, custom, and mental experience (Benedict, 1934)—is taken as a foregone conclusion and not critically interrogated. As a consequence, researchers in the new subfield of cultural psychology (of which I claim membership) have taken a highly *aggregate* view of the relation between persons and cultures, far more interested in the distinctions *between* human communities (often overly reified and caricatured, with political implications) than *within* them (Gjerde, 2004).

My view of culture rejects earlier notions that imply homogeneity within groups in favor of a view of culture as a *linguistic production*—a production that, in turn, *mediates* our experience. It is here that the concept of narrative becomes relevant, for I believe that culture—including its material elements—is produced through the construction of stories about groups, their relationships, and their values and aspirations. What we think of as *custom*, then, is really just a story of what we ought to do in a given situation, and it is the story—and our identification with it—that motivates our adherence to the custom.

To illustrate my point, let us briefly consider Palestinian custom surrounding marriage. I had developed a close relationship over the years with Walid, the older brother of my research participant Mohammed, because we were the same age. During my previous trips, he and I would spend hours discussing family, work, and relationships, and he introduced me to his friends and to a network of other Westerners in Palestine. Walid was a responsible, thoughtful, and cosmopolitan host to me. He spoke fluent English, was anti-ideological (a point that became very relevant in Mohammed's case, which I discuss later in the book) and antireligious, and really had very little care for what he perceived as the antiquated traditions of Palestinian custom.

On one of my later visits to Palestine, Walid had recently married. I was not surprised to find that Dima, his wife, was also not religious (she did not wear the *hijab*), and the two acted very much like equals with one another. Yet, on this visit, I was invited to a series of rituals that are part of Palestinian custom surrounding marriage (in this case, postmarriage). While Walid seemed thoroughly uninterested in these rituals beforehand, as a participant he appeared quite content and even at times elated. I recall watching his wedding video with the family, and Walid's euphoria was palpable, both onscreen and sitting next to me as my guide through the video.

Walid is not a sentimental man. He has no interest in or longing for "tradition." Yet it is clear that he is psychologically affected by his participation in this particular activity or set of activities which we might call *custom*. By participating in these activities, he engages in practice as a member of *Palestinian culture*, coordinating his own personal narrative with his perceptions of a collective narrative of *what Palestinians do*.

Culture, thus, is not something we *have*; it is something we *do*. And it is something we *talk about* doing—both to ourselves and to others—thereby reproducing the material and discursive conditions of a society. In contrast to the way in which we often talk about culture in the vernacular—as someone being of this or that "culture," or about the beauty of Italian, Indian, or Brazilian "culture"—I think of culture as more verb than noun. And to *study* culture, we must be analysts not only of ritual, symbol, and social practice, but also of how individuals make meaning of their participation in the activity of culture. In other words, we need to query individual processes of *narrating* experience.

My view of culture thus weaves together two primary concepts: *language* (and its organization into *discourse* and *narrative*) and *social practice* or *activity*. First, as I have already noted, *narrative* is the anchor of culture. And narrative links individual psychology to *society* and to *group* psychology, for personal narratives do not develop in the absence of an index or a matrix of *possible* stories— narratives that are sanctioned by a community and rendered acceptable.

It is precisely my emphasis on narrative that links my view of culture to Foucault, for Foucault argued that individuals are slaves to *discourse*, that individuals are *subjects* of a clear social *order*, and that social categories are constructed as a part of history, often to meet needs related to social control (e.g., Foucault, 1972, 1978, 1982). Foucault's approach is embedded into my view of culture to the extent that I seek to integrate an acknowledgment of the ways in which individuals become subjects of a socially unjust configuration of identity in Israel and Palestine. In appropriating a vision of identity that reproduces a status quo of conflict, individuals blindly participate in the process of social reproduction specified by Foucault. They unwittingly accept the categories into which they have been placed as *intrinsic* to their being, and it is through *stories* that this process unfolds, rendered salient in the actual structural reality of conflict—a reality in which existence becomes a *question* and therefore a battle to be fought.

Yet, if culture is *produced* and *reproduced* by individuals, we must theorize culture as a *process*. To do so, we must move from a notion of the personal narrative as the salient content of mind (Bruner, 1990) toward a notion of *narrative engagement*. We must study the ways in which individuals navigate multiple discourses about social identity and cultural participation as they begin to develop a personal narrative. The "pure" versions of the Israeli and Palestinian master narratives that introduced this chapter are not, as I acknowledged, static or monolithic. Nor are they the only versions available to youth as they begin to construct life stories. Distinct versions may be narrated to youth through their school history textbooks, or on television, or at the local mosque or synagogue, or at the dinner table.

What interests me most as a *narrative* psychologist is the process by which young people selectively appropriate or repudiate various master stories to which they are exposed. How, when, and why do some Israeli youths emphasize victimization over resilience? How, when, and why do some Palestinian youths legitimize political violence against Israeli civilians while others problematize such acts on moral or religious grounds? These are difficult questions to address, given that they require close access to individual lives and individual processes of psychological experience. But I believe these are essential questions if we are to understand young Palestinian and Israeli lives on their own terms, and if we are to make sense more generally of young lives in contexts of conflict.

Perhaps the key question for me, then, as a *cultural* psychologist, concerns the reproduction or repudiation of conflict. If the conflict between Israelis and Palestinians has essentially constructed two very distinct cultures, both of which unfortunately thrive off of the continuation of conflict in some way by affirming the foundations of a collective identity for both groups, how might young people respond as they begin to construct their life stories? The larger question for me concerns the *reproduction* of culture through individual psychological processes like life story construction. But such processes are inherently *social* and not solely matters of private cognition, which commands a focus on the contexts for *interaction* in the course of young Israeli and Palestinian lives.

My view of how it is individuals come to reproduce culture can be linked to two social scientists whose views are remarkably complementary, even if their thought developed independently at around the same time: Lev Vygotsky and George Herbert Mead. Vygotsky argues that human development occurs through *mediated social activity*, with *language* as a guiding force (Vygotsky, 1934/1986, 1978). The mind is a product of this activity, connecting the material world of culture with the development of the individual. A critical aspect of development, according to Vygotsky, is the internalization of *social speech* to create an *inner speech* that drives thought and action. As this process occurs within an individual, we witness a convergence of practical activity and speech, which Vygtosky (1978) describes as a "unity of perception, speech, and action" (p. 26). In other words, one internalizes an acceptable *language* to organize thoughts and experiences and to legitimize and make sense of action. This language comprises, in my terms, a *master narrative*, and its transformation

from social speech to inner speech (in Vygotsky's terms) represents the reproduction of culture. Mastery of the *discursive* tools available to individuals in
their social ecology is closely connected to *survival*, particularly in contexts of
perceived existential threat or insecurity, for such mastery creates a sense of
cognitive security within the individual (e.g., Giddens, 1991; Kinnvall, 2004).

To put Vygotsky's insights, and my interpretation of them, into the context
of young Israeli and Palestinian lives, we must identify the connection between
language and activity. Thinking again of the master narratives of 1948, these
narratives present a discourse that mediates the actions of young Israelis and
Palestinians, and their actions, in fact, *necessitate* the internalization of social
speech that maintains the conflict—speech that constructs the other in delegitimizing terms. This *delegitimizing* speech, which can become part of the
individual's running narrative of the other, places members of the other group
on a lesser moral and existential plane, thereby justifying acts of violence
(Bar-Tal, 1989, 1990a; Oren & Bar-Tal, 2007).

The most obvious cases of such a process occur among Israeli soldiers
who are forced to commit acts of violence—both physical and psychological—
against Palestinians, as well as among Palestinians who use violence to resist
the Israeli occupation. The soldier and the fighter who fires rockets, throws
stones, or explodes himself at a checkpoint all act with the social speech of the
conflict internalized. They have all crafted their own personal narratives that
make meaning of their position and that motivate and justify their actions.
Speech thus becomes an organizing framework for action, a cognitive filter
through which the material basis of the conflict is reproduced in *both* discourse
and social practice (i.e., violence).

Yet, again, how precisely does this *process* of cultural reproduction unfold?
For my thinking on this question, I am indebted to the legendary Chicago
social psychologist George Herbert Mead and the movement of which he was
a part—*symbolic interactionism*. Guided initially at least in part by Cooley's
(1902) notion of a "looking-glass self," Mead (1934) and his students and colleagues conceived of the development of mind, self, and society through social
interaction (see also Blumer, 1969; Goffman, 1959, 1963, 1967).

Mead (1934) argued that the self arises in consciousness only as it becomes
an *object* to some other. Hence, social interaction is required for the perception
of individuality. Through such interactions, individuals internalize what he
called the "conversation of gestures" considered acceptable or appropriate in a
given community. Childhood "play" becomes the "game" of adult social interaction, with roles and a consciousness of self *reflected* through engagement with
the other. Over time, the individual develops a sense of the self as both subject
(the "I") and object (the "me"), and interactions are framed by an awareness

of each. In every social interaction, there is a delicate balance of the attempted agency of the "I" and the *limitations to that agency* required by viewing oneself through the lens of the "generalized other"—Mead's (1934) concept of "the organized community or social group which gives to the individual his unity of self" (p. 154).

To think about Israeli and Palestinian identity *development*, then, we must think about possibilities of social interaction and the nature of those interactions. Unfortunately, the most common interactions between Israelis and Palestinians are framed within the structural configuration of conflict and its inevitable existential insecurity (Pettigrew, 2003). Consider the interaction of Palestinians in the occupied territories with Israeli soldiers (such as my interaction with Khalid described in the Prologue). Or consider a young Jewish Israeli like Gal, who had witnessed a suicide bombing right before his very eyes, or my experience boarding that coach bus to Netanya, carefully sizing up the Arabs boarding one by one. In these interactions, Israelis and Palestinians witness one another's deep insecurities reflected back upon themselves. In the fear provoked by the other, they find themselves *to be feared*. In a way, these symbolic interactions provide a sense of empowerment to both groups, for they are strong if they are *both subject and object* of fear. In Mead's framework, it is only through coming to see oneself as *feared* (in the case of an Israeli or Palestinian) that one develops a sense of self at all.

Mead's version of symbolic interactionism, though, leaves room for individual agency through the conception of the "I," which suggests that young Israelis and Palestinians might be able to use the context of interaction to reframe the nature of their roles, reframing their own senses of self in the process. For Mead, the "I" is about bringing one's role in the interaction into consciousness and taking control of it. In his own words, "The 'I' is his action over against that social situation within his own conduct, and it gets into his experience only after he has carried out the act" (Mead, 1934, p. 175). Rather than view the individual as *solely* a product of some community, Mead suggests that individuals *respond* to the generalized other they have internalized, and their actions can reconstitute a society in the process: "The individual is constantly reacting to the social attitudes, and changing in this co-operative process the very community to which he belongs" (pp. 199–200).

In performing expected and expectable roles in social interaction, individuals participate in the reproduction of culture. It is only as they "improvise" in the course of these interactions that possibilities for social change occur (Holland, Lachicotte, Skinner, & Cain, 1998), for improvisations of and *challenges* to a received system of symbolic interactions shift possibilities for action. Such acts contest a status quo of intergroup relations.

Symbolic interactionism, and Mead's particular version of it, reveals precisely *how* cultural reproduction can occur through even the smallest of social interactions. Since both self and mind are *products* of a history of interactions with others, there is no "consciousness" apart from social consciousness. Hence, anticipating later movements in European social psychology (Tajfel & Turner, 1979), Mead's framework suggests that there is no identity apart from *social* identity. Within the interactive process of human engagement with one another, individuals reproduce the cultural conditions of their engagement because that is what has *produced them*—their very ideas, senses of self, and ability to communicate.

The obvious application to young Israelis and Palestinians—of great relevance to efforts at contact I discuss in this book—is that, when they meet one another, they do not meet as distinct individuals, with unique autobiographies. Rather, they enter into interaction as members of a rival group, and their social identities are extremely determinative of the course of their interaction (Halabi & Sonnenschein, 2004a, 2004b; Nadler, 2004; Suleiman, 2004a, 2004b). While Mead and other scholars in his tradition considered their perspective on human interaction to be universal, this dynamic of social identity salience seems all the more likely in contexts of conflict—contexts in which groups lack a sense of security, and thus, improvisations within an interaction might be more limited. Yet so much of the content and nature of these processes remain, in my view, as empirical *questions*, matters not fully resolved by social science, and matters surely requiring contextual specificity in their positions and speculations.

We are, then, subjects of culture in a most profound way. As Eagleton (2000) rightly notes, we cannot think of culture and nature as distinct, for culture is a part of the natural world just as much as culture can remake nature through human activity (often in devastating ways). For me, then, culture is more than the material world, more than the products of a "civilized" society; it is, rather, the *mediated activity* that humans create within their material world, and it endures as the stories that sustain that activity maintain their appeal and serve a psychological purpose in the provision of meaning for individual lives. It is precisely the way in which individuals confront this version of culture—stories and their prescriptions for social practice—that I query in this book. And in moving beyond a static view of culture and narrative, I probe past the personal narrative at a single time point toward an investigation of how a special kind of social interaction—contact with the antagonist within the group's master narrative—interrupts or contributes to this cycle of cultural reproduction.

Interrogating Identity

The primacy I place on a concept of culture links me to other social scientists such as anthropologists, sociologists, historians, and perhaps even economists. But social science has no hold on the concept of culture, and scholars in the humanities have taken cultural analysis and critique to be a central intellectual concern. Culture, indeed, has few intellectual boundaries.

What makes my approach distinct as a psychologist is my desire to focus on *individual lives* and to think about the roles of *individuals* in these larger processes of cultural reproduction. Yet, as I have already suggested, most cultural psychologists, while continuing to *assess* individuals, have typically used methods that aggregate the responses of individuals to, say, self-report questionnaires. In such methods, individual variation is considered "error," for statistics seek first and foremost to offer generalizable knowledge about groups, *not* individuals (see Lamiell, 1998; Porter, 1986; Shweder, 1990).

In my view of culture and identity, it is absolutely essential that individual processes are preserved, for my account is based on an analysis of individual *meaning making*. More consistent with earlier approaches in developmental and personality psychology (e.g., Allport, 1924; Erikson, 1958, 1959), I use methods that preserve the integrity of data provided by each individual person. This approach has gone by a number of names in psychology, most commonly *idiographic* (Allport, 1937, 1962), *personological* (McAdams, 1988), or *person-centered* (Gjerde, 2004). Most broadly, this approach falls within the "study of lives" model in personality psychology (e.g., Cohler, 2007; Gregg, 2007; Josselson, 1996; McAdams, 2006), pioneered by Henry Murray (1938).

My emphasis on the idea of *identity* provides me with another major conceptual anchor for my work. It is through the *interrogation* of identity that I study culture, for my lens is squarely focused on individual lives, even as I am a careful analyst of the context within which those lives are positioned. As with culture, identity is a term in great fashion in contemporary scholarly and popular parlance. I am not drawn to the concept for its popularity, though this popularity surely led me to think about my research problem in such terms (social scientists are, after all, products of their times).

Identity is so ubiquitous today because it is the guiding framework of human social organization that emerged out of Enlightenment thought, and it has proven an important political concept in the nationalist movements of the postcolonial era. It was to a kind of identity "purity" that some of the more violent and atrocious nationalist movements of the twentieth century aspired. Nationalism itself, emerging as a new mode of social organization in the postimperial era, commanded the inculcation of a sense of shared community—a sense of a distinct *culture*, marked and motivated by distinct grievances—which was often more a product of imagination than historical fact (Anderson, 1983; Hobsbawm, 1990). But the idea of identity was absolutely essential to motivate a populace to action.

Identity has maintained its importance in contemporary discourse precisely because the problems created by the nationalist era remain unresolved (the Israeli–Palestinian conflict, of course, being a case in point). So even as borders open and the "purity" of identities becomes challenged through access to global media (Arnett, 2002), many groups like the Palestinians and the Israelis continue the fight for identity recognition, for the right to call a distinct and secure *nation*, with identifiable physical boundaries, their own (Khalidi, 1997).

Recognizing the "imagined" basis of identity, or its historical emergence as a social construct, does not, however, suggest the need to dismiss it as an ephemeral concept. As a psychologist, what concerns me most is the way in which identities continue to provide a sense of meaning and purpose, fulfilling vital psychological needs for coherence among individuals (McAdams, 1990, 1997). The meaning provided by a strong sense of identity directly bears upon the views individuals come to hold about war, conflict, and political violence (Barber, 2008, 2009b). In other words, identity is absolutely integral to an understanding of the disputes, challenges, and possibilities that characterize contemporary intergroup relations across the globe, for identity is a central organizing concept that unites thinkers, activists, and cultural participants.

I have been discussing identity in social and political terms, but it is important to note that many psychologists (particularly developmental and personality psychologists) think of identity in terms that are more individualistic. Social scientists generally distinguish between the *personal* identities that make up our autobiographies (e.g., Cohler, 1982; Goffman, 1963; McAdams, 1988) and the *social* identities that speak to our group memberships (Sen, 2006; Tajfel & Turner, 1979). In developing an *integrative* framework for the study of lives in cultural context, I will argue that it is precisely the *convergence* between personal and social identity that we must study if we are interested in larger processes of social change.

We inherit a concern with *personal* identity from Enlightenment thinkers like John Locke (1690/1998) and David Hume (1739/2000), and thus the study of identity is somewhat problematically linked to a Western notion of personhood (Baumeister, 1987). Yet identity as a concept has taken on a broader meaning beyond these European philosophers, and it is a concept in need of integration and synthesis, for, like culture, it is used in rather indiscreet and unspecific ways—a concept we are all supposed to fully "get," for it is so pervasive in discourse.

William James (1890), one of the foundational figures of American psychology, spoke of identity as a "consciousness of personal sameness" (p. 331)—that cognitive experience of waking up one morning and recognizing oneself as the *same* person that woke up the day before, even if one's biography may have changed in the span of a day. For James, identity was a private matter of individual cognition, and its psychological *function* centered on providing a clear sense of *continuity* and, hence, security within individual consciousness.

In his pioneering work on the concept of identity, Erik Erikson (1958, 1959, 1963, 1968) maintains this focus on the psychological function of identity to provide a sense of continuity. But Erikson makes a vital corrective to the Jamesian formulation, so rooted in the individual *privacy* of thought influenced by Enlightenment philosophy. Erikson argues that identity is not simply a matter of individual cognition in cultural isolation. Rather, he posits that the key feature of identity development is its provision of meaning and continuity *to some social group and within some historical and ideological context*. Erikson thus contextualizes, historicizes, and, in some sense, politicizes the development of identity—a move that speaks to contemporary concerns with the politics of identity.

It is no accident that Erikson's theoretical insights were derived in a very interesting historical context in the mid–twentieth century United States—a context in which an entire social order appeared to be in a state of contestation and a culture on the brink of radical transformation. With the massive social and political changes occurring in the United States, it was inconceivable to think of human development apart from social engagement. And given the role of youth in these social movements, it is hardly surprising that Erikson placed such emphasis on the role of youth in social reproduction.

For Erikson, identity was both personal and social. Maintaining James' emphasis on cognition and continuity, he defines identity as "a conscious *sense of individual identity*,... an unconscious striving for a *continuity of personal character*..." (Erikson, 1959, p. 109). But he goes beyond James by also including in this definitional statement the notion of identity as "a maintenance of an inner *solidarity* with a group's ideals and identity" (p. 109; all italics in original). While still decidedly within the realm of individual cognition, this version of identity seeks to integrate a sense of *social* identity, a vision of one's place within some larger group and its ideals and aspirations, thus moving psychology beyond decontextualized mental processes.

For Erikson, history, culture, and society were absolutely key in the individual's development. We must credit him for countering the universalizing discourse of theorists like Freud and Piaget, yet Erikson is just as much a product of his *intellectual* times as he is of his social era. As a consequence, his developmental theory continues the tradition of an ontogenetic sequence, with "ages and stages" (cf. Dannefer, 1984). To be fair, perhaps he is truly one of the pioneers of such an approach, and we ought to appreciate that. But his desire for creativity and relativity in the interpretation of life histories somehow contradicts this drive for the promulgation of a sequential view of human development. For example, Erikson clearly spoke of identity as a "task" to be "achieved," a language then continued by a host of psychologists who took his framework in significant empirical directions (e.g., Marcia, 1966; for review, see Schwartz, 2001).

For my purposes, Erikson's framework is central for a number of reasons. First, his attempt to integrate personal and social identity into a coherent concept parallels my own aims. Second, his insistence on the use of person-centered and ethnographic data to explore his theories resonates with my preferred approach. Finally, Erikson placed the concept of *ideology* at the forefront of his theory of identity, and this instinct rests well with my own observations on the lives of Israeli and Palestinian youth (though I do not think the significance of ideology is restricted to Israelis and Palestinians, or to individuals who inhabit contexts of political conflict). Erikson saw individual life histories as reflective and integrative of the ideas that proliferated an age. Thus, his brilliant case analysis of Martin Luther considers Luther's social movement through a process of ideological identification and commitment (Erikson, 1958).

The study of identity in psychology since Erikson was, until relatively recently, dominated more by derivatives of James Marcia's (1966) adaptation of Erikson's theory than by Erikson himself, mostly owing to the political culture around methodology in American psychology in the latter half of the twentieth century, which came to deride the idiographic and ethnographic methods so central to Erikson's approach. Maintaining Erikson's (faulty, in my view) notion of identity as something to be "achieved" by the end of adolescence, Marcia's (1966) framework categorizes identity *status* along four categorical indices conceptually connected to Erikson's theory. Individuals high in *exploration* and *commitment* are said to be in a state of *identity achievement*; they have openly explored the ideological and occupational possibilities available to them, and they have made a commitment. Individuals high in exploration but low in commitment are said to be in a state of *moratorium*; they are in a process of exploring ideologies but have yet to fully commit to any. Individuals low in exploration but high in commitment are said to be in a state of *foreclosure*; they have come to decisions about ideological commitments without really considering other options. Finally, individuals low in both exploration and commitment are categorized as in a state of identity *diffusion*. Their lives are characterized by a kind of apathy and absence of a drive to examine life's ideological possibilities.

Marcia's (1966) schematic has been appropriated and extensively explored by many scholars, most notably adapted for the study of ethnic identity by Jean Phinney in the 1990s (e.g., Phinney, 1989, 1990, 1991). But I think these frameworks are most appealing because they preserve a fundamental insight from Erikson's original theory. This fundamental insight is that each individual is a *social actor* as he or she develops some internal *sense* of place in the world and embraces a set of expectable beliefs and actions based on that sense. We *explore* the ideological possibilities in our midst, and we *commit* to some over others (or we commit *not* to commit, as may be the case for some).

Like psychologists such as Marcia and Phinney, I also want to retain these concepts from Erikson's thought. Yet I am suspicious of the language of identity *status*. Consistent with my emphasis on the *social* aspect of identity development, I view identity, like culture, as a verb. McAdams (1997) concurs when he discusses the process of *selfing* as a "unifying, integrative, synthesizing process" (p. 56) involving the organization of experience into a coherent life story narrative.

My approach to identity, like my approach to culture, embraces complexity, fluidity, and hybridity. At the same time, it is an empirical approach that necessitates careful attention to the way in which social actors negotiate the identity demands of a culture. Because it is characterized by the globalization of culture through mass media and technological transformation, our late modern era would seem to *require* a reflexive process of identity construction, as a psychological anchor and a source of security (Giddens, 1991; McAdams, 1997; Smith, 1994). As Lifton (1993) argues, individuals have adapted remarkably well to this new metacontext for identity formation—they routinely confront complexity with resilience and construct what he calls "protean" selves.

I would suggest, however, that our propositions about identity in the late modern era must be anchored in observations of actual lives in a variety of places. Such propositions cannot find their only home in the minds of (European or European American) men and women (see Arnett, 2008). I believe we must study individuals in their own right, on their own terms, using the "toolkit" of ideas and methods we have inherited.

I seek to address this empirical need for an examination of actual voices in cultural context. But I cannot make this inquiry in the absence of a clear *paradigm* of culture and identity—a scientific worldview that allows me to interpret the texts of Israeli and Palestinian life stories. Taking an approach to culture that privileges language and activity, and an approach to identity that instinctively recognizes history and culture, I have weaved together a paradigm on the *cultural psychology* of identity that is ambitious in its integration and audacious in its claims for utility in our time.

The Cultural Psychology of Identity

Wilhelm Wundt (1916), typically credited as the founder of the first psychological laboratory in Leipzig, Germany, proposed that psychology required two distinct branches: one that dealt "scientifically" in the laboratory, and one that engaged with the "messiness" of culture. It would take some time for Wundt's vision to be realized in American psychology (and one might argue that, because contemporary American cultural psychologists rely so heavily on laboratory experiments, it has yet to be realized). By the 1990s, however, cultural psychology had (re-)emerged as an intellectual force, with the publication of a number of defining texts for the field (e.g., Bruner, 1990; Cole, 1996; Shweder, 1991). By the 2000s, cultural psychology had a legitimate, if contested, home in the academy (e.g., Kitayama & Cohen, 2007; Nisbett, 2003).

I am most influenced by four strains of thought within cultural psychology, all of which directly bear upon young Palestinian and Israeli lives. First, my emphasis on the documentation of diversity in human experience is rooted in Shweder's (1990, 2003) vision for cultural psychology. He argues against general psychology's notion of a principle of "psychic unity" in mental life, which has historically motivated psychologists to identify universals (Shweder, 1990). What ought to concern us in an increasingly pluralistic world, according to Shweder (2003), is the *distinction* of mental life and the process by which persons and cultures make one another up. In other words, Shweder suggests that we must view person and culture as *coconstitutive*, which is consistent with my views on social reproduction in the context of conflict.

Second, my privileging of the concept of narrative is consistent with Bruner's (1990) vision for cultural psychology. "A culturally sensitive psychology," he argues, "...is and must be based not only upon what people actually do, but what they *say* they do and what they say caused them to do what they did" (Bruner, 1990, p. 16, italics added). For Bruner, culture and narrative are as inseparable as culture and language, for we learn how to make sense of our experience in narration by participating in the rites of a community. In the process, we internalize a way of making meaning of our experience, a psychological mode that anchors thought, feeling, and action.

Early work in this particular renaissance of cultural psychology tended to be more concerned with cultures as relatively homogeneous "packages," probably borrowed from the earlier anthropological concept of culture. Thus, cultures were dubbed as either "individualistic" or "collectivistic" (e.g., Triandis, 1989), "egocentric" or "sociocentric" (Shweder & Bourne, 1982), "independent" or "interdependent" (Markus & Kitayama, 1991), and "holistic" or "analytic" (Nisbett, Peng, Choi, & Norenzayan, 2001). These formulations, unfortunately, tended to suggest a rather monolithic and nondynamic view of the relationship between person and culture. What seemed most missing was *the person.*

Gjerde's (2004) person-centered approach to research in cultural psychology provides a useful corrective to these more aggregate, falsely dichotomized approaches. Arguing against the static notion of "culture," Gjerde (2004) suggests that we must study the relationship between person and culture by examining narratives as "ideology in speech" (p. 152), always positioning the narrator within some larger matrix of power and hegemony. In his view, culture and the individual are coconstructed through discursive practices that reveal either acquiescence or resistance to some status quo of power relations among groups. Hence, Gjerde's vision of cultural psychology is dynamic, dialogic, and integrative of both social structural and individual psychological accounts of cultural participation and practice.

The fourth tradition within cultural psychology with which I identify comes from Vygotksy (1934/1986, 1978) and those who have followed his approach to studying culture as *made* in practical activity (e.g., Gutierrez & Rogoff, 2003; Rogoff, 1990, 2003; Rogoff & Angelillo, 2002; Valsiner, 2001). As I have already noted, this school of thought adopts a dynamic, dialogic view of the relationship between persons and settings. And because *language* is conceptualized as a critical tool for mediation in this view, it represents another ideal anchor within cultural psychology for my analysis of Israeli and Palestinian narratives.

With these general approaches to cultural psychology in mind, I will now outline a particular paradigm that seeks to offer concrete prescriptions for the study of identity and culture, person and social structure, dynamically producing and reproducing one another through the individual's process of narrative engagement. The three most central components to my perspective are *ideology, narrative,* and *social practice.*

Speaking of ideology in more Eriksonian terms as a general or abstract worldview, which comes with a specific set of value commitments, I suggest that the *content* of identity, in cognitive terms, assumes an ideological form. The content of identity is that internalized social speech (Vygotsky, 1978) or generalized other (Mead, 1934) that guides our interactions by *positioning* our-selves within a matrix of possible relations (Harré & Van Langenhove, 1999). The ideological content of our identities thus prescribes the *type* of political and social actors we strive to be. The process by which we come to identify with ideology is, in my view, a process of *narrative engagement*—a process by which we engage with the stories that proliferate in our cultural surround.

It is precisely this process to which I refer when I consider the *ideological settings* of Israeli and Palestinian life stories. According to McAdams (1990, 1996, 2001), the ideological setting of a life story offers the narrator a philosophical, spiritual, and political anchor with which to position herself or himself in a broader collective. Thus, some Israeli youths set their stories within an ideology of secular nationalism (i.e., Zionism), while others internalize a story of messianic or religious nationalism. The exact parallel can be made for Palestinians: Is the life story situated within a larger story about democracy and postcolonial libera-tion (as is that of Fatah and the PLO), or within a story about the significance of Palestine as a holy land in Islam (as in the narrative of Hamas or Islamic Jihad)?

The *structure* of identity as a personal narrative is precisely what allows us to gain a window into the process of cultural production and reproduction. In this view, identity is like a *text* that is told, either in solitude or to some inter-locutor (such as a journalist, a social scientist, or a family member). Unlike a traditional text (such as this book), the text of a life story *develops* over the life course (Cohler, 1982; McAdams, 1996). It is told and retold, and it changes as our psychological needs for integration and coherence require.

Some in psychological science problematize life story accounts precisely because of the phenomenon of "retrospective bias"—the tendency of individu-als to remember the past in ways that are more connected to present needs or the demands of self-presentation than to an *actual* account of past events. But the narrative approach embraces this phenomenon head-on: Narrative psy-chologists are not concerned with actual events but with *individual interpreta-tions* of those events (Bruner, 1986, 1990). Thus, we are interested foremost in how social actors deliberately (or unwittingly) position themselves in a larger matrix of social identity.

Finally, my view of identity privileges the *process* by which this personal narrative develops through social practice and interaction. Individual life sto-ries are as legitimately a part of material culture as, say, a stop sign or a wash-ing machine. They become tools for the navigation of thought and action, but they themselves are the product of successive sequences of thought and action. Personal narrative construction is, in other words, an *iterative* and *interactive* process by which we gradually build a sensible, credible story that frames our feelings, thoughts, and actions in an internalized matrix of possibilities.

Like many cultural psychologists, I view these kinds of mental processes I describe as universal, but I do not view them as suggestive of *uniformity* (Shweder & Sullivan, 1993). To the extent that all human communities have language, and to the extent that members of a community interact with one another, I believe the process of identity development I outline here is a universal one. What I am arguing is *distinct* or *relative* is the *nature* of this process. How self-conscious of a process is it? How complex is it? What factors constrain it or enable it?

It is precisely these elaborative questions that lead me to study young Israeli and Palestinian lives, for the context of conflict undoubtedly bears upon the nature of this process of identity formation. In probing the relationship between master narratives of the group and the personal narratives of individual youths, I seek to query and thus to describe the distinction of this process for Israelis and Palestinians, hopefully contributing to an analysis of the social psychology of conflict and to the cultural psychology of identity.

Experimenting With Identity

In the 1950s, Turkish-American social psychologist Muzafer Sherif conducted a famous field experiment in which he recruited a group of psychologically healthy 11-year-old boys from Oklahoma City for a summer camp at the Robbers Cave State Park (Sherif, Harvey, White, Wood, & Sherif, 1961). According to his original experimental design, the boys were separated into two groups, housed in different parts of the park, and were unaware of one another's presence. In the first phase of the experiment, group formation occurred, and the boys established roles within the group and selected a group name. In the second phase, the boys were made aware of the existence of the other group in the park, and the researchers constructed competitive situations in which the goals of the two groups were in conflict (e.g., an athletic tournament). In the third and final phase, "superordinate" goals were introduced such that the two groups—the "Eagles" and the "Rattlers"—had to work together in order to obtain the desired end (e.g., the necessary pooled resources to get a certain film). Sherif and his colleagues discovered that, through the induction of superordinate goals—goals that could not be met by a single group alone—intergroup hostilities could be dramatically reduced or eliminated altogether.

The implications of Sherif's research for the eradication of conflict were profound. If the *functional* relation between groups (i.e., the incompatibility of their goals) could be transformed, harmony might prevail (Sherif, 1958). The optimism of Sherif's conclusion prevails in contemporary work on

Israeli–Palestinian reconciliation that calls for a reformulation of Israeli and Palestinian identities as *positively*, rather than negatively, interdependent (Kelman, 1999b). To the extent that the conflict endures because of conflicting collective goals, if we can alter the nature of goals so that both groups recognize their interdependence, peace becomes conceivable.

Sherif's pathbreaking work was in many ways a reaction to a competing view of intergroup conflict that emerged in the United States post World War II. In the aftermath of the war and its revelations about the possibilities of human destruction (e.g., the Nazi death camps, the atomic bomb), social scientists began to search for a way to understand motivations for intergroup violence. Following Freud's (1921) earlier account, Theodore Adorno and his colleagues placed great emphasis on the role of a *leader* in motivating a populace for violence and antagonism. They conceived of the *authoritarian personality* as the explanation for such atrocities (Adorno, Frenkel-Brunswik, Levinson, & Sanford, 1950). Only the product of a pathological family environment could go on to seek destruction at the level of precision of someone like Hitler.

Gordon Allport's (1954) perspective on conflict also emphasized the role of individual personality development in prejudice between groups. Writing at the height of the desegregation movement between Blacks and Whites in the United States, Allport (1954) argued that the physical segregation of groups prevented the development of personalities attuned toward harmonious relations between groups. Unlike Adorno and colleagues, Allport saw the "prejudiced personality" as an expectable product of the segregation of groups and not as a "pathological" state, but rather as a *normative* state in a context of intergroup antagonism. But like Adorno and colleagues, Allport privileged the role of the individual personality in the maintenance of conflict and suggested that intervention in processes of personality development might, in fact, reduce prejudice.

Allport proposed an audacious hypothesis for the context of the desegregating United States, a hypothesis that came to be known as the *contact hypothesis*, or *contact theory*. According to Allport (1954), contact could assume a role in the reduction of prejudice at the group level by intervening in processes of individual personality development. He argued that individuals necessarily invoke a cognitive process of *categorization* as they make sense of the world around them; they develop certain mental "maps" about what characteristics seem to go along with being, say, a man or a woman, an Indian or an Israeli, an African American or a European American. We necessarily organize the world population into social categories, and our views of these groups are not value neutral. We bring with these mental images of the category "man" or "African American" an expectable set of characteristics that we think basically defines what it means to be a member of that group—something social psychologists typically call *stereotypes*.

Allport believed that conflicts endured precisely because of these tendencies to view members of a rival group in stereotyped ways that tend to dismiss the variability *within* a group. Thus, a 16-year-old Jewish Israeli might view his Palestinian counterpart as an anti-Semitic religious fundamentalist dedicated to the eradication of the Jewish population. Or the Palestinian might view his Jewish-Israeli counterpart as an aggressive, militaristic individual who would sooner physically displace West Bank Palestinians than grant them independence. These seem like caricatures, of course, but Allport believed that such polarizing visions of the other proliferated in contexts of physical segregation, like the segregated American South, or Israel and Palestine.

The contact hypothesis offered a bold remedy to such psychological tendencies to stereotype and discriminate. If conflict endures precisely because, in the course of personality development, members of a group come to internalize these categorizations of the other—this particular matrix of social identity—then we might be able to influence conflict at the group level through intervention with individuals in the course of their development. Though he did not deny a powerful role for social structural factors, Allport (1961) argued that the *individual personality* represented the most "proximal" cause of conflict, for individual behavior maintains intergroup antagonism.

If we accept Allport's (1961) emphasis on individual, mental factors like personality and categorization as a target for intervention, contact becomes increasingly appealing as a possible remedy for conflict. The basic premise of contact theory is that, *under certain conditions*, contact between group members can reduce the prejudice that fuels conflict. Prejudice reduction occurs through a process of *decategorization* and *personalization*—psychological processes by which individuals come to revise their categorization of out-group members, in large part through personal acquaintanceship in which stereotypes are disconfirmed (see Brewer & Miller, 1984; Miller, 2002).

As critics of the contact hypothesis have suggested, Allport's (1954) original set of conditions under which contact might be effective, along with the numerous additions to this set of conditions that have been added over the years, speak more to the ideal than the actual world of intergroup relations (Dixon, Durrheim, & Tredoux, 2005). For example, Allport argued that *equal status* was a precondition of successful prejudice reduction through contact. But intergroup conflict is consistently characterized by a *struggle* for status and recognition, so it is difficult to imagine a scenario in which conflict exists between two pure, equal rivals. And even if we could, would we want to? So many of the salient conflicts between groups are deeply concerned with matters of power and status—Blacks and Whites in the United States; Hutus and Tutsis in Rwanda; Catholics and Protestants in Northern Ireland; Kurds, Sunnis, and Shiites in Iraq; Israelis and Palestinians.

In my view, the most significant problem with the contact hypothesis is its desire to neutralize power. A major part of social movements like, for example, the Civil Rights Movement in the United States has been to recognize the differential power structure—and its impact on individual lives—that exists between groups. Conflict, then, is often a *symptom of social injustice*. If we only discuss conflict through the lens of individual personality, we miss the larger context within which those personalities develop. Allport's (1961) contention that societal factors represent "distal" causes of conflict is problematic because of the word *distal*—it implies a more remote causal influence, whereas I would suggest that the *root* cause of prejudice lies in the structural inequities that *produce* prejudiced personalities (to use Allport's language). Structural factors like unequal access to resources, institutions, or lack of *recognition*, thus differentiating economic and political possibilities for groups, specify the context in which individual lives unfold. Allport's (1954) original emphasis on the psychological harm of segregation in many ways recognizes this fundamental insight about conflict and social justice.

To return to the groundbreaking work of Sherif and colleagues (1961), it is obvious that they were in dialogue with this more individual-personality model of intergroup relations advocated by Allport. Sherif (1958) argued that conflicts are fundamentally rooted not in individual personalities but in *real conflicts of material interest*, realized and manifested in the incompatibility of goals. The individual psychological processes implicated in the production and maintenance of conflict are, thus, epiphenomena—they appear only as the material conflict between groups is present.

For the scholar and practitioner who want to go beyond the level of individual personality, Sherif's *realistic conflict* theory is very appealing. It has a number of important implications for public policy and social justice. Most fundamentally, it suggests that an equal distribution of resources ought to forestall intergroup hostility, and one concrete way of intervention in conflict situations is to manipulate the functional relationship between groups from a place of competition to cooperation.

What is missing, though, in Sherif's revolutionary account is a recognition of the psychological role of *identity* in conflict maintenance and reproduction. In some ways, Sherif and Allport are positioned at opposite ends of a false dichotomy that pits social and individual forces in a battle for primacy. One of my intellectual aims in developing a paradigm that is concerned with the cultural psychology of identity and conflict is to argue strongly against this dichotomy, to suggest that the individual and social structure are dynamically interacting in a mode of *reciprocal production*. Individuals are, hence, both *products* and *producers* of a particular structural configuration of power and identity, and it is through the *individual* process of narrative engagement that they come to unwittingly participate in this larger reproductive end.

To return, however, to the social psychology of conflict before we depart into the details of the particular study with which this book is concerned, it is important to highlight the vital role that *social identity theory* assumed in rescuing Sherif's vision from its particular brand of social reductionism. Developed in the United Kingdom in the 1970s, social identity theory was the product of Henri Tajfel and his numerous students and colleagues at the University of Bristol (e.g., Tajfel, 1978, 1981, 1982a, 1982b; Tajfel & Turner, 1979, 1986). Recall that Sherif's work relied upon an initial phase of *group formation*. Sherif believed that all new groups had to go through an initial process of establishing roles and hierarchies before their members really came to view themselves as a part of the group (particularly when the group was an artificially constructed one like the Eagles and Rattlers). Tajfel's pioneering work, by contrast, revealed that basic processes of differentiation—and, hence, discrimination—occurred even when social identities were extremely insignificant in actual meaning.

Tajfel and his colleagues developed a particular experimental method to discover this fundamental insight—that *mere categorization* into different groups activates in-group bias. In what became known as the *minimal group paradigm*, subjects were brought into the lab, assigned to a group, and then were asked to do tasks such as provide a certain amount of money to an individual who is a member of the same group or to a different group (Tajfel & Turner, 1986). Time and time again, subjects displayed a clear bias toward members of their own, entirely artificial group. The obvious conclusion is that, *even with the most minimal salience of social identity*, individuals express a bias toward members of their own in-group. This finding is absolutely revolutionary because it suggests that *neither a prejudiced personality nor a real conflict of interest is necessary to activate the in-group bias that characterizes intergroup conflict*. Through this rigorous, systematic program of research, Tajfel and his colleagues were able to persuasively specify the *social-cognitive mechanism* by which conflicts are likely to endure—the significance of social identity in thought, feeling, and action.

The implications of social identity theory for attempts at intergroup contact are profound. As Tajfel and Turner (1979, 1986) explicitly argue, individuals do not approach contact *as individuals*—with distinct personality traits, autobiographies, and idiosyncrasies. Rather, individuals approach interactions *as group members*, and their sense of individuality is actually *reduced* in the intergroup situation, thus creating greater homogeneity within the group. This phenomenon is not, they argue based on their experimental work, exclusive to *actual* conflict situations. Rather, it is a *fundamental, intrinsic* aspect of human interaction. We perceive the world not solely as unique individuals with distinct autobiographies; we perceive the world according to the *possibilities for autobiography* mandated by our group memberships. We never approach an interaction as a free-floating, decontextualized, fully agentic being but rather as a *White male advertising executive,* or a *Black lesbian feminist,* or a *middle-class Pakistani immigrant in London.* Our myriad social identities determine the nature of our thought and action in any interaction.

We cannot, thus, anticipate that young Israelis and Palestinians will come to engage with one another as distinct individuals but rather as inhabitants of a matrix of social identities that bring with them *status-related* implications (Halabi & Sonnenschein, 2004a). Their identities might involve a complex configuration of identification as secular or religious, nationalist or postnationalist, villager or city dweller, kibbtuznik or settler, activist or militant. None of these identities, nor Israeli or Palestinian identity more broadly, fall beyond the gaze of power, for social identities inherently involve a concern with *value.*

The way in which power is integrated into social identity theory is through the *perceptions* of esteem-related sentiments that membership confers. Tajfel and Turner (1986) define social identity as "those aspects of an individual's self-image that derive from the social categories to which he perceives himself as belonging" (p. 16). These social categories, they argue, exist in a larger matrix in society in which some are more highly valued than others. Universally, though, groups strive for *positive* or *optimal* distinctiveness (Brewer, 1991; Tajfel & Turner, 1979) and thus will seek to elevate their perceived value when it is insufficient.

Social identity theory suggests that, in a contact situation, individuals will (a) allow their social identities as group members to supercede their personal identities, and (b) seek to enhance the distinctiveness of their group. In a situation of *actual, intractable* conflict such as between Israelis and Palestinians, we might expect these fundamental psychological processes to be quite salient. As a hypothesis, then, we might speculate that contact between Israeli and Palestinian youth will prime social identity to such an extent that it actually *decreases* the distance between master narratives and personal narratives. Contact might result in a substitution of the personal narrative for a collective story of history and identity that fulfills vital psychological functions.

Israeli social psychologist Daniel Bar-Tal has written extensively about social psychological processes that are unique to situations of intractable conflict. He argues that individuals in a conflict setting internalize a core set of *societal beliefs* that aid in coping with conflict—largely by providing a strong sense of social identity and in-group unity—but that ultimately reproduce the conditions of conflict (e.g., Bar-Tal, 1990b, 1998b, 2000, 2007; Rouhana & Bar-Tal, 1998). These beliefs include *exclusive* claims of legitimacy, victimization, injustice, and the need for security. The "ethos" of conflict, he argues, is dominated by a press to internalize these societal beliefs (Bar-Tal, 2000, 2007; Bar-Tal, Raviv, Raviv, & Dgani-Hirsh, 2009), thereby contributing to the cycle of conflict.

Thus, a fundamental feature of the context of conflict is the *polarization* of identities (Hammack, 2006), with their contradictory interpretations of history (Liu & Hilton, 2005) and functional *negative* interdependence (Kelman, 1999b). And this polarization represents a *normative* feature of conflict, if we accept the fundamental insights of research in the social identity tradition. Since conflict essentially involves a *competition* between identities for power and recognition, a contact situation will only activate this strong need for differentiation and distinctiveness predicted by social identity theory.

In the 1990s, there was an effort to integrate all of these perspectives into a framework called *common in-group identity theory* (e.g., Gaertner, Dovidio, Anastasio, Bachman, & Rust, 1993). Accepting the basic premises of both realistic conflict theory *and* social identity theory, Gaertner and his colleagues argued that the induction of a "common identity" ought to represent the superordinate goal of contact. In other words, the contact situation can be manipulated in order to encourage individuals to see themselves as part of a *new, positively distinct* group—a group that exists at a higher level of category inclusiveness (e.g., Gaertner, Dovidio, & Bachman, 1996; Gaertner, Dovidio, Nier, Ward, & Banker, 1999; Gaertner, Rust, Dovidio, & Bachman, 1996). For example, Israeli and Palestinian youth might be encouraged to view one another as members of a new group—say, peacemakers or activists—that *transcends* the divisiveness of their polarized social identities. This new, common identity does not replace social identity but rather supplements it, such that one is no longer *simply* an Israeli but an *Israeli peace activist*.

Using an integrative framework, Gaertner and colleagues reinterpreted the Robbers Cave study, suggesting that more processes than Sherif initially recognized were at play in the study (Gaertner et al., 2000). They argued that processes of *decategorization* (as predicted by classic contact theory), *mutual differentiation* (as predicted by social identity theory and many of its derivatives), and *recategorization* (the process of identifying with a common identity) all occurred at various stages in the study. Ultimately, they suggest, what reduced conflict between the Eagles and the Rattlers was that they came to view one another as a *common* group.

As we consider the effects of intergroup contact on Israeli and Palestinian life stories, it is vital to keep all of this work in social psychology closely in mind. I would suggest that these empirically derived theoretical perspectives specify at least two concrete hypotheses for our consideration: Is contact more likely to result in a personal narrative that continues to reproduce a master narrative of history and identity, or does contact provide the opportunity to *transcend* such irreconcilable narratives and reconstruct a life story as peacemaker? There is no question that the *desired* end ought to be the latter, and that it is to this end that the American-based programs in which I conducted my research admirably strive—to cultivate a new generation of Israeli and Palestinian youth, who will become leaders committed to peace and coexistence. Yet for me these rival hypotheses require empirical scrutiny, for knowledge cannot be the product of ideal imagination but of the reality of human experience.

The Cosmopolitan Ideal

The larger social issue with which all of these paradigms in social psychology have been concerned is the management of *power, identity,* and *difference* within a given social structure. Scholars like Allport, Sherif, and Tajfel all viewed themselves as contributing to larger concerns of racism, discrimination, war, and genocide. These were the fundamental social problems of the twentieth century, and social psychologists used their own scientific tools to contribute to the dialogue on how to address (or, ideally, eradicate) these problems.

The work of Gaertner, Dovidio, and colleagues links social psychology more explicitly to the late–twentieth century issue that came to be called "multiculturalism." By the 1970s, technological advancement and economic and political disparities across the globe had facilitated the increased migration of populations, and a number of societies could increasingly be described as multicultural in character (Parekh, 2006). Nations like Canada, the United States, and Australia—which were all primarily immigrant or settler societies to begin with—saw the development of social and political movements for the recognition of minority rights and for political and social equality (Verkuyten, 2007). These movements—and the new discourse of multiculturalism that accompanied them—coincided with significant shifts in a number of societies as a result of various movements for liberation, such as the Civil Rights Movement in the United States or the numerous postcolonial movements across the globe.

Notions of *identity* and *culture* have been central to these movements, as they have provided the legitimacy for collective struggle. But scholars, practitioners, and policy makers have differed in the response that they take to the challenge of multiculturalism. The response to such movements falls along a range from full recognition (and accompanying political equality) to forced assimilation.

While psychologists have used the language of "categorization" to explore the cognitive foundations of prejudice, bias, and ethnocentrism, scholars in fields like education and moral and political philosophy have used different terms to develop similar arguments about what our response to identity pluralism *ought* to be. Though it is often implicit, rather than explicit, in their work, such scholars generally take a position similar to social psychologists on the identity-related goals of such efforts.

The argument about identity that I develop in this book can be linked to this line of scholarship in education and philosophy, even though "multiculturalism" is hardly an apt term to describe the crux of the Israeli–Palestinian conflict. Where the study I describe in this book intersects with the multiculturalism movement—and with broader conversations about pluralism, identity, and recognition—it centers on the American attempts to intervene in Israeli–Palestinian relations that I examined as an intimate participant observer. The curriculum of these interventions is closely allied with the frame of multicultural education that emphasizes "unity in diversity" while it presses individuals to abandon their claims to the group in favor of a transcendent, superordinate identity. In its crude form, then, the multiculturalism discourse that infuses the interventions I examine is associated with the recategorization approach in social psychology—if we can get individuals to view themselves as members of a new, superordinate group, prejudice will be reduced, and groups might actually start to get along.

There is a great intuitive appeal to this perhaps unfairly simplistic thesis of multiculturalism. As I suggest throughout the book, though, we need to both identify and challenge some of the underlying premises of this approach. In particular, I suggest that we need to distinguish between the Enlightenment *ideal* of a world without the divides of various social identities, which is really the implication of this thesis, and the *real* world of power, politics, and violence—a world in which social identity can both comfort and mobilize, protect and empower. How we view identity—and whether deconstructing, interrogating, or interrupting identity is appropriate in a given context—says much about our own position in a larger matrix of identity politics. If we come from a place of privilege, I suspect we are more likely to be suspicious of collective identity, for it might prove threatening to our own hegemony. If, however, we come from a place of subordination, I suspect that identity becomes a sacred source of security and, consequently, will be protected and defended to the end.

Schools of thought about how societies ought to respond to multiculturalism are, at base, located somewhere along this axis of identity politics.

They inherently address the question of whether or how much identity transcendence is a worthy goal, and where the balance between recognition and transcendence lies. In this book, I locate the American peace education programs I study as experiments in *cosmopolitanism*. As such, they emphasize the idea of *voluntary and multiple affiliations* we might develop in the world (e.g., Hollinger, 2006). And by seeking to expand the scope of affiliation for young Israelis and Palestinians, they seek to enhance the sense of responsibility they have to one another (e.g., Appiah, 2006).

Cosmopolitanism describes an ideal for human relations in which a recognition of the legitimacy of particularity is balanced by a recognition of our common commitment to one another. The philosopher Kwame Anthony Appiah (2006) expresses the cosmopolitan ideal clearly when he says, "[Cosmopolitanism] begins with the simple idea that in the human community, as in national communities, we need to develop habits of coexistence: conversation in its older meaning, of living together, association" (p. xix). Appiah's vision of a world in which we cultivate habits of hospitality to strangers that specify a set of ethical commitments is, indeed, a noble ideal. And it of course strikes anyone who traverses the boundaries of place as an obvious necessity—and, indeed, an actuality in most parts of the world.

My critical interrogation with the cosmopolitan thesis—or the strand within peace and multicultural education that would seem to rely upon interventions with affiliation—is rooted more in the realities of practice with young Israelis and Palestinians than with any opposition to its ideals. For what American who embarks on an intellectual project such as this would not strive for a cosmopolitanism of character? Yet, like my conclusion about the particular approaches to contact and prejudice reduction that have developed within social psychology, I view cosmopolitanism as a thesis worthy of empirical scrutiny. How precisely do interventions designed in the model of a cosmopolitan American ethos operate, and how does their vision for cultivating more harmonious intergroup relations play out for actual lives? This critical interrogation, I believe, leads us to a deeper and more complex conceptualization of the *meaning* of identity in peace and multicultural education.

Identity as Burden or Benefit?

As is likely already apparent, my work with Israeli and Palestinian youth has taken me beyond initial aims of *description* and *intervention* toward a meditation on the politics of identity. In other words, this work naturally speaks to larger concerns about matters of power, difference, and recognition that reside at the core of conversations about contemporary human relations. In many ways, the form of this meditation is *dialogic* throughout this book, and the reader might find glimpses of my own ambivalence in interpreting the implications of my work for social and political transformation.

My ambivalence is indicated in the question I pose through the title of this section. Like all conceptual tools and discursive means of social organization, identity is not neutral. Were we to view identity as a static object, dehistoricized and depoliticized, we would only contribute to its reification as some kind of "essential" quality. The essentialization of identity is problematic on many grounds, not the least of which is because it can legitimize subordination and persecution along the lines of a "natural" social order (Reicher & Hopkins, 2001), as in the case of "race" during the civilizing projects of colonialism (Memmi, 1972/2000) or "homosexuality" in the pathologization of the nineteenth century (Foucault, 1978).

One of my underlying arguments in this book is that Israeli and Palestinian youth are subjects of a regime of identity essentialism—a regime that, for them, dates back at least to the nationalist era, with its exclusionary ethos for some (e.g., Jews in Europe) and its false promises of "liberation" for others (e.g., Arabs in post-Ottoman Palestine). Like many colleagues who study the consequences of this regime (e.g., Bekerman, 2002, 2005, 2009b; Bekerman & Maoz, 2005), I see young Israelis and Palestinians as locked within this confining and unresolved discourse of nationalism. In many ways, it represents the remnants of an older project of human organization. And, in this way, Israelis and Palestinians simultaneously inhabit a world of fervent nationalism, post-nationalist critique (e.g., post-Zionism, Islamism), and globalization, all the while slaves to the security of an essentialized identity discourse. The conflict, then, subjects them to the kind of existential insecurity that seems to *command* the assumption of a strong national identity. Yet it is precisely the strength of nationalist fervor among Israelis and Palestinians that thwarts the possibility of compromise and conflict resolution.

A fundamental legacy of political conflict is thus the *burden of identity*—the perceived need to identify with the group at all costs, for a sense of both security and solidarity. It makes sense that youth—inhabiting the life course moment in which a social order is either reproduced or repudiated (Erikson, 1968)—are the primary bearers of this burden. And, in fact, studies of peace education in Israel reveal that youth come to the experience with far more openness than the adults who educate them (Bekerman, 2005). In other words, youth suffer the psychological consequences of conflict as they begin to develop their identities—as they come to recognize the positions they inhabit in a given matrix of power and intergroup relations, and the discourses of identity that accompany those positions in their society.

This view of identity as burden makes intellectual sense. After all, as I discuss at length in Chapters 3 and 4, it is certainly historically accurate to recognize that Israeli and Palestinian national identities are themselves (at least in their current incarnations) products of exclusionary nineteenth century nationalism in Europe (in the case of Israel) and of postcolonial configurations of political organization (in the case of Palestine). Yet there are some inherent problems in viewing identity as solely a burden in conflict settings.

First, the view of identity as burden takes as an underlying assumption the idea that conflict is a negative phenomenon. I believe we must problematize the notion of conflict as intrinsically negative and recognize that *it depends on where you stand*. In other words, our own identity positioning determines whether we view a particular conflict as positive or negative. For example, most Americans would now view our various internal conflicts—our Civil War, which ultimately ended the practice of slavery, the Civil Rights Movement of the mid–twentieth century—as positive in that they have resulted in a more just society for all its members. The same can be said of the struggle against apartheid in South Africa. Conflicts that are rooted in the struggles of the subordinated to gain recognition or rights can be viewed as positive, if we oppose the use of power to oppress, enslave, and marginalize. From the position of the subordinated, conflicts such as these were tremendously positive, even if they were accompanied by violence and social unrest. For these struggles contributed to the cause of social justice.

Second, thinking of identity as burden, rather than *benefit*, might subvert the claims of subordinated groups by questioning the basis of collective identity. For the subordinated, identity is not a burden but a *tool for liberation* and a basis upon which individuals are mobilized. Research that reveals the *psychological* benefits of identity-relevant meaning for youth in conflict settings speaks to the positive role of identity at the individual level (Barber, 2009b). Once again, though, it is clear that how we conceive of identity depends very much on where *we* stand. In the United States, for example, critiques of the relevance of racial identity and of sexual identity abound, as our society is increasingly framed as "post-race" (e.g., Gilroy, 2000) or "post-gay" (e.g., Savin-Williams, 2005). Yet there is clear evidence that policy continues to be a tool for the subordination of minority groups, such as policy against same-sex marriage (Herek, 2006). In the case of Israelis and Palestinians, a critique of identity would seem to subvert Palestinian claims for national recognition, thus supporting the status quo of the Israeli occupation.

I think it not only defensible but also entirely appropriate to inhabit both of these intellectual stances on identity simultaneously, and this book in many ways offers a dialogue about identity in conflict. It is a dialogue that I seek to have not only with other scholars and practitioners of peace and multicultural education, but also with youth themselves, as I see some value in bringing to their attention the multiple uses of (and problems with) identity. This dialogue can potentially be deeply unsettling, for it challenges our ideal—inherited from the Enlightenment—to see individuals as self-contained and as capable of their own agentic self-direction. Yet I see in this dialogue a possibility for reconceptualizing how we think of the social and psychological consequences of conflict for young lives, and, perhaps more important, how we might move from a status quo of insecurity and subordination to an ideal of liberation and mutual recognition.

Politicizing Psychology, Psychologizing Politics

In his 2004 essay advocating a person-centered cultural psychology, Gjerde claims that "there is no politically neutral position from where to study culture" (p. 139). Consistent with this view and several critical movements within psychology (e.g., Fox, Prilleltensky, & Austin 2009; Ouellette, 2008; Parker, 2007; Prilleltensky, 1997), I suggest that psychological science cannot reside apart from the political world. All of our research brings with it implications for the world of public policy—from neuroscientific efforts to map various social experiences with brain activity to our structural equation models of survey data and our rich ethnographic descriptions of mental health, homelessness, or schooling. Like Prilleltensky (1994), I do not view the world of science as distinct from the world of *values*, and hence I am explicit in my aim to contribute to theory and practice in Israeli–Palestinian peace-making. In this respect, I am no different from many social and personality psychologists who have attempted to integrate a social justice perspective in their work (e.g., Fine & Sirin, 2007; Kelman, 1968; Lott & Bullock, 2007; Opotow, 2007; Smith, 1969, 2003).

This work is thus more than a description of fieldwork with Israeli and Palestinian youth, or an example of cultural psychology or narrative psychology in action. Rather, it is also a meditation on the science and practice of psychology in the realm of real human problems. As I read the literature in various disciplines to prepare for this study—disciplines like history, philosophy, political science, anthropology, education, sociology—I quickly realized that much work in psychology had become disturbingly insular. Many psychologists have been producing important and relevant work on issues like culture, identity, immigration, and the like. Yet too rarely have I encountered acknowledgment or reference to this work. A classic example for me was a 2006 issue of *Daedalus*, the journal of the prestigious American Academy of Arts and Sciences, on identity in which the only psychologist invited to contribute to the conversation was a neuroscientist. Apparently, social and developmental psychology had little to offer this important colloquy of scholars from fields like history and philosophy.

I believe that a primary reason psychologists have been frequently excluded from participation in important conversations across disciplines lies in some of our problematic disciplinary practices—practices that I seek to resist in this book (as in my career more generally). For example, psychology (particularly in the United States) continues to suffer from an identity crisis. Is it a "science," akin to physics or chemistry, or is it more connected to humanistic inquiry? This fundamental root of disciplinary crisis creates considerable tension in areas like theory (is there any use for it?), epistemology (what counts as knowledge?), methodology (how ought we to obtain that knowledge?), and interpretation (does the scientist play a role?). Contemporary psychology in the United States continues to count experimental methods as the ideal, if not the *necessary*, measure of reliable knowledge, suggesting an alliance with positivist notions of "pure" knowledge that can be obtained in a decontextualized laboratory setting.

It is not my place here to deconstruct the underlying philosophy of science of American psychology. Rather, I want simply to suggest that psychological scientists have much more to offer the real-world setting of social problems when they "descend" from the disciplinary ideals of knowledge production to query human lives in action. This approach requires not only the embrace of new, challenging methods like ethnography and other qualitative strategies, but also the recognition that *context matters for human lives*. Thus, the field setting is a rich site, a "living laboratory" (Bar-Tal, 2004b), for real human concerns and relations. I believe that psychologists will contribute to many more conversations within the academy and beyond its fortified walls when we recognize that the political permeates every aspect of our efforts, and hence, we serve the cause for which we studied in the first place—a passion to make sense of thought, feeling, and behavior—best when we abandon the struggle for a "value-free" scientific enterprise.

An underlying aim of this book is thus to push for a more *politicized* psychology, but I also would like to suggest that the field of politics could gain considerably from becoming more psychological. Historians and political scientists too often, in my estimation, overlook individual subjectivity, preferring instead to let documents or artifacts speak for themselves. Such scholarship makes many assumptions about the impact of politics on individual lives. Individual voices are far too often missing from the analytic gaze, or if they are considered, they rarely rely upon a deep appreciation for psychological theory and research. Narrative psychology is uniquely positioned to resolve some of these dilemmas, particularly since scholars outside of psychology are captivated by the idea of narrative. But I believe that there are many other important contributions psychologists can and should make to larger conversations about identity and violence (e.g., Sen, 2006, 2008), multiculturalism and pluralism (e.g., Hollinger, 2006; Parekh, 2006), and cosmopolitanism (e.g., Appiah, 2006). Just as psychology must be politicized, so too must politics be psychologized, if it is to better speak to the consequences of policy and social structure for individual lives.

An Orientation

In this chapter, I have simultaneously attempted to identify the research questions that guided my work with Israeli and Palestinian youth and to present an overarching framework for the study of lives in conflict. Central to my framework are concepts of *culture*—not as static and reified but as dynamic and practice oriented—and of *identity*. My link between these concepts is *narrative*, because I believe that it is through the *practice* of narration that we become cultural beings and, in the process, reproduce the discursive foundations of a culture. In the tradition of scholars like Vygotsky and Mead, I view mind and society as inexorably linked through the practical ongoing activity of human beings, interacting within and upon a received canvas of cognitive and behavioral possibility.

My commitment to a cultural psychology rooted in power, experience, and activity leads me to analyze young Israeli and Palestinian narratives as texts in the making. The design of my study, involving at least two tellings of the personal narrative in relation to intergroup contact, also allows me to query contemporary practice in peace education and the social psychology of conflict resolution. I hope that my interpretation of these young lives in progress will, perhaps, contribute to larger and challenging conversations within these fields about the nature of intervention in an active and intractable conflict situation.

In order to convince the reader of the credibility of my claims, it is first necessary to detail the intricacies of the study, which include, of course, my own personal narrative as a social scientist and a peace scholar. In Chapter 2, I provide extensive information on the procedures and context of my fieldwork, as well as further information about my personal narrative as a "stranger" (Simmel, 1908/1971) to the Israeli–Palestinian conflict. Part 2 of the book presents the stories of youth in rich interpretive detail. I have devoted a chapter to each of the three major demographic groups I studied—Jewish Israelis, Palestinians from the occupied territories, and Palestinian citizens of Israel— to address my first research question about the relationship between master narratives and personal narratives. Dedicated to preserving the integrity of individual life stories in my idiographic approach, I have selected representative cases from each of these groups for a detailed analysis.

Part 3 speaks to the issue of contact between Israeli and Palestinian youth. I present a chapter that details the history of such efforts, followed by a chapter in which I examine the postcontact narratives of youth through the lens of social identity theory and common in-group identity theory. I conclude the book with an audacious call for research and practice in the social psychology of intergroup relations that resists the temptation to neutralize power and remain blind to structural injustice between groups so as to promote individual explanations for the endurance of conflict. Though it may seem antithetical for a psychologist to make such an argument, it is the social, cultural, and *political* psychologist in me that maintains a watchful eye upon the relationship among power, agency, and social structure.

Any empirical study—and its interpretation—represents a historical endeavor (Gergen, 1973). Knowledge is always produced within some larger social, historical, and political context that influences how it is disseminated and consumed. I claim no transhistorical significance for this work, only perhaps for the general guide for the study of person and culture for which I advocate. The data I present only offer a brief window into the history of the Israeli and Palestinian peoples, but I hope that my account can offer some insight into the more general processes of social reproduction through narrative engagement and cultural practice among youth. At the very least, I hope this work stimulates novel ideas for research and practice with youth from across the globe, for our ever-connected world calls for the talents of curious minds who embrace the infinitude of knowledge and reject the boundaries in place to stifle its creative production.

2

A "Stranger" in the Holy Land

A Position

The purpose of this chapter is to outline my own research practice designed to address the theoretical questions about culture, narrative, and identity posed in Chapter 1. But this chapter cannot simply offer an account of detached research activity, for such is not the story of this project. In this type of project, the *reflexivity* of the researcher is essential (Langhout, 2006; Myerhoff & Ruby, 1992; Tedlock, 1991). That is, I must unapologetically *locate* myself for the audience by telling my own personal narrative and considering the way in which my process of discovery was *coconstructed* by me and my young Israeli and Palestinian research participants (Mishler, 1986).

In social science research, there has long been tension about the role of the researcher. In the experimental tradition that came to dominate much psychological research, careful concern is taken to minimize the "experimenter effect"—the influence of the very presence of the experimenter on the data provided by "subjects" (see Kintz, Delprato, Mettee, Persons, & Schappe, 1965). While such highly controlled studies can often isolate cognitive and behavioral phenomena in interesting and informative ways, they suffer from a lack of real-world location. To what extent do results obtained in a highly artificial laboratory setting (often with a unique sample of college undergraduates in the United States) apply to human inter-actions in the real world (see Arnett, 2008; Gergen, 1973; Sears, 1986)? This question has a long and distinguished history within psychology, with numer-ous debates about the merits of emphasizing *external* versus *internal* validity, generalizability versus situational control (Mook, 1983). Some have suggested that the experimental context itself serves as a context for the enactment of social drama, thus providing information that is *discursively* produced—attitudes and behaviors, for example, that form part of a larger *story* of expect-able social interaction, realized in the psychological laboratory (Moghaddam & Harré, 1982).

Taking a lead from sister fields like anthropology and sociology, qualitative psychology has encouraged researchers to identify and recognize their role in the production of data, rather than seek to minimize it. In other words, because qualitative psychology requires immersion into a particular research context in the real world, "experimenter effects" are simply a natural part of the research process and can, in fact, become useful sources of data in their own right. As I will suggest in this chapter, I believe an analysis of my own position vis-à-vis Israeli and Palestinian youth offers useful information about the identity devel-opment of these youth, who inhabit unique worlds characterized by insecurity and a heightened sensitivity to collective identity (Pettigrew, 2003).

In addition to the issue of my own position and reflexivity, this chapter details the field methods used in the study, including extensive details about the field sites in the two American-based programs and the numerous Israeli and Palestinian communities, as well as details about the interview sample, procedure, and analytic strategy for narrative data. Because of the need for reflexivity and because of the evolving historical context of the Israeli–Palestinian conflict, I have written this chapter in a somewhat different style from typical chapters that describe the methods of a major study. I have attempted to integrate personal narrative, details about historical events in Israel and Palestine during the time of my fieldwork (2003–2007), and a rich description of the field sites and interview methods. My hope is that such a style of presentation very clearly situates the analysis that will follow in subse-quent chapters, while also offering an engaging description of the study and my motivations to conduct it.

The interpretive work necessary in any research endeavor that relies heav-ily on fieldwork and ethnography must be considered through the lens of the researcher. Reflexivity thus requires a clear statement of *position* from the researcher—a reflective narrative of his or her own identity and its connection to the research. Though I may have perhaps begun this work as a classic "participant observer," it cannot be denied that I eventually became an "observing participant" (Tedlock, 1991), and thus what I offer as a product in this book is, at least in part, the narrative of a researcher himself. Alternatively, it may be considered an act of reflexive analysis, but it is without question the account of my own process of *narrative engagement* with the Israeli–Palestinian conflict. Were I to assume another analytic role—that of, for example, the classic detached field-worker, who records but whose presence (and influence) is erased by the conventions of "scientific" practice—I would surely gamble with both the authenticity and the credibility of this book. Such a betrayal would, I believe, accomplish a most undesirable end, yet one that plagues a number of otherwise influential works on the Israeli–Palestinian conflict, whose authors are chastised for their unwillingness to fully acknowledge the impact of their own identity on the research: dismissal on the basis of "bias." I hope that this work can be considered a serious and accurate account of Israeli and Palestinian youth and their role in the larger process of cultural antagonism and political conflict. To this end, I must offer a complete account of my own position in *their* world, and how this position came to bear on my analytic and interpretive practice as a researcher.

Expanding upon Simmel's (1908/1971) classic notion of the social scientist as "stranger," Cressey (1927/1983) argues that the role of the stranger in research requires (a) a delicate balance of proximity and distance to the group or groups under study in the researcher's perceived identity, and (b) the establishment of "prestige" vis-à-vis the groups under investigation. As I will discuss at greater length, I believe my position as a non-Jewish, non-Arab American, coupled with my gender and my occupational status as a psychologist and a researcher, enabled me to conform precisely to this role. That the assortment of social identity labels that could be nominally ascribed to me—American, Christian, Male, Psychologist, Researcher (to name a few)—came to imbue my role with a distinct "strangeness" is most certainly an advantage in a context replete with identity politics. I have come across accounts on this very topic in which the variation in just a few of these labels (e.g., "Jewish" instead of "Christian," "Female" instead of "Male") yields an investigator quite different data (and access to data) than my own. My own collection of social identities seemed to allow me to occupy a kind of "liminal" (i.e., in-between) identity space in the larger context of the conflict, yet one fortunately accorded some measure of both the "balance" and "prestige" that Cressey suggests constitutes the role of the "stranger."

As Simmel argued, the "objectivity" afforded the stranger can lead to a "confessional" attitude among the research participants: in viewing me as a figure of some prestige *outside of* the group, a kind of honesty in the provision of data becomes possible that a member of the in-group may not be able to secure. For example, a taxi driver in Palestine once argued to me passionately for the incompetence of his own people: "Arabs are lazy and stupid.... I would have preferred to be a Jew." It is doubtful, were I to occupy any social identity other than the specific one that I happen to, that I would receive such sentiments.

Yet my position as an American—a citizen of a nation that has played a particular role in the Israeli–Palestinian conflict—cannot be considered one of "neutrality." Rather than impose some differentially "negative" (i.e., among Palestinians) or "positive" (i.e., among Israelis) inflection on my status as a stranger, however, both groups, I believe, came to view me as someone to "win over." It has long been argued that the United States represents the only possible mediator in this conflict, and I believe my American identity actually enhanced my prestige in this way. Yet I am not so naïve as to suggest that my research subjects came to view me *comprehensively* beyond my own social identity. I believe what I came to represent for them—the youth in particular—was the face of the Western, global culture, so dominated by American cultural discourse (e.g., language), artifact (e.g., media), and practice (e.g., consumerism and style).

Each interview, then, must be considered in light of my role as a representative of this global, American-dominated youth culture (Arnett, 2002; Larson, 2002). As youth confided in me their stories, I believe their intended audience extended far beyond me. I believe they recognized in me a figure who could disseminate their stories. So their narratives were carefully constructed with an eye toward a larger, global audience. As I present and interpret these narratives, I attempt to maintain this reflection of position in mind. That my interview data is supplemented by observational and ethnographic data helps to reveal the complications and contradictions in the life stories of youth, illuminating the complexity of identity development in the context of conflict.

In order to place my own reflexivity in the foreground, I present my own personal narrative of engagement with the Israeli–Palestinian conflict. This account will, in my view, provide the reader with important information about my biography that will be of value as I describe my field sites and methods, for I hope to have the reader see the field as I initially saw it, as a canvas on which to make sense of young lives.

A Personal Narrative

Not surprisingly, upon describing my work to colleagues, friends, or acquaintances, their typical response is, if they do not know me, "Are you Jewish?"

or "Are you Arab?" I even had a friend who, midway through the course of this research, had forgotten that I in fact am not Jewish, commenting to me on a Jewish holy day. My multiple travels to Israel had, it seems, confused him. So central has my own elusive identity been to this work.

My research participants are equally, if not more, inquisitive about my identity. I encounter such questions because to look at me, one could speculate that I have some connection to the region. My features are Mediterranean, owing to Italian roots on my mother's side, but I have neither Jewish nor Arab affiliation of any kind. The very fact that I am virtually *always* encountered with this question reveals the necessity of reflexivity in my work.

I value the revelation of both my personal identity, as revealed in what others come to know about my biography (Goffman, 1963), as well as my motivation to conduct such a research project—the two of which are entirely intertwined. For the second question I nearly universally encounter is "Why are you interested in this topic?" To trace the genesis of my intellectual concern with the Israeli–Palestinian conflict, then, one must know something of my own biography.

To say that the environment of my own socialization was lacking in religious diversity is a significant understatement. A Catholic of Italian and distantly British and Dutch origins, I found myself surrounded by Christians as a child in the suburbs of Washington, DC. Diversity in my exposure to religion as a child existed only upon meeting Protestants, who were plentiful where I grew up in the colonial town of Alexandria, Virginia. The Washington area public education system was notorious for having only a few quality schools, so most who could afford to sent their children to private religious schools. I began in an Episcopalian elementary and middle school, moving onto a Jesuit Catholic secondary school. What I can recall most when I consider my own socialization and its connection to my eventual intellectual interest in the Israeli–Palestinian conflict was the complete absence of any perspective at all.

For me as a child, "Israel" had some relevance to the Bible, as did "Palestine," and as far as I knew both represented the "Holy Land" in some way, though naturally I could not locate either geographic locale in its contemporary form on a map, nor was I bothered by such ignorance. Prior to university, I recall having a single Jewish friend in elementary school, naturally having no interest in our cultural or religious differences, only in whether he had the latest G.I. Joe action figures. I am often somewhat embarrassed by the religious exclusivity of my upbringing, particularly since by late adolescence I fashioned myself a person very open to (and increasingly interested in) cultural and religious diversity. Yet, finding myself a person relatively unconcerned with religion at all, I possessed little interest in topics that I interpreted as somehow religious in nature, like the Israeli–Palestinian conflict. (That the conflict itself has little to do with religion was a discovery I would not make for some time.)

As an undergraduate student of psychology at Georgetown, a place quite engaged in topics like the Israeli–Palestinian conflict, I generally avoided such discussions or considerations. At that time in my scholarly career, I viewed psychology as concerned with problems of human development rooted in individual experience, not large-scale political conflicts. I narrowly pursued training in clinical and developmental psychology, with some shallow interest in issues of culture. While my friends occasionally argued and protested, or entered into serious debates on the conflict, I generally withdrew. Of course, it was a different historical era in the course of the conflict: I entered Georgetown in 1994, one year after the historic signing of the Oslo accords just a few miles away from me. Not that I was at all aware of the post-Oslo culture in Israel and Palestine, with its sense of possibility.

I began graduate study in clinical psychology in 1999 with an interest in studying the psychological functioning of ethnic and sexual minorities in the United States. It was not long before I realized that training in mainstream clinical psychology considered culture in highly insensitive and inappropriate ways, viewing the charting of "ethnic differences" along the lines of a "cookbook" of psychological adaptation as its main contribution. I was quite fortunate to, in the midst of my discontent, discover cultural psychology through the writings of Rick Shweder and his colleagues. After my fortunate meeting of Bert Cohler in the process of seeking a clinical placement in a program for which he conducted supervision, the decision to seek formal training in cultural psychology and human development at the University of Chicago, rather than mainstream clinical psychology, was inevitable. It is important at this point in my biography to know the larger sociohistorical context within which my intellectual interests shifted and my lens became focused on Israel and Palestine.

The second Palestinian *intifada* erupted in 2000, coinciding roughly with my work at Loyola University Chicago on a study of urban African-American youth exposed to violence (Hammack, Richards, Luo, Edlynn, & Roy, 2004). As I witnessed the images of the *intifada*—the devastation of suicide bombings in cafés and bus stops, the Israeli tanks bulldozing Palestinian homes—I had a sort of "ethical" awakening as a researcher. I came to realize that, as I began to engage with cultural psychology as a student, research must be socially *relevant*. As I saw these images and followed the journalistic interpretations of these events, I realized the conflict made little sense to me. If it made little sense to me, if these analyses provided in the American media seemed to so vaguely contribute to my own knowledge of what this great tragedy in human interaction was really all about, then surely I was not alone.

I undertook a kind of self-education in the conflict that lasted a number of years (and of course continues today). I came to view my biography as incomplete in its lack of attention to significant international concerns. And I came to resituate my identity as a researcher directly with this intellectual agenda: to examine the psychological features that characterize human development in contexts of political conflict. I came to this problem not for its "negative" undertones. Rather, I came to this problem for its ability to speak to an inherent (and unique) concern of cultural psychology with the complex, dynamic interrelationship of person and culture. But beyond just the relevance of such a problem for cultural psychology as a paradigm or a discipline, I was motivated to pursue this research for its large-scale social relevance. As a scholar with interdisciplinary interests and collaborative aspirations, I came to appreciate the possibility of such a study for its ability to contribute to a larger base of knowledge.

So, before I began this work, if someone were to engage me in a free association task, to the prompt "Palestinian," I would undoubtedly reply, enthusiastically, "Terrorist!" To the prompt "Israel," I would surely offer a response of this sort: "Bible" (a bit less enthusiastically perhaps). I have come to view the lack of knowledge and depth present in my biography prior to this project as a great benefit. It allowed me to "discover" the conflict on my own terms, and the absence of any particular political perspective on the conflict in my own socialization surely solidified the authenticity of my status as a "stranger" in the Holy Land.

Since initiating this research and becoming fully enmeshed in it, my biography has of course been radically altered. Where I once possessed little affect around the topic of Israel and Palestine, I now find myself engaging in such conversations with great animation. I have come to view the information that Americans truly possess about this situation as extremely incomplete, in a way that only my immersion into the conflict through my travels has been able to correct. Thus, when I engage with friends and colleagues now about the conflict, I express a great passion that was once entirely absent. Most importantly, though, I believe I have come to genuinely "feel" with *both* Israelis and Palestinians. While I have gone through an ideological "roller coaster" in my travels through the region, witnessing my own identifications and empathic responses, I believe I have come to appreciate and admire the aspirations of both peoples.

A brief example will illustrate the complexity of my own emotional response to the conflict. After my initial field trip to the region, I was overwhelmed emotionally at the sights and sounds of life in the occupied Palestinian territories.

Traversing numerous military checkpoints, themselves highly problematic for the asymmetrical power relations they establish and reinforce (Gordon, 2008a, 2008b), I found myself crossing from the "developed" world (i.e., Israel) to the "developing" world (i.e., Palestine) in a matter of minutes (or hours, depending on the mood of the soldiers). From nicely paved and well-lit roads to dirt roads strewn with trash and sewage, such a contrast cries for a "stranger" to sympathize with the social and economic plight of the Palestinians (Roy, 2004). But the hardships of daily life for Palestinians speak for themselves and require little embellishment from me: lack of mobility, hazardous living conditions, unemployment, poverty, and so on (Makdisi, 2008). By contrast, I found daily life in Israel to be quite replicable to life in the United States or a European country, with the signs of economic development and success everywhere.

The *differential structure* of the two societies creates an inevitable power imbalance that necessarily instills sympathy for the Palestinians, who do not, after all, even have an independent sovereign state (that is universally recognized, with clearly defined borders). They are subjects of an occupying army and government. They do not possess "freedom" in any sense resembling that of Europe, the United States, or Israel itself.

Yet my emotional response to the conflict was complicated by another factor: a great admiration for the success of Israel. The same sympathy I feel for the Palestinians pervades my emotional response to the plight of Jews before the creation of the State of Israel in 1948. The discrimination and genocide they faced in Europe is without question imprinted in the collective conscience of the Western world. So what is not so astonishing about Zionism as an ideology is its ethnocentric, "Orientalist" (Said, 1978) character (that is far too easy to identify), but rather its *great success*, for Israel does indeed represent a unique culture, with its own language and "ethos," and its own great accomplishments (Talmon, 1970). This, I believe, is quite laudable.

It is easy, I came to realize in my own process of ideological identification, to come to identify with Palestine over Israel. After all, is Israel not merely an extension of colonialism and another instance of the dispossession of an indigenous population (Rodinson, 1973; Said, 1979, 1994)? Are we not, as Americans, radically opposed to the proliferation of such regimes, despite our own national past? But to blindly take this position on Israel is (a) to fail to place Zionism in its particular historical context, at the height of nationalist movements in Europe that specifically *excluded* Jews (Hobsbawm, 1990; Mosse, 1978; Sartre, 1948), and (b) to view Israelis as a monolithic group of "colonialists," which is certainly not the case, given the great ideological diversity that exists within Israeli society (Shafir & Peled, 2002).

The complexity of my own identification with these two peoples has, I believe, enabled me to strike an interpretive balance in this study. My ability to identify with the aspirations of each is, I believe, framed by their parallel psychological needs. Both groups need to express their cultural identities in ways that ensure existential security and national status (Pettigrew, 2003), with all of its representative "liberties" (Fukuda-Parr, 2004; United Nations Development Program [UNDP], 2004). If one comes to view these parallel needs as *legitimate*, as I have come to, then one inevitably identifies with the psychological conditions of both groups.

I do not wish to suggest that I in some way achieved the remarkable ability to engage in interpretive ethnography or fieldwork in some "value-neutral" manner. I believe such practice is impossible in social science, as our values always frame our research questions, procedures, and interpretations (Prilleltensky, 1994). What I do believe, however, is that I successfully attained and maintained the status of a "stranger," striking a balance between nearness and distance from my research subjects and maintaining a level of "prestige" as an American, a psychologist, and a face of the global culture to which Israeli and Palestinian youth so commonly look for influence.

My intention in very honestly presenting my own professional and personal biography vis-à-vis the Israeli–Palestinian conflict was to address from the start questions about my own identity and my motivation to conduct the research. Whether or not the reader identifies with me in this process or in my own desire is likely very much related to his or her own biography. I can only proceed in presenting and interpreting my findings with the knowledge that I have, as it were, "come clean" on my own position. I will not, as I present my findings, shy away from continuing this level of reflexivity in interpretation.

Approaching the Study of Lives

The theoretical perspective I outlined in Chapter 1 specifies a particular methodological approach to the study of culture and identity—an approach that transcends the boundaries of disciplines in the social sciences *and* humanities. Most generally, the study involved qualitative field research in the tradition of sociology (e.g., Goffman, 1961; Whyte, 1943), anthropology (e.g., Evans-Pritchard, 1937/1976; M. Mead, 1928), and social and cultural psychology (e.g., Cassaniti, 2006; Fine & Weis, 1998 Gregg, 2005, 2007). I relied upon techniques of field research (e.g., extensive field notes and interviews) that would allow me to engage in the "thick description" (Geertz, 1973) of a problem—in this case, the identity development of youth in conflict and the consequences of an intervention in this process.

Given my focus on narrative, an emphasis on methodology that is simultaneously ethnographic and *idiographic* (i.e., person-centered) speaks to my view of this project within the larger field of narrative psychology (e.g., Mishler, 1996). It is narrative that anchors the approach of my fieldwork, and hence, it is to the presentations and constructions of self and psychological complexity provided by cultural "actors" that I look for insights. I seek to examine the ways in which "social facts" (Durkheim, 1895/1982) lodge within individual consciousness and serve to organize and negotiate the continuities and disruptions of human development.

Such an endeavor requires a methodological approach that treats individual cases as units of analysis in their own right, so my fieldwork is grounded in the systematic observation of *individuals*, with concurrent analysis of their cultural and historical locations. This case-based method, once popular in psychology, gradually gave way to a more *nomothetic* or *aggregate* view of personality and human development (see Allport, 1937, 1962; Danziger, 1990; Lamiell, 1981). It has become increasingly clear, however, that the production of knowledge about aggregates does not always prove useful in the consideration of individual lives, for aggregate data tends to reduce the variability and complexity of data to a simple "mean," thereby effectively erasing the voices of individual experience (see also Bem, 1983; Lamiell, 1981; Lamiell, Foss, Larsen, & Hempel, 1983; Runyan, 1983).

In the tradition of classic theorists and researchers in psychology (e.g., Allport, 1924; Erikson, 1959; Murray, 1938), I return to a case-based approach at a time of resurgent interest in such approaches—for their ability to provide access to the construction of individual meaning and subjectivity through narration (see McAdams, 1995b; Schachter, 2005). By preserving the data of our "human subjects" as an intact whole, we preserve the integrity of experience as it is narrated, and thus as it is actually lived.

I owe this general methodological view not only to classic social and personality psychologists but also to other social and human scientists whose perspectives informed my design of this study. My *interpretive* approach can be traced directly to social philosophers like Wilhelm Dilthey and Paul Ricoeur, both of whom emphasize the idea of lives as *texts* to be studied and interpreted (e.g., Dilthey, 1923/1988; Ricoeur, 1992), as well as to the general "interpretive turn" that has characterized the social sciences since the 1970s (Rabinow & Sullivan, 1987). Such a view is directly linked to the narrative movement within psychology, which seeks to examine individual meaning making as it occurs through the analysis of personal narratives (Bruner, 1990; Polkinghorne, 1988).

And interpretive approaches have gradually made their way, through narrative psychology and other critical perspectives, into psychological theory and research (e.g., Tappan, 1997, 2005).

In order to access these processes of narrative engagement and identity *development*, I utilized a longitudinal, ethnographic research design that I believed would afford me access to these processes among youth. I began fieldwork in the two American-based programs in the summer of 2003, conducting initial interviews and observations. I traveled extensively in Israel and Palestine in 2004 and 2005, interviewing youth prior to contact and conducting follow-up interviews with youth who had participated in the prior year. In 2006 and 2007, I continued my travels in order to obtain further longitudinal data from youth, residing with families throughout the region and spending considerable time with youth and their social networks.

The Politics of the Field

When I began my fieldwork in the summer of 2003, it was a time of optimism in the history of the conflict. Sadly, the peaks and valleys of the conflict resemble a dramatic mountain range in which great peaks give way to deep descents. I recall working on my first research proposal in the spring of 2003 amid news reports of visits from Israeli Prime Minister Ariel Sharon and newly appointed (at the urging of President Bush, who refused to deal with Palestinian President Yasser Arafat) Palestinian Prime Minister Mahmoud Abbas (a.k.a. Abu Mazen) to Washington. Though largely "sheltered" that summer from news reports in the isolation of the Seeds of Peace camp in Maine, all of us there were keenly aware of the fact that the "road map" was put on the table as a blueprint for progress toward a permanent resolution. Israel's continued settlement construction and assassination attempt on senior Hamas leader Abdel-Aziz Rantisi (unsuccessful for that moment) sparked lively discussion of concern on the prospects of the road map. Abu Mazen demonstrated his influence in the successful brokering of a cease-fire, though many claimed it was in fact imprisoned leader Marwan Barghouti who was able to seal the deal. The fragile cease-fire hardly lasted more than a month, though, and by the summer's end, there were fresh rounds of targeted assassinations by Israel, and a 29-year-old imam from the Palestinian city of Hebron—a man with a family of his own—exploded himself on a bus full of Orthodox Jewish families returning home from prayers at the Western Wall in Jerusalem.

The mood of that first summer of my fieldwork was thus initially, however briefly, optimistic. The two governments, aided significantly by the United States, seemed to at least be talking to one another and moving in a particular direction. Yet a break in the cycle of violence on the ground could not be sustained, with Israelis believing it vital to their long-term security and interest to assassinate Hamas leaders in Gaza, and the Palestinians feeling justified in continuing their bloody *intifada* in retaliation and in defiance of the occupation. The coexistence programs, with their physical and psychological distance from the social structure of conflict, provided sites of isolation for the youth—respites from the intensity of constant shifts in mood and prospect.

The political context leading up to my first field visit to the region in May of 2004 was, not surprisingly, replete with significant events. Mahmoud Abbas resigned his post, replaced by another senior Fatah figure, Ahmed Qurei. Israel suggested that Arafat ought to be deported, and deputy prime minister (later Prime Minister) Ehud Olmert publicly did not rule out the possibility of Arafat's assassination. Edward Said, the Palestinian scholar, icon, and de facto spokesperson to the West, died after a long battle with leukemia. Construction of Israel's controversial separation barrier increased, along with a growing discourse of concern about it in the international community. A brutal suicide bombing in an Arab-owned restaurant in Haifa (in fact, belonging to the family of one of my research participants) frequented by both Israeli Jews and Arabs revealed that no citizen of Israel was immune from possible attack. The popularity of Hamas, the social service and welfare agency with a militant wing that vowed the destruction of Israel, grew in Palestine. Ariel Sharon first spoke of unilateral "disengagement" unless the Palestinian Authority could reign in militants, all the while facing allegations of financial improprieties which threatened to ruin his political career. The once-architect of Jewish settlement expansion in the Palestinian territories, and thus a champion for "Greater Israel," proposed the complete evacuation of Jewish settlements in Gaza. The legality of the Israeli separation barrier came into question, as the United Nations issued a resolution calling for its removal and the International Court of Justice in The Hague considered hearing the case. Finally, on March 22, 2004, Israel assassinated the wheelchair-bound icon and founder of Hamas, Sheikh Ahmed Yassin.

To even the casual follower of the Israeli–Palestinian conflict, this cata-logue of political happenings reveals quite shockingly the transient nature of a political context in conflict. Initial faith in the road map strikes us now as naively optimistic. The very fact of Ariel Sharon and Yasser Arafat as *the* key players in this part of the long saga seems somehow remote. Now both leaders have vanished from the political landscape, and the Palestinian territories are now governed by two feuding entities (the Fatah-led Palestinian Authority [PA] in the West Bank and Hamas in the Gaza Strip). Sharon's ideology of unilateral disengagement has evolved into an entire political party—"Kadima" (Hebrew for "forward")—with a centrist platform and a vow to dismantle a significant number of West Bank settlements. But this strategy has now been called into question, with the Israeli public perception that unilateral disengagement in both Lebanon and Gaza served only to increase the security threats against them. In 2008, Sharon's successor, Ehud Olmert, was forced from power due to charges of corruption, and the Kadima party was ousted in the 2009 elections, replaced by a right-leaning coalition led by former Prime Minister Benjamin Netanyahu. Unfortunately, this new government continues to send conflicting signals about whether it even supports a two-state solution to the conflict—a dramatic policy shift that does not bode well for the possibility of a peace agreement.

I highlight the salience of political change because it most certainly impacts the identities of its youth subjects, as political and ideological changes beget shifts in the discourse of a society. For me in my regional fieldwork, conducted in successive waves from 2004 to 2007, the rapid shifts in political context enabled me to readily detect the ways in which these shifts were impacting individual lives. Was it easier or more difficult to traverse the checkpoints? Were there fewer or more of them? Were sites in Israel more or less fortified? These basic components of the physical culture of the field in fact reflected that all-too-irreducible "ethos" that one cannot help but feel upon immersion into a particular society not his or her own. My fieldwork experience was thus informed by an interpretive perspective on the ways in which the social ecologies of the youth were impacted by the larger political context.

Field Sites in Israel and Palestine

My fieldwork in the region occurred in a number of communities. In most of these communities, I resided with the families of youth. In Israel, I conducted fieldwork in Jerusalem, Tel Aviv, Haifa (with both Jewish and Arab families), Taybeh (an Arab city), and in two different types of rural communities (a *moshav* and a *kibbutz*) in the Gilboa area of the Galilee. In Palestine, field communities included East Jerusalem, Beit Jalla (which neighbors Bethlehem), Ramallah, and Qadas[1] (a small West Bank village). Fieldwork in Palestine also brought me to Bethlehem, Tulkarm, and Nablus for day trips and interviews. It is

---

1 Qadas is the name of a Palestinian village destroyed after the 1948 war. It is used here as a pseudonym for another village in the West Bank. It is the only community of fieldwork that is not recognized by its actual name because of its very small size and the possibility that it could easily be identified as a result.

noteworthy that I did not conduct fieldwork in the Gaza Strip at all, which limited my experience somewhat of Palestine as a field site. Neither coexistence program, however, recruited youth from Gaza during the period of my fieldwork, so the sampling of Gazan youth was not central to the aims of the study. One should take general statements, though, about Palestine, Palestinian culture, and Palestinian identity with something of a grain of salt, as none of my findings are meant to characterize or to represent the lives of Gazan youth.

Nonetheless, one can see by the catalog of communities that a fair amount of geographic diversity was obtained in my fieldwork. For such a tiny piece of land, Israel and Palestine retain a number of local identities that are quite prominent. For example, as I discuss in Chapter 3, growing up on a kibbutz in the north of Israel brings with it a certain "kibbutznik" identity that is quite divergent from that of someone who has grown up in cosmopolitan Tel Aviv. The same can be said of Palestine, where Jerusalemites possess an identity quite distinct of Palestinians from villages like Qadas or even Ramallah, the cosmopolitan Palestinian city. Those from Beit Jalla and Bethlehem, with their larger traditional Christian populations, naturally possess a different local identity than Palestinians from predominantly Muslim Tulkarm. I will briefly detail the demographic and physical characteristics of the primary communities of fieldwork to provide the reader with some detail of the communities.

Jerusalem

As a 2006 report in *The Economist* suggests, this city offers a microcosm of the larger conflict itself. Jerusalem has always been the center point for the numerous conflicts that have characterized this part of the world over the course of human history. In modern times, it has been a site of great identity diversity, where numerous communities of Jewish, Christian, and Muslim religious faith have at times cooperated and at other times been pitted against one another (Romann & Weingrod, 1991; Wasserstein, 2001). The city, referred to in Arabic as *Al Quds* ("the Holy"), contains the holiest religious site for Judaism (the Western Wall of the original Temple). It is the third holiest city for Muslims, as the Prophet Mohammed is said to have ascended into heaven from the *Haram al-Sharif* (the "Noble Sanctuary"), which rests on the Temple Mount. The city holds great significance for Christians as well, as it is the site of Jesus' crucifixion. (His route walked with the cross is marked as the *Via Dolorosa* in the Old City.)

The city is, not surprisingly, a profoundly religious locale, especially when compared to other Israeli and Palestinian cities. The skyline is littered with churches, mosques, and synagogues. Religious Jews, who dress in their distinctive clothing, fill the streets of the West and parts of the Old City. Priests and imams can be readily identified walking the narrow paths of the Old City, located in the East. Yet the current population of Jerusalem is, however divided, quite heterogeneous.

My field visits to Jerusalem were characterized by the salience of its cultural (and national) division. Once divided in half in its entirety prior to the 1967 war, Arabs and Jews could not come together because of the barrier erected between them. Today, that physical barrier is absent, yet its invisible remnants remain. Despite Israel's contention that Jerusalem is the "reunited eternal capital," one does not feel in "Israel" in most parts of East Jerusalem. Although Israel has constructed a number of Jewish settlements around the Arab parts of East Jerusalem, the communities remain entirely at bay. During my first field trip, a good friend and colleague who is Jewish was uncomfortable driving me to the house in which I was staying in East Jerusalem—a place in which I felt extremely comfortable, welcomed, and safe—even though he is no stranger to the Arab population in East Jerusalem, having worked at Seeds of Peace.

I discovered, rather quickly, that Jerusalem indeed remained two quite insular worlds—one Jewish, one Palestinian. The youth who inhabited these worlds were, for all intents and purposes, in fact living in two separate countries. The education system itself was indicative. While Roai, a Jewish Israeli, studied for his *bagrut* examination at the end of high school and prepared for army service on the weekends, Mohammed, a Palestinian, studied for the *tawjihi* examination, an examination used in the Arab Middle East as an indicator of scholastic aptitude, and contemplated his options for university study in Palestine, Lebanon, or Egypt (he ultimately chose Palestine). Mohammed was by no means integrated into Israeli society, even in terms of its institutions. He did, however, possess permanent residency status from the state of Israel, as did all East Jerusalemites after Israel's annexation of the East following the 1967 war. (This annexation remains unrecognized by the United Nations and the international community.)

East and West Jerusalem thus continue to offer a binational socialization experience for youth. The invisible border between Jewish and Arab areas means that, despite their proximity to one another, this is a heavily segregated city. The physical cultures of the two "sides" of the city replicate their two nations. East Jerusalem, like most cities in the West Bank, is dirty, with dilapidated buildings and rubble—in general, poor infrastructure and maintenance of the physical culture. (I should note that this physical state resembled that of West Bank cities but was nowhere near as complete as in those cities and villages, which tended to be on the receiving end of Israeli incursions. Such was not the case in East Jerusalem; it simply was not well maintained.) West Jerusalem, by contrast, was beautiful, leafy, modernized. I often spoke of the experience in my field notes, upon crossing between Palestine and Israel, as my traversal from the "third" to "first" world—from the "developing" to the "developed." Though less dramatic in crossing that invisible border from East to West Jerusalem than in crossing from the West Bank, the feeling of cultural change in crossing that line was nonetheless quite perceptible.

Ramallah

Ramallah, the center of cosmopolitan life in Palestine, is a close distance from Jerusalem (without checkpoints) but feels quite far. With a population of approximately 280,000 (Palestinian Central Bureau of Statistics, 2005), Ramallah is a crowded, densely traversed city, the streets lined with numerous businesses and filled with ubiquitous yellow taxis.

Just with a brief stroll down the famous Rukab Street, Ramallah reveals the incredible diversity of Palestine and its people. Businessmen and women, dressed in European-style fashion, walk beside women in full *hijab* (covered, in the Muslim tradition), young men in tight T-shirts and jeans (again, European style), and older men wearing the traditional Palestinian *kafiya* and holding prayer beads. Nuts, falafel, sweets, and produce are sold on the streets. The city is alive. So alive, in fact, that the notion of a curfew, imposed by the Israeli military during its reoccupation of Ramallah in the early days of the second *intifada*, seems so inconceivable.

Culturally, then, Ramallah is a site of incredible cosmopolitanism in Palestine. Western journalists, tourists, and diplomats mingle with young educated locals at Ziryab, a restaurant that serves both *nargila* (water pipe) and alcohol. Business and commerce abound; nearby Birzeit University serves as the site of higher education and ensures that Ramallah has a large student population. Women and men work together, and there is an air of respect for the diversity embodied here, an acceptance of the multiple lifeways Palestinians may (and do) follow. While the occupation may at times constrain (and even test) this cosmopolitanism, as the life stories of youth reveal in Chapter 4, it is the unity of secular Palestinian nationalism that seems to help retain this ethos in Ramallah.

In the years of my travel to Ramallah, I witnessed major improvements in the physical infrastructure of the city, although it had quite far to go. Nowhere in Palestine was a socioeconomic gap more readily apparent than in Ramallah. Ministers and businessmen occupied a number of newly constructed mansions atop the hill that resembled small villas. Meanwhile, others slept several family members to a room (as was the case for me) and struggled to support one another. The visibility of this disparity helped me to anticipate the rise to power of Hamas over Fatah following Arafat's death and Abu Mazen's inability to improve life for ordinary Palestinians.

Qadas

A small village in the West Bank, Qadas typifies the Palestinian village of today. Getting to the village from anywhere in Palestine necessitates crossing several checkpoints monitored by Israeli soldiers. At the time of my first visit, to enter the village, one needed to pass through an entry gate attended by Palestinian security forces. My driver exclaimed, as we approached the gate, "Aha! A Palestinian checkpoint!" (The Israeli checkpoint is, not surprisingly, the subject of extreme disgust and disdain among Palestinians. It serves as a constant reminder of the occupation and the unbalanced power dynamics between the two peoples.)

The entry to Qadas is adorned with Palestinian flags. On my second visit to the village, a number of green Hamas flags began to dominate, as the village became a Hamas stronghold over the course of 2005. It is noteworthy that in my return trip to Qadas in the midst of the 2007 factional war between Fatah-dominated PA forces and Hamas fighters in Gaza, the green Hamas flags had disappeared from the streets of Qadas. A poster of Sheik Ahmed Yassin remained on the roadway but was significantly faded by the sun. The road into the village is, like most of the roads in Palestine, in terrible shape. Potholes and unpaved sections abound. The streets are littered with trash, the walls covered in graffiti. Posters of Palestinian martyrs (*shahid*) were ubiquitous in 2005, featured at times in marquees resembling advertisements or movie posters. Qadas always seemed to me a great distance from the cosmopolitan center of Ramallah.

However "militant" the village may have been, or become, during the course of my fieldwork, in most ways it resembled a very typical Mediterranean village to me. The structure of social life was relatively conservative, with most women wearing the traditional Palestinian dress of that area (a beautiful color), and most focusing on their roles as wives and mothers. The adult children of a family would, as in other Mediterranean villages (e.g., in Italy), construct a house for their family above that of their parents, resulting in clustering of residences by family throughout the village.

An ethos of struggle and conservatism may have filled the air in Qadas, not to mention a degree of religious observance I had not witnessed in other parts of Palestine (e.g., the regular praying of family members at the appropriate times), but the residents of this village were no exception in the realm of "Arab hospitality." As in other Palestinian communities, I was made to feel quite at home, with plentiful amounts of food and assistance in all my needs. Of course, my host mother's conviction on several occasions that I really ought to become Muslim—that in fact she prayed for me to become one—seemed to reveal the distance in tolerance for religious diversity this village occupied from a city like Ramallah.

Beit Jala and Bethlehem

Beit Jala and Bethlehem lie just outside of Jerusalem. Both communities possess significant historical sites to Christianity and continue to be home to a number of Christian Palestinians. Bethlehem in particular remains a major tourist destination, with its regular welcoming of Christian pilgrims at Christmas. Despite the fact that tourism continued—to an extent—during the second *intifada*, it is difficult to sit in Manger Square and not notice the absence of giant tour buses that this city really *should* see, given its historical significance.

Beit Jala and Bethlehem resemble most other Palestinian cities and towns in their appearance, with the occasional rubble from either an Israeli incursion or the infrastructural neglect of the Palestinian Authority. Yet the Christian families that I worked with in this area noted the difficult and complex relations between Muslims and Christians—a phenomenon quite distinct to this area, as all the other Palestinian areas in which I conducted fieldwork were overwhelmingly Muslim.

Both of these communities witnessed significant activity during the second *intifada*. On my first night in Beit Jala during one of my field trips, the father of Peter, one of my research participants, pointed to the hills that their balcony overlooked toward Bethlehem. The house of a suicide bomber, destroyed by Israel after his attack, was visible on the hill. "They came in with a plane and just blew it up!" said Peter's father. "They tried to rebuild it, but the army just kept coming and blowing it up again, and we could see it each time right here from this balcony."

The next day, Peter's father took me to a most depressing site just outside of Bethlehem. "You see," he explained with his deep smoker's voice, "before the *intifada*, Bethlehem was really growing fast. We had busloads of tourists coming. It was a good time." He pointed to a large building by the roadside. "That was to be a mall," he said. "It's completely built, but they never opened it, because then the *intifada* started."

At last we arrive at the site he had been wanting to show me. It is a site of major historical significance, he said. I described what I saw next as a "most fascinating tragedy" that night in my field notes. We arrived at King Solomon's pools—historical reservoirs constructed by the Jewish king, as Peter's father explained to me. It is here that this tragic site emerged. I have certainly seen ruins before, in Greece, Italy, and Turkey, of empires long past and grand buildings weathered by time, but I had never seen something quite like this: a contemporary ruin.

In the 1990s, when a cold peace had set in and Palestine began to possess some autonomy—on its way to full sovereignty in the minds of its inhabitants—all kinds of development projects had begun. Naturally, the Palestinian economy was expected to rely significantly on tourism for its revenue. Bethlehem would likely be the capital of its tourist economy, given the uncertain status that Jerusalem would assume in the final settlement. In 2000, Manger Square underwent a $200 million share of renovations in anticipation of new possibilities for the city, with the dawn of a new millennium for Palestine. Sometime in the 1990s, in this time of economic idealism, construction began on what would become a resort at King Solomon's pools—surely a major tourist destination. As I stared at the empty edifice in front of me, a skeleton with grand arches and crumbling walls, despite the clear recency of its construction, a feeling of profound tragedy overcame me.

It did not really matter that now the siege that occurred in the Church of the Nativity in April 2002 had given way to an extended period of calm. Bethlehem was a destination for only the few determined tourists, not for the hordes destined to fill the grandiose rooms of the resort at King Solomon's pools or, perhaps more modestly, the hotel rooms in the city itself. Today, these hotels remain significantly underoccupied, with most tourists making day trips to Bethlehem but staying on the other side of the barrier that cages in Bethlehem.

It is in the midst of this physical culture, with its economic realities, that a particular psychological ecology of development consumes the lives of the inhabitants of Beit Jala and Bethlehem. Perhaps more than any other Palestinian area, these communities began to experience the optimism of the emerging state of Palestine in an economic way more remote to other communities. In these communities, the loss of possibility and of economic development creates a most pernicious feeling of pessimism and failure. The occupation, with its debilitating unpredictability and "caging in," naturally receives full blame for this state of regression in the culture of these communities (Gordon, 2008a, 2008b; Makdisi, 2008; Roy, 2004).

Yet there is a way in which hope remains in Beit Jala and Bethlehem. The sharp, refurbished Bethlehem Peace Center consumes an entire block of

Manger Square. The sights and sounds of construction abound. One can hear a number of international languages on the streets, including English and French. The coffee house that Peter and his brother took me to on my last night is clean and open for business, selling alcohol in addition to the traditional coffee, tea, and *nargila*. I ordered a Taybeh beer, Palestine's "microbrew," and a nargila. Bethlehem, like Ramallah, possesses a kind of cosmopolitanism and a yearning for intercultural contact unlike other communities in Palestine.

It was in the midst of this unique social ecology, with its perceptible tragic decline but hopeful return, that three young men who participated in my study resided: Peter, the son of a Muslim father and Christian mother, both of whom work inside of Israel and thus are far from insulated from other identities; Luca, the son of Christian parents whose families have been merchants in the heart of Bethlehem for generations; and Osama, a Muslim whose best friend became a "martyr for Palestine" in the second *intifada*.

Tulkarm and Nablus

My fieldwork brought me to some communities in Palestine for day trips only. Tulkarm and Nablus, both of which are major urban centers, represent two of these communities. In these cities, I met with school officials and families and conducted formal interviews with youth. I describe these cities together, as they possess a number of similarities.

During the period of my fieldwork, accessing Nablus was generally a prohibitive challenge. I was, however, determined to visit the city, with a population of approximately 325,000 (Palestinian Central Bureau of Statistics, 2005), and famous for its *kanafeh*, the delicious Palestinian dessert made of shredded wheat, nuts, cheese, and honey. The driver I had hired to take me from Qadas to Nablus in his yellow Mercedes taxi warned me it would be a bumpy ride. He failed to mention how strangely beautiful it would be as well. As we traversed the ruins of an old Israeli military outpost on what had once been a road, now a pothole-filled field of dirt and gravel, the stony mountains of the West Bank ascended in the background.

During the course of the second *intifada*, Nablus had essentially become sealed off from the rest of the world. An Israeli tank stood at the paved road where a prominent sign pointed, in English, Hebrew, and Arabic, "Nablus" (in Hebrew, *Schechem*). So there was no way to reach Nablus apart from gaining access to the mountain roads, which required some careful maneuvering on the part of my driver. Somewhat surprisingly, by taking these roads (or nonroads), we avoid any checkpoints at all. One of the first sights as we enter the city are the ruins of what was once a mammoth police station, reduced to

FIGURE 2.1 Emblem of Palestinian Islamic Jihad.

rubble in one of the sieges on the city. It was, like Bethlehem, the infrastructure of a *possible* society, now in ruins. Across the street is, quite prominently, a massive painted rendition of the Islamic Jihad symbol (Figure 2.1), with its blood-red map of Mandate Palestine, superimposed over Jerusalem's Dome of the Rock, and flanked by fists and guns.

That this emblem, along with the emblem of Hamas (Figure 2.2), was initially ubiquitous throughout the West Bank during my fieldwork, is hardly surprising. The strength of resistance movements in Palestine seemed to grow as a function of discontent with the peace process in the 1990s, and by the *intifada* and Israel's formidable response in parts of Palestine like Nablus, discontent had given way to despair. The conditions for recruitment into such movements were ripe during the course of my fieldwork, and the symbolism of

FIGURE 2.2 Emblem of Hamas.

these movements, with their violent imagery and clear claims to all of Mandate Palestine, reflect the growing polarization of Israelis and Palestinians.

Nablus thus presented itself somewhere between Qadas and Ramallah to me, in terms of its "ideological" culture. In Qadas, the symbols of Hamas and Islamic Jihad were painted into every wall on my walk from my house into the heart of town. Posters of martyrs, many of whom were suicide bombers, adorned the same walls, where in perhaps a village with a different kind of economy there might hang advertisements.

In Ramallah, the symbols and posters were certainly present, along with the requisite antioccupation graffiti. But at times in Ramallah, I felt as though I almost had to look for it. It seemed less ubiquitous (though varying some-what across the period of my fieldwork). Nablus was somewhere in between, but without question a place of greater ideological insulation than Ramallah, likely owing to its physical isolation.

I chose to present Nablus and Tulkarm together as field sites for this reason: they are very similar in both their physical and ideological culture. The signs of military incursions abound in both cities. And yet, between the incur-sions, there is a vibrant life. The commercial avenues of both cities are filled with people, buying fruits and vegetables, sipping coffee, and playing cards. These are major urban centers, though Tulkarm's population is significantly smaller than that of Nablus, at approximately 130,000 (Palestinian Central Bureau of Statistics, 2005). There are hints of a cosmopolitanism of another time, particularly in Nablus, where a massive villa overlooks the city. Yet these cities are clearly severely bruised by the incursions that have taken place since the start of the *intifada* in 2000.

It was in these cities of ideological insularity, physical dilapidation, and daily struggle that Tamer, Lubna, and Omar negotiated their identities over the course of my fieldwork. Though I came to know them somewhat less inti-mately, owing to my more limited fieldwork in these communities, it was clear to me that the ecology of their daily lives impacted their narratives-in-formation in profound and unfortunate ways. Replete with stories of fear and loss as they experienced repeated incursions by the Israeli army, the narratives of these youths revealed an intimate confrontation with the occupation, and the ways in which such a challenging ecology of development came to bear on their own identities.

Tel Aviv

After an extensive stay in the West Bank, I always longed for Tel Aviv, a city where one could easily forget that a conflict of any kind existed. Dotted with trendy cafés, restaurants, gyms, bars, nightclubs, and shops, the streets of

Tel Aviv reveal a genuine cosmopolitan allure. As my field notes revealed, my arrival in Tel Aviv was usually accompanied by a sigh of relief. No more checkpoints, no more bumpy roads and dirty showers. This was a city of the West, with its skyscrapers, beautiful sandy beaches, and vibrant culture.

The field experience is often disorienting, as one traverses great distances in geography, thought, and behavior. So the occasional experience of the familiar, such as I was able to have in Tel Aviv, offered a respite from the necessary inhibitions of other areas in Israel and Palestine. No longer did I need to excessively concern myself with self-presentation; the cosmopolitanism of Tel Aviv meant that I could express my own identity with greater authenticity. Identity diversity was simply more acceptable in this city, the undeniable cultural capital of secular Israel.

It was in fact on the grand Rothschild Boulevard, with its massive leafy trees and carefully restored Bauhaus mansions, that I came to view Zionism for its remarkable achievements, not for its oppression of the Palestinians. I suspect this revelation stemmed from just how impressive Tel Aviv is as a city and how laudable the culture of Israel appears from this vantage point, this grand boulevard on a pleasant summer evening, on a stroll after a first-class meal at a French restaurant. As in any cosmopolitan city, where a tradition of cultural collision results in harmonious fusions, rather than disruptions, of ways of living, Tel Aviv was home to multiple lifeways. Mizrahi (i.e., Jews of non-European origin) and Ethiopian immigrants mingled with Russians and Jewish tourists, guest workers from Thailand, and Israeli natives whose grandparents had established this Jewish settlement down the street from the major Palestinian port city of Jaffa.

Tel Aviv as a field site thus represents a highly modernized, urbanized city. Economically and culturally, it is the center of Israeli society. And with its physical culture—its clean, leafy streets, expansive beaches, and thriving boutiques, cafés, and restaurants—Tel Aviv is without question the center of cosmopolitanism in Israel. It is a place where identities do indeed collide, and seem to do so in ways that are accommodating and open. It is no surprise, then, that my interviewees from Tel Aviv inevitably identified as "left-wing" ideologically and were perhaps the most exposed to identity diversity among their peers. That exposure, however, rarely extended to Arabs, but they were nonetheless ready for such engagement.

Taybeh

Twenty minutes from Tel Aviv lies an Arab city called Taybeh (the largest of several towns with the same name across the region). Just in the distance, Tulkarm is immediately visible, revealing the close proximity to the West Bank.

For me, in the course of my fieldwork, the two locales always seemed quite distant. Ideologically and economically, they indeed were. Culturally, they were both Palestinian, serving as home to people with identical cuisine, identical wedding rituals, identical *nargila* cafés where men would assemble each evening to smoke and play cards. Yet they were far from identical in other elements of their social ecologies beyond some of these shared cultural practices.

Taybeh is and has always been inside of the Green Line—the official armistice line declared following the 1948 war that created the State of Israel. One evening, after a barbecue hosted by the family of one of my closest colleagues, I queried her father about why Taybeh, of all the Palestinian villages and cities that were erased overnight in that war, remained. He told me, "We in Taybeh were strong. We fought when the Jews came here, and we pushed them out. We didn't just run like all the other towns. So they said they wouldn't push us out. But of course that meant we became Israeli."

That Taybeh became officially an Israeli city means a great deal for the identities of its inhabitants, especially compared to their fellow Palestinians in areas that did not become part of Israel, such as West Bank communities like Tulkarm. Though in Taybeh I feel quite strongly as if I am in a distinctly *Palestinian* city, with older women often wearing the traditional dress of the region and old men driving donkey-led carts of fruits and vegetables, there are notable differences between Taybeh and Palestinian cities in the West Bank.

The distinctions between Palestinian communities inside and outside of Israel center on ideological and economic factors. In terms of the physical culture of Taybeh, it indeed resembles a Palestinian city like Tulkarm, even in its state of disrepair. In Taybeh, roads are often crumbling, and sewage fills the streets in rivers. Trash abounds. Yet the absence of political graffiti and martyr posters immediately distinguishes Taybeh from a place like Tulkarm. While Taybeh may *look* a bit in need of economic development, its inhabitants are in fact in a good economic position, particularly compared to Palestinians beyond the Green Line. Most of the adults in Taybeh, including many women, have jobs outside of the city, in places like Tel Aviv. Everyone in the city speaks fluent Hebrew, for they deal quite regularly with Jewish Israelis in their daily lives. Arabic is the language of the home and of the community, but Hebrew is recognized as the language of the country. There is no desire, ideologically speaking, for them to be a part of Palestine as opposed to Israel. In all of my interviews with youth from the city, as well as all of my conversations with adults and adolescents in Taybeh, not a single inhabitant supported such an idea, even though they all viewed themselves as members of a subordinated minority inside of Israel. They were all quite critical of Israel's "ethnocratic" character that favored Jews over Arabs (Abu-Saad, 2004; Ghanem, 2002; Rouhana, 1997; Yiftachel, 2000). Ideologically, though, they aspired to be anti-ideological. That is, they preferred to remain silent.

The silence of the Palestinian Israelis, particularly in cities like Taybeh, is connected to the fact that these communities lived under a military administration in Israel until 1966 (Tessler & Grant, 1998). Though they may have, as my colleague's father put it, "fought the Jews," the sacrifice for them to stay in their city was that they become subjects of the Israeli state—a Jewish state. The new Israeli administration naturally viewed all Arabs as hostile. Thus, the system of military administration was at least temporarily necessary, so that a realistic threat assessment could be discerned. During this time and after, these communities have been carefully observed by Israeli intelligence, and thus, the inhabitants of these Arab communities have, over time, come to recognize the value in avoiding politics. These communities favor the economic benefits, and the benefits of staying in one's community, over any political aspirations to, say, "liberate" the entirety of Mandate Palestine. In fact, it is perhaps *because* of their economic success and the freedom they have to maintain their local cultural practices that they seek to maintain the particular status quo, or work *within*, rather than *against*, it.

The taboo against political discourse was readily apparent to me in my fieldwork in Taybeh. Yet its sustainability was threatened by a new generation of Palestinian-Israeli youth whose anger and frustration at the ongoing perception of subordination and discrimination within Israel, as well as the continued occupation of their Palestinian brothers and sisters just beyond, has infused their identities with more political awareness and interest (Louër, 2003; Rabinowitz & Abu-Baker, 2005). It will come as no surprise, then, when I detail the stories of youths such as Laila, Jibril, and others from this and other Arab villages inside of Israel, that their narratives reveal both the challenges of negotiating multiple identities, as well as the frustrations of the political evasion of a previous generation.

Haifa

A 45-minute train ride along the Mediterranean coast from Tel Aviv, Haifa is contrasted with this other coastal city in both its topography—it is exceedingly hilly—and its cultural character. Ofra, one of my Jewish research participants from Haifa, once shared with me that Israelis refer to Tel Aviv, in a comparison to New York City, as "the city that never sleeps" and to Haifa as "the sleep that never cities." In a way, she is quite right. Even though Haifa is a large city, on the Mediterranean coast just like Tel Aviv, it has a decidedly slower pace of life.

Often dubbed "the city of coexistence" in Israel, Haifa is home to both Jews and Arabs. It is, as some call it, an "integrated" city, even if the two communities within the city generally segregate by neighborhood. Jews spend their nights out at the Carmel Center, atop Mount Carmel, while Arabs stroll Ben-Gurion Street, down by the water, with its beautiful view of the Baha'i Temple. My fieldwork revealed that segregation is in fact alive and well in Haifa, but I have to confess it certainly represented the closest thing to integration that could be witnessed in the region.

A story from my fieldwork helps to differentiate, politically and ideologically, some of the major communities in Israel, particularly Haifa. A significant amount of my fieldwork in Israel and Palestine occurred in 2005, the year of the Gaza disengagement (i.e., forced evacuation of Jewish settlements in the Gaza Strip). As the disengagement approached, an "orange" movement began in Israel (the color of orange being adopted as it had been in Ukraine). Orange came to represent opposition to the disengagement. In particular, orange ribbons on the antennae of cars or tied to the backpacks of students indicated opposition to the plan and, in most cases, a conviction that the Jewish settlements in Palestine ought to remain (and perhaps even expand). Essentially, the orange movement was a prosettler movement. I was struck in my visit to the Ben-Yehuda shopping district in Jerusalem during one of my field trips by the ubiquity of orange. I thought to myself that surely Israel was going to have a big problem if this many people were opposed to the disengagement.

By the time I got to Tel Aviv on that trip, I had learned that there was in fact another movement: the "blue" movement, which signaled support for the disengagement and a general left-wing political stance. I would not say I saw as much blue as orange during that field trip, though it is difficult to know how many left-wing Israelis chose to stay "colorless" during that period, recognizing the inevitability of disengagement. Yet when I got to Tel Aviv, I was greeted (not surprisingly) by a significant amount of blue. When I arrived in Haifa shortly thereafter, I discussed the disengagement plans with Ofra's parents in their living room. To my surprise, Ofra's mother had not even heard of the counter-color movements. I found that even the parents of the Arab families with whom I stayed in Haifa had tended not to know about these movements, or to perhaps have only vaguely heard of them.

Haifa, then, represents a kind of ideological oasis—a complete counter to a place like Jerusalem, where physical segregation and ideological polarization are in plain sight. In Haifa, these structural and psychological forces do indeed exist (it is, after all, still in the midst of a conflict zone). But in Haifa, these forces are a bit more hidden from view. There seems to be a culture of coexistence in the city, in theory if not always in practice.

Many of Haifa's Palestinian residents are, in fact, Christian, which stands in contrast to most of the Palestinian cities and villages in Israel (Nazareth being the other city with a large Christian population). Haifa is also surrounded by a number of Arab villages, some of which are Druze (the mystical sect of Islam) and others of which are Christian. Haifa, then, makes for an interesting site of identity collisions in Israel, a place where a multiplicity of cultural and religious identities coexist in a fragile state of general harmony, occasionally shattered by the inescapability of the conflict.

The Gilboa

The final formal site of fieldwork in Israel occurred in two types of rural communities in the fertile Galilee, near Mount Gilboa. I refer to the area simply as "the Gilboa," as the communities are too small to be named, to preserve the confidentiality of my research participants and their families. These communities represent, culturally and ideologically, the aspirations of Zionism in its most socialist form.

I conducted fieldwork in two types of cooperative agricultural communities in the Gilboa: a moshav and a kibbutz. In a moshav each family operates its own plot of land and keeps its profits. By contrast, in a kibbutz, the land is collectively owned, the profits are collectively shared, and all aspects of life are essentially collectively controlled. Meals occur not at a family dining table but in the communal kitchen. Youth live in houses together, away from their parents (for reviews of these communities, see Avgar, Bronfenbrenner, & Henderson, 1977; Sofer & Appelbaum, 2006; Spiro, 1956, 1975).

The extent to which these cooperative systems have been maintained varies considerably, particularly among kibbutzim. It happens that there was wide variation among the three kibbutzim in which I conducted some measure of fieldwork. One of these kibbutzim in fact was quite faithful to the cooperative practices of the original ideology. The other two were less faithful.

Gal's father, Eli, the chain-smoking slight man with the weathered face and the vivid memory of the bus on which a bomber exploded himself right in front of him and Gal, described the gradual erosion of the kibbutz ideology this way:

> Look, the people who came here at first, they were totally idealistic. They were young; they were naïve. In the end, people want capitalism, at least some kind of capitalism. People *want* to own their own things; it just wasn't realistic. And the young people, they don't wanna stay here. They wanna go off, away from here, though they think it's a nice place to grow up.

With its natural beauty, idyllic setting, and proud heritage, these communities seem, indeed, a fine place to grow up. But Eli is quite accurate, based on my interviews with youth, when he says that there is little interest in spending one's adulthood in these places. Eli, like other parents on the kibbutzim and the moshavim, worry about the future of these communities, particularly their economic sustainability.

I have said something about both the physical culture and the existential viability of these communities in the Gilboa. Let me now say something about their ideological character. Traditionally, inhabitants of these communities have affiliated very strongly with Israel's foundational Labor party. Its ideology was always their ideology. Its secularism and its pragmatism always resonated with their aspirations for a cooperative Jewish society. They have, therefore, generally favored peace with the Arabs and the "land-for-peace" concept. They have little interest in "Greater Israel." They are quite content with the Jewish state they have now, minus the conflict with its Arab neighbors. They are quite literally a few kilometers from both Jenin and the Jordanian border. The barrier constructed by Israel—in this part of it, clearly a "fence" and not a "wall"—runs behind the apple orchard belonging to the family of Ezra, one of my research participants.

Physically, then, the inhabitants of the Gilboa are quite close to the Palestinians. Culturally, they could not be farther away, in custom and lifestyle. Yet ideologically, perhaps because of their proximity, the members of these communities are willing to compromise. The youth, then, of these communities can readily be labeled "left-wing," and the encounter with Arabs in the coexistence program creates new challenges for their identities, rooted in the "venture in utopia" (Spiro, 1956) that frames their social ecologies of development.

Field Sites in the United States

My immersion into the lives of Israeli and Palestinian youth and the American attempt to intervene in their life course began in the summer of 2003. Fortuitously, the timing of my own interests coincided with the founding of a new program in the suburbs of Chicago, Illinois, and with my offer of a group facilitator position in this program and the larger, better known program of which it was somewhat of an offshoot—Seeds of Peace International Camp in Otisfield, Maine. In 2003 and 2004, I conducted facilitation at Seeds of Peace with youth from other conflict zones, while conducting participant observation and interviews with Israeli and Palestinian youth. At Hands of Peace, I served as a group facilitator for Israeli and Palestinian youth in their inaugural year (2003) and then assumed the role of program director from 2004 to 2006, an administrative role that facilitated my participant observation and provided me with an intimate knowledge of the program and the individuals involved in its design and implementation.

In describing these major sites of my field research, I wish to guide the reader carefully through these programs as I came to know them. Thus, my account will detail the history, philosophy, and rites of participation for each. As a cultural psychologist, it was impossible for me not to come to view these programs as "cultures" in their own right—sites of distinct discourse and practice. Each represented a distinct social system, with a hierarchy, norm structure, rituals, symbols, and language. Each *commanded* of youth a certain practice. I will, therefore, discuss these field sites as distinct cultures within which youth came to participate.

Seeds of Peace

HISTORY, PHILOSOPHY, AND CULTURE OF THE PROGRAM Although Israelis and Palestinians are gripped by seemingly infinite cycles of violence, such is not the inevitable state of their relations. War and conflict emerge from governments, not people. Ordinary Israeli and Palestinian people, inhabitants of a land of mutual significance, can coexist in peace, if only they can come together to "humanize" the other and legitimize their collective narratives. Israelis and Palestinians can coexist, but only by transcending the ideological rigidity of what divides them—those "negatively interdependent" (Kelman, 1999b) master narratives of history and collective identity. Through meaningful contact, in a neutral setting where both groups are accorded equal status, such transcendence of identity polarization can create a new generation of leaders whose personal identities are attuned to peaceful coexistence.

This narrative represents the underlying story of programs like Seeds of Peace. If Israeli and Palestinian youth are socialized in the context of identity polarization, in which their commitment to a master narrative of social identity is expected and supported by the obstinacy of the conflict itself, then programs like Seeds of Peace present a third narrative—the narrative of coexistence. Its story is one of optimistic, idealistic possibility. With the ubiquitous motto, "Treaties are negotiated by governments; peace is made by *people*" (Seeds of Peace, 2010), this third narrative relies on an ideology of liberal value pluralism (Galston, 2002), cosmopolitanism (Appiah, 2006), and individual-driven social change. And with its focus on intervention during adolescence, the narrative primes a decidedly American cultural model of adolescence itself, so eloquently posited by Erik Erikson in a number of his writings (e.g., Erikson, 1968) and reinforced by other social theorists of youth in the 1960s and 1970s (e.g., Keniston, 1971, 1972; Mead, 1970).

Respect for diversity, the legitimacy of justice and equality, the existential legitimacy of national identities, and the recognition of relativity in narrative—of historical interpretation and collective story-making—represent the ideological components of the narrative of coexistence. It is a new narrative for Israeli and Palestinian youth—one that rejects identity polarization and the salience of social identity in favor of a "transcendent," common identity (Gaertner & Dovidio, 2000). That common identity is imparted in the recognition of *sameness* that can occur through intergroup contact. As youth come to recognize that little besides their conflicting master narratives in fact polarizes them, they may come to achieve ideological distance from these master narratives and, in this way, to break the cycle of narrative reproduction that maintains the conflict.

I present this third narrative—a narrative of possibility—as a "hypothesis," for it represents the aims of these American-based coexistence programs[2]. In the case of Seeds of Peace, it is rather explicit, in fact. As Seeds of Peace founder John Wallach (2000) notes in his account of the program,

> [Seeds of Peace] is about changing attitudes, ending the fears and prejudices that have prevented entire generations from getting to know one another; in short, it is about "rehumanizing," not dehumanizing, the enemy. (p. 13)

Wallach frames the process of transformation meant to occur at the camp as a "journey from fear and suspicion to understanding and trust..." (p. 13), but he does not question that

> Most reach their destination: a new level of compassion for one another as human beings. When they return home, they are well on their way to becoming the true leaders of a new generation that is as committed to fighting for peace as their predecessors were in waging war. (p. 13)

Naturally, the idealistic appeal of the third narrative offered by programs like Seeds of Peace encourages such audacious statements. But Seeds of Peace, I came to realize early on in my preparation for fieldwork and during that initial summer of 2003, in fact remained a "hypothesis" largely untested by

---

2 It is important to note that Hands of Peace is an "offshoot" of Seeds of Peace in its basic curriculum and philosophy; so much of the detail on Seeds of Peace as a field site is relevant to Hands of Peace as well.

anything approaching "science." It had, if you will, "coasted" in its existence for its noble idea—one of great appeal to those American funders who would support the cause of educating Israeli and Palestinian youth to respect existential diversity.

Founded on the eve of the Oslo accords in 1993 by liberal Jewish journalist John Wallach, with extensive connections across groups in the Middle East, Seeds of Peace has always been decidedly idealistic in its aims. Staff recollect that in the inaugural summer of the program, the need to have facilitated dialogue sessions actually escaped John Wallach, whose idea was merely to bring Israeli and Arab youth (from across North Africa and the Middle East, but with the largest concentration from Palestine) together to recognize their commonalities rather than to engage in any serious or substantive discourse about the conflict that consumed their lives. "Make one friend" was always Wallach's slogan for the youth, and we will revisit it when we consider the postcontact narratives of youth presented in Chapter 7. Needless to say, the focus of the program has shifted to incorporate a loosely structured (and loosely monitored) dialogue program and has gradually opened itself up to systematic evaluation.

RITES OF PARTICIPATION From its inception, Seeds of Peace has worked collaboratively with governments to select participants for the program and to guarantee their safety. Such collaboration has always secured the legitimacy of the program; it is more difficult to receive criticism of bias toward one side or the other if both sides officially support you. This method of participant selection works well for the aims of Seeds of Peace: the two governments[3] aim to send youths who will be the best "representatives" of their respective nations, thereby ensuring a measure of ideological diversity among the youth by encouraging those who are not necessarily "propeace" to attend.

In Israel, the qualifications are largely academic, and this generally guarantees a diverse group of youth (though Ashkenazi Jews, or Jews of European origin, are typically overrepresented). In Palestine, the qualifications are academic but also dependent upon social network and political affiliation. As part of every interview I conducted, I assessed each individual's personal motivation to participate in the program. The diverse motivations expressed by

---

3 Though its focus has always been on the larger Arab–Israeli conflict, Seeds of Peace does work with youth from other regions of war and conflict (e.g., Cyprus, India, Pakistan, Afghanistan). For the purposes of this study, only the portion of the program that focuses on Israel and Palestine will be discussed and considered. During the summers in which I conducted fieldwork, approximately 85% of the total youth participants were engaged in dialogue on the Israeli–Palestinian conflict and the larger Arab–Israeli conflict.

youth suggested to me that these youth were not universally committed to peaceful coexistence. In fact, a number of youth from both groups endorsed motivations such as wanting to "convince the other side they're wrong."

Once selected in the region, both groups undergo preparatory seminars that are designed to ensure their readiness for the encounter. Though I was unable to observe such seminars, I received a number of reports on them from my interviewees. Laila, a 16-year-old Palestinian citizen of Israel[4], reports that the seminar presented a narrative of Israeli history that contradicted her knowledge of the Palestinian narrative:

> We had this seminar in Jerusalem before we came.... The seminar was about the history of Israel and everything. I knew the history of Palestine, and then I learned the history of Israel. I was kind of unhappy because I totally disagreed with them in the seminar. But I shut my mouth, you know. I couldn't speak. I felt like they were kind of preparing us for war and not for peace, so it was kind of difficult for me.... They have this *totally different* history of the Palestinians.

Laila's experience of the preprogram seminar reveals the complex position of the Palestinian Israelis, with their immediate access to both historical narratives. The problematic nature of their dual identity will recur, particularly in the context of Seeds of Peace, in which they are official members of the Israeli delegation and are hence expected to "behave" like Israeli citizens.

Youth arrive at the camp in "delegations" and are greeted in each instance by an enthusiastic group of staff. As they descend the stairs of the bus, the head counselor or another senior staff member politely removes all symbols of national identity adorning the youth. Typically, these include necklaces with the Star of David, representing the national symbol of Israel, or Palestinian *kafiyas* or bracelets featuring the Palestinian flag. All of these symbols are permitted to be worn on the last night of camp, but for now, the youth are to be stripped of the symbolic gestures that communicate their commitments to a national identity. It is part of a larger project of identity "restructuring" that occurs at the camp.

Each delegation is escorted from the bus to the lawn overlooking the lake, in which they are told the origin story of Seeds of Peace (recounted now by the

---

4 The Palestinians who remained inside the borders of the newly declared State of Israel in 1948 and were granted citizenship (though with limitations) go by a number of identity labels. Traditionally they were called "Israeli Arabs" or "Arab Israelis," depending on the desired emphasis of the namer or the named. More recently, many have preferred to renew their sense of Palestinian cultural identity by taking on the label "Palestinian citizen of Israel" (Ghanem, 2002). In this book, this group will be referred to as "Palestinian Israelis."

soft, nurturing voice of Bobbie Gottschalk, a former social worker who was one of John Wallach's collaborators in founding the program). They are also introduced to the narrative of the new cultural system in which they will be (re) socialized. Bobbie tells them:

> When you drove into Maine, when you crossed that border, there was a big sign. Did anybody see the sign? It said on it, "Maine, the way life should be." At camp, we try to make this a reality for you. We try to make *this* the way life should be. So after tonight, you'll all be wearing the same green Seeds of Peace T-shirt. This is very important, because it shows that you're all equal. Everybody at camp is equal. All of you with each other, even with the staff. There is no inequality here.

At camp, the "difference" of identity undergoes an attempted erasure through a radical restructuring of social ecology. Underlying this attempt is, most clearly, a liberal American cultural model of intergroup relations that relies on a humanist ethic of identity pluralism: Identity diversity is worthy of reciprocal respect, and it is the environments of youth that polarize them. Here, in a place that could not resemble "home" less for either Palestinians or Israelis, they might come to witness the elements of their identities that are united: in eating, sleeping, playing; their commonalities as boys or girls, as human beings.

And so Israeli and Palestinian youth come to be subjects of a common experiment in the social psychology of identity and intergroup relations: the attempt to restructure identity through the transformation of external reality. The social structure of the conflict itself is stripped of its perceptible quality in anything but memory—which of course remains salient for the youth. The differences between youth become obscure, as they undergo a series of rituals that encourage the "loss" of identity and the "gain" of a new one—they begin the socialization process of *becoming a "Seed."*

An excerpt from my field notes the day after the youth arrived from their long journey tells the story as it first occurred to me: "Today the kids began to lose their identity by receiving the green Seeds of Peace uniform. One group at a time, they learn the Seeds of Peace song—the 'anthem.'" The remainder of Day 2 is spent orienting to the camp. It is not until Day 3 that camp begins in earnest, and the identity-restructuring rituals continue.

A key ritual of camp—one that marks its formal initiation—is called "flag-raising" (Figure 2.3). In this ritual, all of the youth file outside the camp to its front gate, where the flags of all nations represented at the camp hang. One by one, each group stands together, sings its national anthem, and raises its flag. Once all flags are raised, the youth sing the Seeds of Peace song together and

FIGURE 2.3 Flag-raising ritual at Seeds of Peace camp.

file back into the gates of camp, leaving, they are told by camp director Timothy Wilson, their national identities behind.

Returning staff had, I must admit, poisoned me to this ritual long before I had actually witnessed it. Their claim was that it tended to cause unnecessary turmoil, particularly for the Palestinian Israelis, who tended to be conflicted about which group to join in song for the national anthem. While they are Israeli citizens, the content of the national anthem presents significant problems to their Palestinian identity:

> As long as the Jewish spirit is yearning deep in the heart,
> With eyes turned toward the East, looking toward Zion,
> Then our hope—the two-thousand-year-old hope—will not be lost:
> To be a free people in our land,
> The land of Zion and Jerusalem

(available at www.stateofisrael.com/anthem)

Ideologically, then, there can be no connection to this anthem for the Palestinian Israelis, for its contents refer to a collective identity that is foreign to them and to their defeat in achieving their own Palestinian nation.

At the same time, the Palestinian Israelis are completely unfamiliar with the Palestinian anthem:

> My country, my country
> My country, my land, land of my ancestors,
> Guerilla[5], guerilla, guerilla
> My nation, the nation of eternity,
> With my determination, my fire, and the volcano of my revenge,
> With the longing in my blood for my land and my home,
> I have climbed the mountains and fought the wars,
> I have conquered the impossible and crossed the borders,
>
> My country, my country, the nation of eternity,
> With the resolve of the winds and the fire of the guns,
> And the determination of my nation in the land of struggle,
> Palestine is my home, Palestine is my fire, Palestine is my revenge,
> And the land of the eternal
>
> My country, my country, the nation of eternity,
> I swear under the shade of the flag
> To my land and nation, and the fire of pain,
> I will live as a guerilla, I will go on as a guerilla,
> I will end as a guerilla, until my country returns
> My country, my country, the nation of eternity

(available at www.mofa.gov.ps/arabic/Palestine/anthem.php)

With its references to "pain," "revenge," "struggle," and a "guerilla" identity, the Palestinian national anthem is clearly derivative of the experience of Palestinian loss and dispossession (Said, 1994). It is also clearly rooted in the founding ideology of Arafat's Fatah party, which has dominated Palestinian politics. The initial emphasis of the Fatah platform was explicitly rooted in the adoption of "guerilla" tactics to fight the occupation of Mandate Palestine (Harkabi, 1968/2001). The contents of the Palestinian national anthem also strongly echo key documents such as the Palestinian National Charter (Palestine National Council, 1968/2001).

---

5 *Fida'i (fedayeen)*, typically translated as "guerilla" or "revolutionary."

It should be quite apparent that the contents of each of these national anthems, regardless of the challenge that the very ritual itself presents to Palestinian Israelis, is highly problematic for any kind of peaceful coexistence between Israelis and Palestinians that entails the mutual recognition of identity. The Israeli anthem represents the classic discourse of Zionism and commitment to a Jewish state in the land known as Palestine until 1948. The Palestinian anthem is both violently reactive to Zionism and reflective of a national identity that emphasizes suffering, struggle, and violent resistance. The discourse reflected in these anthems is extremely divisive, so perhaps the notion of leaving these discourses safely behind—outside the gates of camp—is not such a bad idea after all, if it is indeed possible.

The new, third anthem, sung by youth as they file back into the camp, represents the common, superordinate identity of a "Seed":

> People of Peace, rejoice, rejoice,
> For we have united into one voice,
> A voice of peace and hate of war,
> United hands have built a bridge between two shores.
> We on the shores have torn down the wall,
> We stand hand in hand as we watch the bricks fall.
> We've learned from the past and fear not what's ahead,
> I know I'll not walk alone,
> But with a friend instead.
> I am a Seed of Peace, seed of peace, a seed of peace
> I am a seed, a seed of peace
> I am a seed, I am a seed of peace
> Peace, peace, peace, peace

Most notably, this anthem refers to the common identity of a "Seed" ("I *am* a Seed of Peace") as "united" against "war" and a "bridge" between the polarized identities that maintain the conflict. The reference to friendship is also key, consistent with Wallach's (2000) founding philosophy. His notion was that only through friendship with the enemy could the stereotypes and negative attitudes toward the out-group really diminish, consistent with social psychologist Tom Pettigrew's (1998) reformulated contact theory, in which cross-group friendship is considered central.

These early rituals at camp thus serve the purpose of contributing to the larger "reacculturative" design of the program. If the problem that creates the Israeli–Palestinian conflict is decidedly located not *within* individuals, particularly *young* individuals, but rather in their *environment*—that is, the social structure that surrounds them—then a radical restructuring of environment will, at the very least, "de-essentialize" the perception of the "enemy." Youth should come to view members of the out-group as *individuals* who share many common features with them, such as an interest in soccer or swimming, Eminem or Britney Spears. In social psychological terms, youth will undergo a process of *decategorization* in which, through interpersonal acquaintanceship, their stereotypes of the out-group disintegrate (Brewer & Miller, 1984; Miller, 2002).

Seeds of Peace is consumed with the project of fashioning a new common identity among the youth: that of a "Seed." By no means does this project some-how *necessitate* the abandonment of national identity. Rather, consistent with common in-group identity theory in American social psychology and its ability to reduce intergroup conflict (Gaertner et al., 1999), the goal is to preserve in-group identity but to "add" the perception of a higher level of category inclusiveness (e.g., we may be Palestinians or Israelis, but we are all *human*). Participants undergo a process of what Gaertner and his colleagues call iden-tity *recategorization*, placing themselves in a new group that shares an identity with the out-group. In Chapter 7, I will explore in greater detail the ways in which youth engaged with the new culture of Seeds of Peace either accommo-date or resist the inculcation of the identity supplement of a "Seed." This brief preliminary account of the early rituals of camp has, I hope, sufficiently intro-duced the ideological project of Seeds of Peace. Let me now provide more detail on the curriculum of the program.

As camp begins in earnest, after the flag-raising ritual, the youth settle into what will become a stable activity routine for the next 3 weeks. Each morning the ringing of a loud bell awakens them, and they file to the outdoor audito-rium in which camp director Tim Wilson, an African-American man and former civil rights leader in Maine of incredible presence, makes announce-ments and, more critically, delivers daily lectures on how he perceives the pro-cess to be going. He recounts stories from his own childhood experiences with racism, inequality, and intergroup conflict in the United States, solidifying the connection between the American social project to reduce intergroup conflict among racial groups (Pettigrew, 2008b) and the project of "assisting" those in the Middle East to do the same. Given his stature and authoritative presence, the campers are consistently focused and silent. Then the youth eat breakfast together at a preassigned, mixed-group table.

As Wallach (2000) describes, the youth interact in three distinct groups at camp designed to maximize intergroup contact and exposure to a number of out-group members: (1) the "sleeping" group who reside in a bunk together, (2) the "eating" group who eat together for each meal, and (3) the "talking" group who meet once daily for dialogue about the conflict and intermittently during the program for physical "group challenge" activities. Thus, social identity at the camp is reorganized (away from strictly national identity) in a multitude of ways, demonstrating possibilities in social identity diversity to the youth.

The remainder of the day is spent in scheduled blocks of sports, artistic activities, and the dialogue sessions themselves. On the field and in other contexts at camp, youth become members of even more groups, such as sports teams or a group working on a particular art or drama project. Again, the purpose here is to get youth working toward goals that transcend the conflict they in fact have with each other as a consequence of their particular national identities. The one place in which the *actual* social identities of youth as Israelis or Palestinians are clearly primed is the dialogue session.

The dialogue program at Seeds of Peace possesses its own history. As noted, the need for facilitated dialogue was not immediately apparent to Wallach in 1993, and it was introduced in the second year. Since the inception of the dialogue program, a number of facilitation methods have been used, with no set guidelines for facilitators. According to the official documents distributed to facilitators in 2003 and 2004, a general "flow" to the dialogue program at Seeds of Peace is intended to proceed in three stages.

In the first stage, the goal is to develop trust among group members and to cultivate personal knowledge of one another. The conflict is typically not directly addressed, at least by the facilitators themselves, during this first phase. Naturally, the conflict arises immediately in dialogue, as youth indicate even their communities of origin (e.g., Palestinian youth claiming to live in "Palestine" immediately sparks fury among the Jewish Israelis). The second and most extensive phase of the dialogue program involves a more direct focus on the conflict, covering topics such as the two historical narratives (typically a lengthy part of Phase 2), identity and interpretation, and mock conflict resolution. The final, quite brief phase concerns preparation for the readjustment home. This phase typically involves either direct conversation or role play of possible scenarios upon the return home (e.g., reaction of friends and family to a "new self").

The dialogue sessions contribute to the general reacculturative efforts of the program by providing a safe space for processing the experience. But they also serve the important function of directly confronting the conflict and, in that confrontation, assaulting the polarized identities that youth possess as they enter the camp. The exercises on history and identity are designed to instill in the youth a relativistic (or at least pluralistic) view of history. A sample "Walk Through History" exercise (Table 2.1) illustrates.

TABLE 2.1 Sample Responses to "Walk Through History" Exercise

Israeli	Year	Palestinian
"State of Israel Declared Independent"	1948	"The Land of Palestine Occupied; Families Killed; People Expelled"
"Israel Victorious Over Arab Enemy Invaders"	1967	"Israel Rapes the Virginity of Palestine and Seizes It in Total"
"Terrorists Strike: *Intifada* Begins"	2000	"Sharon Disrespects the Muslim People, Instigates the Palestinians to Rise Up!"

In the table above, consider the differential interpretations of 3 key years in the history of the conflict: 1948, 1967, and 2000. In this exercise that I observed, youth were instructed to create newspaper headlines that depicted what was happening around these key events. They worked in separate national groups and thus did not have access to each other's narrative until they came together. Exposing the negative interdependence of historical narrative serves to highlight the relativity of historical interpretation to youth. In theory, recognition of this relativity might lead to a decrease in the salience of master narratives, as youth come to see the narratives they have been presented as incomplete or one sided.

While many of the activities and curricula of the dialogue program contribute to the larger project of common in-group identity construction, an interesting change in the program occurred during the course of my fieldwork with the increase in facilitators from the region. The leading center for training dialogue facilitators in Israel, *Neve Shalom/Wahat al-Salam* (the School for Peace), has developed a specific philosophy that is grounded in social psychological theory and research. That theoretical foundation happens to be social identity theory (Tajfel & Turner, 1979). As Nadler (2004) describes it:

> The work at the School for Peace reflects a perspective that is closer to the social-identity approach. It is predicated on the view that unequal power relations between Jews and Arabs are the key factor in understanding the conflict between these groups within the Israeli context and beyond. The work within the parameters of this model aims to lead Arabs and Jews to genuinely and openly address the inequality and the power differences that exist between them.... [T]he School for Peace model view[s] relative power as the nexus through which greater understanding of the conflict between groups can be achieved. (p. 28)

So the School for Peace model has a particular aim that, in theory, can contribute to "greater understanding" between Arabs and Jews: the unequal distribution of power. This focus adheres to the social identity approach in its emphasis on group status, but it also adheres in its focus on the dialogue participants *as group members* rather than *unique individuals*:

> This model emphasizes that a genuine dialogue that may produce social change is one that occurs only between two conflicting groups and not between individuals who happen to belong to groups in conflict.... This work aims to promote an encounter between secure identities. It represents an emphasis on interidentity dialogue about power and equality between Jews and Arabs, rather than a personal meeting between Jewish and Arab individuals. (Nadler, 2004, p. 29)

True to a social identity approach, facilitators trained in this model view the encounter as occurring not among individuals, with particular life stories and unique engagements with master narratives of history and identity. Rather, the dialogue occurs between groups, as the intergroup experience primes social identity over and above personal identity.

The fact that Seeds of Peace increasingly relied on facilitators from the region (particularly in 2004), most of whom are schooled in this model, introduced an interesting element to the larger project of the camp and its regional follow-up program. It appeared to create a more complex blend of underlying philosophical approaches, to some extent leading Seeds of Peace more toward a "mixed" model of peace education (Maddy-Weitzman, 2005). Yet in some ways, as I saw it in my fieldwork, the two approaches created confusion among the youth. On the one hand, they were supposed to somehow "lose" their identities: to leave behind their national identities at the front gates of camp. On the soccer field and basketball court, in the bunks and the dining tables, they were to see themselves as all part of a larger, more diverse team. Yet many of the facilitators were seeking to achieve just the opposite psychological effect: getting youth to recognize the *distinctiveness* of their identities and the legitimate differences between one another, so as to foster greater awareness of mutual legitimacy.

Seeds of Peace thus relies first and foremost on a common in-group identity model. Yet in the dialogue session, the youth were to prime their national identities again; they were to serve as representatives of their group. One might argue that this blend helps to inject a dose of realism into the curriculum at Seeds of Peace, but my impression is that it created more conflict between facilitators and other (American) staff. In fact, the summer after I completed fieldwork at Seeds of Peace there was apparently a "revolt" (or "*intifada*," as one of my Palestinian colleagues dubbed it) of facilitators, which resulted in the dismissal of all of them. As we consider the postcontact narratives of youth most explicitly in Chapter 7, we will explore further the impact of these sessions upon their own understanding of personal and social identity.

The ultimate ritual in which the construction of a new common identity is cultivated at Seeds of Peace is the closing ritual of "Color Games." Adapted from the popular American camp finale, "Color Wars," Color Games involves the creation of two larger teams that compete for 3 days intensively in a number of sport and challenge activities. During these 3 days, no dialogue sessions are held, and what has become the routine, regimented camp schedule is essentially erased as youth stay up late planning their strategies for the next day's challenges. It is an intense period of adrenaline-infused intergroup competition.

The programmatic strategy underlying Color Games is to (a) demonstrate the fluidity of social identity (someone's bunk mate and best friend one day may be an "enemy" the next), and (b) facilitate intergroup cooperation (between Israelis and Palestinians, not between the two Color Games teams) through the "superordinate" goal of winning the games. The Games culminates in a kind of ritual "baptism," if you will, as all campers and staff storm into the lake in celebration and, reuniting as the external imposition of their divergent social identities is removed, sing the Seeds of Peace anthem in unison. An excerpt from my field notes conveys the perception of an onlooker:

> The winning team was announced followed by what appeared to me a "baptismal" rite. Prompted by the counselors, the winning team led the whole camp into the lake. Kids were coerced to submerge, despite the freezing temperatures and their clear state of exhaustion. It seems to me like a rite of passage in which the identity shift to "Seed" is complete by reflecting successful completion of the Color Games, itself another identity ritual in which identity is somehow "given up." To me the rite seemed to represent a kind of ultimate acquiescence to the Seeds ideology. Those who resisted were essentially coerced, literally dragged into the water.

My critical reaction to the ritual at this point in my fieldwork was linked to my own concern with a number of key observations at camp.

I came to view the culture of camp, with its distinctly liberal American ideology, as highly problematic for youth socialized in the context of conflict. The "third" narrative presented by Seeds of Peace is one of respect for diversity and identity pluralism, anchored in a radical perspectival approach to history. Ideologically, this narrative is rooted in our own experience with intergroup conflict (e.g., racism and segregation), and the vast social psychological literature on intergroup relations has precisely this American history in mind (e.g., Brewer & Miller, 1984). My ethical concern as a researcher, and as an observing participant, was centered squarely on the psychological challenge that indoctrination of this new, superordinate identity narrative creates for youth. I use the word "indoctrination" for its authenticity here, not for some kind of dramatic intent. There is at camp a rather pernicious "press" to identify with and internalize the identity of a Seed. The coercive participation in rituals such as the post–Color Games "baptism" is just a minor example. Staff and facilitators, not to mention the ubiquity of Wallach's "Make one friend" mantra, seek to instill this third narrative into the consciousness of youth through discourse and practice. While the context of camp substitutes an ecology of conflict with an ecology of cosmopolitanism, it does so with just as strong a drive for conformity among youth. It constructs an artificial, highly contrived narrative of identity—one disconnected from the reality of conflict.

I will reserve further analysis of the context of Seeds of Peace for Chapter 7, but I trust the reader has been at minimum introduced to a critical perspective on the ideology to which participants are expected to become resocialized. I would be unfairly critical were I not to acknowledge that, despite the disconnection of camp itself from the conflict, an extensive follow-up program was developed in the late 1990s by former counselor Ned Lazarus, himself now a scholar of these kinds of interventions. Originally based in Jerusalem, the follow-up program has undergone a number of evolutions in focus and philosophy. But it must be noted that the effort of the follow-up program is precisely to address the problematic distance of the camp (both physically and ideologically) from the region. Providing a safe place for continued intergroup contact, in a highly segregated parcel of land, is certainly foremost in the minds of staff.

Hands of Peace

HISTORY, PHILOSOPHY, AND CULTURE OF THE PROGRAM   Let us now consider a very similar enterprise, but one more explicitly integrated into an American cultural context. Hands of Peace was the idea of Gretchen Grad, a University of Chicago–educated businesswoman-cum-housewife in the northern suburbs of Chicago. As she often describes the genesis of the idea in a number of public forums, the idea sprang from her own experience with pluralism and religious diversity. Her neighbor and best friend, Deanna Jacobson, happens to be Jewish. Grad, a Protestant Christian (a member of the liberal United Church of Christ), took great pleasure in the fact that her children were exposed to religious diversity at young ages, owing to this friendship. An avid follower of international affairs with a supremely poised presence, Grad decided that youth from Israel and Palestine, in addition to members of her own liberal community, could perhaps gain much from exposure to cultural and religious diversity through such a program.

In the tradition of cosmopolitanism and the idealism of cooperation through contact, Grad viewed the possibility of such a program to transform individual lives through exposure to "others" unlike themselves. She approached Jacobson about the idea, who successfully persuaded her synagogue to cosponsor the endeavor. The two women then approached the local mosque, which agreed to the interfaith venture and appointed a Palestinian-American woman to complete the triumvirate of what became known locally as the three "soccer moms" working for peace in the Middle East. The three women approached Seeds of Peace to assist in getting the first summer's program off the ground, and the program quickly achieved independence in operations.

Far from removed from a recognizable culture, Hands of Peace is deeply embedded in the suburban culture of a politically liberal, diverse metropolis. Here amid the expansive shopping centers and new developments of "McMansions"—the physical culture of suburbia that Erikson (1968) once described as "safe and remote" but "bland" (p. 298)—lies the nexus of middle-class liberal America. Physically, then, the culture of Hands of Peace is one that, similar to Seeds of Peace (but in radically different ways), resembles nothing of either Israel or Palestine. It is interminably flat—a topography quite foreign to Israelis and Palestinians, even those who reside on the coastal plain who are quickly transported to the mountains with a brief drive. The expansiveness of the place is also quite alarming to youth from a land of relatively diminutive size (Israel and Palestine are about the size of New Jersey and Delaware combined). The fact that a journey from Glenview to downtown Chicago can take an hour by car is shocking to them—Jerusalem and Tel Aviv are only 45 minutes apart, and Jerusalem and Ramallah are (absent military checkpoints) only about 20 minutes apart.

Naturally, another key aspect of the physical culture of Hands of Peace that is quite divergent from both Israel and Palestine is the enormity of the homes in which youth reside. Hands of Peace blends standard American summer "day camp" with "hospitality" program in that participants reside with host families in the local communities while coming together for the majority of each day. Typically those families who are able to serve as a host to such youth are quite well-off financially and thus have rather large homes. Expressions of awe are not at all uncommon as the youth arrive at their host family residences. David, a Jewish Israeli who lives in a rather cramped Haifa apartment with his parents and two siblings, had his own "suite" in a home that overlooked Lake Michigan in Wilmette for the duration of the 2-week program in 2005.

The novelty of the physical culture, while instantly revealing the economic discrepancy between the societies (particularly for Palestinian youth, whose emerging country occupies a far lower level of economic development than Israel), also serves to excite the youth. Participants in both Seeds of Peace and Hands of Peace, owing to the criteria for admission, are typically middle-class youth from the region; they are all subjects of globalization, fluent English speakers, consumers of the global youth marketplace. So for them, the visit to America and their residence in the homes of affluent families are like a dream realized. This physical culture, then, brings with it an economic one. As global consumers, this generation of youth is lured by the affluence of American culture, even as that affluence itself is something of a caricature. Though it may be a kind of caricature—or, at least, an incomplete representation of American culture—it infuses the culture of Hands of Peace physically, economically, and socially.

The social ecology of Hands of Peace is thus the American suburb as we know it. Unnaturally clean streets, carefully manicured lawns, driveways with glimmering sports cars and SUVs, and, above all, good public schools. So it makes sense that such a program would be born out of the liberal idealism of these communities—places where a level of cosmopolitanism and an ethic of pluralism infuse the identities of their citizens, at least in the liberal discourse if not necessarily always in its practice.

It is, therefore, quite readily perceptible that the culture of Hands of Peace in its more ideological, rather than physical, form should resemble that of Seeds of Peace. A key difference, however, is that Hands of Peace has its origins in the commitment of a largely middle-class Christian community (as opposed to the elite liberal Jewish-American community of which John Wallach was a member). Even though she was successful in enlisting the support of her Jewish friend Jacobson, and the endorsement of Jacobson's synagogue, Grad struggled over the years to maintain the support of the local Jewish community, who witnessed a far greater threat to their Jewish identities in welcoming Palestinian youth and hearing their stories than seemed psychologically manageable. As the sponsoring synagogue changed hands to a rabbi who had lived in an Israeli settlement in East Jerusalem, gradually the institution and its community withdrew support for the program. Jacobson herself quietly diminished her own role, despite a highly visible presence and level of involvement in the first summer of the program in 2003.

In addition to the difficulties of maintaining the support of the Jewish community, the collaboration of the local Arab and Muslim community could not be sustained after the first summer of the program. Nuha Dabbouseh, the

Palestinian American whom the mosque had appointed as its representative to the program (Dabbouseh was in fact dubbed a "cofounder" for purposes of public relations and legitimacy in the local Arab and Muslim community), recommended that the mosque withdraw its support after she perceived Grad and Jacobson to be culturally insensitive to her requests for program policies that were respectful of Islam (e.g., a more strict dress code). Beyond what appeared minor "slights" or instances of "imbalance" to the local Jewish and Muslim communities, it was abundantly clear to me that institutional support for such a program created far too many threats to identity, at least in these suburban communities. The inability to predict the interplay of their own identity politics seemed to render the continued participation of the Jewish and Muslim institutions (i.e., the mosque and the synagogue) untenable.

But the fact that Grad and her Christian community remained firmly at the helm of the organization, supported, of course, by those American Jews and Arabs who were willing to risk a level of alienation from their religious institutions to remain active in the program, ensured the program's endurance. In fact, for Grad, a richer appreciation of the challenges posed by such a program seemed to set in, and the idealism with which she founded the program seemed to transform with this recognition of the reality of the conflict. What therefore happened, it seemed to me as an observer, was a far more expansive attempt to appease various "camps" in the organization. A kind of factionalism emerged with the efforts of Grad and other leaders to live out the virtues of cosmopolitanism and to consider a multiplicity of voices and perspectives on the actual program itself.

This brief historical narrative of Hands of Peace offers an inside view of the contestation of the very foundation of the program itself. In the 2-year debate over whether to become an entirely independent nonprofit organization (it originally existed as a subsidiary of Glenview Community Church, Grad's congregation), the identity of the program was certainly at stake, particularly around its emphasis on an "interfaith" versus "intercultural" focus. (An emphasis on interfaith dialogue suggested a religious basis for the Israeli–Palestinian conflict, which tended to distress the regional staff and the youth themselves, who, like most of their peers, lived relatively secular lives.) Yet the contestation over organizational identity hardly, in my estimation, affected the essential culture to which the youth were exposed in the course of participation.

The culture of Hands of Peace, not surprisingly, mimicked that of Seeds of Peace in a number of ways. The use of a uniform served to highlight for the youth their status as a new group with a common, superordinate identity. The mission statement of Hands of Peace, despite undergoing the occasional minor revisions over the course of my fieldwork, was always quite clear in its ideological foundations and allegiance (unscientifically, that is) to the common in-group identity model of intergroup contact:

> The mission of Hands of Peace is to foster long-term peaceful
> coexistence among Jewish-Israelis, Arab-Israelis, and West Bank
> Palestinians by bringing young people from the Middle East together
> with American teens in an *interfaith setting*. We strive to promote this
> mission by creating opportunities for the participants—young
> people from the Middle East, local teens, host families, staff, and
> volunteers—to seek the *mutual understanding that comes from face to face
> encounters* by: (1) Exposing teens and host communities to cultures other
> than their own for the purpose of *recognizing our common humanity*;
> (2) Promoting the ability of participants to give and receive *differing
> perspectives* in a respectful manner; (3) Developing *a personal commitment
> to promote intercultural relationships*; (4) Educating home communities
> about the need for continuing dialogues to foster peaceful coexistence.

> (Hands of Peace, 2006; italics added)

The italicized portions of the mission statement serve to draw the reader's attention to the ideological features of the program.

First, the immediate statement of an "interfaith setting" reflects the desire on the part of the organizers to view the social ecology of the program as one of primarily *religious* diversity. Cultural diversity is certainly noted but, owing to its later placement in the statement, receives a slightly lesser degree of emphasis. This insistence of framing the program as *interfaith*, it should be noted, was met with resistance even among members of the Steering Committee[6] upon the recognition that most of the youth participants from Israel and Palestine were not religious. There were also, as noted, concerns about the conflation of religion and nationality by framing the program as primarily "interfaith" in nature, which might contribute to the somewhat common misconception that the Israeli–Palestinian conflict is largely a religious conflict between Jews and Muslims.

Regardless of these concerns, Grad's commitment to her religious congregation, as well as that congregation's significant financial contributions to the program, necessitated an insistence that the program retain its original interfaith focus. As will become clear upon detailing the rites of participation, this focus was never very well integrated into the program's curriculum. It should,

---

6 The Steering Committee was the primary governing body of Hands of Peace during my fieldwork.

however, be noted that the alliance with the three congregations (which ulti-mately reduced to two and then only one—the Christian church) possessed implications for the physical culture of the program: many key events (includ-ing the dialogue sessions in the first year) occurred at the church, synagogue, and mosque themselves.

The second key component of the Hands of Peace mission statement that I wish to highlight is the contention that "face-to-face" encounters *intrinsically* result in "mutual understanding." In social psychology, rigorous experimental work has suggested that, upon mere exposure to a stimulus (e.g., a particular word or sound), individuals appear to develop a positive attitude toward it—an effect that has been replicated across populations and with animals (Zajonc, 1968, 2001). This basic idea about the relationship between exposure and sentiment can be connected to Allport's (1954) original model of intergroup contact. However, unlike in highly controlled laboratory studies on the mere exposure effect, the vast literature on the psychological outcomes of contact is less definitive.

A meta-analysis of quantitative studies of contact suggests that, indeed, it is generally associated with prejudice reduction, even in the absence of all of Allport's (1954) conditions (Pettigrew & Tropp, 2006). However, there are clearly conditions in which contact does not result in prejudice reduction or "mutual understanding" between group members, and exploring the *variability* of contact outcomes and processes is vital to the evolution of social psychologi-cal research on this topic (Dixon et al., 2005; Pettigrew, 2008a). In other words, we must approach the relationship between "face-to-face" encounters (i.e., con-tact) and "mutual understanding" as a *question* rather than an *assumption*.

The mission statement of Hands of Peace reveals the program's commit-ment to a common in-group identity (again, implicitly) model of intergroup contact and the same basic ideology as Seeds of Peace. The focus in the state-ment on getting participants to recognize their "common humanity" reveals a desire to, in social psychological terms, initiate a cognitive recategorization process of social identity in which the youth will come to view Israeli and Palestinian national identities as a part of the superordinate "common human" identity. The emphasis on promoting the ability to tolerate "differing perspec-tives" and to foster "intercultural relationships" reveals the ideological project of the program as connected to cosmopolitanism: through the recognition of pluralism in perspective and identity, achieved through relational exposure to such difference, a higher level of "identity consciousness" is achieved. It is precisely this "higher level" that embraces an ideology of peaceful coexistence.

So we come to view the ideological project of Hands of Peace, like Seeds of Peace, as intimately connected to the larger American project of liberal pluralism and its embrace of cosmopolitan values in human consciousness (Hammack, 2009). Fundamental to this project is both (a) the reduction in salience of one's social identity—an internalized master narrative that only serves to polarize and insulate, and (b) the induction of a common in-group identity at a "higher" level of category inclusiveness: that of "Hand" most prox-imately and ultimately that of "Human." It is in this recategorization of iden-tity that the possibility of a new generation of "transcendent" (Kelman, 1999b) identity narratives might flourish.

RITES OF PARTICIPATION Having established the essential material and philosophical foundations of the program, let us explicitly consider the rites of participation: the actual goings-on of the program, from the moment of recruitment of the youth to their reintegration home after the program. Hands of Peace relied on the support of Seeds of Peace to recruit youth in their inaugural summer of 2003. Seeds of Peace did so by soliciting former participants and their siblings who, for whatever reason, had not been accepted by their governments to participate in Seeds of Peace but desperately wanted to. This recruitment strategy worked quite well for Hands of Peace, as the idea of having participants who were in fact somewhat acquainted with the nature of a coexistence program meant that there was less at stake in the program's experimental beginnings.

After the first summer, a school-based recruitment strategy was initiated in the region in which the organization developed relationships with a small number of schools from across Israel and Palestine. Presentations were made once a year by American staff, and interested youth applied online. Every attempt was made in recruiting a delegation to balance a number of factors. For example, among the Palestinian delegation, there was a desire to balance Muslim and Christian youth, as well as youth from large cities like Ramallah or Nablus and those from villages. Among Jewish-Israeli applicants, there was a desire to balance geographic locale as well as "ethnic" origin (i.e., Ashkenazi versus Mizrahi). Beyond the consideration of demographic dynamics, how-ever, there was a genuine attempt to recruit an ideologically diverse group of youth. That is, there was an active desire to avoid taking youth who seemed somehow already committed to peaceful coexistence. While many participants may have been "predisposed" to such ideological commitments, there was an attempt to assemble a delegation that mirrored as closely as possible the actual population of Israel and Palestine.

Once selected, the participants underwent at least one preprogram orientation in Jerusalem with regional staff and former participants. These were important sessions for them to become initiated into the larger group

of active program alumni, thereby beginning the process of identity restructuring (i.e., of belonging to a new *social category*). Their participation began in
earnest as they departed from the region to Chicago. The politics of identity
immediately played out in the journey. I will offer two examples, both of
which derive from the fact that one's travel documents are highly determinative of the experience one will have in both leaving the region and in entering
the United States.

Since identity is so central to the conflict itself, and therefore to Israel's
very security, it is impossible for certain cultural practices (like entering and
exiting the country) in Israel to really embody the values of the multicultural
democracy it may strive to be. The *screening* of identity is thus central to the
process of airport security in Israel. Security agents at Ben-Gurion embody
more American Secret Service agents than anything resembling a Transportation
Security Administration employee examining the baggage X-ray screen in
mind-numbing nonchalance. Airport security is, for Israelis, a *science*—and
one of vital existential significance.

The significance of identity in the process of leaving Israel means that the
identity of the passenger is key to one's experience in the airport. Upon arriv-
ing to the airport, security agents appear every 20 to 30 feet and ask for a passport and details on the nature of one's visit to Israel. When one enters the
airport and undergoes that initial "interrogation" by the security agents, one is
then "marked" with a color-coded sticker. As best I could discern, pink indicated low-risk, yellow indicated medium-risk, and red indicated high-risk. (As
revealed by this color scheme, airport security was fairly overt in its classifications. This color-coded system has now been changed to a numeric one.) Not
surprisingly, one's identity was entirely predictive of one's sticker color: Jews
invariably received a pink sticker, Arabs a red one, and "unidentifiable" travel-
ers such as myself (i.e., non-Jews and non-Arabs of any nationality, including
American) a yellow one.

When I first traveled through Ben-Gurion and was extensively quizzed
about the "origin of my surname" and whether it may have any Arab origins
(explicitly asked by security agents), I initially sort of laughed off the event as
the paranoia and lack of trust of one random security agent. When the same
exact ritual occurred *every time* I left the country, I finally realized the discern-
ment of any Arab origins at all was fundamental to the science of Israeli
security, and the relevance of my own identity in the perception of Israelis was
constantly affirmed in this experience.

The Hands of Peace participants who travel through Ben-Gurion include
all Israeli citizens (i.e., both Jewish and Palestinian citizens of Israel) and
Palestinians who reside in Jerusalem and therefore have permanent resident

status in Israel. They typically have passports issued by Jordan and an Israeli travel document that permits them to travel in and out of Israel. (Jerusalemite Palestinians possess the coveted "blue ID" that maximizes their ability to pass through checkpoints and to cross between Palestine and Israel. They are the one group that essentially has complete freedom of movement, as Palestinian Israelis are prohibited from entering the territories without approval from the Israel Defense Forces (IDF).)

The initial encounter with airport security highlights most poignantly the identity dynamics of the conflict, as all of the Arab participants undergo a different, far more lengthy security process than Jewish participants. Psychologically, that this event commences the program immediately highlights the perceived power imbalance of the Palestinian youth. Ali, a 16-year-old Palestinian from East Jerusalem, describes this experience on the day he arrived in Chicago:

> Today we witnessed the discrimination. First our car was stopped and searched at the airport. Then all the Jews just walked right through, while all of us Arabs were searched, practically strip searched. This is our lives as Palestinians. We're always struggling, always fighting. It's really depressing.

The experience in the airport serves, then, as a catalyst for the identity salience that will consume the coexistence program. The politics of exit from Israel are, unfortunately, closely mirrored upon entry to the United States, where Israeli citizens again receive preferential treatment. Palestinians who travel with the Israeli delegation experience detention upon entry to the United States, where they are required to undergo an entrance interview with the Department of Homeland Security. In my years of fieldwork, Israeli citizens never needed to undergo such interviews (including Arab citizens).

Palestinians who hold a "green ID" and a passport issued by either Jordan or the Palestinian Authority are not permitted to travel from Ben-Gurion (at least without overcoming significant bureaucratic obstacles). Rather, their best option is to depart from Jordan to reach destinations outside the Middle East. As a consequence, the Palestinian delegation for Hands of Peace begins their journey to Chicago 2 days prior to the Israeli group. They do so because they must traverse the West Bank route to Jordan, passing through numerous Israeli checkpoints and then eventually the Jordanian border. According to the staff who served as chaperones for the youth, this journey is exhausting and fraught with numerous possibilities of potential obstacles, including delays at checkpoints and the border. Thanks to good planning and political connections in Jordan, the group successfully made the journey to Amman in each of my years of fieldwork with little incident. They then fly directly to Chicago.

Unfortunately, even though this Palestinian group experiences little in the way of identity discrimination upon their exit from Jordan, the entry to the United States is anything but a welcoming one. It is the policy of the Department of Homeland Security to register all Palestinians and Jordanians who enter the country. As a consequence, the Palestinian delegation spends up to 4 hours following arrival in Customs and Immigration at Chicago waiting to be interviewed and registered. My colleague Amin, a chaperone to the group, summarized his experience as follows:

> It's what we're used to, us Palestinians. It was very disappointing for us, though, because we were expecting to be welcomed. We are a group that is working for peace, and we think of America as a great land of freedom and democracy. To be singled out like that—which we knew we were because we saw other foreigners walk right through—it reminded us that we are Palestinians. We know we face this at home, by the Israelis and the Jordanians and everyone, but we didn't think we'd face it here.

The very experience of travel to Chicago itself thus primes key aspects of the master narrative of identity, particularly for Palestinians. The narrative of oppression and discrimination, of victimhood, is thus rendered salient even before the youth enter the dialogue session with Israelis.

Once in Chicago, the traumas of travel are rapidly left behind them as youth are in awe of the vast expanse, cleanliness, and affluence of the suburban community in which they will spend the next 2 weeks. The exact welcome ritual varied from year to year during my research. In 2003, when both groups arrived in the morning, the day was spent at a local park where youth played softball, basketball, and made bracelets and engaged in other types of activities. In 2004, when both groups arrived in the late afternoon, something a bit more "ritualistic" was attempted. A formal welcome dinner was organized and, at a point late in the evening, all of the youth were gathered in a separate room from the families, given their official program T-shirts, and then introduced (amid energized applause) anew to the families wearing their purple program T-shirts. Obviously this kind of ritual was more explicitly "initiative" for the youth and much more explicitly ritualistic, closely mirroring the concept of flag-raising at Seeds of Peace: thanks to a uniform, they are all now part of a new group, possessing a new social identity as a "Hand." In 2005, such a ritual was no longer possible, as the security situation at Ben-Gurion necessitated that youth receive their program T-shirts in the region so that (in theory) they could proceed through security more expeditiously. But a formal program dinner and welcome still occurred in which the new participants were highlighted as a new group. This latter pattern continued in 2006 and 2007.

The early days of Hands of Peace are spent in basic relationship- and trust-building activities both in and out of the dialogue sessions. In the sessions, this phase typically involves the use of name games and basic interpersonal sharing, although this experience can even prime a direct conversation about the conflict. Outside of the sessions, youth eat and play together in outings like mini-golf or ice-skating. This initial phase culminates in the "teams challenge" course, an outdoor group-building challenge course that requires youth to work together.

Like Seeds of Peace, Hands of Peace has an "anthem" that the youth learn in the very first days of participation and then perform at various points throughout the program. Its lyrics affirm the basic foundation of the program's ideology:

> We are people from different nations,
> But now we're learning how to live as one.
> We just wanted our voices to be heard,
> No more enemies to fear,
> Working together we can reach the highest heights,
> Keep this in mind and peace is near.
>
> (Chorus) Hands of Peace, we're building a bridge,
> Put your hand in mine.
> Trust in me, we'll change the world.
> We are people from different nations,
> But now we're learning how to live as one.
>
> Coexistence is more than just a word,
> Meet me halfway and that's a start.
> With your commitment and with honesty and time,
> You will feel a change of heart.
> (Chorus)

The song suggests a unity in the national pluralism of the group. It conveys a respect for diversity, while simultaneously identifying the need for cooperative interaction. Its goals are infused with emotion, with its poignant ending, "You will feel a change of heart." Such emotional transformations, it suggests, are possible only once the values of coexistence—and the new narrative of a common identity—are internalized.

All of these early experiences serve very well to "acculturate" the youth to the program—to its basic structure, its essential characters, its social and political ideology. Outside of the dialogue sessions, the goal is to construct a new group, and the ability to do so is facilitated by the fact that these youth are all subjects of a global youth culture, fueled by similar interests and tastes in music and film (Arnett, 2002). As such, finding common ground does not pose a formidable challenge, so long as discussion of the conflict (which primes in-group identity and reminds the youth of their differences from the larger group) does not occur.

As the second phase of dialogue gets fully under way, the youth address the conflict head-on, focusing on discussions of stereotypes, history, and identity. This phase culminates in a full day of religious service observation. The youth attend Friday services at a local mosque and then discuss Islam with congregation members and staff. They then attend Shabbat services at a local synagogue, followed by a typical ritualized Shabbat dinner. It should be noted that the synagogue has always been of the Reform or Reconstructionist variety, neither of which are popular in Israel. Thus, the ritual is often quite different to what even Jewish Israeli youth have experienced at home.

Although these rites of participation are designed to be purely observational in nature, the lines often blur between "observation" and "participation," as even observation of services poses some requirements of the youth. For example, female participants who are menstruating are forbidden from entering the prayer area of the mosque, even just to observe. Females also need to cover their heads, regardless of whether they are Muslim. Some youth interpreted the need to comply with these rules as oppressive, but in general the mosque observation was welcomed by the non-Muslim youth, most of whom had never stepped foot inside of a mosque and had little knowledge of Muslim religious practice.

Observation of Shabbat services proved more problematic for the group for several reasons. First, for Palestinian youth, the very idea of stepping into a synagogue brings about feelings of guilt and disloyalty, as Jews in general are viewed as the aggressor and the synagogue itself represents an institution of oppression. The experience thus typically created unique challenges for the Palestinian participants. Unfortunately, the encouragement by the rabbis for youth to actually *participate* rather than simply observe the service over the years also created tensions for the youth (as well as tensions between the program staff and the rabbis). For example, in 2003 Palestinian youth were asked spontaneously by the senior rabbi to approach the altar and light a series of candles. In this way, they were asked to become participants in a service that was already quite psychologically difficult for them to attend. An even more basic problem with Palestinian attendance at Shabbat services is the content of the service itself, with constant reference to "the people of Israel" and the "return to the land of Israel." For better or worse, the content of the Shabbat service strikes the Palestinian participants as essentially Zionist, affirming their attendance of the service as guilt ridden.

These midprogram rituals thus challenge the common identity being constructed by priming national identity. Though initially intended to contribute to the program's aim to expose youth to different faith traditions and rituals, and in this exposure to facilitate their recognition of a common identity, they in fact interrupt the process of common in-group identification. The resumption of social activities—a series of barbecues and other events—reinstates a sense of common identity, if only ephemerally.

National identity is thus primed during the course of the program, albeit unintentionally by the organizers. As the second week of participation begins in earnest, it becomes increasingly difficult to segregate the content of the dialogue sessions with the social activities outside of them that serve to develop a common identity. Yet by "Handshake Games," a ritual mimicking Color Games at Seeds of Peace, the triumph of the common identity becomes readily apparent.

Handshake Games consists of an entire day's worth of sports, games, and other challenges. Youth are divided into mixed groups (i.e., dialogue groups are divided, good friends are separated, sex and nationality are balanced) for the day's competition. It is a day of fun and laughter, with the youth acting as good friends and teammates. The following night, youth work together for "Culture Night," the ultimate ritual revealing the cosmopolitanism that infuses the ideology of the program.

For Culture Night, youth work together to cook their favorite recipes from home. The families are then treated to a feast of food, including traditional Palestinian fare like *makloube* and *kibbe* and Jewish dishes like *schnitzel* and *latkes.* The evening culminates in performances that represent their distinct cultures in some way. The Palestinian *debka* folk dance is standard fare, along with a number of traditional Israeli songs. With Culture Night, there would seem to again be a kind of priming of social identity, but in fact the Israelis and Palestinians are very encouraging of one another, watching intensely as the other performs, or asking members of the other group about the various dishes prepared for the dinner. There is a way in which, with this ritual, the program seems to have succeeded in getting youth to appreciate cultural difference, though we must remember that such appreciation occurs in a social structure that is quite divergent from the actual context of conflict.

The final three evenings of the program are spent in social activities. A party for participants only (i.e., no host families) occurs the night following Culture Night, and the Farewell Dinner the next night. The Farewell Dinner brings together families that have been involved and major community donors. After the meal itself, attendees are treated to more performances from the youth (some repeated from Culture Night, but now perfected), as well as speeches about their experiences in the program. By this point, the youth feel so connected to one another that the idea of their imminent departure is extremely disappointing to them. Tears run down their faces as the Farewell Dinner performances conclude with a group rendition of the Hands of Peace song. That final lyric—"Now we're learning how to live AS ONE!"—is shouted passionately in unison. The next morning the youth gather at the church before the bus departs for the airport. They sign each other's T-shirts, write in each other's journals, and spend quiet one-on-one moments together. As the tears return, it is clear to me that the program has, in its way, and despite its many diversions into territories that could further polarize the youth, succeeded in psychologically affecting participants in its intended way.

Owing to the major psychological process the participants undergo during the program, the return home is typically a traumatic one. There is also, naturally, the realization of travel from what has become a kind of ideological "utopia," with its new narrative of coexistence, to a place of conflict and identity polarization. At this point, I wish only to inform the reader of the ways in which youth can and do intersect again with the program after its conclusion in Chicago, rather than to address the experiences of youth postprogram, which will be discussed in detail in Chapter 7.

Youth who choose to remain active in the program can do so in two ways. First, there is a program listserv to which they can send messages to the entire group. Second, there are semiregular follow-up meetings in Jerusalem for all alumni (though typically targeted to the immediate preceding year's alumni). These are conducted by the regional staff who accompanied youth from Israel and Palestine to Chicago. They consist of both socializing and typically a dialogue session. The attendance of West Bank Palestinians at these meetings is, unfortunately, infrequent owing to the difficulty of travel to Jerusalem. (They require special permission and must endure the numerous checkpoints in order to get to Jerusalem.) In Chapter 7, we will consider the ways in which the new narrative of coexistence is or is not sustained by continued participation in the program in these contexts—far removed from the original physical and ideological culture of Hands of Peace itself.

The Interviewees

Out of the approximately 450 youths I came into contact with over the course of my fieldwork, I recruited a sample of 45 to study intensively through interview and ethnographic methods. Tables 2.2 and 2.3 provide demographic summary data that illustrate the identity diversity of the sample. Table 2.2 summarizes participants by overall identity group (i.e., Jewish-Israeli, Palestinian-Israeli, and Palestinian) and sex.

The ultimate interview sample was thus demographically diverse and representative of most of the identity groups that reside in Israel and Palestine. Missing, of course, are the voices of youth from smaller identity groups, such as the Druze who reside in various areas in the north of Israel. Also notably

TABLE 2.2 Characteristics of the Interview Sample: Identity Group and Sex

	Sex		
Identity Group	Male	Female	Total
Jewish Israelis	7	10	17
Palestinian Israelis	5	7	12
Palestinians	10	6	16
TOTAL	22	23	45

The identity label *Jewish Israelis* refers to all youth who are Jewish citizens of Israel. *Palestinian Israelis* refers to all youth who are Palestinian Arab citizens of Israel. These youth are the descendants of the indigenous Palestinian Arab population that in 1948 remained in the territory that became the State of Israel. The label *Palestinian* refers to youth who reside in the Palestinian territories occupied by Israel following the 1967 War. These territories include East Jerusalem, the Gaza Strip, and the West Bank.

TABLE 2.3 Demographic Characteristics of the Interview Sample

Jewish-Israeli (n = 17)	N
Ashkenazi	13
Mizrahi	4
Urban	11
Rural	6
Palestinian-Israeli (n = 12)	
Christian	4
Muslim	7
Druze	1
Urban	4
Village or rural	8
Palestinian (n = 16)	
Christian	4
Muslim	12
Urban	13
Village or rural	3

missing are voices of youth from Gaza, from refugee camps, and from Jewish settlements in the occupied territories (with one notable exception).

This interview sample, while not fully representative of the population of Israel and Palestine, represents a "theoretical" sample of Israeli and Palestinian youth. A theoretical sample, in the parlance of grounded theory qualitative research (e.g., Glaser & Strauss, 1967), is recruited to address a specific research question and thus may in fact be a "nonrepresentative" sample of a larger population. Given the second research question of this study—change in the life story following intergroup contact—I needed to target a sample of youth who participate in such programs. The use of such a sample to address my first research question—the relationship of "big" stories in a culture to the "small" stories of a personal narrative—means that I must be tentative in making definitive claims about that relationship based on this study. But qualitative research is not really intended to make generalizable claims. Rather, it is meant to allow for a certain richness of theoretical analysis and individual-level data that large-scale quantitative research simply cannot provide. The youth who comprise the interview sample—geographically and religiously diverse, though largely middle and upper-middle class—are generally representative of those youth who participate in such American-based programs.

It is important to note that certain groups overrepresented in my interview sample tend to be overrepresented in the programs themselves. Specifically, Ashkenazi Jews outnumber Mizrahi Jews substantially in these programs, likely owing to the educational criteria necessary for securing admission to the programs and the differential treatment of Mizrahi and Ashkenazi Jews in Israeli society, which may impact educational success (see Leichtman, 2001; Mizrachi, 2004; Shavit, 1990). In addition, Muslims outnumber Christians substantially among Palestinian participants. Such an imbalance both reflects Palestinian society, which is majority Muslim, and the desire on the part of these programs to compose a delegation of youth that essentially mirrors the demographics of the society as much as possible. (Hands of Peace, for example, routinely receives applications from more Palestinian Christians than it can possibly accept in order to maintain some representativeness of the actual demographics of Palestine.)

Interviewees ranged in age at first interview from 14 to 18 years. In 2003, interviewees were recruited in collaboration with staff at Seeds of Peace, who insisted on a very limited number of interviews (seven in total). At Hands of Peace in 2003, 2 of the 12 participants from the region who had formerly been participants at Seeds of Peace were selected as interviewees, as the focus at that point in the project was primarily on Seeds of Peace, as well as one new participant who had never undergone contact before. In 2004, Seeds of Peace permitted me to recruit interviewees randomly from two dialogue groups, which resulted in the recruitment of eight additional interviewees. All participants in the Hands of Peace program in 2004 and in 2005 ($n = 27$) were successfully recruited as interviewees.

The Interview Procedure

In the tradition of grounded theory interviewing (Charmaz, 2006; Glaser & Strauss, 1967), the interview protocol changed over the course of my fieldwork, as I sought to "test" some of the theories that were emerging from the data. Despite some variation in content of the interview, a number of factors were standardized across administration. All of the 45 interviewees completed a "life-line" drawing at the beginning of each interview. In this task, interviewees were prompted with the following instructions:

> What I'd like to ask you to do is to draw a line that represents the events of your life. The line should go up when it was a good time in your life, and down when it was a bad time in your life. You can write as much information as you like on the line. You can do this quietly to yourself, and then we'll talk about it.

Interviewees then completed the life-line drawing, similar to a life satisfaction chart commonly used in life course research (see Giele & Elder, 1998; Runyan, 1980). The life-line presents a visual plot of life experience that essentially places the life-story narrative in a visual form. My intent in starting the interview with this procedure was to encourage integrative reflection among my interviewees prior to their telling of the life story. In addition, life-lines were useful as I conducted formal analysis of narratives.

After completing the life-line, interviewees were instructed to tell the story of their life using the line. They were prompted throughout this portion of the interview to provide as much detail as possible, and I intervened to ensure that a complete picture of each element in the story emerged. Items from the formally constructed interview protocol, including a modified version of McAdams' (1995a) Life Story Interview, were ensured coverage in this process. If items in the protocol were not spontaneously covered by the telling of the life story, I asked them of interviewees after their initial telling.

The resulting interview data was rich in content, providing basic demographic and family information as well as the key events of life (e.g., peak experience, turning points, nadir) and the meaning interviewees made of those events. Personal and political ideology was assessed in great detail, particularly with specific reference to the conflict and the various political ideologies in the respective societies of the youth (e.g., Hamas vs. Fatah, Labor vs. Likud).

I conducted all interviews in English. For the occasional moments when interviewees were unable to express themselves in English, I instructed them to speak in their native language. These portions of the interview were then later translated by research assistants fluent in either Hebrew or Arabic. In some longitudinal interviews conducted in the region, I included a native research assistant in the interviews to assist with translation as needed. Interviews conducted at Seeds of Peace and Hands of Peace occurred in a variety of available locations, all of which were private, which ensured the interviewees comfort to speak openly. Interviews in the region were conducted either in the homes of interviewees or in public locations such as cafés. Every attempt was made to secure as much privacy as possible for interviews conducted in public spaces. The duration of interviews ranged from approximately 1 to 3 hours. All interviews were audiotaped and transcribed verbatim, with corrections made in some cases for comprehensibility, given that interviewees were not native English speakers.

Interviewees narrated their life stories at various points relative to their participation in the coexistence program. Of the 45 youths interviewed, 42 were interviewed at least twice. Interview administration proceeded according to two general patterns. The absence of a more systematic sampling design and interview administration was both deliberate and uncontrollable. It was deliberate in the grounded theory tradition: as theories emerged from various sources of data, the research design adapted (Glaser & Strauss, 1967). It was uncontrollable in the sense that, in order to secure permission from the two programs themselves, I had to abide by the limitations they imposed on when interviews could be conducted.

The most common pattern involved the administration of a life story interview about 1 month prior to program participation, conducted in Israel or Palestine. Interviewees were then observed during their participation in the coexistence program, as I assumed a participant observer role each summer. Then I conducted a brief postprogram interview to assess immediate reports about the contact experience. Finally, I conducted a second life story interview in Israel or Palestine within 2 years of completing participation. Due to difficulties in locating some youths, this longitudinal interview was sometimes conducted as many as 3 years following program participation.

Due to issues of feasibility and the unavailability of information on program participants beforehand, I conducted some initial life story interviews at the start of the coexistence program in the United States. For all of the 42 youths with whom I was able to remain in contact over the course of the study, I spent considerable time with them and family members during my continued travels to the region, often residing with them for some length of time and conducting brief informal interviews and home observations.

As with many projects that rely upon qualitative methods and immersion of the researcher into the population under study, this study lacked what many scientists would call a "systematic" design. Given the logistical challenges of mounting this kind of study, though, I opted to sacrifice systematicity for fluidity and richness, all the while remaining aware of the possible limitations that such an approach might bring with it. As I came to realize, though, my ability to address the research questions was enhanced by the multiple points in time relative to program participation that youth were interviewed. As I present the narratives of youth in the following chapters, I will make every attempt to contextualize my data with specific reference to program participation, so that the reader can judge my interpretations fully informed.

Analytic Strategy

The primary focus of data analysis in this book is the individual narration of the life story at two data points—prior to or at the start of participation in contact, and 1–2 years postcontact. Guided by an *interpretive* approach pioneered by early scholars such as Wilhem Dilthey (1900/1976) and by more recent psychologists who use qualitative methods (e.g., Tappan, 1997, 2005), I treated each personal narrative as a "text" to be interpreted. I analyze three specific aspects of each narrative in my interpretation: (1) *form*, (2) *thematic content*, and (3) *ideological setting*. The focus on these three indices is inspired by theoretical and methodological approaches to narrative research.

In an early treatise on narrative analysis, Gergen and Gergen (1983) posit that life stories assume particular forms associated with literature. For example, some life stories take the form of a tragedy, in which the overall tone and the destiny of the protagonist (i.e., narrator) are characterized by misfortune. Other life stories assume a form more associated with romantic literature, in which the protagonist overcomes adversity to triumph. My analysis of the life stories presented in this book adopts this approach to formal analysis, while also using classifications suggested by more recent scholarship in narrative studies (e.g., Lieblich, Tuval-Mashiach, & Zilber, 1998; McAdams, 2006).

The second focus of narrative analysis was on the major themes that characterize the life story. Given my interest in the connection between collective and individual narratives, I focused on four themes present in the collective narrative of each group in order to assess their integration into the individual life story. These four themes were identified based on a review of the literature on Israelis and Palestinians and an analysis of key historical documents (e.g., political statements and speeches). For Jewish Israelis, these themes included *historical persecution, existential insecurity, exceptionalism,* and *delegitimization of Palestinian identity.* For Palestinians, themes included *loss and dispossession, existential insecurity, resistance,* and *delegitimization of Zionism and Israeli national identity.* In Chapters 3 and 4, I detail the basis of these themes in the historical literature and political archive on Israel and Palestine.

Finally, I analyzed the *ideological setting* of each life story in order to determine the political perspective of each youth within her or his own society and regarding the conflict in general. In his landmark theory of identity, Erik Erikson (1959) advanced the idea that ideology is a major component of identity formation. McAdams (1993, 1996) integrates this emphasis on ideology in his life story theory of identity, in which he argues that all life stories are set within some abstract system of beliefs or worldview that comprise an ideology. In the context of the Israeli–Palestinian conflict, this ideological setting of the life story would seem to assume even greater significance, given the presence of competing ideologies within each group that, at least in part, exacerbate the conflict.

In order to assess my second research question, the narratives of youth collected 1 to 3 years following their encounter with members of the rival group were analyzed using the same procedure: the form, thematic content, and ideological setting were examined, treating each life story as a text. Then these components were contrasted with the earlier life story of each participant to examine change in personal narrative construction.

As I noted earlier, my analytic approach is anchored in a tradition in personality and social psychology typically called the "study of lives" approach. This methodological perspective, which seeks to retain the integrity of individual-level data by focusing on the whole person and not aggregating across cases, was pioneered by Henry Murray (1938) and Gordon Allport (1937). It is a tradition that is alive and well today in contemporary psychological research (e.g., Cohler, 2007; Gregg, 2007; Josselson, 1996; McAdams, 2006), particularly among those who identify with a narrative approach.

While the personality and developmental psychologist within me wants to focus very sharply at the level of the individual and to avoid aggregation of narrative data, the social psychologist within me wants to address issues that are fundamentally about *groups* and *group membership.* Thus, I fuse both holistic, idiographic approaches to narrative analysis with what is often called a *categorical* approach (e.g., Lieblich et al., 1998). While I am interested in interpreting narrative data based on my observations of individual, person-specific processes and experiences, I am also deeply interested in interpreting narrative data *across* individuals who belong to a particular group (in this case, Israelis, Palestinians, and Palestinian Israelis).

The chapters that focus concretely on the presentation of narrative data (Chapters 3, 4, 5, and 7) will apply this integrated approach to narrative data analysis—this focus on both person-level and group-level interpretation—to the two primary research questions of this study. Recall that the first research question is concerned with the relationship between what I call "master" narratives (those big stories that youth encounter about their national groups) and the personal narratives youth are in the initial stages of constructing. My second research question concerns the way in which the experience of contact seems to affect life story construction over time.

Both of these research questions speak to the need to consider patterns both *within* and *between* individual youths. Chapters 3, 4, and 5 offer case studies of youths from each of the three groups under study in order to address the first research question. Chapter 6 further contextualizes contact between and Israelis and Palestinians, while Chapter 7 then returns to the narratives of youth collected following participation. Rather than present a series of individual case studies, in Chapter 7 I categorize the outcome of contact on the life story according to two dimensions and then provide illustrative narrative data from my analysis.

The purpose of this chapter was to offer some authentic, reflexive description of my activities as a cultural psychologist and as a "stranger" to the Israeli–Palestinian conflict. I trust that my fusion of personal narrative as a researcher with a description of the fieldwork, the interviewees, and the procedures of data collection and analysis has sufficiently satisfied the desire of the reader to know something of me and of the context of this study. It is now to the voices of youth, expressed in their narratives of identity-in-formation, that we turn for insight into the cultural psychology of youth in conflict.

PART II

Stories

"By the mere fact that he forms part of an organized crowd, a man descends several rungs in the ladder of civilization. Isolated, he may be a cultivated individual; in a crowd, he is a barbarian—that is, a creature acting by instinct."
—Gustave Le Bon (1895/1969), *The Crowd: A Study of the Popular Mind*, pp. 27–28

"To be in a viable culture is to be bound in a set of connecting stories, connecting even though the stories may not represent a consensus."
—Jerome Bruner (1990), *Acts of Meaning*, p. 96

3

"Jewish in My Blood": Stories of Jewish-Israeli Youth

In Chapter 2, I provided an outline of the field methods used in this study. As the detail provided in that chapter suggests, field methods result in a vast amount of data for analysis. In order to focus on the first research question that drove the study—the relationship between master narratives and personal narratives in a context of intractable political conflict—I focus on two primary sources of data in the analysis presented in the next three chapters. First, I analyze historical documents (e.g., original Zionist texts) and political speeches, along with my own observational data collected during the course of my fieldwork, to identify the basic form, thematic content, and ideological setting(s) of the master narrative of history and identity to which contemporary youth are exposed. In each of the next three chapters, I begin with a presentation of this master narrative, and I am careful to identify the ways in which it is currently contested within each group. Then I present case studies in which I seek to demonstrate the utility and vitality of a methodological approach that fuses ethnography and idiography.

Recall that *idiographic* methods seek to focus, as much classic work in personality and social psychology once did (e.g., Allport, 1924, 1965; Murray, 1938), on the whole person. While most contemporary methods in psychology rely upon aggregate data (e.g., mean scores on a self-report measure of some psychological construct), an idiographic approach restores psychology's concern with the dynamics of *individual* experience and development. The point here is not, of course, to make broad, sweeping generalizations about populations (as is the purpose of aggregate statistical methods). Rather, psychologists who embrace idiographic methods are more interested in the "noise" that characterizes human development— the points of tension, the unexpected, the mysterious. Those of us who remain committed to a holistic approach to studying individual lives believe that the best window into the dynamics of human personality—with all its coherence and contradiction—is the voice of the person her- or himself, captured through methods that can allow us to analyze a life in its "complete" form.

The thrust of my first research question centers on the role of culture and context in individual development. As I discussed in Chapter 1, "culture" is a somewhat slippery concept that has, at times in its intellectual history, been used in ways that unfairly homogenizes groups and even delegitimizes or makes claims about the relative value of groups. On the other hand, the idea of a shared culture among group members can contribute to a sense of solidarity and security, thus highlighting and supporting the distinctiveness among human communities.

My window into the relationship between culture and personal identity is the idea of *narrative* or story. As I argued in Chapter 1, to identify connections between the "big" stories (or "discourse") that circulate in a cultural community and the "small" stories that reveal an individual's integration of lived experience is to query this dynamic relationship between person and culture. This kind of analysis reveals the way in which individuals appropriate or repudiate the big stories transmitted by a prior generation. And in the context of a long-standing, intractable conflict like the Israeli–Palestinian conflict, we (unfortunately) have a "living laboratory" for exploring such complex questions in social psychology (Bar-Tal, 2004b). Because collective narratives contribute to the continuation of conflict (Bar-Tal, 2007; Hammack, 2008; Kelman, 2007), the empirical exploration of the *process* by which youth engage with these narratives provides valuable insights into the current phase of the conflict. Let us now turn directly to this analysis of the relationship between collective narrative and personal story-making, beginning with Jewish-Israeli youth.

The Master Narrative of Jewish-Israeli Identity

An Introduction

The story of Israel is a story of emancipation and regeneration, of the rescue and resurrection of a threatened cultural identity (Halpern, 1969; Hess,

1862/1997; Pinsker, 1882/1997). It is a tale of suffering and success, of vulnerability and perseverance, of the emergence of power and strength out of weakness and persecution (Gamson & Herzog, 1999). It is a classic narrative of "descent and gain" (Lieblich et al., 1998) in which great tragedies precede resilient triumphs (Talmon, 1970).

In its simplest rendering, the master narrative of Jewish-Israeli identity begins many, many years ago, when the Kingdom of Israel existed and thrived, only to be destroyed and its people sent into exile around the world. The form of the story gradually ascends as the success of Jews in the Diaspora reveals their contributions to civilization, in spite of inhabiting a state of minority permanence in these societies. Then the narrative takes a tragic turn, as these host societies come to persecute the Jews, seeking a kind of national "purity" in the age of nationalism (Hobsbawm, 1990). Systematic pogroms result in the forced migration of Jews to contexts of greater safety.

The pace of this migration cannot be swift enough, as the ultimate nadir in this collective story—the Holocaust—fulfills the promise of vulnerability and lack of a fully realized national identity. This tragedy, however, serves as the final impetus for the peak experience of the master narrative—the "revitalization" of the State of Israel, a Jewish state, a safe haven for the Jews of the world, and a model for democracy in the region. Though existential threat remains, the sustenance of the Jewish state replaces vulnerability with *strength*, persecution with *preservation*, and mortality with *might*.

Formally, then, the Israeli master narrative represents a *redemptive* story. A redemptive narrative is one in which the protagonist (in this case, the Jewish collective) emerges from formidable struggle with greater strength and resolve, having mastered difficult challenges (McAdams, 2006). Yet the memory of tragedy and victimization infuses the narrative with a sense of existential insecurity, thus constructing the master narrative as always in a *possible* place of contamination.

Based on my analysis of historical and political documents, as well as my own ethnographic data, I suggest that the master narrative of Jewish-Israeli identity contains four primary themes: (1) historical *persecution and victimization* of the Jews; (2) *existential insecurity*, thus revealing the need for a strong security establishment and defense institution (i.e., military) in order to protect the collective; (3) the *exceptionalism* of Jewish Israelis, in their economic, military, and moral success, as well as their commitment to democracy; and (4) the *delegitimization* of the Palestinians. This latter trope at its extreme is characterized by *existential denial* of an indigenous Palestinian identity, well represented by former Israeli Prime Minister Golda Meir's assertion in a 1969 interview in *The Washington Post* that "There were no such thing as Palestinians" ("Golda Meir Scorns Soviets," 1969).

Contestations

Though I would argue that Israeli youth continue to be exposed to and influenced by this master narrative, I do not mean to depict this master narrative as a kind of static cultural artifact. Rather, I believe that master narratives are always in states of dynamic contestation. This view, in fact, underlies the empirical project I undertake in this book to chart the relation between master and personal narratives, for it is in the *dialogue* individuals have with such narratives of history and collective identity that processes of social stasis and change occur.

Beyond this intellectual argument, though, it is important to note that there is little that is "static" about Israeli society. In other words, Israelis are anything but monolithic as a people. Ideologically speaking, Israel has a plethora of political parties, which in fact often hinders the ability of its governments to take decisive action, given the number of constituencies that need to be satisfied.

Several scholars have sought to map the complexity of contemporary Israeli society by identifying distinct segments of society. Lemish (2003) divides Israeli identity among four primary groups, including the Palestinian citizens of Israel. Considering the three Jewish communities, he identifies (1) an *ultra-orthodox* community (approximately 9% of the total Israeli population), who live relatively autonomously from the institutions of the state and in many ways are opposed to the dominant stream of Zionism; (2) a *national-religious* community (approximately 15% of the population), who believe strongly in the concept of "Greater Israel" and Jewish settlements in the occupied territories and hence are the most ideologically polarized vis-à-vis the Palestinians; and finally (3) the *secular* Jewish community (approximately 50% of the population), who represent the descendants of "hegemonic" Labor Zionism (Kimmerling, 2001; Shafir & Peled, 2002), Ashkenazi elites who are more committed to secular nationalism than to the religious aspects of Judaism. As Shafir and Peled (1998, 2002) argue, these ideological rifts in Israeli society are represented in discourses of "citizenship" in the society.

But there is much more identity diversity in Israel than that created by ideological differences and discourses of citizenship. Despite attempts to construct Israel as somehow "ethnically unified" as a Jewish state, it is without question a pluralistic place, a nation of immigrants from diverse cultures in Eastern and Western Europe, North Africa, the Middle East, and, more recently, Ethiopia. Long considered a key source of identity diversity (see Hofman, 1970), a significant divide in Israeli society continues to exist between Ashkenazi and Mizrahi Jews, and differential "ethnicity" in this regard is the source of status differences and a stratification hierarchy in Israeli society (Leichtman, 2001; Mizrachi, 2004; Shafir & Peled, 1998). That is, the Israeli identity narrative is really dominated by the Ashkenazi Jew, and Israeli society continues to operate, as it always has in some way, on a model of assimilation (Mizrachi, 2004)—what Shafir and Peled (1998, 2002) refer to as an "incorporation regime."

The Israeli historian Baruch Kimmerling (2001) argues that the increasing pluralism of Israeli society challenges the idea of an enduring coherent national identity. He suggests that collective identity is in a place of continuous conflict within contemporary Israeli society. Yet, like the common claims of collective process often made by historians, philosophers, political scientists, and the like, Kimmerling makes many assumptions about the consequences of these larger social transformations for individual lives.

Rather than view social processes like immigration or pluralism, discrimination or subordination, as entirely determinative of individual subjectivity, I am inclined to view such processes as dialogic. That is, I believe that we inhabit social worlds that severely restrict and restrain many possibilities for thought, feeling, and behavior, yet I believe we challenge the construction of those worlds through our own processes of *engagement*, or *activity*, within them. Hence, though in principle I agree with the notion that a coherent and unified Israeli identity may be challenged by these larger social processes, I view the sustenance of a master narrative of Israeli identity as an empirical question—one that is entirely accessible through the personal narratives of youth.

The piece of the Israeli master narrative that would seem to be the most contested is, quite understandably, its *ideological setting*. Since the emergence of a new historiography that has disrupted the foundational myths of the state (e.g., Morris, 1987, 2001; Shlaim, 2001), there has been a growing movement within Israeli society that questions and challenges the received discourse of the conflict. A segment of the Israeli populace has embraced an ideology of "post-Zionism," in which it is argued that the need for a "monoethnic" Jewish state has outlived its usefulness and in fact prevents Israel from regional integration (Cohen, 1995; Kelman, 1998; Liebman & Susser, 1998; Silberstein, 2008). Post-Zionism deploys a new discourse in Israeli society that directly challenges the master narrative. In this way, as an ideology, its existence increases the field of discursive possibilities for Jewish-Israeli youth. They may, for example, learn the master narrative in school, only to be offered a critical evaluation of it by their post-Zionist parents at home. Again, the extent to which the *contested* nature of Jewish-Israeli identity in fact has a significant impact upon contemporary youth is very much an empirical question.

In sum, I do not view a master narrative of Jewish-Israeli identity as static or reified but rather as dynamic and always in a state of contestation. In fact, I believe it is through an analysis of individual life stories that we come to examine and understand this dialogic process of *social* and *cultural* development as it unfolds, for life stories provide a vital window into the process of narrative engagement youth undergo. As we see how the complexities, contradictions, and contestations of larger discourses are navigated within individual processes of life story construction, we gain access to a larger process of culture in action.

Before I properly consider this process through the stories of youth, I want to say more about the key thematic content of the Israeli master narrative. I want to guide the reader through my process of analysis by carefully illustrating the evidence for my claims about these four salient themes—historical persecution and victimization, existential insecurity, exceptionalism, and delegitimization of Palestinian identity. Following this more complete detail about these themes, I present the cases of four Jewish-Israeli youth in depth in order to examine the key theoretical questions about narrative, culture, and identity I have outlined.

Theme 1: Persecution and Victimization

In the nineteenth century, as the moment of great empires began to fade, groups began to unite along perceived cultural, linguistic, and "ethnic" lines to construct "imagined communities" (Anderson, 1983). In this "golden age" of nationalism (Hobsbawm, 1990), myths about the reawakening of "primordial" nations were rampant (Suny, 2001), and new structures of power and subordination emerged. In Europe, Jewish identity challenged the myth of unified, primordial communities. As discrimination turned to exclusion and subordination, and prejudice to violence, a Jewish political response began to crystallize.

Early Zionist thinkers, not surprisingly, appropriated the exclusionist nationalist discourse of the day to argue for the revitalization of a Jewish state. In *Rome and Jerusalem*, Moses Hess (1862/1997) argues that the Jews of Europe, who had favored assimilation into European culture (and thus the erosion of a Jewish identity), constitute a primordial nation that could be "reawakened" and "restored" to greatness in Jerusalem:

> The Jewish people will participate in the great historical movement of present-day humanity only when it will have its own fatherland. As long as the great Jewish masses remain in their position of inequality, even the relatively few Jews who have entirely surrendered their Jewish

identity in the vain attempt to escape individually from the fate of the
Jewish people, will be more painfully affected by the position of the Jews
than the masses, who feel themselves only unfortunate but not degraded.
(pp. 137–138)

Hess, of course, is not conceptualizing a primordial Jewish nationalism
out of some inevitable diasporic identity crisis among Europe's Jewry. There is
evidence that Europe's rapidly assimilating Jewish community was, by and
large, quite content with the privileges of European identity (Kimmerling,
2001). Rather, it is important to recognize that the idea of Zionism is reactionary. It is reactionary in the sense that its development was dependent upon the
growth of European nationalism that explicitly *excluded* the Jews (Mosse,
1978).

The experience with rising anti-Semitism in Europe began to write a tragic
chapter in the history of the Diaspora. At the height of their contributions to
civilization, at a time when Jewish intellectuals and scientists seemed to achieve
remarkable success in Europe and a Jewish culture coexisted in harmony with
other local ones, their sense of "home" was radically disrupted—largely by the
shifting discourse on identity and power that came to consume nationalist
Europe. Leo Pinsker, another foundational figure of Zionism, describes this
experience in his 1882 essay, *Auto-Emancipation*:

> The Jewish people has no fatherland of its own, though many
> motherlands; it has no rallying point, no center of gravity, no government
> of its own.... It is everywhere a guest, and nowhere *at home*. (Pinsker,
> 1882/1997, p. 183, italics in original)

Pinsker, like other architects of Zionism, is reacting to the growing reality of
Jewish victimization and persecution in the context of an orthodox nationalism
in Europe, with its growing notions of "racial purity."

Zionism, then, is best viewed as a national movement that emerged
in reaction to the persecution and victimization of Jews in Europe. In his influential essay, *The Jewish State* (1896/1997), Theodore Herzl crystallized the sentiments of other European Zionists when he said, "I consider the Jewish
question neither a social nor a religious one.... It is a *national* question"
(p. 209; italics added). The "nation-building" ideology of Zionism thus probably owes its emergence less to some irrational primordialism than to the very
real experience with subordination, victimization, and persecution in Europe.
Reactionary though it may be, there is no question that Zionism, like other
nationalist movements of the nineteenth and twentieth centuries, can be conceptualized as classic primordialism, in which a discourse of national identity

is rooted in the belief in some inherent national status long lost or eroded (Suny, 2001).

Zionism and the settlement movement in Palestine began long before the ultimate moment in the history of Jewish persecution in Europe—the Holocaust—but it is the Holocaust that served as the final impetus for the creation of a new Jewish identity. The Holocaust indeed serves as the ultimate story of Jewish victimization in the Israeli narrative (Caplan, 1999; Stein, 1984); it reveals the *necessity* of Israel's existential legitimacy. It fulfills the tragic prophecy of Zionism. It permeates Israeli culture and saturates its identity discourse, framing the politics of Israeli national identity (Moses & Moses-Hrushovski, 1997; Zertal, 2005).

Collective suffering, persecution, and victimization may reside at the core of the Jewish-Israeli identity narrative, and in fact reveal the necessity of a distinct Israeli primordialism for existential security, but there are other tropes in the master narrative that, perhaps owing to the passage of time and the success of Zionism as a national project, appear more salient for contemporary youth. The historical experience of victimization in the Diaspora led to an entire reconceptualization of Jewish identity and the emergence of the "Jew as Fighter" (Zeruvabel, 1995): the emergence of Jewish "militancy" (see Figure 3.1). The potentially *contaminating* effect of historical persecution and victimization in the Jewish-Israeli master narrative is thus mitigated through the cultivation of strength in the face of existential insecurity.

Theme 2: Existential Insecurity

The second major theme of the Jewish-Israeli master narrative centers on existential insecurity—closely related to the collective memory of persecution in Europe, but made salient in the violent struggle for self-determination, independence, and recognition. The sense of existential insecurity is manifest in the security beliefs that Jewish Israelis endorse (Bar-Tal, 1998b, 2004b, 2007; Jacobson & Bar-Tal, 1995), particularly the "siege mentality" (Bar-Tal & Antebi, 1992a, 1992b) that pervades Israeli society.

Yet, the sense of existential insecurity does not serve to contaminate the Jewish-Israeli master narrative, for the *response* to insecurity actually serves to *reposition* Jewish identity from *victim* to *fighter*, thus making the critical transition from the Diaspora identity to the Israeli national identity (Zeruvabel, 1995). In other words, the theme of existential insecurity actually serves to *redeem* the Diaspora narrative of Jewish victimization by *motivating* individuals to participate in an activity central to the making of this new identity—military service.

FIGURE 3.1 A prestate recruitment poster for Jewish soldiers (circa 1941–1945).

This particular theme of the master narrative thus prescribes a particular *practice* that contributes to collective identity. Cultural practice, certainly central to the inculcation of any identity (Holland et al., 1998), is absolutely essential to the sustenance of an identity under perceived existential threat. In Israel, practice related to the cultivation of security beliefs is quite centrally integrated into the life course of *all* its Jewish citizens through compulsory military service. Institutionally, the IDF emerged out of a consolidation of various militias in prestate Israel. No aspect of the life course was perhaps more central to the youth in this study—the male youth in particular—than the years of military service that preceded university (see Ben-Ari, 1998; Kaplan, 2006; Seginer, 1999). Soldiers—as ubiquitous in Israel as the sun—are figures of national reverence. They ride buses and trains for free; they are given special discounts at shops, hostels, and restaurants. Their stories consume entire pages of daily tabloids, with tales of heroic sacrifice beside stories of coping apart from families. Existential insecurity is thus realized in the institutionalization of the Jewish-Israeli life course itself, and the stories of youth reveal the prominence of the contemporary Israeli identity as Fighter, rather than as Victim, in the Israeli master narrative.

Existential insecurity has framed the collective experience of the Jews since the first *aliyah* (i.e., wave of immigration) to Palestine in the late nineteenth century. Thematically, it provides *continuity* with the collective memory of victimization in Europe (and, later, other regions from which Jews would emigrate), while simultaneously redeeming the narrative from its possible nadir of existential annihilation. In the collective *response* to insecurity through military action, Israelis live this redemption. As they respond to threats to their legitimacy and coherent identity—threats from Hamas in Gaza, Hezbollah in Lebanon, or the leaders of Iran—they reverse the vulnerability, defenselessness, and powerlessness of a prior generation.

In the course of my field research, youth engaged with this theme of the master narrative in at least two ways. First, my fieldwork was conducted during the second Palestinian *intifada*, amid continuing attacks against Israeli civilians. Thus, the youths in this study—youths like Gal, whose story I introduced in the Prologue—lived with the possibility of existential uncertainty in their daily lives. Second, I worked with all of the youth in this study just a few years prior to their military service; my first interview with them typically occurred when they were 15 or 16 years old. Hence, as I followed them over time, I watched as they prepared for military service. In some instances, they looked to military service with suspicion or disdain, but almost all were eager to engage in the practice necessary to fulfill their national identities, to participate in the act of collective redemption for a dark history of weakness.

Theme 3: Exceptionalism

The third major theme of the Jewish-Israeli master narrative I will highlight is the notion of exceptionalism—the view that the Jews constitute a special, "chosen" group. In those early Zionist texts, like Hess' *Rome and Jerusalem*, the call to Zion is the call to a higher moral order, to a nation that can be looked at for not only its material but also its moral successes, such as the abolition of "race and class oppression" (Hess, 1862/1997, p. 137).

The idea of Jewish-Israeli exceptionalism likely owes much of its origins to eternal stories of the "Chosen People" (Stein, 1984), but perhaps more recently to the success of Zionism itself, in its existential fulfillment. Talmon's (1970) essay, "Israel Among the Nations," casts the efforts of Zionism, culminating in the creation of the State of Israel, as "the most remarkable and most constructive achievement of the Jewish people..., and one of the great feats of universal history" (p. 3).

It is precisely this *remarkability* of the achievements of Zionism, as well as Israeli society since the establishment of the state, that infuses the master narrative of Jewish-Israeli identity with a concept of exceptionalism. Jewish Israelis view themselves as a "special" people—a people who, despite the "hostility" of their origins and current surrounds, have demonstrated not merely *resilience* but *progressive sustenance* in their ability to secure their own national and cultural existence. As Mizrachi (2004) argues, this component of the master narrative of Jewish-Israeli identity has traditionally referred more to the hegemonic Ashkenazi class of Israeli society, with the Mizrahim expected to be "nurtured" (*tipuach*) sufficiently to come to embody this aspect of the Israeli identity.

Exceptionalism infuses the master narrative of Jewish-Israeli identity and reinforces in-group solidarity by highlighting the distinctiveness of the group. Like other elements of the master narrative, the idea of exceptionalism in achievement cultivates a kind of isolationism that polarizes Jewish-Israeli identity in its regional context, particularly when this exceptionalism, as it often does both historically (e.g., Hess, 1862/1997) and in contemporary Israeli discourse, takes on an ethnocentric (i.e., Eurocentric, Orientalist) character (see Mizrachi, 2004; Said, 1978). The exceptionalism of the Jewish Israelis, at its most ethnocentric extreme, serves to delegitimize Palestinian identity, arguing that the Jews have a connection to the region "from time immemorial" whereas "the Arabs" served only as temporary inhabitants at best or "squatters" at worst (e.g., Peters, 1984; cf. Finkelstein, 2003), awaiting the end of the "third exile" (Pinsker, 1882/1997) of the "Chosen People."

Theme 4: Delegitimization of Palestinian Identity

Probably no other social psychological process is more characteristic of conflict than delegitimization. Israeli social psychologist Daniel Bar-Tal (1990a) defines delegitimization as "the process of categorizing groups into extremely negative social categories and excluding them from acceptability" (p. 65). Delegitimization, as a key component in the larger psychological process of conflict reproduction, has cognitive, affective, and behavioral consequences for intergroup relations.

A delegitimized group is conceived hierarchically below one's own group. Its members are reviled, dubbed as "evil" and not worthy of humane treatment; they are, in fact, *less than* human (Oren & Bar-Tal, 2007; cf. Haslam, 2006; Haslam, Loughnan, Reynolds, & Wilson, 2007). As Bar-Tal (1990a) argues, delegitimization facilitates moral exclusion (Opotow, 1990, 2007), which essentially provides justification for a group's acts against a rival group and its members. Delegitimization is thus a key part of the psychological cycle of violence.

Israeli delegitimization of the Palestinians occurs within the broader context of *Orientalism*. Orientalism in its broader thesis argues for the hegemonic
construction of "the Orient"[1] and "the Oriental" in relation to the Occident
(Said, 1978). The Orient is viewed through the lens of European ethnocentrism
as a place for civilizing, and the Oriental is thus a character *to be civilized*. The
failure of early Zionist writing to fully acknowledge the indigenous population
in Palestine likely had more to do with the proliferation of Orientalism as given
in European discourse than with some attempt to hoodwink the masses into
Palestine's complete emptiness. Zionism was, of course, Orientalist in nature,
being a product of European nationalism.

Even Erik Erikson (1959), in one of his characterizations of Israel, seems
to neglect the existence of an indigenous population in Palestine, having internalized the Orientalist conception of its "emptiness" and "unclaimed" status:

> These European ideologists [the Zionists], given—as it were—a *historical
> moratorium* created by the peculiar international and national status of
> Palestine first in the Ottoman Empire and then in the British mandate,
> were able to establish and to fortify a significant *utopian bridgehead* for
> Zionist ideology. In his "homeland," and tilling his very home soil, the
> "ingathered" Jew was to overcome such evil identities as result from
> eternal wandering, merchandising, and intellectualizing and was to
> become *whole* again in body and mind, as well as in nationality.
> (Erikson, 1959, p. 172, italics in original).

Erikson quite clearly explicates the Zionist vision of national regeneration in
this passage, with its emphasis on revising identity through the redemption of
a "spoiled" land—a land of uncertain status, a land in need of "tilling."

Orientalism has a long history in Israel. In his analysis of anthropological
study of the Palestinians, Israeli anthropologist Dan Rabinowitz argues that
early anthropology contributed to the "Oriental othering" that was necessary to
construct a coherent, exceptional Israeli national identity (Rabinowitz, 1992,
2001a, 2002). Specifically, he suggests that anthropological interpretations of
Palestinian culture served to construct a clear out-group that essentially provided a perfect counteridentity to the Israeli national identity under construction. Palestinian culture was characterized as "traditional" in its familial and
general social structure, in contrast to the new Israeli culture, which was

---

1 As Said (1978) notes, American readers will be less familiar with the use of the "Orient" and the "Oriental" to
refer to the Near, rather than the Far, East. In European discourse and in academic parlance in both North
America and Europe, the Orient refers largely to the Near East (e.g., to be an "Orientalist" in anthropology would
refer to one whose work centers on areas such as Turkey, Palestine, Egypt, and the like).

"modern" and "metropolitan" (Rabinowitz, 2002). Palestinian political culture was characterized as "unequal," with its tendency to emphasize social relations and the power dynamics of those relations over an "equal" system like democracy. Rabinowitz argues that Israeli anthropologists unwittingly served the identity needs of the nascent Israeli society by constructing contrasting identities that in fact polarized Israelis and Palestinians even further.

Delegitimization through Orientalism was also nurtured by the institutions of the state. In his study of school textbooks in Israel from the prestate period to the Oslo accords, Bar-Gal (1994) reveals the ways in which Palestinians were fashioned in the larger project of Israeli national production (see also Bar-Gal, 1993; Bar-Tal, 1998a; Bar-Tal & Teichman, 2005). He discovered that, by the 1920s, textbooks used with Jewish youth constructed the Palestinian Arabs in highly ethnocentric, Orientalist ways. In the 1920s and 1930s, a delegitimization project appeared in full-force in Jewish textbooks. Not only were the Arabs presented as backward, lazy, savage, and exotic, they were also presented as diffuse in their identity. That is, the argument against any real existence of a Palestinian identity was presented concretely in the education curricula of prestate Jewish schools in Palestine. As one textbook reads, "Their common language does not create a single nation of them, for the inhabitants of the Orient can be divided not by their language but by their religion" (Brawer, 1936, p. 73, cited in Bar-Gal, 1994, p. 226). The contents of these textbooks reveal a desire to incite psychological distance between Jews and Arabs, as well as a desire to suggest the homogeneity of the people of "the Orient," encompassing land far beyond Palestine. The connection of the "inhabitants" of Palestine, as they were called in those prestate textbooks (Bar-Gal, 1994), to the inhabitants of other neighboring lands could frame the Palestinians as diffuse in their national identity status; their "nationality" was not Palestinian but perhaps "Oriental."

With the founding of Israel in 1948 and the establishment of a national curriculum, the contents of textbooks changed. Once referred to as *inhabitants*, the Palestinians were now referred to as *minorities* (in pre-1967 Israel). The issue of the Palestinian refugees and the overnight disappearance of numerous Palestinian communities during the war (see Abdel-Nour, 2004; Morris, 1987) are simply ignored in the early state textbooks, according to Bar-Gal (1994). The Palestinian Israelis are, after a period of being identified as "enemies," constructed rather paternalistically in the textbooks. The Arab citizens are presented as benefiting greatly from Zionist success and being afforded more rights than their brethren in other Arab-ruled countries. They are also openly discussed as a "demographic threat" in textbooks, including those used in Arab schools in Israel (Bar-Gal, 1994).

It is important to view the construction of the Palestinian in Israeli discourse as fulfilling Israel's need to construct a new national identity that argued for the *distinctiveness* of the two identities. The fact that the Palestinians, and Arabs in general, continue to be viewed in an Orientalist frame speaks to the endurance of Orientalism as an ideology that fulfills political *and* psychological needs (Said, 1978). Delegitimization of the Palestinians in Israeli discourse contributes to the perception of righteousness, benevolence, and exceptionalism in the master narrative of Jewish-Israeli identity. But perhaps even more importantly, delegitimization provides a moral framework for Israelis to justify political violence against Palestinians in the occupied territories, as well as the continued subordination of its own Palestinian citizens (e.g., Oren & Bar-Tal, 2007).

In addition to studies of educational materials such as textbooks, there has been a growing (but still relatively limited) study of delegitimization among young Jewish Israelis. Studies that have directly examined the endorsement of delegitimizing beliefs suggest considerable variability among Israeli youth based on factors such as demography, political ideology, and emotion (e.g., Halperin, Bar-Tal, Nets-Zehngut, & Drori, 2008; Sagy, Adwan, & Kaplan, 2002). Many studies do not assess delegitimization directly but rather factors assumed to be associated with it, such as stereotypes and prejudice. Studies with Jewish-Israeli children have revealed that negative stereotypes of Arabs are present by age 3 or 4 (Bar-Tal, 1996), that Palestinians are judged most negatively relative to other Arabs (Bar-Tal & Labin, 2001), and that children even express a desire to inflict violence on Arabs at a very young age (Bar-Tal, 1996). For Jewish Israelis, the tendency to express in-group favoritism and out-group delegitimization appears to emerge as early as preschool and then to diminish in middle childhood, only to return quite strongly in early adolescence (Teichman, 2001; Teichman & Bar-Tal, 2007). Not surprisingly, such negative stereotypes are accentuated during specific major conflict-related events, such as a Palestinian attack inside Israel (Bar-Tal & Labin, 2001). Jewish Israelis who are particularly affected by the ethos of conflict demonstrate information processing characterized by stereotypes of Palestinians as extremely aggressive (Bar-Tal et al., 2009). These studies reveal the extent to which the Arab in general, and the Palestinian in particular, is constructed as an antagonist in the master narrative and internalized at a very young age.

At its most extreme, the Jewish-Israeli master narrative goes beyond Orientalism in its treatment of the Palestinians and, in fact, undertakes an entire delegitimization project. To reiterate, delegitimization functions as a form of out-group categorization in which a highly negative image places the group outside the realm of an acceptable human group (Bar-Tal, 1989, 1990a;

Oren & Bar-Tal, 2007). At the extreme, delegitimization can take the form of existential denial of the Palestinian people or a rejection of the geographic terms used by Palestinians, such as the naming of *Palestine*.

As noted in the beginning of this book, the very naming of the region and the labeling of a place called "Palestine" truly sums up the conflict itself. While Palestinians want to insist that *some* piece of land can still be legitimately called Palestine, it is completely unacceptable (or, at least, quite provocative and reproachable) in the Jewish-Israeli narrative to refer to anything called "Palestine," except perhaps in historical terms. As Lemish (2003) notes, in 1977 the geographic designation "Land of Israel" (*Eretz Israel*) was redefined to include the Palestinian territories occupied in 1967. The terms "occupied territories" or "Palestine" are in fact prohibited in government-supported media or textbooks (Lemish, 2003). The desire to geographically define the region in such a way as to exclude the aims of that rival nationalist movement, to deny the legitimacy and the *possibility* of Palestinian identity, would seem to reproduce a status quo of conflict, rather than to move toward peace, reconciliation, and mutual recognition.

Summary

The story of Jewish-Israeli identity is a story that begins with suffering, persecution, and victimization and ends with glorious triumph, righteous indignation, and moral exceptionalism. Along its narrative path of descent and gain, in its attempt to construct a coherent, compelling, and sustainable in-group identity, it offers a polarizing contrast in the construction of the Palestinian as (Oriental) enemy. The story has a clear protagonist and antagonist, with the necessary discourse to credibly frame these characters as such. The seemingly indefatigable existential threat posed by the Antagonist (Palestinian) to the Protagonist (Israeli) infuses the narrative with a definable theme of *insecurity*.

This master narrative is, based on my fieldwork, accessible to contemporary youth through its infusion in both discourse and practice. In discourse, one can locate it in textbooks, in media, in conversations on the street, in cafés, and at the dinner table. In practice, it is realized in the symbolic interactions that frame Jewish–Arab relations both in Israel and in Palestine (e.g., checkpoints). It is also realized in Israel in the cultural practice of commemoration (Ben-Yehuda, 1995; Zerubavel, 1995), whether during national holidays or ritualized field trips for youth (e.g., to the Nazi concentration camps; Feldman, 2008), and the life course period of military service. The question remains and will now be thoroughly explored: In what ways do youth appropriate this master narrative as they begin to write their own life stories?

The Stories of Youth

Yossi: The Ambivalent Pragmatist

I first came to meet Yossi in the summer of 2003. At age 15, he is a tall, slender, athletic boy with military-short hair, dark eyes, and a confident presence. An Ashkenazi Jew whose family is quite secular, Yossi grew up in the suburbs of Haifa—that idyllic "city of coexistence." Mirroring the Jewish-Israeli master narrative in form, his life story offers a classic account of descent and gain, with nadirs followed by ever-increasing upward slopes.

The complexity of Yossi's identity is immediately revealed as he begins his life story and reveals the family's story of immigration to Israel:

> I was born in Dushanbe, it's the capital city of Tajikistan, and my both grandparents—from both sides I mean—they came from Ukraine to there. So, I know I'm kind of Russian but was born in Tajikistan and came here to Israel.

Like many Jews who, in the twentieth century, fled from persecution in places like Russia, the story of Yossi's family is one of *necessary* migration. In this way, with the common family story of immigration to Israel as a *flight from persecution*, the theme of persecution and victimization is encoded into the life story narratives of youths like Yossi.

Yossi's earliest memory, at age 2, reveals the perception of existential threat that begins at a very early age and creates a narrative tone of fear for Jewish-Israeli youth:

> We moved to Israel from Tajikistan exactly 2 weeks before the Gulf War started. And I remember that every evening, we used to go in our rooms and put on the masks and seal the rooms. I remember I didn't like it at all, and sometimes when I put the mask too tight I just had to take it off, and I was puking all of the time. I hated it. I really hated it when I was little.

The experience of possible death is thus perceptible at a very early age for Yossi. Affirming the theme of persecution and victimization, this experience in the narrative immediately positions Yossi's life story in a state of threatened existence. A need for *protection* and *security* naturally flows from such positioning.

The first descent in Yossi's life story occurs at the death of a family member, his great aunt, to natural causes. The lowest point in his narrative—the nadir—involves an experience common to adolescents in the industrial and postindustrial world: a negative school experience (see Eccles, 2004):

> In fifth grade, I had an awful teacher and hated her. Then I changed schools, and I felt like I lost all my friends. Then I found out that I have

new friends; it's a better place with better teachers. By the way, they fired the teacher after I left, because everybody hated her.

Yossi's narrative follows the descent-and-gain, or redemptive, pattern precisely in his ability to use challenging events as an opportunity for making cumulative gains. The challenge of transfer to a new school is followed by a successful gain in the recognition of his ability to make new friends. In this experience, he has learned a valuable social skill. From the moment of this realization, the trajectory of his narrative assumes a stable ascent. Skiing in Austria and his attendance at Seeds of Peace represent peaks on the ever-ascending course of his life story. The peak experience of his life is his younger sister's birth.

In terms of his life experience, then, Yossi's story reveals the narrative of an adolescent traversing what ought to be considered highly "normative" ups and downs: immigration to a new country, the death of a family member, the birth of a sibling, troubles with school, success in friendship building, and exciting travels. But Yossi's first memory—the memory of the first Gulf War—reveals that this life story is being constructed in a particularly unique cultural context.

In narrating his life story, it is not until we come to questions of the meaning of identity and of Yossi's decision to participate in Seeds of Peace that we come to a greater understanding of the ideological setting his story is beginning to assume. It is also only upon this further probing that we come to realize the impact of the perception of threat—as understood through his experience with Palestinian attacks during the second *intifada*—on Yossi's narrative.

First, on the meaning of being Israeli, Yossi constructs a narrative of the elements that comprise a collective identity and identifies the ways in which he fits into this collective:

> I think [being Israeli is about] speaking the language [Hebrew], all the
> education stuff, living in this country and speaking this language, and
> having friends that are Jewish, and being Jewish yourself—you know
> what, you don't *have* to be Jewish. It's just a way of life in Israel, and
> I think when you live this way of life, it doesn't matter if you like it or not,
> and sooner or later you just have to act the same way you see these life
> ways demand you to behave somehow.... The whole way of life that
> makes you an Israeli includes the religion, it includes the language,
> it includes everything, the clothing.

To be Israeli, then, in Yossi's mind, is first and foremost about *language* and *culture*. Interestingly, Yossi reveals some ambivalence about the role of being *Jewish* and the role of *religion* in Israeli identity. Initially, being Jewish seems foremost, but then he qualifies his statement with no explanation, no reference, for example, to the Arab citizens of Israel. But ultimately his final definition of Israeli identity places religion at the forefront.

Yossi's ambivalence reveals that his ideas about Israeli identity are in a process of formation. He has been exposed to a number of discourses in Israeli society—on identity and on citizenship (Lemish, 2003)—and he remains in a process of selective appropriation:

> We're not a religious country.... I'm Jewish in my blood; I don't really believe in all this stuff about religion, like I gotta pray and stuff. I don't believe in this. In Israel, we have the Islam, the Christians, but when you're talking about the Jewish people, you're talking about two large groups—the Orthodox Jewish, and the secular Jewish, which are a lot more than the Orthodox. What brings everyone together is this country. There are problems between the Orthodox and the secular, but what makes us all together is that we live in this country. *We have the same enemy.* They're attacking us both. Not only Orthodox people die, not only Jewish people die, even Arab people die.... We have so many different ways of life, so many different cultures in Israel. But what brings everyone together is that you live in Israel, that you're an Israeli. Maybe we can call it, having the same problems. It makes you all together in some kind of way. [Italics added.]

In this portion of his narrative, Yossi makes a number of very critical statements for understanding the way in which Jewish-Israeli youth construct their national identity. First, being Jewish is an *ethnic* or, perhaps more appropriately, a *racial* matter. Yossi is "Jewish in his blood." It does not really matter how religious he or any other Jewish Israeli is; they are united in a "blood line." Yossi also makes reference to a key contributor to identity polarization *within* Israeli society: the religious–secular divide. He also mentions, as an afterthought, that Israeli identity includes members of other "religious" communities (Muslims and Christians). But most critically, he identifies the *existence of an enemy* as the key uniting force in Israeli identity. It is precisely the fact that the victim of a bombing can be religious, secular, or even Arab, that constructs a coherent unity amidst prodigious identity diversity. Even in the midst of growing pluralism in Israeli society (Kimmerling, 2001), all Israelis are united against a common enemy—the Palestinians.

It is here, in this part of Yossi's narrative, that we can see the ways in which the conflict assumes an important *identity function* in Israeli society. The conflict with the Palestinians in fact is fundamental to the construction of a unified, coherent Israeli identity that possesses some kind of *distinctiveness* from the surrounding Orient. As Yossi suggests, having an enemy in fact helps to reduce the tension within Israeli society that naturally stems from its intrinsic pluralism. To cultivate a coherent identity for a nation of immigrants requires a clearly identifiable language and culture, as well as some readily identifiable "Other" identity that can be easily contrasted (see Rabinowitz, 2002). To produce and reproduce a coherent Israeli identity, the conflict is perhaps essential.

Before we consider the ideological setting of Yossi's life story most concretely, I want to present an important part of his narrative that indeed reveals the unique challenges of the Israeli life course. The perception of existential threat that infuses the master narrative of Jewish-Israeli identity is rooted in the very real experience of Palestinian attacks in Israel. In fact, a bus bombing in Haifa provides Yossi with the primary motivation to participate in Seeds of Peace:

> While I was on a field trip with my school, a suicide bomber killed himself on the bus in Haifa.... It really came together with the explosion—the terrorist act—so I wanted to go [to Seeds of Peace]. At the beginning, when I thought of the children that were killed, I thought about [Seeds of Peace], all the Palestinian children who would be here. I wanted to go here. I wanted to talk to them. I wanted to see their side. I wanted them to see my side.

The experience of a proximal attack—relatively uncommon in Haifa during the second *intifada*—serves as the catalyst for Yossi's interest in intergroup contact with Palestinians, to try to understand their motivation for conducting such attacks and to try to express his perspective as a Jewish Israeli.

Reflecting on what daily life is like in Israel, having to cope with the possibility of an attack, Yossi reveals the sense of resilience and defiance that has come to consume the Israeli discourse:

> My mother is so scared. She won't let me ride the bus or something to see my friends.... Now she's a little bit more calm because she realizes the situation, and if you show you're frightened, the terrorists will achieve their goal: to frighten us, to make us think they're stronger than us. This is not right. So now I can go with friends to the mall and stuff, and to parties, and I can ride the bus and stuff. But you know, you always live in fear, that the next person who walks into the bus will just jump in and explode himself. And this is not the kind of fear you want to live in.

The possibility of attack indeed creates an initial response of fear and anxiety, as my own field experience revealed to me. Though my own method of coping with this possibility—this very real, perceptible threat to one's existence—leaned more toward denial and rationalization, Jewish Israelis like Yossi seem to utilize a kind of defiant coping, quite similar to the American determination to resume air travel after 9/11, in which giving into anxiety is interpreted as a kind of "treason." To continue one's life as normal is the "patriotic" response. In the case of young Jewish Israelis, and for reasons that are vital to national security and sustained national *existence*, resilience and defiance are necessarily incorporated into the self-narrative.

Let us now consider the ideological setting of Yossi's life story at the age of 15. First, Yossi's interest in contact with Palestinians says much about the flexibility of its setting. He is an interested and willing interlocutor who recognizes the legitimacy of a Palestinian identity, even if such recognition is somehow "conditional":

> I know that by words, just talking to them once or twice, won't change their minds. But maybe when they'll see my point of view, they'll get something and I'll get something. Because they call the suicide bombers "freedom fighters." I don't really understand why. I just wanna get it. Maybe it's because I wanna understand the enemy, cause if you have an enemy, you gotta know him, if you wanna beat him or something. No, not beating, that's not what I meant. If you wanna live with him peacefully, you have to understand. If he opens a war against you, you gotta know his ways to fight back. I mean, you can't fight terror with terror. This is not the answer. But you can fight terror with strikes against the terrorists.

In Yossi, then, we see a genuine desire to *understand* the Palestinians. Because he has constructed the Palestinian as the antagonist of his life story—the enemy—Yossi reveals that a part of this motivation for understanding is to be able to stand strong *against* the Palestinians. Yet it is clear that he is still negotiating the specific role that the *imago* (McAdams, 1993) of the Palestinian will assume in his narrative. Will this experience with intergroup contact come to create a more realistic, less stereotyped, and more legitimized Palestinian character in his story, or will it only come to affirm and reproduce the status quo of identity polarization between groups?

Ideologically, Yossi sees himself as a "man of peace." He says, "I don't like violence.... Especially in what's going on in the last years. I don't like it. I really don't like it." He expresses a curiosity about the Palestinians and about the conflict and a genuine will to understand its origins. And perhaps most crucially, he demonstrates a conditional acceptance of the legitimacy of Palestinian claims:

> I do believe in the right of the Palestinians to have a country, and I think the education that I receive has a part in this, and I do believe in it. I think they should have a country. It's better for them, and it's better for us. 'Cause if a country will stop all the terrorism, I'll agree for it. I want peace—well, even if it's not peace, I just don't want these terrorist acts to continue. This is the first thing. After that, [the Palestinians] can do whatever [they] like.

Yossi, in keeping with left-wing Israeli political discourse, supports Palestinian independence, but he places the onus of conflict resolution on the Palestinians, arguing that "terrorist attacks"[2] must cease before the Palestinians can have full independence. This conditional recognition of Palestinian nationhood relies on the negatively interdependent interpretation of victimhood that characterizes the narrative stalemate between Israelis and Palestinians (Kelman, 1999b). Israeli youth, appropriating part of an accessible master narrative, interpret themselves as victims of Palestinian "terror," while Palestinian youth interpret themselves as victims of Israeli military occupation, with its own brand of power imbalance and dispossession. Thus, while we ought to view Yossi's conditional recognition of Palestinian statehood as certainly positive with regard to likely conflict reduction, we must recognize the problematic nature of its conditionality, reproducing a stalemate of narratives.

The conditionality of Yossi's acceptance of the Palestinians becomes clearer as we discuss with greater specificity his perspective on the prospect for peace:

> I think the first thing, they should stop the terrorist attacks against us. The whole thing started because of the terrorist acts against us.... They actually started it. They fired first. They were the first to use suicide bombers.

Yossi's narrative may reveal a measure of ideological flexibility, particularly in his recognition of the legitimacy of claims for Palestinian statehood. Yet his narrative of the conflict conforms very closely to a master narrative in which

---

2 Labeling Palestinian actions as "terrorist" is problematic for recognizing the legitimacy of the Palestinian master narrative, which views Palestinian violence against Israelis as acts of "resistance" (for further discussion, see Battin, 2004; Pape, 2005). Seeking a kind of mutual recognition of these competing narratives, I will avoid condoning one label or another in my own interpretation and so will suggest some distance between these labels and my interpretations with the use of quotation marks, indicating that such labels are part of the in-group discourse about the out-group.

Israel is the victim of Arab aggression. He fails to recognize any validity in the Palestinian counternarrative of, for example, what sparked the *intifada* (Sharon's provocative visit to the *Haram al-Sharif* [Temple Mount]) or what needs to occur for peace (the end of the Israeli occupation and Israel's recognition of Palestinian independence). In this way, Yossi's apparent initial pragmatism seems to give way to a life story narrative that reproduces the ideological conditions of conflict; his conditional and tentative recognition of the Palestinians mirrors the mainstream, post-Oslo discourse in Israeli society.

One of the most concrete ways in which Yossi reproduces the delegitimization of the master narrative of Israeli identity is his stance on the naming of "Palestine." The way in which Yossi, though he professes to support Palestinian independence, seeks to invalidate the use of the name "Palestine" among Palestinian youth says much about the salience of his own social identity and his desire to construct a narrative that "works" in the discourse of Israeli society:

> Of course, I think that I'm right—that my country's right. Everybody thinks that his country's right. Let's start from the first thing [Palestinians at camp] say, when they say, "I am from Palestine." I mean, there is no such country named Palestine. You can check the UN. There is no country written in the UN notebook called Palestine! There *is* such country called Israel. So he can say, "I'm a Palestinian from Israel." But when you say, "Hi. I'm from Palestine." "Jerusalem, Palestine" or something, it hurts the people that are from Israel and are from Jerusalem.... This is the problem: they don't have a country, and they feel like they have it. And they're speaking like there is no Israel!

The naming of Palestine is, for Yossi, a threatening act. He interprets the use of the term Palestine by Palestinians as entirely invalidating the existence of the state of Israel. What he fails to see is the delegitimizing nature of his request to have Palestinians refer to themselves as "Palestinians from Israel." He also fails to acknowledge the counternarrative of the land: that Israel's control of the *entirety* of Mandate Palestine is unjust and that Palestinian nationalism deserves its own fulfillment alongside Israel. Interestingly, the premise of this counternarrative (i.e., the Palestinian narrative) was accepted by Zionist leaders who agreed to the UN partition plan of 1947, but the legitimacy of its fulfillment is now contested in the Israeli master narrative.

If we agree that "to name is to know" (Strauss, 1959/1997), in the sense that it is through *naming* that we come to *identify* something in cognition, then the inability of Yossi, and of most Jewish-Israeli youth, to name "Palestine" as a geographic possibility can only be interpreted as part of the delegitimizing theme of the master narrative. That is, the unwillingness to acknowledge the *possibility* of Palestine—for, truly, it is possibility, rather than actuality, that is being expressed when Palestinian youth use the term—contributes to, and is in fact fundamental to, the reproduction of conflict through narrative. Yossi may be ideologically flexible and open to the Palestinian narrative, but he displays a defiant rigidity when confronted with the actual content of the counter-narrative. The strength of this rigidity speaks to the salience of his social identity as a Jewish Israeli and to his relationship with the master narrative.

Considering Yossi's narrative in relation to the master narrative of Israeli identity, its redemptive form mirrors the master narrative, and much of the key thematic content of the master narrative is present to some degree. For example, Yossi's family story of necessary migration to Israel primes the tropes of both historical persecution and existential insecurity. His account of life during the *intifada* is constructed within this larger theme of existential insecurity, and Yossi's resilient response is consistent with the construction of a strong, "new" Jewish identity to stand in contrast with the perceived weakness of the Diaspora Jewish identity. Though his narrative suggests a measure of pragmatism in his willingness to recognize Palestinian claims for national identity fulfillment, thus moderating the degree of delegitimization that might have consumed his narrative, the conditionality of his legitimization poses challenges to possibilities of peace through mutual recognition.

Noa: The Kibbutznik

Noa is a 14-year-old Jewish Israeli from a kibbutz in northern Israel. As we sit outside on the balcony of her apartment—an apartment communally owned by the kibbutz—dramatic views of the mountains and the fertile valley surround us. The mountains of Jordan are within sight; the border is not far. The separation barrier that, in this part of Israel, essentially follows the Green Line of the 1967 armistice agreement and is quite accurately a "fence," is just a few kilometers away. So is Jenin—the Palestinian city known during the second *intifada* for producing a number of bombers. But Noa's kibbutz feels like a world away from all of this. Its setting is pastoral, its natural beauty serene, its utopian vision undeniably admirable, even if rapidly fading.

It should be no surprise that, ideologically speaking, Noa's upbringing was quite left-wing. Kibbutz culture is and always has been rabidly secular. Part of a historic project in economic and social communalism, the people of the kibbutzim considered themselves secular pioneers (see Spiro, 1956). They had a vision—without question a utopian one, particularly when viewed through a lens that recognizes the triumph of capitalism in the twentieth century. Their vision, influenced by the social movements in Europe from which all of them had emigrated, was of a "scientific socialism" (Spiro, 1956) in which man's connection to labor, and to one another, was returned to a natural state of symbiosis. Their goal was to construct a whole new identity—that of the *Sabra* (Almog, 2000; Neslen, 2006; Spiro, 1975), the first generation of actual "Israelis"— who would fulfill the utopian vision of social and economic equality.

Contemporary residents of the kibbutzim are typically left-wing not just economically and socially but also with regard to the Israeli–Palestinian conflict. Secular and pragmatic, they tend to view the achievement of a Jewish state in 1948 as complete and the idea of "Greater Israel" as problematic for the safety and security of Israel. Noa's family is no exception. Describing her own political socialization, she says, "Most of the things that I know about politics is from my brother, and so, I don't know, he's very on the left side, and so I just heard from him and from my family."

Noa comes from a long line of kibbutz residents on her father's side, her great-grandfather having emigrated from Russia. Her mother is a Diaspora Ashkenazi Jew who immigrated to Israel for Noa's father. Noa's life story begins with the faint memory of loss at the divorce of her parents. Pointing to the first descent in her life-line, Noa says, "This is where my parents got divorced, so I think it was a bad time, but I can't really remember." Difficulties with her parents' divorce returned when she was age 10. Describing the second descent in her life-line, she says, "When I was like 10 years old, I remember that I started having problems with the fact that my parents got divorced, but I got used to it and worked it out."

The third of Noa's descents reveals the overall pattern of her narrative, like Yossi's and like that of the Jewish-Israeli master narrative, of descent and gain:

> This is when I'm in the seventh grade, and I remember that I *hated*
> the seventh grade because you become the youngest again, and I was so
> shy. I'm not a shy person now but I was back then, and I hated this
> about myself. It was a bad year. And then the eighth grade was good.
> I loved it.

The transition to a new year at a new school, where the developing social skills of an early adolescent are still being tested and reformulated, creates a crisis for Noa. But as with her previous challenges in the story, the resolution of this crisis is a successful adjustment, with accrued confidence in her ability to manage life's challenges. As the form of her life-line revealed to me, the challenges become psychologically more significant with age, the peaks and valleys larger and larger.

The final low point in Noa's life story centers again on her family. She describes it as follows:

In the beginning of the ninth grade, I remember having a terrible, terrible time because my brother was supposed to fly to the USA for a year of community service, and he lost his passport two days before his flight, and all the time there is so much stress and everyone was so angry and really, it wasn't a pleasant time.... Everyone was so nervous, and my mother and I, we had these horrible fights all the time because she was so stressed and I was, and we were always fighting. In the end, it all worked out and he was able to go. And overall the ninth grade was really great—the best—which is why the line goes up again.

The nadir of Noa's life story to date thus involves essentially a single family incident and its impact on family dynamics for a brief time. Noa's greatest challenges, then, involve mastery of life's inevitable ebbs and flows. In her own words, "Normally, I just love my life, but it has its ups and downs."

Noa's life story, like Yossi's, conforms to a redemptive, descent-and-gain pattern in which challenges are mastered, and a sense of cumulative gain infuses the tone of the narrative. Impressionistically, Noa is an extremely vivacious, outgoing young woman whose challenges with family struggle and self-reported "shyness" are hardly perceptible. Spending significant amounts of time with Noa and her mother, however, reveals the depth of emotional challenge that characterizes Noa's narrative, in a way not apparent in her interactions with peers.

Noa's mother, perhaps owing to her own life challenges, presents a radical contrast with Noa's vibrant outgoing persona. She is quiet and calm, cool and collected, but beneath the surface a perceptible melancholia is readily apparent. Between the divorce and other family struggles—including the emotional needs of Noa's brother currently serving in the army and struggling significantly—Noa's mother projects a quiet resignation to life's fortunes. Noa's contrasting confidence in traversing the "ups and downs" often appeared to me to frustrate her mother, with her cynical outlook on life's possibilities.

Noa's story is thus one in which the main characters—her family members—have in fact created challenges and struggles that she finds herself having to negotiate. But her tendency to see the resolution of these challenges in optimistic terms, in terms of inevitable satisfactory resolution, reveals the overall optimistic tone of her narrative, even for her own sense of confusion. As we conclude the interview, talking about her feelings of safety and security in Israel, she says, "You can never feel really safe because everything can happen. But usually I don't feel scared." After a long pause in which she seems to reflect upon the entire interview, she adds, "It seems like I'm a really depressed girl, but I'm not."

Considering Noa's narrative and its relation to the master narrative of Jewish-Israeli identity, clearly it mirrors the redemptive form of the master narrative. But it is possible to see some ideological and thematic distance. In fact, Noa's life story has no references to persecution and victimization. Its references to the army are mostly in more negative terms, rather than any serious emphasis on Israel's need for security. There are no references to Jewish exceptionalism per se, and little discussion at all of Arabs or Palestinians. Her social identity as a Jewish Israeli is not, I would suggest, incredibly salient. What is salient is her *local* "kibbutznik" identity, even as the sustenance of that collective identity is in a process of erosion.

I do not want to suggest that this lack of national identity salience is necessarily typical of youth from the kibbutzim and moshavim in which I conducted fieldwork, for the youth in my interview sample did indeed display heterogeneity in this regard. But Noa's story is actually quite close to that of the other *females* from the kibbutz whom I studied, whose stories favor a local identity over a national one. The sex difference in social identity salience among Jewish Israelis is an important one, and one that I will consider at greater length. But, to stay with Noa's story for the time being, I want to highlight the ideological setting of her story, even in its most nascent stage at the young age of 14.

I noted that Noa comes from a very left-wing family—a family opposed to Jewish settlements in the occupied territories and supportive of claims for Palestinian statehood. This political perspective is transmitted to Noa through the stories of army service from her two brothers:

> My brother would talk with me about the conflict with the Arabs, and he would tell me how they would make him go to Arabs' houses and tell them to leave their house. And he was telling me these stories in a perspective like "this is bad, this is wrong, this is *morally* wrong."

Noa is introduced to the conflict through the stories of her older brothers, both of whom resented having to serve a country whose policies they saw as immoral toward another group. As a consequence, it is not surprising that Noa is ideologically very much in favor of Palestinian statehood:

> I think that Israel should give the Arabs those territories that we took from them. I think the Arabs should get their own separate state. This is the situation: there is a small piece of land [for] both cultures and religions. We should live together, and if we can't do it together then we should do it separate.

Before she has even met Palestinians, Noa displays a real desire to compromise and an authentic pragmatism about the conflict. She does not, as the master narrative might have encouraged her to do, delegitimize the national aspirations of the Palestinians. She sees their struggle as entirely legitimate, and she even seems to assign Israel a level of responsibility for the resolution of the conflict. The first step, according to her, is for Israel to return the territories to the Palestinians. Unlike Yossi's conditionality, Noa seems rather unequivocal in her conviction that Israel, not the Palestinians, holds the key to peace.

The ability of Noa to construct a narrative that conforms very little to the master narrative of Jewish-Israeli identity reveals the extent to which this master narrative is contested and, perhaps, on the "decline" (Kimmerling, 2001). But it is also, I believe, connected to the unique social ecology of Noa's development. The kibbutz is certainly a unique place to grow up. It is, as Noa notes in her life story, quite insulated from the realities of the conflict:

> We live in an area [where] all those bombings and stuff aren't really
> here. I mean, it's everywhere, but it's not like in Tel Aviv or Jerusalem.
> It isn't affecting our daily lives, but it is. It's affecting our lives because
> guys from the kibbutz have to go to the army and serve in the territories,
> and these friends of my brother's got killed in Hebron. So that's really
> hard.

To spend any time at all in Noa's community truly feels like an oasis—both physically and psychologically. My impression of it as an area relatively unaffected by bombings may have been affirmed by Noa's account, but it was certainly shattered by Gal's story, which I presented in the Prologue. Yet, Noa's perspective is that the conflict affects her daily life more in the sacrifices the young community members serving in the IDF must make, rather than any specific existential threat she encounters in her life.

It is not, then, as if youth from the kibbutz and moshav have no exposure to or experience with the conflict. The "situation," as it is commonly called among both Israelis and Palestinians, consumes every aspect of existence in the region. Yet what Noa's story demonstrates, I think, is the way in which Jewish-Israeli youth can, with the support of a local identity narrative, question and even reject elements of the master narrative that frames the larger discourse of Israeli society. In this local identity narrative, the outright repudiation of conflict is possible. We turn now to the story of Roai, a Mizrahi raised in one of the largest settlements in the West Bank. Not surprisingly, the contrast between his life story and that of Noa could not be more significant.

Roai: The Settler

I first met Roai in the spring of 2004, 1 month prior to his participation in Hands of Peace. We met at a popular café on the campus of the Hebrew University in Jerusalem. I used this café frequently to conduct interviews. I still recall quite vividly the psychological ritual of this experience. I would always approach the café, with its large outdoor area in front, very cautiously. The security guard often seemed to notice my hesitation and began to stare me down when I was still at quite a distance. Public places like cafés in Jerusalem inevitably rouse feelings of anxiety at a possible attack. After receiving the requisite, if cursory, search by the security guard, I would always struggle with the decision of where to get a table for my interview—not out of concern for privacy, as *ought* to be the case, but rather out of a concern for my survival. I often reasoned that, were we to sit in the outside area, we could see a bomber coming and perhaps even make a quick escape. Then, I would consider whether settling inside, as far as possible from the front door, might be the safest locale for us, as perhaps the bomb would not be strong enough to affect us from a distance. How ridiculous this thinking seems to me now. Yet it felt very real and, in fact, necessary, even if entirely illogical, at the time. Such was my glimpse into the daily realities of life under conditions of threatened existence.

A Mizrahi whose mother was born in Morocco and his father in northern Iraq, Roai is a handsome, athletic young man with fashionable sunglasses, dressed in jeans and a T-shirt, and an iPod in his ear. He immediately seems older than his 16 years. Roai's life story begins very calmly, with a steady but slowly progressive form. He connects this time in his life with a period of relative stability in the conflict: "We had a very quiet time in the country." The peak experience in his life story occurs during a 2-year period (1998–2000) in which his father, a tour guide in Jerusalem, had significant work. During this period, Roai and his family traveled to the United States for a month, which he describes as "a very good time" in his life.

The year 2000 marks the beginning of the tragic descent of Roai's narrative, with the commencement of the second Palestinian *intifada*. The tourists stopped coming to Jerusalem, which was the focal point for the start of the uprising, so his father suddenly found himself out of work. Then, very suddenly in 2002, Roai's father passed away, having suffered a severe heart attack while in the midst of his routine morning jog. For Roai, not surprisingly, this event is the nadir in his life story. He claims now, 2 years on, to be coping well, saying, "It's getting better."

When I spend time with Roai and his family at their home, it is clear to me that his father's death has forced Roai to mature more quickly. He has two younger brothers and a quiet, fragile mother. He has, since his father's death, assumed responsibility for the family, emotionally if not financially. To spend any significant amount of time with this family, there can be little doubt that Roai has taken on the role of "man of the house."

Formally, then, Roai's narrative reveals a stable equilibrium that is disrupted by both political and personal events. His positive evaluation of the political situation as a child contributes to this stability, which is followed by a brief period of sustained ascent, then by a tragic regress owing initially to the dramatic change in the conflict and culminating in the death of his father. Yet a sense of stability ultimately returns to the narrative, as Roai constructs a story that possesses coherence and acceptability for his role in the family.

In contrast to Noa, political events figure prominently in Roai's narrative. Here we can again recognize the salience of local identity among Jewish Israelis. While Noa resides in the midst of Israel's (crumbling) utopian experiment, far away from the epicenter of the conflict, Roai resides in a Jewish settlement in the West Bank, just outside of Jerusalem. The view from his community is a Palestinian town, with its identifiable absence of red-tile roofs in favor of ubiquitous satellite dishes, the barren but stunning mountains of the West Bank, and a shepherd herding his flock in the valley below, his head wrapped in a red-and-white *kafiya*. Roai's social ecology, both physically and ideologically, lies a great distance from Noa's.

Noa has known no Arabs in her life, catching only occasional glimpses at rare moments. Roai, however, recalls his first memory about the conflict as follows:

> Since I live in the settlement, we had a checkpoint right outside. If we wanted to go to Jerusalem, we had to go through the checkpoint. But for me it wasn't a big problem because I'm an Israeli. But I saw the Palestinians waiting there, in the sun, and that's the first time I thought about us and them.... I remember asking my father why they are waiting and we are not. He said they have to be checked. I asked why, but he just said they have to be checked. Now, of course, I know why.

This early experience seems to arouse within Roai a genuine interest in understanding the conflict—its origins, its characters, its differential structure. Certainly nowhere is this structure more readily apparent than inside of the occupied territories themselves—a place most Israelis never see. (Since the start of the second *intifada*, Israeli citizens are forbidden to enter the territories, except for residents of the settlements and those who obtain special permission.)

Roai's life story thus contains within it actual, not theoretical, interactions with Palestinians. In fact, his attendance at a selective Jerusalem school places him in direct contact with other Jewish Israelis, Palestinian citizens of Israel, and Palestinians from the occupied territories. Ideologically, then, Roai's life story reveals more complexity than one might expect, given the social ecology of the settlement and the right-wing ideology of most of its inhabitants. His story allows for the possibility of transcending identity politics, if only in his basic exposure to other narratives.

Similar to Yossi, Roai accepts the idea of Palestinian statehood, seemingly rejecting the delegitimization of Palestinian identity contained in the master narrative of Jewish-Israeli identity. But also like Yossi, Roai's is a conditional acceptance. His narrative of Israel's history reveals its foundation in the need for Jewish protection through national sovereignty, though he does not hesitate to acknowledge the existence of the Palestinians and their own desire for national self-determination:

> In 1948 we established our own country, but there were a lot of Arab communities—the Palestinians were here, and they also wanted to build their own country. They started fighting us with the Arab neighbors. Four wars we had, and now today we are still fighting them. The main reason we wanted a state was the Holocaust—that's why we came here and tried to build our own country.

While Roai clearly recognizes the existence and legitimacy of Palestinian identity, he conforms to a master narrative of "conditional recognition" that frames the post-Oslo Israeli discourse and that is appropriated by many Jewish-Israeli youth:

> I think that the Palestinians have to get their own state, but not in such as this condition—like today, they are attacking us. We need to have it quiet before we are letting them to build their own country. No attacks from the Palestinians, and then we will talk about the peace process. And it will not be a fast movement. It has to be for a long time.... But I think that they must have their own country.

Roai's conditional acceptance of the legitimacy of Palestinian aspirations for statehood reveals a level of ideological confusion. On the one hand, he seems to truly believe that the Palestinians constitute a distinct, national identity group deserving of their own country. He does not seek to delegitimize their existence. He does not see their existence as necessarily threatening his own. Yet his stance remains one of classic paternalistic Orientalism—that the Arab must be "tamed."

During the second *intifada*, the Israeli discourse about the failure of peace talks at Camp David placed blame squarely on the Palestinians, and on Yasser

Arafat in particular (Dor, 2003). Information about Arafat's rejection of the deal, as presented by the Israeli government at the time, essentially initiated this discourse by arguing that the Palestinians had been offered the best deal imaginable and had rejected it without making counterproposals (Bar-Tal, 2004b). The Israeli interpretation, officially speaking, was that the Palestinians indeed did not seek peace but rather the destruction of Israel as a Jewish state (hence the insistence on the right of return for Palestinian refugees to Israel, not just Palestine).

Roai's view of the start of the *intifada* conforms very closely to this narrative of Camp David:

> A time when I was very, very angry about the conflict was in 2000 when the *intifada* started. Yeah, because it was after Camp David when we tried to talk with them about the peace process, and we gave them a lot of good conditions before they are building their own country. But they wanted to return their refugees to Israel, and they didn't let it go, and we didn't want to give them this right, because then Israel would not be a Jewish state. There would be too many Arabs. They don't understand how important this is to us.

Roai believes in the legitimacy of Palestinian nationalism, but not at the cost of threatening Israel's identity as a Jewish state. Here we see the extent of Roai's ideological flexibility. He is open to Palestinian nationalism, so long as it does not threaten the maintenance of Israeli identity.

For Roai, to be Israeli first and foremost means *to go to the army*. This experience is, in his prearmy adolescent view, the ultimate in identity fulfillment. It should hardly be a surprise, given the existential insecurity in the master narrative that creates the conditions for a militaristic state (Kimmerling, 2001), that Roai, like all of the Jewish-Israeli boys in this study, anxiously awaits his military service, looking forward to the day when he can fully *become* Israeli. When asked about what it means to be Israeli, Roai reveals a hierarchy of factors that comprise, in his estimation, a coherent social identity:

> That's a hard question. To go to the army, that's to be an Israeli. We're serving in the army, we're speaking Hebrew, we are Jewish. Religion has a major part in Israel. What else? Being in the conflict, *that's* Israeli.

For Roai, then, after military service, it is language and Judaism—ethnically and, for him, religiously—that comprise Israeli identity. The final element he identifies, though, is a very important one: Israeli identity is rooted in the experience of conflict itself. Having to traverse the daily anxieties of possible attack, internalizing the perceived existential threat of an entire collective identity—these factors in fact construct a coherent Israeli identity. Like Yossi, Roai views simply "being in the conflict" as a fundamental unifying feature of Israeli identity.

In terms of the master narrative, then, the experience of persecution and victimization resides within Roai's narrative, but only as it serves as the root cause for what he views as the most essential aspect of Israeli identity: the need for security. The identity fulfillment in performing military service enables the social practice needed to fully qualify as an Israeli. It is a rite of passage, and certainly one with greater resonance for boys than for girls, given the connection between masculinity and nationalism (Nagel, 1998; see also Golan, 1997; Sasson-Levy, 2003). As we will see when we return to Roai's life story in Chapter 7, when we consider the impact of intergroup contact on his narrative, other elements of the master narrative become salient. But for now, at age 16, 1 month before contact with his Palestinian peers, it is the theme of existential insecurity that, despite his ideological openness to the Palestinians, conforms most closely to the master narrative.

Before we depart from Roai's story, let us conclude with his own key reflections on the ideological setting of his life story. As noted, Roai lives on a settlement in the West Bank. Currently, however, he attends a prestigious high school in Jerusalem, which has exponentially altered the political discourse to which he is exposed. Ideologically, he inhabits two very divergent worlds, and he is still determining how to negotiate them:

> All the ideology of my school is to be with the Arab neighbors ... to live in peace. ...My friends from my town, they are a little more militant than me, and my friends from school are the opposite of me. Their ideology is the opposite of my ideology. It's a bit opposite because they think we should give them the state and not fight them and not make all the action in Gaza and the West Bank.... [My friends from home], they think that we should fight them now, and all the Arabs are killers and something like that.... It's very hard to think from a different way while you're always living in one place and you can't hear the other side, or meet people from the other side. It's very hard.

In this very direct admission of his ideological struggle, Roai reveals the deep ambivalence in the setting of his life story. Up to this point in his narrative, he has generally advanced conditional acceptance of Palestinian identity. For him, this conditional acceptance—this notion that Palestinians can and should achieve independence, but only under certain conditions specified by Israel—can be seen as a "compromise ideology." It is, for the moment, the ideological location that is essentially at the center of the two poles to which Roai has been exposed in his upbringing. On the one hand, the ideology of the settlement is, as he describes it, "militant." The Palestinians are viewed as "killers" and sinister characters; the legitimacy of their narrative, and their very existence, is called into question. There are no compromises for a settlement. Peace is not even really possible with such a savage enemy—one that needs to be controlled.

On the other hand, the context of Roai's prestigious high school seems to espouse a left-wing ideology that is distinct from that of the settlement. As he describes it, the students there desperately want peace and view Israel's continued occupation as unjust. They believe in the return of the territories in exchange for peace—highly problematic for Roai since he in fact lives on a settlement *in* those territories. What we can discern from this direct statement on his ideological identifications is that Roai is in fact quite ambivalent. Exposed to competing discourses within Israeli society on the conflict and on the legitimacy of Palestinian identity, he has come to a compromise ideology that is, given the social and political ecology of his upbringing, actually quite remarkable. Yet he continues to struggle with these ideological poles, even as he speaks with such conviction and confidence as he presents his life story to me. This struggle is evident in the way in which he ends the interview, reporting that it is indeed "very hard" to think differently than the way one has been brought up to think, to embrace a discourse one has always been encouraged to reject. The ways in which his ideological "compromise" withstands the reality of his approaching military service, not to mention his forthcoming contact with Palestinians, will be considered when we revisit his narrative in Chapter 7, 1 year later.

Ayelet: The Cosmopolitan

The portrait of Jewish-Israeli youth sketched so far in the stories of Yossi, Noa, and Roai certainly reveals key points of convergence. There are numerous ways in which the narratives of these youth contain themes that reflect the master narrative of Jewish-Israeli identity, particularly in their redemptive form and in much of their thematic content. But there have also been important sources of divergence. I suggest that these sources are largely based on the diversity in *local* identity that exists within Israel. So we saw that Noa's social ecology of the kibbutz is quite distinct from Yossi's social ecology of the Haifa suburb, or Roai's Jewish settlement in the West Bank.

The pluralism of Israel's local identities is key to understanding ideological identifications among youth and, thus, divergence in the ideological setting of life stories themselves. Roai has engaged his entire life with a right-wing—"militant," as he calls it—ideology that delegitimizes Palestinian identity. Noa has had just the opposite experience, with her exposure to the kibbutz narrative of pragmatic reconciliation with the Palestinians. We come now to another local culture in Israel and to the life story of one of its inhabitants, Ayelet.

Ayelet has spent her entire life in the cosmopolitan cultural capital of Israel—Tel Aviv. With its beautiful Mediterranean coast lined with radiant sandy beaches and trendy bars and restaurants, the Tel Aviv identity is certainly distinct from other locales in Israel. At age 16, Ayelet first narrated her life story to me on a hot Tel Aviv afternoon in 2004, at a popular café where several languages could be heard throughout our interview.

Ayelet's narrative, true to the Jewish-Israeli master narrative, assumes a redemptive, descent-and-gain pattern in its form. The first descent, which also consists of Ayelet's first vivid memory, occurs with the divorce of her parents at age 4:

> I had a pretty rough time because my parents broke up. They got divorced when I was like 4 years old. You know how it is, kids can't really understand the reason. So I found a nice little way to deal with that. Every time somebody pissed me off or something, I didn't think twice, I just hit him. And so kids didn't really like me for that.

As a consequence of her belligerent behavior, Ayelet reports that she had few friends during her childhood. The divorce of her parents seems to have quite classically resulted in significant emotional and behavioral problems for her—a common occurrence in many cultures (for review, see Emery, 1988; Kelly, 2000; McKenry & Price, 1995; cf. Bilge & Kaufman, 1983).

Ayelet's life story achieves gains after this difficult early descent with the increase in her perceived social competence. By age 11, she reports having achieved a peak experience of social acceptance and "popularity" among her peers, which positively impacts her self-confidence:

> I was like 11 years old, which is like fifth grade, when kids started to understand that sometimes you should give a second chance, sometimes you miss things in life.... Then, when I was in sixth grade, the last one of the elementary school, that was the best. I got so popular and everybody liked me and since then, it just went way up.

For Ayelet, we see the significance of peer approval in her personal narrative from a young age. The divorce of her parents creates formidable challenges for Ayelet, which interferes with her ability to form and maintain friendships with her peers. But transcendence of these challenges, and mastery of the ability to become socially competent with her peers, has created a strong sense of self-confidence in Ayelet. Her peer relations assume a significant role in her construction of self, which will become problematic for her in the year following Hands of Peace, as we will see in Chapter 7. Yet, for now, Ayelet interprets the mastery of this ability as absolutely central to the positive tone of her narrative. Out of challenge she has developed a strong sense of self and her ability to cultivate and maintain close relationships. From descent, she discovers a way to ascend through shifting the source of her self-confidence from her family to her peers.

While this strategy works for Ayelet for some time, the nadir in her life story again centers on her family and, more specifically, on her relationship with her father:

> Then [life] went really down, because that was the time when my dad left Israel.... On my fifteenth birthday, I got to see my dad is not totally who I thought he is. I found out exactly who is my dad—that he stole money from my mom, money that was actually for me, when I was older and stuff.... It was a hard time to find out that my dad stole money and did so many terrible things.

The difficulties between her parents resurface in Ayelet's life story at age 15 with the simultaneous departure of her father from Israel to the United States and the discovery of many of his wrongdoings. Ayelet considered her father a "best friend" as a child and reported feeling much closer to him than to her mother. But now her father's behavior has forced her to reevaluate those relationships. She has recast her mother as a victim, but one whose strength has helped Ayelet to cope with the loss, not only of the physical presence of her father but also of the image of him she had carried for many years:

> My mom worked so many years, kicked her ass, and I am who I am today because of my mom—not because of my dad. He was a great dad, he was a best friend and everything, but come on, the one that was really there for me in hard times was my mom.

While Ayelet identifies the strength of her mother as a source of her own identity, her resilience and recovery from this nadir seem to reflect her own abilities to master the challenge of coping. Referring to that difficult time in her life story, she says,

> Basically, there is a hole inside. But you grow up, you move on, you learn to accept things. The purpose is not crying about the milk that went off the table, it's to see how you can get a new glass! And that's what I'm trying to do—forgive my dad and actually to go see him.... After that time, [life] went way up, because I started to look at the positive way of

life.... Basically, I did it on my own. It's kind of, to be proud of myself, that I hold myself so tight. I guess that life can offer you so many things and sometimes you're down, sometimes you're up—that's the way of life. You can't always be up. It's not possible. And then you'll not be a strong person if you don't go through things and see things.

As a method of coping with life's inevitable challenges, Ayelet has adopted a decidedly problem-centered approach (Lazarus & Folkman, 1984), and she uses the stresses in her life to make cumulative gains in her ability to adjust and adapt.

Because of the success of her coping strategies, Ayelet's narrative is, in tone if not necessarily in form, essentially a progressive story. Speaking of the current challenge she faces in her schoolwork with difficulties in mathematics, the progressive, positive tone of Ayelet's narrative is readily apparent:

I decided that no matter what, no matter what price, I'm going to be successful. Whatever I want, I will do. There's nothing that's going to stop me. And probably I will have to work for it—very hard. But hey, when you get to be successful and you're stopping for a second and looking back and say, "Wow! Look what I did!" And that's what gives you the most power to keep going.

As a consequence of her challenges and her ability to cope and adapt to them, Ayelet views the current challenge before her—improving her performance in mathematics—as entirely surmountable. She possesses extraordinary self-confidence and self-efficacy (Bandura, 1997). This kind of resilience and the self-narrative she has constructed—of someone who can effect change in her own life through cultivating a strong sense of agency—shape the ideological setting of her life story.

In contrast to Roai, for whom the conflict is quite physically perceptible in his daily life, Ayelet's life story reveals no connection whatsoever to the conflict. Upon probing, however, it becomes abundantly clear that her story does possess an ideological setting—albeit one still in formation—that is quite connected to her *local* identity as an inhabitant of cosmopolitan Tel Aviv:

I'm kind of in the middle. I think we should all just learn to live together. It's such a small country. And with all the bombings and things, eventually we're not going to have an Israel. We're going to have chaos; we're going to have nothing. And people dying for no reason, I just believe that somebody's got to put an end to that.... I just hate the thought—we are coming from a place where we've been hated all our lives. The Holocaust, wherever we go, we still have it. So people that go through such a thing are supposed to understand that thing.... We're part of a group that feels hated, so we shouldn't be hating another.

Though the trope of persecution and victimization, culminating in the Holocaust, is a theme from the master narrative that resonates for Ayelet, she appears to take a critical stance on the conflict and identifies a contradiction in the Jewish-Israeli master narrative. Unlike Yossi and Roai, Ayelet appears to go beyond a *conditional* recognition of the legitimacy of Palestinian identity and even views her own group as partially responsible for the continuation of the conflict:

> This is where I live and these are my neighbors, and you have to choose whether you want to live in a fight and make your life miserable, or whether you want to try and make a solution. I know you can't find a solution for everything; you need both sides for that. It takes two to tango, yes? I just sometimes feel like they stabbed us with a knife in the back. But we're not totally white in that thing. We're not totally good. So I really hope that the kids of this generation will have the chance to change it.... Maybe one day, you know, there'll be peace. It's got to happen, eventually. Though it seems like kind of a dream, one might say, but I really believe you can do it. You just need to be willing and have the strength for that.

The existence of the Palestinians is a foregone conclusion for Ayelet, as she refers to them as "neighbors." She reveals some ambivalence about them, having been exposed to one of the most common discourses about Arabs in Israel—that they cannot be trusted and are prone to betrayal. But so far in her narrative it appears that, ideologically, she is very attuned to peace and coexistence with Palestinians. She is already quite willing to assume some responsibility for the conflict on the part of her in-group.

Ayelet's narrative of the conflict itself also reveals a great deal about the current ideological setting of her life story:

> They were here first [the Palestinians]. We came and took this land from them because God—whoever wrote the Bible—said that this is our land. But if you look at it the other way, in their Bible, in the Koran, this is their land.... We just came from Europe here after the Holocaust before we settled down here and we started to take control of their lives. I understand their way of thinking right now—of the Arabs. Come on, they were here, they were having a nice life, and then we came and we started to take control of everything. Jobs, and basic social life. So I can totally understand how they feel.

Based on these initial parts of our discussion about the conflict, my impression of Ayelet was that she hardly "needed" the experience of intergroup contact to expose her to alternative discourses of the conflict. She seemed to have developed a narrative of the conflict that was quite sympathetic to the Palestinians. Yet, as she continued to describe her views on the conflict—particularly on the matter of its resolution—it became clear to me that the ideological setting of her life story was still very much in formation:

> The problem is that everyone is looking at the past instead of looking at the future.... This is the situation right now; crying about it won't help you achieve anything. I just think Israel is supposed to be a place for everybody—Jews and Arabs. They will have to understand that they can't kick us out. We will have to understand that this is our neighbors, and whether we like it or not, half of them actually live here, inside of Israel. We need to coexist with Arabs, just live with them, no politics or nothing.

The extent to which Ayelet's ideological identifications contain a measure of pragmatism is called into question by her utopian vision of a one-state solution to the conflict. When I query her about the possibility of two states, Israel and Palestine, side by side, she reveals that perhaps her engagement with the master narrative of Jewish-Israeli identity is more significant than I had at first realized:

> I don't really understand [the idea of a two-state solution] because I don't understand why they need a country, because they have so many. They have Egypt, Syria, so many Arab countries. Why can't they live there? We have only one. No matter where we go, everybody's gonna hate us, no matter where we going to go.... It's not like they're different—Syria and Egypt and all of those countries—it's all Arabs. I mean, they're part of it, they're not supposed to *feel* different. And they could totally live there—Egypt and Syria are *huge*. Iraq even.... For the Jewish people, we have only one country. There's nowhere we can go basically. This is where we live.... There's no place for Palestine, and there's no place for making it here. And I kind of understand them, because they are kind of in the place where we were before, when we didn't have anywhere to go, and then the Holocaust happened and whatever, and so we have Israel. Basically what they care most about is Jerusalem, so the ones that really care about it, stay here around Jerusalem, and be happy about what they have and stop complaining about what they don't have. People always look at the empty half of the glass instead of the full half! That's the

stupidity of people, they never appreciate what they have, they always want more, and that's greedy.

Quite alarmingly, given the initial sympathetic tone Ayelet reveals in discussing the Palestinians, she now seems to be sympathetic to that most "right-wing" effort in the Israeli discourse: population transfer. Displaying significant out-group homogeneity in her understanding of the Arabs, she rejects the national and cultural distinctions Arabs themselves make, as "Egyptians," "Syrians," "Palestinians," and the like. She rejects the notion that the Palestinians indeed constitute a unique social identity apart from Egyptians or Syrians and, in this way, seems to delegitimize Palestinian identity.

Ayelet's view of Palestinians thus conforms to an extent with the delegitimization of Palestinian identity contained in the master narrative. Clearly, though, she is ambivalent and, at the age of 16, is still in the process of making decisions about which aspects of the master narrative to appropriate and which to repudiate. For now, though, her view of the Palestinians can be described as classically Orientalist, particularly in the paternalism that underlies the elaboration of her one-state solution:

[The Palestinians] need to stop complaining about the things they don't have. They need to stop and think about what they do have. And they have each other, and they have families. I think if we go through them, if we help them, because they barely have technology. Half of them doesn't even know what a computer is. So if we help them, all around Gaza, build them houses, give them games, give them money a little bit, something like that, I think it will be better. It's all about helping each other. Sometimes Arabs can be all the way around there. I've heard stories, some people say, "We give one finger, they want the whole hand." They have to be fair if we gonna be fair. Both sides equal.

Ayelet has internalized the power imbalance in identity that Orientalism as an ideology establishes. She sees her in-group—Jewish Israelis—as wealthier and more developed, economically and socially. She adopts a paternalistic benevolence with regard to the Palestinians, certainly with a genuine sense of generosity. Perhaps the greatest irony in this excerpt from her narrative is the way in which she concludes it. Having established with Orientalist precision the *inequality* of status between Jews and Palestinians, she reverts to a discourse of equality, suggesting that the Palestinians will have to do *something* in exchange for all of this assistance.

The ideological setting of Ayelet's narrative is like the pattern of a quilt in the midst of its design. Fragments of one pattern shift to another, as the artist abandons original designs for new pathways, then decides perhaps the original ones were best. Any ideological setting of a life story in adolescence is likely to assume this quality, particularly with exposure to such a myriad of ideologies in a place like Israel. A life story currently in the early stages of conscious construction, Ayelet's narrative reveals deep ambivalence about its reflection of the master narrative of Jewish-Israeli identity, with its characteristic form and content.

On the one hand, the redemptive form of Ayelet's narrative conforms very closely to the master narrative. In its content, we see glimpses of familiar themes—of the need for a Jewish state because of the history of persecution and the belief that there is nowhere else for the Jews of the world to *safely* call home, of the exceptionalism of the Israelis, as revealed in her internalized Orientalism. When it comes to the Palestinians, what seems initially to be a rejection of the master narrative—a recognition of the Palestinians and a genuine sympathy for their plight, as well as an expressed *identification* with their experience—gives way to a greater degree of conformity by the narrative's end. Ultimately, Ayelet suggests that, in a way, Palestinians do not even exist as a unique identity group and certainly cannot have a state of their own. They should, rather, be a part of Israel in some kind of apolitical fantasy of coexistence.

Ayelet's narrative may reveal significant ambivalence in its ideological setting, but her willingness to consider counternarratives and to engage in the conversation of discourses that consumes the conflict reveals her cosmopolitan identity:

> The key to everything is to accept the different. I might disagree with the other side; you can disagree with a person, but I'll never see that as a negative. I'll never take it and say, "No. You're wrong. You're definitely wrong and no, I'm not about to listen!" The whole point of it is success with the other and the other opinions, even if you don't agree with them. You're not always supposed to agree with others, you just have to accept their opinions.... You can see I'm a very peaceful person—against war, basically.

If cosmopolitanism condones, ideologically and culturally, a coexistence of conversations (Appiah, 2006)—a willingness to accept the multiplicity of discursive possibilities and the identities that they construct—we can see in Ayelet the promise of conflict repudiation, rather than reproduction. Yet the ideological ambivalence of her currently constructed life story—prior to contact with Palestinians—reveals an identity very much in an active process of formation, and its course is difficult to predict. We will return to Ayelet's story in Chapter 7 to examine the consequences of contact for her personal narrative.

Summary: The Cultural Psychology of Jewish-Israeli Youth

Recall that the first research question that guided this study was concerned with the relationship of the "big" stories that circulate in a society and the "small" stories of a personal narrative of identity. In Chapter 1, I argued that this research question fundamentally speaks to the *cultural psychology of identity,* as it provides us with a framework for understanding the way in which identity is simultaneously a *product* and a *producer* of the discourse that defines "culture." In other words, I suggest that the *personal* narrative represents a *textual mediator* of cultural reproduction (Wertsch, 1998, 2002), as it is through individual life stories that *reflect* a particular master narrative that the discursive conditions of culture are enacted and reproduced.

In this chapter, I applied this theoretical focus on the role of individuals in the maintenance and reproduction of culture to the context of conflict and to the life stories of young Jewish Israelis. The portraits of four youths presented in this chapter were meant to illustrate the complex process of identity construction that contemporary Jewish-Israeli youth undergo, along with some of the discursive *challenges* provided by the context of conflict and its inevitable sense of existential insecurity.

The stories of Jewish-Israeli youth collected for this study reveal narratives of personal redemption that closely mirror the master narrative of national identity, with its larger story of collective redemption. The tendency to construct personal narratives of redemption links Israelis to other cultures in the West (e.g., McAdams, 2006), suggesting an affiliation with Western notions of personhood (see Baumeister, 1987). Yet the stories of youth strongly suggest the salience of *local* identity over *national* identity, particularly as youth determine the ideological settings of their narratives. Local identity also determines the extent to which the conflict has a predictable impact on their daily lives. Only Roai, who lives on a West Bank settlement and commutes to Jerusalem for school, has significant exposure to the actual social structure of the conflict. For Noa, Yossi, and Ayelet, their exposure is almost entirely relegated to particular *discourses* about the conflict, rather than to the conflict's tangible physical realities. This pattern was similar across youth interviewed in this study: only those who resided close to or in the occupied territories had integrated experiences closely related to the conflict or to the Palestinians into their life stories. The prominence accorded to political events in narratives like Roai's speaks to the differentiation of Jewish-Israeli identity across local contexts.

The portraits of Jewish-Israeli youth offered here demonstrate the unique identity challenges created by conflict. Dealing with the possibility of attack on a bus, or hearing stories of siblings in the army, Jewish-Israeli youth meet the challenges of conflict by constructing stories that reveal resilience, strength, and defiance. No matter what the challenge—the loss of a family member, difficulties at school, a parental divorce, the possibility of Palestinian "terror"— Jewish Israelis rise to the challenge with *strength*. This image of Jewish-Israeli identity is meant to contrast sharply with the identity of Jews in the Diaspora (Zeruvabel, 1995).

The thematic content of youth narratives reveals key points of convergence with the master narrative. The theme of Jewish persecution and victimization is consistently present, if sometimes only deployed to justify the need for a Jewish state. The need for security is internalized among all the youth in this study, with the recognition of continued existential threat. The idea of Israeli exceptionalism is closely connected to the delegitimization of Palestinian identity. But this delegitimization, a legacy of Orientalism and its Eurocentric posture toward the Middle East, is contested within the narratives of youth. Yet what can at first appear to be a surprising legitimization of Palestinian identity frequently becomes conditional—and conditional in ways that fail to acknowledge the power asymmetry inherent in the conflict (Rouhana, 2004).

The tendency for youth to diverge from the master narrative on the theme of Palestinian delegitimization parallels shifts in Israeli political discourse that began with the Oslo accords. Those accords represented an official recognition of the legitimacy of Palestinian claims for statehood, and it is noteworthy that contemporary youth appear to have internalized this new discourse on Palestinian identity. Yet Oslo policy can be described as "transitional," given that it specified an interim agreement of principles rather than an actual peace agreement. The perceived failure of Oslo policy to achieve a reduction in conflict has resulted in a discourse of ambivalence in Israeli society. That both Israelis and Palestinians are locked within the liminal discursive conditions set by the Oslo accords—representing a kind of semirecognition of mutual legitimacy and identity—is perceptible to contemporary youth as they begin to construct life stories. Narratives of Israeli youth reveal the reproduction of this deep ambivalence toward the Palestinians and the conflict more generally.

The cultural psychology of contemporary Jewish-Israeli youth is thus characterized by considerable *ambivalence* as the discourse of the conflict makes its gradual way toward identity recognition of the Palestinians as a distinct national group. As I will argue later with regard to peace and conflict transformation, it is the recognition of *identity distinction*, coupled with implications for collective action in the interest of peace and social justice, that both Israelis and Palestinians must embrace to achieve a genuine state of coexistence. That contemporary Jewish-Israeli youth continue to struggle over the degree of distinction they are willing to accord the Palestinians reveals the power of the master narrative as a mediator of personal narrative construction. Youth cannot write their individual life stories apart from the lens of historical persecution and existential insecurity that characterizes the master narrative of Jewish-Israeli identity.

As youth write these stories of ambivalence, they are participants in the reconstruction of a master narrative of identity, even as their stories appear as *products* of a received discourse of conflict and intergroup relations. Through the practice of life story construction, young Jewish Israelis appear to reproduce the status quo of the conflict in its current pernicious place of confusion and seemingly interminable "transition" since the Oslo accords. Even though the youth in this study were intrinsically motivated to pursue intergroup contact with Palestinians, their personal narratives revealed a highly ambivalent, perhaps superficial concern for peace and coexistence. I will reserve further analysis of the narratives presented in this chapter and will for now be content to consider the life stories of Palestinian youth, in order to gain a fuller picture of the *interdependent* nature of Israeli and Palestinian identity in the reproduction of conflict.

4

"It's Not a Normal Life We Lead": The Stories of Palestinian Youth

In Chapter 3, we began to consider the first research question that framed this study—the question of the relationship between a master narrative and the individual life stories of youth in their early stages of construction—through an analysis of four young Jewish Israelis. I presented a version of the Jewish-Israeli master narrative—the "big" story that dominates accounts of history and collective identity in Israeli society. I also highlighted the way in which this master narrative is both nonmonolithic and contested in contemporary Israel. The narratives of youth revealed the role of local context in creating variations in the identification with the master narrative and its ideological setting. It was clear from this analysis that youth engaged with different versions of this master story in constructing their own personal narratives, yet it was also clear that the Palestinians continue to represent the antagonist in their collective narrative. Though the discourse has shifted in Israeli society away from the outright delegitimization of Palestinian identity, the stories of youth revealed the "transitional" characterization of Palestinians in contemporary Israeli society. As indicated by policies like the Oslo accords, the claims of Palestinian nationalism are now recognized but accorded a "conditional" legitimacy by which Israel's security needs assume priority over the fulfillment of Palestinian statehood.

In this chapter, I will apply the same analytic strategy to the question of contemporary Palestinian identity development. I will examine the form, thematic content, and ideological setting(s) of the master narrative of Palestinian history and identity. Then I will present four case analyses in which this relationship between the big stories of a collective and the small stories constructed by youth is queried. Here we will gain another window into the cultural psychology of identity—the process by which individuals construct identities in and through an engagement with "culture," understood primarily through the provision of linguistic "tools," such as narrative, that specify possibilities for social practice (e.g., Bruner, 1990; Holland et al., 1998; Vygotsky, 1978).

The Master Narrative of Palestinian Identity

An Introduction

The master narrative of Palestine assumes a tragic form. Articulated by Palestinian scholars like the late Edward Said (1979), the thematic content of the collective narrative presents a story of a peaceful people, harmoniously inhabiting a place of religious pluralism, whose rights for dignity and national self-determination were violated as a consequence of Zionism's success (e.g., Said, 1979). In this frame, the Palestinian master narrative is a story of struggle and loss, subjugation and occupation, dispossession and despair. But it is also a story of resistance and resilience, of righteousness and liberation, of steadfast survival. In this section, I will elaborate and provide documentary evidence for the basis of this characterization of the form and content of the Palestinian narrative.

Like the form of many tragedies, the Palestinian narrative begins at a point of ideal imagination—a time in which people of different religions and ideologies coexisted, united in a language and cultural tradition. According to the master narrative, this harmonious state of affairs is disrupted by Zionism (Said, 1979), which the Palestinians frame as a colonial political program and ideology (Rodinson, 1973). Thus Zionism and its fulfillment in the realization of an Israeli state are interpreted as a disruption in the possibility of Palestinian self-determination following four centuries of Ottoman rule.

The Palestinian master narrative is infused with a number of key themes. I will highlight four of these as they relate to the discursive encounters of contemporary youth. First, the core of the narrative centers on the experience of *loss and land dispossession*. Second, the theme of *resistance*, grounded in the perceived *injustice* of this loss, pervades the narrative and redeems its sense of powerlessness. Third, the *existential insecurity* of Palestinian identity, and the insecurity of everyday life in Palestine, represents a significant trope in the narrative. Finally, the *delegitimization of Israeli identity* serves the classic role of dehumanizing the enemy (Bar-Tal, 1990a).

Contestations

It is important to note that, like the Jewish-Israeli master narrative and master narratives in general, the Palestinian master narrative represents a dynamic discourse in a perpetual state of appropriation and repudiation. In other words, its form, thematic content, and ideological setting are contested among cultural participants. As I will suggest, the primary site of contestation of the Palestinian master narrative is its *ideological setting*, manifest in the fierce political competition between the secular nationalist Fatah party and the religious nationalist Hamas party. While in some ways this contestation is related to larger struggles in the postcolonial world, and to the rise of religious fundamentalism more generally (see Herriot, 2007), my treatment of this issue will focus very concretely on the Palestinian context, since I believe that this ideological struggle from within is best understood in its local context of origination. Rather than deal extensively with this issue at this point, I will integrate discussion of it throughout this chapter, and consideration of this issue is central to my analysis of the individual life stories of Palestinian youth.

Just as I relied upon extensive documentary evidence to illustrate the thematic content of the Jewish-Israeli master narrative in Chapter 3, in the pages that follow I rely upon historical and political documents to construct a comprehensible master narrative of Palestinian identity for the reader. Just as some of the documentary evidence I relied upon in Chapter 3 no doubt deeply offended readers of Arab or Palestinian descent, no doubt that some of the documentary evidence that follows, spoken by leaders and architects of Palestinian political movements, will offend some readers of Jewish origin. I trust that in the passionate response to these documents, the reader of any origin will quickly come to recognize the role of emotion in the maintenance of conflict, as well as the way in which stories can simultaneously comfort one group, providing an anchor for thought, feeling, and action, just as they evoke a deep sense of antagonism in another. In our own response to the content of these storylines, I believe we can begin to appreciate the profound psychological experience of war and conflict for contemporary youth.

Theme 1: Loss and Dispossession

According to the Palestinian narrative, the struggle for Palestine and its national destiny culminated in the loss of the 1948 war, which turned 700,000

Palestinians into refugees overnight and transformed the landscape by erasing entire villages (Morris, 1987; Sa'di & Abu-Lughod, 2007). With the resolution of "the Jewish question" emerged a whole new question—the question of Palestine and of the Palestinians (Arendt, 1973; Said, 1979). The Palestinian scholar Edward Said (1979) describes this trope of the narrative in his book, *The Question of Palestine*:

> The Muslim and Christian Palestinians who lived in Palestine for hundreds of years until they were driven out in 1948, were unhappy victims of the same movement whose whole aim had been to end the victimization of Jews by Christian Europe. Yet it is precisely because Zionism was so admirably successful in bringing Jews to Palestine and constructing a nation for them, that the world has not been concerned with what the enterprise meant in loss, dispersion, and catastrophe for the Palestinian natives. (p. xxxix)

The success of Zionism as a solution to the Jewish "problem" in Europe thus resulted in the displacement of injustice, according to the Palestinian narrative. In this frame, the condition of the Jews in Europe—increasingly alienated and persecuted—was addressed at the expense of another, the Palestinians. The consequence for the Palestinians—displaced and dislocated by the usurpation of their land, their dignity, their national identity—has been, in Said's words, a "catastrophe."

Some of the most prominent voices of the Palestinian experience since 1948 have been those in exile, most notably the late Edward Said (1979, 1994, 2000, 2003). The experience of loss and dispossession—of the loss not only of one's physical land but of the ability to express freely his or her *national* and *cultural* identity—forms a key part of the Palestinian master narrative, particularly for those in exile (Aoudé, 2001). Given the success of constructing and maintaining a coherent sense of Palestinian national identity, in spite of the absence of territorial sovereignty (Khalidi, 1997), the emphasis of loss in the Palestinian narrative is decidedly on the *land*, rather than collective identity (e.g., Christison, 2001; Khalidi, 1997; Lynd, Balhour, & Lynd, 1994; Rubinstein, 1991; Said, 1979, 1994).

The *land*, its liberation and reclamation, is thus central to the master narrative. In fact, in his speech to the UN General Assembly in 1974, Yasser Arafat argued that the conflict was entirely reducible to land dispossession:

> [In 1947] the General Assembly partitioned what it had no right to divide—an indivisible homeland. When we rejected that decision, our position corresponded to that of the natural mother who refused to

permit King Solomon to cut her son in two when the unnatural mother claimed the child for herself and agreed to his dismemberment.... The roots of the Palestine question lie here. Its causes do not stem from any conflict between two religions or two nationalisms. Neither is it a border conflict between neighboring states. It is the cause of a people deprived of its homeland, dispersed and uprooted, and living mostly in exile and in refugee camps. (Arafat, 1974/2001, pp. 173–174)

The land, then, is a vital character in the Palestinian story, and its loss is the ultimate tragedy of the narrative. The perceived injustice of this loss forms the basis of Palestinian *resistance.*

As the conflict between Jews and Arabs in Palestine was at its peak in the 1930s, and a civil war loomed, the Arab historian George Antonius reflected in his 1938 classic *The Arab Awakening* on the connection of the Arabs to the land of Palestine:

The rights of the Arabs are derived from actual and longstanding possession, and rest upon the strongest human foundation. Their connection with Palestine goes back uninterruptedly to the earliest historic times.... The Arab claims [to Palestine] rest on two distinct foundations: the natural right of a settled population, in great majority agricultural, to remain in possession of the land of its birthright... (Antonius, 1938/1965, pp. 390–391)

Antonius summarizes the Palestinian narrative as Zionism and its national project created a heightened state of insecurity among the indigenous population. In framing the concept of land possession in terms of historical continuity and morality, he offers an early interpretation of the injustice of Zionist aspirations that will anchor the collective Palestinian narrative. Less than a decade after the publication of his seminal book, that "longstanding possession," in fact, came to an end.

Dispossession of the land is not, thematically, just a historical relic of the Palestinian story; it is very much alive in the everyday discourse of Palestinian lives today (Gordon, 2008a, 2008b). Stories of loss and trauma pervade popular Palestinian discourse, particularly among residents of the refugee camps (Awwad, 2004). For those displaced by the wars, particularly the 1948 war, it is customary to retain the antique key from one's original house. My friend and colleague Khalid always identified himself as a "refugee" from Haifa, even though his family had lived in Tulkarm since the 1948 war and he had become a resident of Ramallah. Stories of dispossession abound and are reawakened in the contemporary context of Israel's construction of its separation barrier, which has confiscated a great deal of Palestinian land (Gordon, 2008a, 2008b; Makdisi, 2008; Roy, 2004).

In the Palestinian narrative, then, the creation of Israel represents a disruption in the continuity of their relationship with the land. The psychological experience of this disruption is reproduced from generation to generation through the master narrative, with its emphasis on land dispossession. The land and its reclamation thus constitute the central core of Palestinian identity, and it is in resistance that the Palestinian narrative seeks to fulfill its possibility for redemption.

Theme 2: Resistance

If the "catastrophe" of Israel's success creates in the Palestinian narrative a radical disruption, it is the idea of *resistance* that rescues the narrative from the depths of tragedy. In resistance, hope is not lost for the righteousness of the Palestinian cause and for a reversal of fortune. Through resistance, despair turns to possibility, fatalism to optimism, vulnerability to agency. Resistance confers power, and with that power, the redemption from suffering, oppression, and victimization.

The nature of Palestinian resistance and its course is intimately linked to the historical context in which it developed following the 1948 and 1967 wars. Once the dream of pan-Arabism had faded with the significant loss of the 1967 war, a distinct Palestinian resistance movement began. For inspiration, that movement looked to other postcolonial liberation struggles, such as the Algerian War (Harkabi, 1968/2001; see Fanon, 1961/2004). The perceived success of these movements convinced the Palestinians of the value of such a program.

The new Palestinian revolutionary identity was embodied in the doctrines of the organizations that emerged following the 1967 war, most notably Fatah and the Palestine Liberation Organization (PLO). The seventh point in Fatah's "Seven Points" document reveals this connection clearly:

> The struggle of the Palestinian People, like that of the Vietnamese people
> and other peoples of Asia, Africa, and Latin America, is part of the
> historic process of the liberation of the oppressed peoples from
> colonialism and imperialism. (Fatah, 1969/2001, p. 131)

Fatah's ideological platform—which originally centered decisively on the eradication of Zionism and, hence, Israel itself—assumes the discourse of a "Revolutionary War waged on guerilla warfare lines" (Harkabi, 1968/2001, p. 121).

As the Palestine National Council (1968/2001) proclaimed in its original charter, the cultivation of a new revolutionary Palestinian identity among youth was absolutely essential to the success of the movement:

> It is a national duty to bring up individual Palestinians in an Arab revolutionary manner. All means of information and education must be adopted in order to acquaint the Palestinian with his country in the most profound manner, both spiritual and material, that is possible. He must be prepared for the armed struggle and ready to sacrifice his wealth and his life in order to win back his homeland and bring about its liberation. (p. 117)

The production and reproduction of a new Palestinian was considered vital to this new phase of the national movement—one in which pan-Arabism was rejected in favor of an "indigenous" Palestinian solution. Palestinian liberation became part of the postcolonial struggle, and resistance, *in spite of* loss, its new dominant trope.

It is important to note that this discourse of resistance not only provided an important sense of legitimacy to Palestinian identity and the Palestinian struggle, but also a moral justification for the use of force against Israelis. The related theme of *injustice* that pervades the Palestinian master narrative legitimizes resistance to Zionism and to Israeli occupation. A mantra of Palestinian discourse on peace has long been "Peace with Justice." The notion of injustice stems directly from the perception of Zionism as an outgrowth of European colonialism (Rodinson, 1973). We will return in a moment to this perspective on Zionism as we consider Palestinian delegitimization of Israeli identity. For now, it is only vital to view Palestinian resistance as rooted in the perception of an unjust incursion—and domination—of their homeland.

Injustice, of course, breeds legitimate resistance, according to the narratives of other postcolonial encounters and struggles for independence. Discursively, then, acts of violence against Israelis are not interpreted in the Palestinian narrative as "terrorism" in the sense that the term has come to connote, for that interpretation implies a lack of legitimacy—a kind of chaotic, meaningless intent to harm. Palestinian acts of violence are, rather, interpreted as forms of "resistance" in the master narrative. Yasser Arafat makes this argument in his 1974 speech at the UN:

> Those who call us terrorists wish to prevent world public opinion from discovering the truth about us and from seeing the justice on our faces.... The difference between the revolutionary and the terrorist lies in the reason for which each fights. For whoever stands by a just cause and

fights for the freedom and liberation of his land from the invaders, the settlers and the colonialists, cannot possibly be called terrorist; otherwise the American people in their struggle for liberation from the British colonialists would have been terrorists, the European resistance against the Nazis would be terrorism, the struggle of the Asian, African and Latin American peoples would also be terrorism, and many of you who are in this Assembly Hall were considered terrorists. This is actually a just and proper struggle consecrated by the United Nations Charter and by the Universal Declaration of Human Rights. As to those who fight against the just causes, those who wage war to occupy, colonize and oppress other people—those are the terrorists, those are the people whose actions should be condemned, who should be called war criminals: *for the justice of the cause determines the right to struggle.* (Arafat, 1974/2001, pp. 176–177, italics added)

In this opportunity to present the legitimacy of the Palestinian cause to the international community, Arafat articulates the Palestinian master narrative. According to him, the Palestinian struggle is rooted in a just cause and consists of resistance to Israeli "terror," with its systematic expansionism, exclusionism, and oppression of the indigenous inhabitants of the land. Resistance is, in the master narrative, entirely justifiable and, in fact, vital to the preservation of human rights and the self-determination of all postcolonial subjects.

The idea of Palestinian resistance constructed a redemptive foil to the tragic Palestinian master narrative. Relying on the discourse of other liberation movements, it promulgated an idealistic end goal: the emergence of a democratic Palestinian state in which the rights of all citizens—Jews included— would be equally accorded. The Palestinian narrative of emancipation, then, was a romantic one in which the outcome was to "restore" a level of democracy and pluralism. The final objective of Palestinian resistance is, as articulated by Fatah (1969/2001), "the restoration of the independent, democratic State of Palestine, all of whose citizens will enjoy equal rights irrespective of their religion" (p. 131). Such a claim, of course, obscures the fact that Palestine never was an independent sovereign democracy and could not therefore be "restored." Nevertheless, the claim illustrates the way in which a *story* of Palestinian society before Zionism had been constructed as a place of identity pluralism.

As I have suggested, like contemporary Jewish-Israeli identity, Palestinian identity is far from monolithic and is, in fact, contested. While Fatah and the PLO have dominated Palestinian discourse and can legitimately be credited with scripting the narrative of resistance, a formidable challenge has arisen in more recent times with the ascent of political Islam and groups like Hamas and Islamic Jihad (Lybarger, 2007; Mishal & Sela, 2006). These organizations explicitly call for an "Islamic state" in Palestine and do not embrace the same secular vision that consumed the initial liberation movement. It remains to be seen how the youth of Palestine engage with these contested narratives of the vision for the state, but the discourse of both "factions" indeed legitimizes violent acts against Israelis as "resistance."

The involvement of youth in the first Palestinian *intifada* (Barber, 1999a, 1999b, 2001, 2008, 2009b; Bucaille, 2004), which culminated in what was initially perceived to be the beginning of the end of Israeli occupation in the West Bank and Gaza Strip, reveals the success of this attempt to fashion a Palestinian identity of resistance. Brian Barber's work with Palestinian youth serves as an excellent example. Barber, an American developmental psychologist, discovered that involvement in political violence during the first *intifada* was not always associated with negative psychological outcomes and that Palestinian youth instead reported *great meaning* in their involvement in the *intifada* (Barber, 1999b, 2001, 2008, 2009b). Involvement in political violence served as an important source of social integration (Barber, 2001, 2008, 2009b). Youth saw themselves as part of a legitimate, enduring struggle for self-determination.

Political violence actually had a positive interpretation for Palestinian youth of the first *intifada*. Participation in violence meant that they could fulfill their identities as Palestinians through meaningful social practice—suggesting a deep internalization of the narrative of resistance. Their commitment to the idea of resistance had, in fact, "protected" them from the challenges to psychological well-being that the context of conflict can naturally create (Punamäki, 1996). The fact that their resistance may have resulted in imprisonment was hardly problematic for the Palestinian, as imprisonment is viewed as a rite of passage in the Palestinian life course and a site of education about the Palestinian movement (Barber, 1999b; Peteet, 1994).

It is important to note that Palestinian youth continue to be affected by the trauma of war and conflict. In fact, there is a significant literature that reveals the negative impact of the prolonged conflict on the psychological development of Palestinian children and adolescents (e.g., Abdeen,.Qasrawi, Nabil, & Shaheen, 2008; Baker & Shalhoub-Kevorkian, 1999; Elbedour, 1998; Elbedour, ten Bensel, & Maruyama, 1993; Garbarino & Kostelny, 1996; Haj-Yahia, 2008; Qouta, Punamäki, & El Sarraj, 2008; Thabet & Vostanis, 1999; Zakrison, Shahen, Mortaja, & Hamel, 2004). Yet children who are socialized in conflict appear to identify at young ages with the strength of its cause (Jagodić, 2000), thereby, at minimum, ascribing a sense of meaning and purpose to the violence associated with it (Barber, 1999a, 1999b, 2009b; Barber, Schluterman, Denny, & McCouch, 2006).

Israeli psychologist Michelle Slone has discovered an interesting pattern regarding the impact of political violence on Israeli and Palestinian youth (e.g., Slone, Adiri, & Arian, 1998). For Israeli youth—Jewish and Arab alike—a clear linear relationship appears to exist between exposure to adverse political events and psychological symptoms. More exposure is associated with more negative symptoms. By contrast, a curvilinear relationship exists for Palestinian youth, whereby youth with moderate exposure report the highest levels of symptoms, and youth with the highest exposure appear "buffered" from the negative impact of violence. Psychologists like Slone discuss this differential impact in terms of coping, suggesting that the Palestinians have adopted coping strategies that are highly effective at high levels of exposure to political violence (see also Punamäki & Puhakka, 1997). But another interpretation, of course, is consistent with Barber's (2009b) emphasis on the *meaning* of political violence. Suffering at the hands of the Israeli army is, for Palestinian youth, perhaps a rite of passage in the same way that military service is for Jewish-Israeli youth: it serves to secure the internalization of an identity of resistance.

The trope of resistance in the master narrative thus serves a number of important social and psychological functions for Palestinians. First, it reconfigures Palestinian identity and associates its endurance with *strength* rather than *weakness* (notably similar to the reconfiguration of Jewish identity that occurred through the establishment of Israel). Second, it produces subjects who are willing to sacrifice themselves for the Palestinian cause of national liberation. Its allure is precisely in its reconfiguration of power and its refusal to acquiesce to a state of subordination and domination. Finally, resistance provides the inherent struggles in Palestinian daily existence with a sense of meaning and purpose. The struggles of Palestinians can be reinterpreted, on an axis away from *suffering* toward *emancipation* (again, much as the Israeli master narrative sought to configure before its own fulfillment). Yet it is ultimately existential insecurity in the daily lives of Palestinians and in their sense of identity fulfillment that legitimizes the need for resistance in Palestinian discourse.

Theme 3: Existential Insecurity

By now most readers will have observed some of the important similarities between the Israeli and Palestinian master narratives. No tropes contained within the two narratives overlap as much as that of *existential insecurity*. Just as the construction of an Israeli identity was intended to ensure the ontological survival of Jewish identity, the Palestinian master narrative is consumed with the sustenance of a fragile Palestinian national identity.

With the success of Zionism and the failure of Palestinian national identity to achieve its recognition, Palestinian identity has been relegated to the status of a *question* in the master narrative (Said, 1979). This lack of security in national identity, Palestinian historian Rashid Khalidi (1997) argues, creates a sense of anxiety in the Palestinian consciousness and, in fact, is affirmed in the experience of existential interrogation that Palestinians routinely undergo—at the border crossing, the checkpoint, the airport:

> This condition of suspense in which Palestinians find themselves at borders means that as far as the world, or at least a large part of it, is concerned, the Palestinian's identity remains in question. This identity is therefore a source of anxiety to governments and their security authorities.... At a time when internal and international barriers to free movement of people and ideas are crumbling rapidly in many places, those barriers remain in place for Palestinians.... The fact that all Palestinians are subject to these special indignities, and thus are subject to an almost unique postmodern condition of shared anxiety at the frontier, the checkpoint and the crossing point proves that they are a people, if nothing else. (Khalidi, 1997, pp. 4–5)

The existence of Palestinian identity is structurally threatened by the lack of freedom of movement and of full recognition in the global consciousness, according to Khalidi. But, according to Khalidi (1997), it is precisely in this threat—this state of "suspense," as he calls it—that the existence of Palestinian identity is in fact secured, for the identity perils that they must experience together construct a community of shared subordination.

The theme of existential insecurity in the Palestinian narrative is thus intimately connected to the social structure of the Israeli occupation (Gordon, 2008a, 2008b). Many have argued that the experience of life under military occupation became significantly more threatening since the outbreak of the second Palestinian *intifada* in 2000 (Collins, 2004). This *intifada*—far bloodier and seemingly more intractable than the first—has been characterized by prodigious collective punishment to the Palestinians for attacks in Israel (Kelman, 2007). This punishment has included the reoccupation of a number of cities and towns granted autonomy during the 1990s. This reoccupation has harmed communities that were in the process of economic and cultural development (Gordon, 2008a, 2008b; Makdisi, 2008; Roy, 2004).

Existential insecurity is therefore not *abstract* in the lives of Palestinians during the second *intifada*; it has been *tangible* in the daily reality of their existence. At its extreme, this trope of the master narrative has come to create what Reuter (2002) calls a "culture of death" among Palestinians, a culture in which life is seen as so temporary and rich with trauma that the notion of self-sacrifice, or "martyrdom" (*shahid*), is not considered exceptional. The discourse and status of martyrdom seems to imbue a sense of meaning in death under conditions of existential uncertainty and seeks to redeem the collective narrative from a place of contamination by positioning martyrdom within a discourse of "resistance" (Abdel-Khalek, 2004; Allen, 2006; Naaman, 2007).

Theme 4: Delegitimization of Israeli Identity

There are many significant tropes in the Palestinian master narrative, but all of them essentially rely upon the existence and success of Zionism and its embodiment in Israeli identity. That is, the key themes of loss, dispossession, and resistance rely upon the fulfillment of Zionism and its consequences for the Palestinians (Said, 1979). The very existence of an Israeli national identity is thus framed as the antithesis of a secure Palestinian identity. Such is the state of negative interdependence of Israeli and Palestinian identities (Kelman, 1999b). And so it seems somehow *logical* that the legitimacy of Israeli identity could not be acknowledged, for that acknowledgment would obviate the ideology of Palestinian liberation. The case for Palestine is a case *against* Israel; in a democratic, secular Palestine, there is no need for Jewish separatism, according to the secular nationalist version of the Palestinian narrative.

Recall that in the Palestinian narrative, Zionism is interpreted as an extension of European colonialism: the Zionist national project, a colonial one (Rodinson, 1973; Said, 1979). Said (1979) characterized the struggle between Palestinians and Zionism as "a struggle between a presence and an interpretation, the former constantly appearing to be overpowered and eradicated by the latter" (p. 8). By this he suggested that the Palestinians had a claim to Palestine in their *presence*, whereas the Zionist claim to Palestine rested on an historical *interpretation*—the notion that the Jews possessed a distant but powerful connection to the land. Again, we can look to Arafat's 1974 speech at the UN for a treatment of the subject:

> The roots of the Palestinian question reach back into the closing years of the nineteenth century, in other words, to that period which we call the era of colonialism and settlement.... This is precisely the period during which Zionism as a scheme was born; its aim was the conquest of Palestine by European immigrants, just as settlers colonized, and indeed raided, most of Africa.

Just as colonialism heedlessly used the wretched, the poor, the exploited as mere inert matter with which to build and to carry out settler colonialism, so too were destitute, oppressed European Jews employed on behalf of world imperialism and of the Zionist leadership. European Jews were transformed into instruments of aggression; they became the elements of settler colonialism intimately allied to racial discrimination.

Zionism is an ideology that is imperialist, colonialist, racist; it is profoundly reactionary and discriminatory; it is united with anti-Semitism in its retrograde tenets and is, when all is said and done, another side of the same base coin.

Zionism encourages the Jew to emigrate out of his homeland and grants him an artificially created nationality.

When we speak of our common hopes for the Palestine of tomorrow we include in our perspective all Jews now living in Palestine who choose to live with us there in peace and without discrimination.... We invite them to emerge from their moral isolation into a more open realm of free choice, far from their present leadership's efforts to implant in them a Masada complex. (Arafat, 1974/2001, pp. 171–172, 181–182)

In this speech, Arafat reduces Israeli identity to an "artificially created national-ity" and its subjects as victims of a racist colonial movement. He seeks to dele-gitimize the perceived need for a national identity among the persecuted European Jews who immigrated to Palestine. The Israeli narrative is, in Arafat's frame, an empty one, contrived by the "Zionist leadership."

In the Palestinian narrative, Israeli identity is considered an extension of Western imperialism, founded in an Orientalist, ethnocentric, and racist ideol-ogy. The Palestinian National Charter, that document which instructed Palestinians to raise their children in a "revolutionary manner," to prepare them for "armed struggle," states the case against Zionism:

Zionism is a political movement organically associated with international imperialism and antagonistic to all action for liberation and to progressive movements in the world. It is racist and fanatic in its nature, aggressive, expansionist, and colonial in its aims, and fascist in its methods. Israel is the instrument of the Zionist movement, and a geographical base for world imperialism placed strategically in the midst of the Arab homeland to combat the hopes of the Arab nation for liberation, unity, and progress. (Palestine National Council, 1968/2001, p. 119)

According to the Palestinian narrative, then, an Israeli identity is an illegitimate identity, founded upon aggression, antagonism, and strategic disposses-sion. It is, in this way, considered a false identity, and one worthy of eradication—according to the Palestinian narrative.

Though the Palestinian master narrative denounces and delegitimizes Zionism and Israeli identity, it is important to note that it seeks to distance its critique of Zionism from claims of anti-Semitism. The narrative seeks to "intercept" such critiques by positing a distinction among Zionism as an ideology, Israel as a national identity, and the Jewish people and religion. The second of Fatah's (1969/2001) "Seven Points" articulates this distinction:

> *Fatah*, the Palestinian National Liberation Movement, is not struggling against the Jews as an ethnic and religious community. It is struggling against Israel as the expression of colonization based on a theocratic, racist and expansionist system and of Zionism and colonialism. (p. 130)

The master narrative thus seeks to delegitimize Israeli national identity while recognizing the legitimate existence of a Jewish religious and ethnic identity.

Arafat (1974/2001) argues that the Palestinian struggle for liberation is also a struggle for the liberation of Jewish identity:

> Since its inception, our revolution has not been motivated by racial or religious factors. Its target has never been the Jew, as a person, but racist Zionism and undisguised aggression. In this sense, ours is also a revolution for the Jew, as a human being, as well. We are struggling so that Jews, Christians, and Muslims may live in equality enjoying the same rights and assuming the same duties, free from racial or religious discrimination. (p. 176)

According to Arafat, the struggle against Zionism and against Israel is an emancipatory one not just for Palestinian identity but also for Jewish identity. The Palestinian master narrative, in this claim, seeks to elevate its democratic project to a higher moral space than Israel in its aims to construct a state for *all* the identities of the region, not just one. Palestinian (secular) nationalism is thus framed as an *inclusive* nationalism, Zionism and Israeli nationalism *exclusive* in their ideological foundations (see Peleg, 2004).

The Palestinian master narrative thus delegitimizes Israeli identity on both historical and ideological grounds. It constructs the Israeli national identity as an artificial one, and one with less legitimate basis than the Palestinian national identity. But beyond this characterization, it is the perceived ideological content of the Israeli identity that most delegitimizes it in the Palestinian narrative. In its perceived content, Israeli identity is framed as exclusionary and discriminatory; it favors its group members and is, therefore, an ethnocentric identity. According to the Palestinian narrative, this aspect of Zionism conflicts with democratic principles and the idea of universal human rights, in which multiple identities are granted equivalent dignity. With its in-group-specific ideological foundation Israeli identity is perceived as antagonistic and therefore in conflict with the postcolonial project of liberation with which secular Palestinian nationalism sought to ideologically locate itself.

Summary

The Palestinian master narrative contains a number of tropes that exceed the four briefly outlined here. Yet most of these tropes are centered on the trauma of loss and dispossession. Victimization, oppression, powerlessness, humiliation, and indignity all stem from this experience. Resistance as a responsive trope injects the narrative with the possibility of redemption, though it also predicts further loss to the extent that it requires self-sacrifice and martyrdom to achieve its thematic strength. And this notion of resistance relies upon the systematic delegitimization of an Israeli identity—the framing of Israeli identity in a place of lesser moral or existential worth than Palestinian identity.

I want to return, for a moment, to the idea of master narrative *contestation*, and to offer more precision about contemporary challenges to this classic narrative of secular Palestinian nationalism. A coherent master narrative is, of course, always a fragile construction, for social change and the competition of discourses ensure its contestation (Gjerde, 2004). The Palestinian case is no exception to this general rule. In fact, its genesis was complicated by, on the one hand, a tradition of *localism* over *nationalism* in Palestinian identity before Zionism (Tamari, 1999) and, on the other, competition between a pan-Arab nationalist discourse and a distinct Palestinian national discourse (Khalidi, 1997). Today, the introduction of an Islamist discourse into the mainstream of Palestinian society has rendered the master narrative extremely fragile (Lybarger, 2007), particularly since the death of Arafat and the growing disenchantment with the Fatah-led Palestinian Authority. The central focus of contestation in contemporary Palestinian discourse is, as I have suggested, in the ideological setting of the master narrative.

The original Palestinian narrative was set in the ideological context of other secular postcolonial liberation movements in the mid–twentieth century. The goal of such movements was popular liberation, followed by socialism and democratic rule. The current point of contestation in the Palestinian master narrative centers on the ideological foundations of the narrative, with the discourse of political Islam and religious nationalism now seriously vying for primacy (see Esposito, 1997).

Following the Islamist philosophy of Sayyid Qutb (1953/2000, 1960/ 2006, 1964/2006), a major intellectual architect of Egypt's Muslim Brotherhood movement in the 1950s and 1960s, social and political organizations like Hamas and Islamic Jihad call for an Islamic state in the entirety of Mandate Palestine. In this vision of religious nationalism, Islam is considered the ideal ideology for the framing of a national consciousness that responds to the shortcomings of secular nationalism.

Focusing specifically on Hamas, the dominant of the Islamist movements in Palestine, the way in which the philosophical and ideological approach of the Muslim Brotherhood was appropriated was in the call for an Islamic state. The organization's 1988 charter illustrates the way in which their ideology was manifest in a new discourse on Palestinian nationalism:

> The Islamic Resistance Movement is a distinct Palestinian Movement which owes its loyalty to Allah, derives from Islam its way of life and strives to raise the banner of Allah over every inch of Palestine.... [Peace] initiatives, the so-called peaceful solutions, and the international conferences to resolve the Palestinian problem are all contrary to the beliefs of the Islamic Resistance Movement. For renouncing any part of Palestine means renouncing part of the religion; the nationalism of the Islamic Resistance Movement is part of its faith, the movement educates its members to adhere to its principles and to raise the banner of Allah over their homeland as they fight their Jihad.... There is no solution to the Palestinian problem except by Jihad. (Hamas, 1988/2001, pp. 341–342)

Ideologically, then, Hamas seeks to reconstruct the master narrative of Palestinian identity around *religious*, rather than *secular*, nationalism. The ascendance of religious nationalism is by no means confined to elements of Palestinian society, nor is it confined to Islam (see Herriot, 2007; Kinnvall, 2004). Its emergence is largely credited to the failure of secular nationalism, for Palestinians as well as many other groups, to achieve credible gains both socially and economically in the postcolonial period.

The distinction between the secular nationalism of Fatah and the religious nationalism of Hamas creates a major contestation over the ideological setting of the Palestinian master narrative as it is currently constructed and disseminated through the discourse of Palestinian society. Youth are intimately exposed to both discourses, and the ideology in which they choose to set their own life stories remains an empirical question that I will examine through an analysis of life stories.

As I consider the personal narratives of Palestinian youth, I examine the ways in which the master narrative of Palestinian identity is appropriated in its form, thematic content, and ideological setting. This analysis reveals the role that Palestinian youth assume in the reproduction of conflict through their own process of identity development, intrinsically bound to a mediational process of narrative engagement and the construction of a personal narrative of identity. The consideration of only four of these life stories in their totality only begins to shed light on the Palestinian experience, yet an in-depth analysis of these four cases, selected for their representativeness of the larger sample, provides idiographic specificity to the problem at hand.

The Stories of Youth

Ali: The Unlikely Islamist

With his baggy shorts, baseball cap, and iPod, Ali looks like a typical American teenager. The first day I met him, he engaged with me, in his fluent English, about some of his favorite movies, like *The Matrix* and *Lord of the Rings*. He is, in fact, a 16-year-old Palestinian Muslim from East Jerusalem. His appropriation of American style, his consumption of American products, his fluent mastery of English and French, in addition to his native Arabic and some Hebrew, all attest to his residence in the "global village." Ali is, without question, a subject of globalization. From a wealthy Palestinian family who are apolitical and anti-ideological, Ali has, by most standards, an exceptional status as a young Palestinian.

Yet despite his privilege, Ali's life story does not present itself as a narrative of progress or ascent. It is, rather, true to the tragic form of the Palestinian master narrative. With its tone of despair and depression, loss and anger, and vengeful resistance, Ali's personal narrative at age 16 conforms quite closely to the master narrative of Palestinian identity, and Ali has appropriated much of the discourse of this narrative into his life story.

Ali's narrative assumes a stable form until age 4, when the first Gulf War began. His story is grounded in the foundational tone of fear that characterized that historical moment in the lives of both Palestinians and Israelis, connected in the mutual fate of potential annihilation (e.g., Elbedour, 1998; Lavee & Ben-David, 1993; Lavi & Solomon, 2005; Milgram, 1994):

> I wasn't really aware of everything, but I remember it. The gas masks, and I remember my little brother was like, 2 or 1, and they had to put him in this plastic box or something. And I was really scared.

> I remember that.... You could hear the alarm everyday, the sirens.
> I remember crying sometimes.

Ali's first memory is thus the first descent in his life story. It is a time at which the idea of existential insecurity is awakened for him—the notion that his life is not secure and that he and his family live a fragile existence as Palestinians.

The form of Ali's narrative ascends as he professes to have slipped into a period of political unconsciousness, dismissing the threats in his social ecology and attempting to live a "normal" life: "I was a kid, so I wasn't aware of the situation, just normal life, school, making friends. [Life] starts going down when I grew up." With the emergence of political consciousness and the birth of a sophisticated understanding of "the situation," Ali's life story begins its tragic decline:

> I didn't really start to care about other people until I was like 12 years old. But then I came to know about the whole thing, and it's really depressing. It was like, to see how people are humiliated.... And then the *intifada* started. It's like, when you're a 16-year-old, I'm a 16-year-old Palestinian ... and it's so hard. It's hard to be who you are.

For Ali, the increase in his political awareness became a "depressing" influence on his life story. The conflict and its pernicious psychological structure lead him to the perception that his identity is somehow "blocked." He cannot fully express his identity as a Palestinian, which is probably connected to his residence in East Jerusalem (Klein, 2004). From 12 years on, Ali's narrative contains one tragic story after another—stories of his own experience, but even more so of the collective experience of the Palestinians. His privilege has, to some extent, shielded him from the harsh realities of the conflict, and he experiences a sense of guilt as a result.

Formally, then, Ali's narrative mirrors the tragic Palestinian master narrative with uncanny precision. His story, saturated with the tone of fear and the experience of identity insecurity, is an archetypal Palestinian story. As we consider in greater detail the thematic content of his narrative, the link between his story and the master narrative becomes increasingly apparent.

Dispossession of the land is a central theme in Ali's life story. In connecting resistance to this loss, he reveals the extent to which he has appropriated the master narrative of Palestinian identity:

> It's like we're supposed to fight for every inch of the country. It's ours, and they took it by force. We're gonna take it back by force, if we can. But we, we can't take it back by force! We don't have money. We're not allowed to have an army, weapons, nothing! This is why we use the

freedom fighters.... I believe, if we're not gonna get our land back, we don't have to make peace. Everyone should fight until they die.

In this brief excerpt from his narrative, we see quite readily the axis upon which Palestinian identity is constructed and, quite successfully, reproduced among youth: the *unjust* dispossession of the land ("It's *ours*, and they took it by force"), and the *just* cause of Palestinian resistance, symbolized during the second *intifada* by the "freedom fighters." In this excerpt, though, the theme of Palestinian *powerlessness* is also apparent. For Ali, the inherent *weakness* of the consistent *loss* of the Palestinians is not fully reversed through resistance, as perhaps it is intended to be in the master narrative.

Ali endorses the practice of suicide bombing as a legitimate form of resistance, though he professes that he would never become a "fighter" because of his family. As he says, "I don't wanna mess up their lives," causing yet another disruption in their own narratives:

> And how come do they call the suicide bombers "terrorists" and not the Israeli government? They started all the violence! They invaded Palestine! It's like, we're just defending ourselves. What else can you do?! If your wife was raped and killed, your mother and father, your whole family was killed in front of you, and you were humiliated, your wife being raped in front of you, and your home destroyed, and you have no reason to live, and all the hate, and you have all the hate inside you, and all you could think of is revenge, right?! ... It's wrong, but it's the *only* way. And it's like every Israeli has to join the army. It's like, so no one's innocent.

Ali appropriates the master narrative when he rejects the label of "terrorism" to describe Palestinian acts against Israelis. These are, rather, acts of "resistance"—and a *legitimate* resistance at that—in the frame of his narrative. As he notes, "They started all the violence! They invaded Palestine!" In this narrative frame, Israel is the aggressor and antagonist and the Palestinians only defending themselves and their legitimate cause for liberation from occupation and oppression.

But Ali also reveals the current phase of Palestinian resistance as a time grounded in perceived desperation. He presents a narrative of the suicide bomber as the ultimate victim, and thus someone who has "nothing to lose." It is this characterization that approximates the Palestinian "culture of death" (Reuter, 2002) of the second *intifada* (see also Grossman, 2003; Naaman, 2007). In many ways, Ali shares the same sense of collective depression, despite the fact that he has not experienced these kinds of traumatic losses: "We don't believe that we have a good life," he says, "We live, like, we have no

reason to live." Yet Ali reveals his own ambivalence about the practice of suicide bombing—justifying it as a legitimate tactic on the one hand, but claiming
that it is somehow "wrong" on the other. Desperate circumstances, in Ali's
formulation, require desperate measures, and the use of "human bombs" is
indeed the result of utter desperation.

Ali's characterization of the Palestinian collective experience, as well as the
obstacles of his own life story, reveal powerful perceptions of insecurity,
trauma, and humiliation—all at the hands of Israeli soldiers (see Giacaman,
Abu-Rmeileh, Husseini, Saab, & Boyce, 2007):

> [As a Palestinian in East Jerusalem,] you're so humiliated, discriminated
> against, everywhere…. Checkpoints everywhere you go, soldiers looking
> at you. You are not allowed to look at soldiers. You get beat up if you do
> anything. If you do … you're fucked up. You can't be yourself. And if you
> do, you're in danger. Like a guy was shot next to my house, just because
> a soldier felt like killing somebody…. Like a month ago, I was going
> through the checkpoint, and the soldiers were just training, practicing
> how to shoot and stuff. They were pointing the guns at us, and they
> started shooting but the rifle was empty. They didn't care. It was so scary.

The structure of the conflict, with its ubiquitous checkpoints that serve to reinforce the power differential of the conflict (Gordon, 2008a, 2008b), creates
regular traumas for Ali and essentially blocks his ability to express an identity:
"You can't be yourself," as he says. As an East Jerusalemite, a member of a
subordinated identity group within Israeli society (East Jerusalem was officially
annexed by Israel and its residents granted "permanent residency" but not
citizenship; this annexation remains unrecognized by the international community), Ali's identity is under constant threat by Israelis who seek the de-
Palestinization of Jerusalem and insist on its Jewish identity (Klein, 2004; see
also Romann & Weingrod, 1991).

Ali is particularly influenced not only by his own experiences but also with
stories of Palestinian suffering that proliferate in the larger society—on the
streets between friends and on the Internet:

> A friend of mine was shot—not a friend of mine, someone I know—was
> shot because he was walking in the street during curfew, and he was
> killed. That was really, really terrible. Yeah, he's my friend's best friend.
> It's so fucked up. And you get to hear lots of stories. They show it on the,
> they show it on the Palestinian TV. It's so weird, like, the media's so
> biased. You hear about every suicide bombing, right? But you never
> heard about what the soldiers are doing.

Palestinians like Ali, who are somewhat more distant from the nexus of violent confrontation with Israeli soldiers, know the stories of loss and trauma in the second *intifada* through stories in the media and through friends. The salience of these stories commands a sense of identification, as the existential security of one's *identity*, if not one's actual life, is considered at stake.

Ali experiences only glimpses of identity insecurity—at checkpoints most notably. But the plight of Palestinians in the West Bank resonates with him and forms a crucial part of his own narrative. Identifying the West Bank as "the most dangerous place you can live," he explains the inherent insecurity of daily existence there:

> 'Cause you never know what happens, even if you are in the middle of your house. An F-16 could just come and shoot! They bomb houses. Little babies get killed with their family. It's so scary. There's this guy, Ahmed, he's a singer, a Palestinian singer. There's a song about a little girl that was on the roof of her house, and the Israeli soldiers were shooting and she was shot and died. He made a song about her. She's like an innocent little girl that had nothing to do with anything! I think she was 5 or 4. Yeah, it's heartbreaking.

The stories of Palestinian struggle in the *intifada* are extremely salient to Ali, who reports feeling a sense of guilt that, as an East Jerusalemite, he "suffers less" than his West Bank compatriots.

Ali's narrative reveals the significance of stories of collective suffering—and their proliferation in the discourse of contemporary Palestinian society—as fundamental to youth identity development. These stories infuse Ali's personal narrative with its tragic form and tone and its particular ideological setting. Early in its development as an organization, Fatah noted, "Our operations in the occupied territory can never reach the stage of the aspired revolution unless all Palestinian groups are polarized around the revolution" (cited in Harkabi, 1968/2001, p. 130). In spite of his secular and apolitical upbringing, in spite of the discourse of his family—a Westernized family who are pragmatic and not ideological—Ali has indeed become "polarized around the revolution." His life story is saturated with the thematic content of the master narrative that seeks to ensure this polarization.

Perhaps most surprisingly, given the secularism of his family, Ali has appropriated the discourse of political Islam into the ideological setting of his life story:

> And there's this thing in Islam, if someone dies for his own country, he's like, these are the best people. If you die for your country, you go straight

to heaven. That's what we believe. It's in the Koran also.... The whole Islamic population is supposed to fight for Palestine because, you know, there is the prophet Mohammed was there. It's a holy land.

Considering his narrative in the context of his larger social ecology, Ali's identification with political Islam seems unlikely. While refugees and Palestinians in the West Bank and Gaza have experienced great hardships during the second *intifada*, Ali's family has suffered little. They own a profitable business that caters to Westerners in Jerusalem. Ali's mother, with her uncovered hair and her stories of extensive world travels, is clearly a member of the Arab elite. Ali, like his parents, acknowledges that he does not practice Islam. Yet it is precisely his sense of privilege as a Palestinian that makes him all the more motivated to appropriate an Islamist variant of the master narrative of Palestinian identity.

The unanticipated ideological setting of Ali's personal narrative, with its clear connection to a religious nationalist version of the Palestinian master narrative, reveals the success of movements like Hamas in the Palestinian territories. By the second *intifada*, organizations like Hamas had come to quite successfully lure youth to their ideological discourse by presenting an empowering, viable alternative to Fatah, with its perceived corruption. Hamas' provision of social services was central to building a credible movement that could attract youth (Mishal & Sela, 2006).

It is perhaps because Ali feels *incomplete* as a Palestinian, because he feels unable to fully express an identity, that he seeks to appropriate a version of the master narrative that he perceives as most "popular" among his generation—at this particular historical moment[1]. This sense of *inadequacy* as a Palestinian stems both from the uniqueness of his socioeconomic privilege and his status as an East Jerusalemite. The following excerpt from his narrative illustrates:

> The most disturbing thing is, like, little kids, throwing stones. It's like, you see the courage in your people. And I'm really proud of being a Palestinian. I'm *really* proud. It's like, you see men in 8-year-old children. *Men. Real* men.... I live in East Jerusalem, it's different there. I think these children are better than me. Better. Better than me.... They're like men, *real* men.

Ali's sense of *inferiority* as a Palestinian from East Jerusalem—his sense that he does not undergo the same kind of daily trauma that affects Palestinians in

[1] It is noteworthy that the popularity of Hamas declined considerably following the 2007 factional war between Fatah and Hamas in the Gaza Strip. My interview with Ali occurred in the summer of 2003.

the West Bank—likely motivates his identification with a discourse that he *perceives* to represent the master narrative of Palestinian identity. As an elite, he may be shielded from elements of this *experience*, but its master narrative is too compelling to repudiate. It is a narrative, rather, that commands identification in the meaning and purpose it can provide young Palestinians who perceive the powerlessness in their midst. The identification with the master narrative restores power and a sense of agency through its call to resistance and justice.

In sum, Ali's personal narrative closely mirrors the Palestinian master narrative in its tragic form and much of its thematic content. The theme of collective dispossession and loss infuses Ali's account of his life, as he discusses the consequences of life under occupation. Resistance is deployed in his narrative to reverse the sense of powerlessness that results from living in occupation, with its restrictions on life's possibilities. Experiences with the violence associated with the second *intifada* place Ali's narrative in a place of existential insecurity, as he routinely fears for his own life. But, more important, he clearly identifies with the *collective* existential insecurity that frames the master narrative of Palestinian identity, as he expresses the inability to develop an identity that has any value or sustenance in the matrix of social identities in his midst. In his call for a reclamation of the land, Ali delegitimizes Israeli identity by challenging the legitimacy of Israeli sovereignty. Finally, the ideological setting of Ali's life story in an Islamist frame stands in contrast to the ideological context of Ali's upbringing in a secular cosmopolitan family and to the original master narrative of Palestinian liberation, with its secular nationalist focus.

Adara: The Pious Villager

As is customary upon my arrival to Qadas, a small West Bank village under full control of the Palestinian Authority, I am greeted by an entourage of young children, who seem to find great excitement in the arrival of any foreigner. Such is the carefree pace of life in Qadas and the eventlessness of the place. Or perhaps it is the unusual attention I wish to pay to the village's inhabitants, whose lives unfold in relative predictability and insularity, aside from the occasional military incursion from the Israeli army. Summer evenings are spent on the driveway-cum-patio, with delicious mint tea and the requisite smoke of the apple-flavored *nargila*. Winter evenings, the family huddles around the makeshift fire in the TV room, which doubles as a dining room and a bedroom for Adara and her older sister. Lemon trees and spices grow in the family's garden, which serves three generations of the family, with houses stacked on top of one another like Legos in the traditional village method. The family olive grove is a short drive away.

I sleep in the spacious living room on a thin mattress on the floor. Several of the children compete to sleep in the room with me. One memorable night, little Hassan wins the competition, and he is entranced by my laptop, on which I am furiously writing the day's field notes. He brings a CD to me and begs me to let him show me his new favorite game. As the program starts, I am somewhat taken aback by its content. The key characters are Sheik Ahmed Yassin, the Hamas founder and spiritual leader, and Abdel-Aziz Rantisi, the political leader of Hamas. They have both just been assassinated prior to this particular visit in 2004. The goal of the game seems to be to fight the Israeli soldiers before they kill Yassin or Rantisi. Visually, it is stunningly similar to the popular American game, *Grand Theft Auto*. But its contents are far from fantasy in the minds of young Palestinians like Hassan. The game depicts an actual reality for them, and it affords them an early start in learning the content, characters, and configurations of the Palestinian master narrative.

Nowhere is the Palestinian master narrative more resonant than in villages like Qadas. Physically isolated from Israel and the rest of the world, an insular discourse in the service of producing identities of resistance is carefully deployed. Posters of the *shahid* are ubiquitous, as are the flags and symbols of Hamas and Islamic Jihad[2]. The popularity of these organizations and their ideologies is probably enhanced by virtue of the fact that this is a deeply religious place. Nowhere else in Palestine did I witness people waking early to pray at the mosque, or interrupting their daily routines to bow toward Mecca. And nowhere else did I encounter such a proliferation of songs and symbols of Palestinian resistance.

Adara's family describe themselves as refugees from a coastal city occupied by Israel in 1948. The antique key to their home hangs on the wall of their modest home in Qadas. Adara's mother spends most of her time with me lamenting about "the Jews" and what they have done, how they have schemed and robbed the Palestinians of their land and their dignity. In between these diatribes, she implores me to convert to Islam, the "true revelation" and the only possibility for my salvation.

Qadas, then, offers a social ecology in which an Islamist version of the Palestinian master narrative would likely have appeal. Stories of Palestinian struggle and suffering proliferate in the discursive field to which youth are exposed from very young ages. In the midst of this social ecology, 16-year-old Adara, a quiet, deferent young woman, devotedly covered in a *hijab*, like nearly

---

2 As I indicated in Chapter 2, in a return visit to Qadas in 2007, after the violent takeover of the Gaza Strip by Hamas, the Hamas flags that adorned the main street of the village during my earlier fieldwork had been removed. A large poster of Sheik Yassin remained on the street but was faded by the sun.

all the women in her family, has begun to construct her personal narrative and ground it in an ideological setting.

Adara's narrative begins with the forgotten happiness of childhood. Quickly, though, her story assumes the tragic form of the Palestinian master narrative:

> I think when I was a baby I had a good time. But then, I was 5 years, 6 years, at that time it was the occupation, and I became aware of it, and it was so bad.

Adara's political awareness begins at an earlier age than Ali's, and with that awareness the tone of her story becomes grounded in the struggle of life under occupation.

Asked to divide her narrative into chapters, Adara identifies two: a "good" chapter and a "bad" one. Tragically, she says, "I think the bad time is more than the good time." Her first memory reveals the only role the Israeli will assume in her life story—that of a soldier:

> When I was a child, always soldiers were there. They came to our house to take my brother. I remember I was 4 years old. The soldiers came to our house. I was in another room, and they stayed the whole night waiting for my brother to come home. And my mother, she was crying. It was a terrible experience.

As it turns out, it is only one of many encounters with the occupation for Adara and her family, most of whom have chosen exile over the limitations imposed by Israel. But a small number of family members, including Adara, remain in Qadas, forced to reckon with the obstacles of life under daily occupation.

Although she cannot identify a peak experience in her life story, Adara does purport to experience happiness, but that happiness is entirely contingent on the status of the occupation and of Palestinian suffering:

> When I see the news and there will be no people killed from the occupation here in Palestine, I am so happy. I am like, "Oh, it must be like this always." Without killing or the separation wall.

The perpetual descent of Adara's narrative—its abyss—is also rooted in the experience of life under occupation:

> It's extremely hard, the checkpoint. And from 2003, the life is always going to be difficult and complicated, with the separation wall. So we can't go to Jerusalem to visit Al-Aqsa Mosque, to visit other holy sites. So always when you want to go to another city in Palestine, you see the

Jewish settlements, and I feel so bad, when I see the Israeli flag here in
Palestine. Because Palestine is our land.

In this excerpt from Adara's narrative, the connection between the tragic form
of her life story and the difficulty of Palestinian life more generally is explicit,
given the social structure of military occupation. Her connection to the land—
and her sense of alienation from it as a consequence of the occupation and the
Israeli settlements in the West Bank—is also clear.

The experience of the occupation in a place like Qadas—where the population is quite literally caged in by the structure of occupation (Gordon, 2008a,
2008b; Makdisi, 2008; Roy, 2004), with soldiers right outside the gates of
town—commands a method of coping with its daily challenges. For Adara,
drawing and writing are methods she employs to channel her emotional response
to the occupation. She shared with me one of these drawings (Figure 4.1), which
offers a graphic summary of her perception of daily life under Israeli occupation. In this drawing, Adara draws a scene from her daily life that she claims to
have witnessed: a Palestinian being beaten by Israeli soldiers at the checkpoint.
The rings of the Olympic symbol are replaced here by handcuffs, which for
Adara symbolize the imprisonment of the occupation for Palestinians.

In its basic content, then, Adara's life story closely mirrors the master narrative of Palestinian identity, with its focus on cumulative loss and trauma as

FIGURE 4.1 The "Palestine Daily Olympics," by Adara (2005).

the master trope, and tragedy as the guiding tone and form of the story. The ideological content of Adara's narrative also closely conforms to the master narrative. She makes a number of references to dispossession of the land and to the land as legitimately belonging to the Palestinians. Interestingly, though, she is firmly committed to a two-state solution to the conflict and willing to recognize Israel and to concede that the entirety of Mandate Palestine is not a realistic goal for reclamation:

> We are here in Palestine, we are helpless.... We want the world to believe that Palestine is our homeland. Palestine *is* our homeland.... Palestine is our land, so I don't like these feelings [that the conflict creates]. I think that Israel–Palestinian conflict is complicated.... But we are two nations, we must decide to stop killing and live peacefully in the two separated countries in 1967 borders.

Adara longs for the tranquility of life without occupation. As a compromise in her ideological setting, she seems to have exchanged willingness to acknowledge the legitimacy of Israeli identity, as realized in the existence of a Jewish state, with the possibility of emancipation from the occupation. While many other Palestinians in the course of my fieldwork would emphasize that the occupation includes all of Mandate Palestine (like Ali, for example), Adara seeks only the liberation of the territories occupied in 1967. In this way, she is clearly more closely aligned with the secular nationalist ideology of Fatah than the Islamist ideology of Hamas.

A central theme of the master narrative is the existential threat of identity insecurity, as symbolized in structural encounters Palestinians undergo such as the checkpoint (Gordon, 2008a, 2008b). This theme resonates strongly with the experiential content of Adara's narrative, and her drawing reveals the extent to which such *insecurity* is at the forefront of her consciousness as an adolescent. Insecurity consumes her narrative when she identifies the struggles of life under occupation, beginning with her childhood memories of soldiers coming to her house to look for her brother. The fact that the occupation comes to create for youth in Qadas a kind of insecurity and unpredictability is extremely disruptive, socially and psychologically. For, as I have described it, Qadas is a place of great eventlessness. It is a simple village, and lives are lived in relative simplicity. But the occupation introduces a layer of complexity that reverses the "natural" flow of life and reframes the "life space" (Lewin, 1951) of Qadas' inhabitants.

It is not, however, simply stories of the daily life of Qadas' inhabitants that influence the life stories of youths like Adara. Rather, it is the highly effective dissemination of stories throughout Palestine, as noted in the consideration of

Ali's narrative, that serves to ensure an ideological setting, as well as a thematic reproduction, that conforms to the master narrative of Palestinian identity. In discussing her favorite film, Adara describes it as follows:

> It's talking about the Palestinians in 1948 when they are getting, they got out of Palestine and they go to Lebanon and Egypt and Jordan. It talks about the story, and about the soldiers. It talks about the children of Palestine. Some children were lost from their parents. When you see these things, you feel sad about them. Because it's a hard feeling to be without your parents. Maybe the child, his parents are still here in Palestine. Sometimes a family from Israel has taken this baby and made him Israel, Jewish.

In film, then, Palestinian youths like Adara are exposed to the master story of Palestinian identity and to its tragic foundations in the "Catastrophe" (*al-Nakba*) of 1948. The story offers in alluring simplicity the construction of a protagonist (the innocent Palestinian) and an antagonist (the vicious Israeli) that is appealing to youth and that essentially resonates with their daily experience of the occupation, in which the only Israelis they come to know are soldiers. The mechanism of identification and reproduction is, as revealed in Adara's story, *affective*, its contents possessing a deep emotional resonance that constructs social identity and in-group solidarity.

In her engagement with Palestinian literature and poetry as well, Adara comes to internalize the discourse of the Palestinian master narrative:

> I'm reading now a book by a Palestinian writer about Palestine, and about the war here in Palestine and in Lebanon. The writer who wrote this book, it's so nice because he wants to make the people understand what the Israelis want from the Palestinians. Maybe we can understand them, the Israelis. Every story finished in Israel, and the plans Israel has.... When you read the book you can understand many clues about the occupation, from the beginning until now.

> I like the poetry of Mahmoud Darwish.... There's this poem about Israel, he says, "You are stealing my children. You have stolen my whole church with my ancestors, and the land which I cultivated, along with my children, and you have left us with nothing except for these socks." He talks about the true stories, how they have stolen our land. And sometimes our children.

The perception of the conflict as the unjust dispossession of her people's land is firmly secured through her engagement with these texts—these sites of discursive reproduction that are highly effective for both their emotional salience and their resonance with the structural conditions of the occupation itself. Such stories affirm the *imago* (McAdams, 1993) of the Israeli as a brutal, inhuman antagonist acting against the Palestinians.

The most significant family story transmitted from generation to generation in Adara's family is the experience of dispossession in 1948, when her parents were forced to flee their placid seaside village for Qadas. But this story is too vivid, too real and raw for Adara. It is not just an ideological abstraction or the tale of collective loss, like the stories described in the poems of Mahmoud Darwish. It is, rather, a story that arouses great emotion in Adara and in all of her family members, for it is the great tragedy in the narrative of the family. When I ask her about the story, she says, "I don't like this story. Many are crying in this story. And when my parents talk to me about this, they are so sad. And me, too. It is too sad."

We find in Adara's story, still in its formative stages of construction, a connection with a number of stories accessible in the discourse of her particular social ecology. These stories are quite appealing to Adara in their thematic content. They provide a larger perception of group struggle and loss that serves to construct a coherent tragic narrative and to imbue Adara's experiences of life under occupation with collective meaning. The inculcation of a tragic narrative—a narrative that focuses on loss, dispossession, and injustice—is necessary if one is to also cultivate a narrative of resistance, for the two are mutually contingent. Yet in Adara's story we find little in the way of resistance. Instead, Adara seems to possess a kind of resignation to tragedy, or at least to the futility of Palestinian organized resistance. This perception, though not explicitly acknowledged by Adara, is likely connected to something I briefly alluded to earlier: Adara's older siblings, including that brother who was always being hounded by the Israeli army, have all become exiles. They have moved to countries in Europe and North America.

Because of her family's experience with Palestinian resistance—initial involvement followed by resignation and then exile—Adara has perhaps internalized a sense of futility in resistance. Ideologically, as noted before, she supports a two-state solution:

> We need to live peacefully, and to separate the countries in 1967 borders, so that if we can find a good result…. I think this is good for the Palestinians, for Israel. We need this. And of course, without separation wall.

Interestingly, even though Adara strongly supports a two-state solution to the conflict, she purports to identify more with Hamas than with Fatah in terms of her politics. Yet, as she confesses this identification to me, which I do not find surprising given her religiosity and the fact that Hamas has, in fact, provided a number of social services to the youth in Qadas, she seems to do so with a sense of guilt: "I think that [Fatah] is good, but sometimes I feel Hamas."

It is noteworthy that my initial interview with Adara took place in the summer of 2005, before Hamas assumed power in the Palestinian Legislative Council (PLC) and before their forcible takeover of the Gaza Strip created a context in the West Bank in which one could not safely express allegiance to Hamas. But clearly, at this point in her identity development, Adara is more aligned ideologically with Fatah, even if the Islamic nature of Hamas at times appeals to her. Her ideology more closely resembles the classic Palestinian master narrative, with its focus on the liberation of Palestine, without any allusion to religion. Yet, of course, the ideological setting of her life story is only beginning to be constructed, and it remains to be seen the path it will eventually assume.

Adara's story ends with a central message that speaks to the extent to which the master narrative is quite powerfully embedded in her voice and her experience. Describing the theme or message of her story, and the impression that it will have on an audience, Adara describes it as follows:

> [People will think about my story,] there is a nice story. When you read it, you can feel good. You feel you are good now, at first, but then you feel not so good because then you, the whole story about the Palestinians, you can't, you shouldn't feel good in the story about the occupation, the separation wall, about the killing here. About the situation. So it's not so good a story.

Adara's personal narrative is thus a story that was not meant to be a tragedy. It is the story of a good life, with great possibility. Yet the tragedy of collective struggle looms and infuses the story. The story of Palestinian suffering should, in Adara's thinking, create in the audience a sense of sympathy in the tragedy. In this important concluding passage of her narrative, Adara reveals the extent to which her life story is intimately connected to the Palestinian master narrative, with its tragic form and thematic content.

While Adara's life story conforms rather closely to the master narrative in its tone and form, as well as much of its key thematic content, it is worth noting that in two important ways her story diverges from the master narrative. First, there is little in her narrative about resistance. She seems relatively resigned to Palestine's historic loss and willing to compromise for peace. In this way, she already possesses a measure of pragmatism and willingness to transcend the polarization of identities created by conflict. Second, she does not seem to invalidate or to delegitimize Israeli identity. Though she emphasizes time and time again that "Palestine is our land" and that it was taken unjustly, she does not refer to Zionism or to Israeli national identity as explicitly illegitimate. She does not question the existence of Israel, nor does her two-state solution to the conflict suggest that Israel might not exist. On these dimensions, Adara's personal narrative demonstrates points of contestation in the Palestinian master narrative, as the legitimacy of violent resistance and the lack of recognition of Israel have become increasingly interrogated as worthy elements of the narrative over time.

Adara's life story reveals the way in which youth are dynamically engaged with the content of a master narrative as they begin to construct their own personal narratives. Beyond the elements of the master narrative that Adara clearly reproduces, such as its tragic tone or its thematic focus on loss and land dispossession, what is most interesting about her story is its *idiographic complexity*. Without knowing the holistic picture of her life—most notably the encounters with the Israeli army that her older siblings had—it would be difficult to comprehend her surprisingly pragmatic ideological perspective, her willingness to recognize Israel, and her dismissal of resistance as a legitimate response to the occupation. The contrast between the personal narratives of Ali and Adara reveals the ways in which the content of personal narratives cannot always be anticipated by the social ecology of development. Although Adara lives an ideologically insulated life, she is far more pragmatic and open to the possibility of peace and coexistence than Ali, whose privileged status in Palestinian society creates within him a kind of compensatory reaction as he sets his life story in a particular ideology.

Luca: The Christian Fighter

The two stories presented so far have both been the stories of Palestinian Muslim youth. Let us now consider the narrative of a Palestinian Christian youth—someone for whom the Islamist discourse on Palestine, with its calls for an Islamic state, can have no resonance by virtue of its exclusionary ideology. Luca is a 16-year-old from the West Bank city of Bethlehem. The son of a carpenter and small-scale entrepreneur, Luca's life story begins in conflict:

> The first day I was born my parents could not take me to the hospital because it was a Palestinian holiday, where people remember the day the Israelis came.... My father suffered and they both suffered to take me to the hospital in Jerusalem.... The soldiers wouldn't let anybody move, and this was the day my life started. Just my mother only, they wouldn't let my father go to the hospital.

Luca's narrative begins in the social structure of occupation. The fundamental task of getting to the hospital for childbirth is disrupted by the conflict, and his life story thus begins in complete engagement with the conflict.

Luca's narrative assumes in its form immediate tragedy upon his birth and its complications, the story of which has been passed down to him from his parents. As the conflict becomes more psychologically remote, the form of his life story (as revealed by his life-line drawing) briefly ascends and stabilizes. Yet the formal trajectory of Luca's narrative is inevitably downward as it makes a gradual descent toward a present-day nadir. This period of ascent and stability occurs during the first *intifada* and the subsequent aftermath of the Oslo accords. As Luca describes it,

> [The first part of my life] was during the first *intifada*. And the situation was getting better day by day until the peace agreement, and then it's back to normal for 2 or 3 years. And then it got worse and worse until now, and now we have the second *intifada*. I got injured in the second *intifada*.

Luca's story is entirely connected to the political context of his life. His life-line drawing is essentially a map of the conflict itself, perceived through the lens of a young Palestinian. Experientially, he cannot escape the conflict.

The second *intifada*, still raging during our interview in the summer of 2004, is the great nadir of Luca's story. It is a time in which the fragility of his very existence was called into question during the siege on Bethlehem 2 years earlier. That period of reoccupation is vividly imprinted into Luca's life story:

> You know when they occupied Bethlehem we can't go out of our homes. So I was riding my bike and a jeep was passing by. He called me, the soldier. I ran as much as I could, but there was something in the way, and I hit it, and flew in the air before I came down. This is one of the times I got injured.

The events of Luca's life which determine the form of his narrative cannot be dissociated from the master narrative of Palestinian identity, or its ideological setting, for Luca's experiences mirror the experiential content of the master narrative itself.

In describing his life during the second *intifada*, Luca highlights Palestinian suffering and insecurity:

> We don't have anything. We don't have zoos, parks, nothing.... And it's a terrible life. It's like a jail. You can't do anything. Even in jail, people

don't worry about their food. But us, we're worried about our food, how we're going to drink water. The Israelis control everything in our lives.... And now, the new, what's called the new separation wall, makes a big difference. Smaller jail. Every time, smaller and smaller. They're trying to cage us in. Until we just disappear.

The "abnormality" of Palestinian life is well represented in this excerpt from Luca's narrative, with his insistence on the deprivation of Palestinian life under Israeli occupation and its comparison to imprisonment. But what is perhaps most thematically significant in this excerpt, in terms of his story's connection to the master narrative, is the pervading sense of existential insecurity that is revealed. The perception that the Palestinians indeed have no control in their own lives, that the "Israelis control everything," including the water, leaves Luca with a sense of threatened existence. His conviction that the separation barrier just creates another phase in the Israeli attempt to eradicate the Palestinians—"until we disappear"—reveals the extent to which he identifies with the pervasive sense of existential insecurity in the Palestinian master narrative. Yet this identification is secured in the structure of the conflict itself, in the concreteness of the separation barrier and its location inside of the Green Line, in the checkpoints and closures that complicated Luca's very birth (see Gordon, 2008a, 2008b).

Existential insecurity may lie at the root of Luca's narrative, with the challenge of getting to the hospital for his own birth, but it has been consistently affirmed during the course of the second *intifada*. Describing life under occupation, Luca says,

It's terrible. You can't imagine, everyday, how we go to school. And whether we're going to school or not. If the school is destroyed or not. Even if we're in school, we hear shooting, we are confused all day, we can't concentrate, we don't understand anything. But Palestinians have a really hard life. You're going to wake up the next day, and the house is going to get blown up. You know, it's always, Israelis always say it's a mistake. "We hit this house, we thought it was a terrorist house." ... The beginning of the second *intifada*, they were shooting a lot, and my house was shot over 30 bullets. It came in the windows. It didn't hit anyone. There's some nights when we didn't sleep at all.

Luca must deal with the uncertainty of daily life as a young Palestinian. Schools may come and go, as will stray bullets and even houses. With this uncertainty in daily life and its experiential content comes a perception of existential insecurity, of life in constant threat.

As Luca describes his motivation to engage in intergroup contact with Israelis, the thematic proximity of his personal narrative to the master narrative is striking:

> I want to show all the people that Palestinians are suffering. The Israelis occupied our land. They don't have any rights, no human rights. They use all the ways to torture us. Plus, freedom fighters are not terrorists because they are fighting for the country, and we don't have an army. I [want] to show all the people, Israelis, Americans, Jews, any nationality, I want to show them all what Palestinians are actually going through, how much we suffer.

The unjust dispossession of the Palestinians from their land, despite the fact that Luca and his family indeed remain in possession of their original home in Bethlehem, is a central message that Luca seeks to communicate in his life story. In Luca's narrative, the Palestinian cause is a just cause, and actions against Israel are legitimate, justifiable, and cannot credibly be labeled as "terrorism." In Luca's story, Palestinians suffer under the harsh, unjust Israeli occupation, and resistance is both normal and justifiable. Consistent with the Palestinian master narrative, Luca is determined to reveal the righteousness of the Palestinian cause to all whom he encounters (including me). His personal narrative is a vessel for this cause, his document of lived experience a testament to the collective struggle of his group.

Speaking more directly of his personal experiences in the second *intifada*, Luca identifies being an adolescent during this historical moment as beneficial to his own personal connection to his social identity as a Palestinian:

> [The *intifada*,] it's a bad thing, but it's a good thing because it made, the second *intifada* made me stand for Palestine. The first *intifada* I was small, I didn't understand much. But now, I like understand more about it. People are dying for their country, for Palestine, and I think the second *intifada* was good too because people are fighting, not like the first *intifada* because now we have suicide bombers and the first *intifada* was just throwing rocks and small things. And now, we have small weapons.... Plus the whole world gets to know what's happening now in Palestine.

Luca identifies the second *intifada* as formative in his connection to his national identity, which he sees as extremely beneficial. He also views the second *intifada* as a better and more effective demonstration of Palestinian resistance, revealing his connection to the ideology of active Palestinian resistance as a method of opposition to the occupation. He sees the first *intifada* as a passive movement in which the Palestinians did not possess weapons and did not use the suicide bombers, which he sees as more effective.

Clearly, then, Luca identifies strongly with the thematic content of the master narrative of Palestinian identity, including a focus on the unjust dispossession of the land, the existential insecurity of Palestinian identity under occupation, and the legitimacy of armed resistance. Though he does not explicitly delegitimize Israeli identity or call for the destruction of Israel, he implicitly does in his argument for the unjust dispossession of Palestinian land. Not surprisingly, his is the discourse of a secular nationalist Palestinian resistance. As a Christian, he cannot identify with the Islamist discourse that has emerged as a viable competitor for ideological identification among youth. Yet, at the same time, as a religious minority in Palestine, in a discursive field that has become increasingly Islamist, there is a way in which, like Ali (but for very different reasons), Luca has to "prove" he is fully Palestinian.

In Israel, the Palestinian Christians are often described as more "Westernized" and "moderate" (see Horenczyk & Munayer, 2007). Many Jewish Israelis would confide in me over the course of my fieldwork that it is the Muslims who are really "the problem." So for youth in the process of constructing a personal narrative that is somehow acceptable in the frame of one's larger social identity, being a Palestinian Christian poses a unique challenge. The call to identify with the master narrative can perhaps be even greater among Christian youth who, like Luca, struggle with their minority status within Palestinian society. In the classic social identity paradigm, members of a minority group may use the strategy of individual mobility to counteract the perception of lower status (Tajfel & Turner, 1979). In the context of a majority Muslim population, Luca may in fact employ strategies of ideological identification that place him at an equal status to Palestinian Muslims. His appropriation of the discourse of the master narrative may be influenced by his minority status within Palestinian society.

However, we can only speculate on Luca's particular *motivations* to construct his personal narrative in close proximity to the master narrative. It is important to note that the social structure of the occupation does not discriminate based on religious identity in Palestine, which is quite evident in Luca's life story. The reason that his personal narrative is so thematically proximate to the master narrative may speak more to the uniformity of Palestinian experience in the context of occupation. Thus, Luca's narrative may say more about the broad psychological consequences of occupation than about his minority status within Palestinian society.

Luca's account actually supports this latter interpretation—this notion that the experiences of contemporary Palestinian youth do not differ along the lines of religious identity. When confronted directly with the question of how being Christian impacts his experience of life in Palestine, Luca says,

> I am the one guy that was throwing rocks, everyone throws rocks, because you want to do something for your country. It doesn't matter if someone's Muslim or Christian, or this myth like only the Muslims are involved in the shooting and fighting, it's not true, 'cause we're all Palestinians.

Luca's religious identity as a Christian is, at least at this moment in his life story construction, quite remote in his narrative. It is nothing more than a linguistic marker of identity; it has no experiential impact on the substance of his story as he currently frames it for me. According to Luca's narrative, being a Palestinian is about *suffering* as a Palestinian in solidarity, regardless of one's religion, and actively *resisting* the Israeli occupation.

Luca's narrative highlights the interesting additional challenge in identity development that exists for Palestinian Christians. As a minority group, they must negotiate their identifications with a master narrative of Palestinian identity that at times excludes them. For youth at a particular moment of identity formation, the need to feel part of the larger national group, to fully identify with *and be recognized* as a member of the social identity of "Palestinian," may outweigh other identifications and consume the entirety of the life story narrative. The need to belong is simply too significant, especially when existential threat is a daily component of lived experience.

On the one hand, Luca's narrative illustrates this process for Palestinian Christian youth—this need to internalize the master narrative in order to fully "pass" as a Palestinian. Yet on the other hand, Luca's story, and its experiential content in particular, demonstrates the extent to which the structure of the conflict possesses quite salient effects on the daily lives of Palestinian youth, irrespective of religious identity or community. Bethlehem may be a "Christian" city (it is not, in fact, majority Christian but has a Christian identity because of its significance to Christianity), but it is still a city in the occupied West Bank. It remains a city surrounded by Israel's massive separation barrier, nowhere more visually ominous than at the entrance to the city. It remains a city in which the Israeli military presence hovers, a city that has been witness to significant activity, and even more significant economic impact, during the second *intifada*.

The narrative tone of Luca's story closely mirrors that of Ali and Adara in its emphasis on the tragedy of Palestinian existence. Ideologically, we saw in Adara the seemingly genuine desire for a peaceful resolution of the conflict, as well as a de-emphasis on Palestinian resistance in her narrative. In Luca's story, we see the same kind of support for resistance that we witnessed in Ali's narrative. As I queried Luca about his thoughts on suicide bombers toward the end of our interview, he revealed the frustration and rage that underlie the tragic tone of the Palestinian master narrative:

> [The suicide bombers,] they're depressed. *I'm* depressed. I'm here,
> I don't know. I feel that I'm going to explode.... I don't know, it makes
> me angry.... I would kill any Israeli, I don't care. Being Palestinian, and
> living the Palestinian life, going through hundreds of checkpoints,
> getting beaten by soldiers ...

Luca's narrative is thus more than merely tragic and despondent in its tone and form; it is on the brink of an overwhelmingly furious anger. This anger is, for Luca, channeled into his support of armed acts of resistance.

In sum, Luca's personal narrative closely mirrors the tone, form, thematic content, and ideological setting of the Palestinian master narrative. Like the master narrative, Luca's life story assumes the form of a tragedy. This form is retained by the history of existential insecurity and sense of loss that pervade his personal narrative. Luca expresses strong support for armed resistance against the occupation, but the ideological setting of his story conforms more closely to the traditional secular nationalist ideology of Fatah than its Islamist competitors. Luca's Christian identity assumes a role in solidifying this ideological setting, but it may also motivate a strong identification with and reproduction of the Palestinian master narrative, given that it confers minority status within Palestinian society. As in the cases of Ali and Adara, Luca's narrative sensitizes us to the idiographic complexity of young lives and their relationship to a complex social ecology and its matrix of social identities, with the differential status and meaning associated with those social categories of identity.

Lubna: The Survivor

At one point or another during the course of the second *intifada*, most Palestinian cities have witnessed some level of Israeli reoccupation, with soldiers and tanks taking control of the streets, brutal fighting between soldiers and fighters, and the imposition of a strict curfew. Lubna, a 15-year-old Muslim from Nablus, has, like Luca, had to endure life under such circumstances.

The daughter of secular, professional parents, Lubna is, like many of the youth in this study, a subject of globalization. She spends most evenings on the Internet, chatting with friends. She speaks fluent English; she does not wear a *hijab*. But she lives with vivid memories of some of the greatest challenges the conflict has created, as Nablus has been the site of many Israeli incursions during the second *intifada*. Like many residents of Nablus, she has come to view her life with great unpredictability and without the guarantee of continuity, not just for her own threatened existence but also for those of her friends, many of whom have either been imprisoned or "martyred."

Prompted by the explanation of my research, Lubna begins the telling of her life story by spontaneously sharing the story of a book she is currently reading:

> I hope that you will tell people what you saw here. It's a coincidence because yesterday I was reading a book that has maybe 200 pages.
> I finished it in 2 days, so it was really good. It was about two boys. One of them was real cool, he was a singer, and his brother was, his personality was so weak, so when the *intifada* came, everything was different.
> The cool boy went to fight against the Israelis, and the brother, he lost his cat and went looking for it in a settlement, but there he was arrested by the Israelis. And soldiers caught him and he had to stay in jail. After he went out of it, he became a different person. He was, he had a real strong personality and then he started working with the ambulance so he saw many bodies and he hated very much the Israelis.... His village that was near the great wall in Israel. So they gave him a paper that their house would be destroyed. The wall has to be! A tractor came and destroyed their house, and a little girl, she was British, she stood in front of the tractor but it ran over her and crushed her.... The boy tried to escape from the soldiers in the ambulance, but they shot him, and his father said, "My little boy is a martyr."
>
> After I read this story, I was just thinking so much about our situation. I kept thinking, why this was the end? All the stories are supposed to end, "They lived happily ever after." But the only answer I thought was that this was our life, and the suffering never ends in Palestine. Welcome to home.

The narration of Lubna's life story is framed by her engagement with literature that goes to great length to reproduce the Palestinian master narrative, with its emphasis on perpetual loss, powerlessness, and interminable suffering. The boy who immediately joined the Palestinian resistance movement as a "fighter" was "cool," while his brother found in the imprisonment rite of passage a "strong personality." The prison served as an important site of education and socialization for him (see Barber, 1999b; Peteet, 1994). And the story essentially contains within it almost every symbolic encounter connected to Palestinian suffering, at least as constructed during the second *intifada*: the wall, the bulldozer, land confiscation, and brutal disrespect for human life on the part of the Israelis (with the allusion to the Rachel Corrie incident in which a young American woman was killed while serving as a "human shield" to try to stop the demolition of a Palestinian home in Rafah in the southern Gaza Strip).

That a 15-year-old from Nablus, whose life story is saturated with memories of direct confrontation with the conflict, should be consumed with such stories is hardly surprising. The deployment of these stories in Palestinian society serves not just the purpose of inculcating the master narrative. Rather, it also provides affirmation of a collective experience with the structure of the conflict. It is comforting for Lubna to learn that Palestinians as a collective suffer and struggle as she does.

Let us also not omit the important context of her narration and the way in which this excerpt from her narrative began: "I hope that you will tell people what you saw here." Introducing her own personal narrative with the story of this book says much about what it is she wants to communicate *to me*. In fact, in no other interview was the construction of the *interview event* more apparent to me than with Lubna. I draw the reader's attention to this to remind the reader that each life story was narrated with the knowledge of my own identity and what that identity meant to those being interviewed. It is clear that Lubna hoped that I would faithfully communicate the suffering of Palestinians in a way that could elicit great sympathy in my primarily Western audience.

Lubna's life story begins at a low point. In a story similar to that of Luca, Lubna's father could not be present at her birth. He was, in fact, in prison. The tone of her narrative is thus grounded in a sense of loss and injustice—the loss of having a "normal" birth situation, unjustly deprived to her because of the conflict. Lubna is a child of the first *intifada*. But since the culmination of that uprising is viewed as the partial liberation of Palestine, with the creation of the PA and semiautonomy in the West Bank and Gaza, Lubna interprets the end of the *intifada* around age 12 as the peak experience in her narrative—a time of possibility for the end of Palestinian suffering.

The time of hope and optimism that occurred after the first *intifada* was extremely short lived in Lubna's narrative. She describes the descent of her story as beginning with the second *intifada*:

And then at 12 years old, there was the *intifada*. I was in the sixth grade. I remember when it started, we had to, everything got closed. We didn't go to school for 3 weeks. I was at my grandmother's house, and I saw the picture of the Al-Aqsa mosque, that Sharon went there. I couldn't explain what was happening in my mind.... All I was thinking of was when will this end?

For Lubna, the beginning of the second *intifada* would commence a dark and tragic chapter in her life story, one replete with stories of fear, suffering, and existential insecurity. They are also stories of loss—loss of friends to imprisonment and "martyrdom," loss of freedom, and loss of childhood itself:

> I remember there was a funeral of a martyr. It came next to our house, and, so, you know, the guys always hold the guns and start shooting because they are angry, so I was very frightened and, I don't know, it was the first gun shooting I heard, because it was near our house.... It was really tough to live in the sixth grade. In school you would hear the gun shooting. The principal would come in and say, "Come on, you have to go home now." And maybe we get really happy because the school ended but deep in us, it's tough. To know the reason is not good.... And then I was in seventh grade, in 2002, we had the invasion.

Lubna's memories of life during the second *intifada* are consumed by fear and insecurity, as well as the perceived unjust deprivation of a "normal" adolescent life, like being able to attend school. But no experience would be more traumatic for Lubna—nothing would arouse greater feelings of existential insecurity—than the 2002 invasion and reoccupation of Nablus by the Israeli army.

"The tanks are coming," Lubna says as she recalls precisely the moment at which the invasion began. She could hear them in the distance. Nablus was gripped by a frenzy of fear. In her mind, her death and the death of those dear to her were imminent:

> They're going to kill the people from Nablus.... So it was scary.... And then there was many guns shooting. And the bullets were powerful because it sounded really loud. And there was explosions, the electricity gone. A long night. After the long night, I didn't want to walk out. The first day we had to stay in the room. Because everybody knew that if you open the window and they saw you... So we had to stay in there [in the house]. It was very scary. The first day we had food. The first day it was fresh. The second day it became a bit stale. The refrigerator was off, 'cause of the electricity. My mother made beans. It was good, but after a couple of days it started to get bad. So soon there was no food and everyone was so hungry.

The tone of fear in Lubna's narrative is rooted in the concrete experience of existential insecurity as a consequence of the Israeli invasion of Nablus. The invasion left Lubna psychologically scarred, with images of dead bodies in the Old City once the incursion had ended and the curfew lifted. Images of death and destruction pervade Lubna's life story, given the trauma of this and other military incursions into Nablus that have been frequent since the start of the *intifada*:

> The most part I remember [after the invasion], when I went to my school, almost destroyed.... You know, the maps, they see Palestine, they cut it off. In the playground, there were tanks and they took all the people there that they want to take to jail. They stay there, and ruin the playground. And now the school will have to clean all of it.

A once stable institution and the most significant physical site in her social ecology apart from home—the school—now lay in ruins, with the maps of Palestine desecrated, symbolizing for Lubna the desire to negate Palestinian identity entirely.

Unfortunately, the 2002 invasion of Nablus was not a momentary disruption in Lubna's life story. Since that invasion, there have been numerous others, and more memories of fear, death, and destruction. As a consequence, no trope is more significant in Lubna's narrative than that of existential insecurity. Her life as an adolescent under military occupation and almost constant siege has cultivated within her the consciousness of a fragile existence and a threatened identity. She has witnessed, time and time again, the loss of friends either to imprisonment or death.

In its tragic form and its traumatic tone of fear and insecurity, Lubna's story conforms closely to the Palestinian master narrative. The tropes of loss, dispossession, and existential insecurity are as pervasive in her personal narrative as they are in the master narrative of Palestinian identity. She summarizes the sense of injustice constructed by the Israeli occupation in a desperate plea for the restoration of rights and dignity to Palestinians:

> The Palestinian children always have the wish to live and the right to eat, to travel, to live freely in their cities and their country, and like every other people in the world, just wish to go to the playground.... Why we always ask for the rights which we should have? For a school to study in, to be safe in there.... Everyday we ask God to bring us back our liberty..., and we are always thinking about the idea of my friend and his arrested brother or sister.

Lubna identifies strongly with the idea of injustice embedded within the Palestinian narrative (Said, 1979). She views the continued occupation as a source of fear, insecurity, and trauma in her own life story, as in the stories of those around her.

Interestingly, her narrative diverges from the master narrative in two key ways, quite similarly to Adara. First, she speaks little of resistance as a legitimate response to the occupation. But she is conflicted. She is torn between the ideology of her parents, who are "living peacefully," as she says, and her friends, who "live the resistance." Her narrative contains little in the way of expressing support for any kind of armed resistance, and she advocates for a negotiated two-state solution to the conflict. Lubna's internalized pragmatism about the conflict is summarized in this excerpt from her life story:

> So maybe I'm not against the negotiations, and I'm also not against the self-defense.... It's our destiny, to live side by side with Israel. If you want to live peacefully, you have to give up some things.... You know my mother once told me, it's like Japan, when they were beaten in the second World War, after the two bombs in Hiroshima and Nagasaki, they gave up. It's not that they are weak, but they were fighting against the strongest power in the world. So they gave up. Until now they're beating many countries in economics, cars.... I'm not against to go and fight, but not like people do it sometimes. If they have to do this thing, they can go to the settlements.

Though she identifies the Palestinian cause as just, she also seems to acquiesce to its inevitable failure, at least in its original ideological vision. Thus, the second way in which her personal narrative appears to diverge from the classic master narrative of Palestinian identity centers on her legimitization of an Israeli national identity. Lubna acknowledges the existence of Israel and implicitly accepts its right to exist and, hence, the legitimacy of an Israeli identity "side by side" with a Palestinian identity. These ideological convictions naturally lead her to seek opportunities for intergroup contact with Israelis, for she genuinely believes in the possibility of a peaceful negotiated solution.

Lubna's life story is the tragic narrative of a young Palestinian whose life experience has been characterized by unpredictability and existential uncertainty. Hers is a life course interrupted, with curfews and schools in ruins. While these traumatic experiences have guaranteed the internalization of key elements of the Palestinian master narrative—its tragic form and thematic content—there are fundamental ways in which Lubna's ideological identifications diverge from the master narrative. Owing mostly to the influence of her pragmatic, secular parents, Lubna has come to see Palestinian resistance as a losing cause and one that seems only to increase the suffering of Palestinians. Yet, as the ideology of her peers competes for attention in Lubna's narrative, she remains conflicted, the ideological setting of her personal narrative not fully formed.

Summary: The Cultural Psychology of Palestinian Youth

To understand the cultural psychology of contemporary Palestinian youth, we must query the process by which they come to narrate their life experience. As I emphasized in Chapter 1, my view of cultural psychology is one that privileges the concept of narrative, for its ability to link individuals to their participation in some larger unit of social practice. As youth begin to construct individual life stories, they employ a discourse of credibility and fidelity to the master narratives of social identity with which they identify. One of the central questions I seek to address in this book concerns the *proximity* of these personal narratives to master narratives of collective history, identity, and experience. In this empirical project, we come to view the ways in which youth are simultaneously *products* and *producers* of a master narrative, architects of an evolving discourse that provides a sense of meaning, unity, and purpose to their participation in some collective (Bruner, 1990; Cohler, 1982; McAdams, 1990, 1997).

In the case of Palestinian youth, I am particularly interested in the ways in which their membership in a group living in an active, multigenerational conflict under military occupation commands a particular conformity to the master narrative. But the personal narratives of youth reveal the dynamic relationship between culture and narrative, calling into question essentialized versions of cultural psychology (Gjerde, 2004). What is most evident in the narratives of youth is a *process* of narrative *engagement*—an active experimentation with the appropriation of certain elements of a master narrative over others. Furthermore, the narratives of youth reveal the dubiousness of the concept of a monolithic master narrative itself, for their stories suggest the active rescripting of several elements related to legitimacy and ideology.

Representative of the other personal narratives of Palestinian youth I have collected over the years, the stories of Ali, Adara, Luca, and Lubna reveal points of both convergence and divergence with a master narrative of Palestinian identity. As adolescents in the midst of negotiating ideological identifications, consolidating commitments, and scripting preliminary life stories, they are in the process of constructing a narrative that will anchor the course of their lives. The personal narratives they ultimately come to construct will serve as an interpretive lens in their daily lives, filtering their cognitions, emotions, and behaviors through a matrix of personal and social meaning (Barber, 2009b; Bruner, 1990; Cohler, 1982; Hammack, 2008; McAdams, 1990, 1996, 2001).

Most fundamentally, the youth in this study have internalized the central historical narrative of Palestinian identity that has framed their collective struggle for national liberation in the twentieth and early twenty-first centuries.

This narrative is a decidedly tragic one, replete with tropes of loss and unjust dispossession (e.g., Said, 1994). This sense of loss is connected not only to the physical land itself, but also to the perception of existential threat that the trauma of continued loss has cultivated. Although these youth all identify with the historical narrative of Palestinian dispossession, it is perhaps the trope of existential insecurity that is most salient in the stories of contemporary youth, their lives in relatively regular danger owing to Israeli military operations in the occupied territories since the start of the second *intifada* (Pettigrew, 2003).

Interestingly, two central themes in the master narrative were at least partially contested among youth in the study. The legitimacy of armed struggle and resistance to the Israeli occupation is not universally appropriated by youth as they construct their personal narratives. Though few are outright critical of Palestinian resistance, they all allude to the problematic nature of it, particularly in the common form of suicide bombing it has taken during the second *intifada*. Some youth, like Adara and Lubna, seek a peaceful, negotiated solution that does not require armed struggle. But even these youth are conflicted, at times arguing that resistance is "self-defense" for acts of violence committed against Palestinians by Israel. From their internal conflict about the legitimacy of resistance naturally flows an acceptance of Israeli identity. That is, to concede that resistance and the liberation of all of Mandate Palestine is futile, as youth like Adara and Lubna do, and to embrace the possibility of a peaceful resolution through negotiation and a two-state solution, one necessarily acknowledges the legitimacy of Israeli identity. So the second significant point of divergence from the master narrative of Palestinian identity seems to center on a willingness to acknowledge the existence of a Jewish state and an Israeli national identity, so long as such acknowledgment is reciprocated by the Israeli willingness to legitimize Palestinian identity.

An additional interesting source of divergence among youth centered on their internalization of either a traditional *secular* narrative of liberation—the ideological setting of the Palestinian master narrative as it emerged through the discourse of Fatah and the PLO in the 1960s—or an *Islamist* narrative that has emerged with the growth of organizations like Hamas and Islamic Jihad beginning in the 1980s. Interestingly, among the cases presented here, it was Ali, the son of very secular Muslims, who had internalized the Islamist narrative of liberating all of Mandate Palestine in the name of Islam. Adara, the daughter of devout Muslims from a very religious village, seemed to set her personal narrative more in the secular ideology of Fatah, recognizing the religious pluralism of the Palestinian people.

The ideological setting of Ali's personal narrative may represent a kind of compensatory reaction to his parents' secularism (like Luca's to his religious identity), which he perceives as unpopular at the time of narrating his life story to me, as well as to his own sense of privilege within Palestinian society. Thus, he may feel the need to somehow "prove" his Palestinian identity through appropriation of the most polarizing discourse available, for he does not truly "feel" like an authentic Palestinian. Regardless of the individual motives for Ali and Adara, though, what the contrast in their stories reveals is the extent to which the *ideological basis* of the Palestinian master narrative is very much in question among contemporary youth. The ideology of Fatah has not provided the kinds of significant gains that Palestinians have longed for, and the way in which they have run the PA is sharply criticized among Palestinians, now that the immunity of Yasser Arafat has vanished with his erasure from the political scene (see Lybarger, 2007). As a result, many Palestinians are currently exploring the possibility of Hamas, whether or not they embrace its exclusionary Islamist narrative. Youth are increasingly exposed to this alternate narrative, and the ideological setting of the Palestinian master narrative itself is thus a point of collective contestation.

In spite of elements of divergence from the master narrative among youth in this study, we can readily see the ways in which the Palestinian master narrative is reproduced in the personal narratives of youth, particularly in its tragic tone and form. The mechanism of reproduction may be discursive, as youth engage with the stories available in their immediate surround, but it is also secured in the continued confrontation with the structural conditions of the conflict that Palestinian youth continue to endure (Gordon, 2008a, 2008b; Makdisi, 2008). That is, the master narrative of Palestinian identity is not *merely* reproduced through discourse, though we see in the stories of these youth powerful identifications with the stories available in their social ecologies. It is, rather, reproduced and rendered salient in the experiences with *personal* loss and insecurity that characterize the ongoing activity of the Israeli occupation. The stories of youth are saturated with intimate experience with the conflict itself, even among those who encounter the structure of the conflict with somewhat less frequency, such as Ali.

In sum, the cultural psychology of Palestinian youth is characterized by a dynamic engagement with a tragic master narrative of collective identity. Its contents resonate with youth because of their continued personal experience with the Israeli occupation. The personal narratives of youth in their early stages of formation suggest a strong identification with the master narrative, both in terms of form and content, and the ideological settings of these life stories reveal possibilities for both the reproduction of intergroup conflict and its possible amelioration through the ideology of a new generation. Yet these narratives also reveal important ways in which the master narrative is currently contested among youth, and the ways in which the master narrative itself might be evolving toward a less polarized position ideologically, perhaps mirroring the increase in pragmatism that has framed the general evolution of Palestinian politics under the PLO and Fatah-led PA (Mohamad, 2001).

Yet the structure of the conflict remains, with its barriers to economic and social development in the Palestinian territories (Gordon, 2008a, 2008b; Kelman, 2007; Pettigrew, 2003; Roy, 2004). The development of Palestinian identity therefore relies upon the conflict and its reproduction, for it is the conflict that consumes its master narrative, as well as the identities of youth (Elbedour, Bastein, & Center, 1997). The narratives of Palestinian youth presented here reveal this deep connection between identity and the conflict, between self and context, between person and culture, cocreated through discourse and social practice, and embodied in narratives of personal and social identity.

5

"I Had a War With Myself": Palestinian-Israeli Youth and the Narration of Hyphenated Identities

In his semiautobiographical novel, *Dancing Arabs* (2004), Sayed Kashua's "antihero" protagonist, a young Palestinian citizen of Israel, reflects on his experience at a predominantly Jewish high school:

> In twelfth grade I understood for the first time what '48 was. That it's called the War of Independence. In twelfth grade I understood that a Zionist was what we called *Sahyuni*, and it wasn't a swearword. I knew the word. That's how we used to curse one another. I'd been sure that a *Sahyuni* was a kind of fat guy, like a bear. Suddenly I understood that Zionism is an ideology. In civics lessons and Jewish history classes, I started to understand that my aunt from Tulkarm is called a refugee, that the Arabs in Israel are called a minority. In twelfth grade I understood that the problem was serious. I understood what a national homeland was, what anti-Semitism was. I heard for the first time about "two thousand years of exile" and how the Jews had fought against the Arabs and the British.... In twelfth grade, the kids in my class started running in the parking lot, getting into shape for the army. They were taken to all sorts of installations and training camps, and I received a bus pass and a ticket to the Israel Museum. Sometimes soldiers in uniform came to our

school to talk with students, and I wasn't allowed to take part. Our teacher always apologized. He was embarrassed to have to tell me it wasn't for me. In twelfth grade I understood I wouldn't be a pilot even if I wanted to be, not only because I wasn't fit and my grades weren't good enough. There was no way they would even call me up for the screening tests. I sure had a good laugh at my father. (pp. 117–118)

As Kashua's (2004) protagonist illustrates, Palestinian citizens of Israel navigate two distinct narratives of identity as they encounter the "weight of the hyphen" (Zaal, Salah, & Fine, 2007) and come to realize their status as a subordinate minority in Israel. Kashua's protagonist does not fully internalize the discourse of his larger society until the twelfth grade, when he becomes aware only through his encounter with Jewish Israelis of the narrative of the dominant culture.

In this chapter, I examine the personal narratives of Palestinian-Israeli youth using two valuable theoretical concepts. First, I call upon the idea of *hyphenated selves*, recently developed by Michelle Fine, Selcuk Sirin, and their colleagues in a pathbreaking study of Muslim-American youth post-9/11 (Fine & Sirin, 2007; Sirin & Fine, 2007, 2008; Sirin et al., 2008; Zaal et al., 2007). Second, I employ Elli Schachter's (2004, 2005) conception of an identity *configuration* to examine the narratives of Palestinian-Israeli youth as they negotiate disparate discourses in Israeli society. Both of these theoretical frameworks provide a useful way of making meaning of the life story narratives of Palestinian-Israeli youth—narratives that are uncomfortably positioned within the larger identity politics of Israel and Palestine.

Certain key features of the Palestinian-Israeli story are readily apparent in the excerpt from Kashua's (2004) novel: exposure to disparate narratives, maintained through segregation of Arabs from Jews; and constrained life course possibilities for Arab citizens, who are kept at a distance from fundamental identity building institutions like the IDF. The collective Palestinian-Israeli story is thus one of *exclusion*—from the dominant culture, its national narrative, its institutions, its normative life course. Yet, territorially, the Palestinian citizens are a part of Israel, and thus their master narrative is characterized by the frustration of exclusion and all of its implications for their own life course possibilities.

The Master Narrative of Palestinian-Israeli Identity

Beyond exclusion, the story of the Palestinian citizens of Israel is a tale of dispossession and containment, of quiet struggle and determination, and of prodigious identity complexity. Unlike the Palestinian narrative, it is not a story of resistance and national liberation. The roughly 160,000 Palestinians who remained in the territory that became Israel overnight in 1948 underwent a radical disruption in their master narrative of identity. One night, a majority in their homeland; the next, a minority in a new one. Discursively stripped of their Palestinian identity through the creation of a new identity label—"Israeli Arab" (Rabinowitz & Abu-Baker, 2005), the new "Palestinians in Israel" were granted citizenship but were ruled by a military administration until 1966 (Tessler & Grant, 1998). Though they secured citizenship and its essential benefits, there were and continue to be a number of ways in which they suffer from institutional discrimination and unequal status compared to Israel's Jewish citizens (e.g., Peleg, 2004; Sa'di, 2004; Tessler & Grant, 1998).

Since 1948, the Palestinian citizens of Israel thus experienced the trauma of *al-Nakba*, the "Catastrophe," with all of its displacement and dispossession (Sa'di & Abu-Lughod, 2007). Families were split into pieces, with members fleeing to neighboring countries, all of which remained hostile to Israel. The consequence was devastating for families, who could not reunite (Rabinowitz & Abu-Baker, 2005). Their new life in the Israeli state was characterized by military rule of their towns and villages, with lack of freedom in mobility.

Their story since the end of military administration in 1966 has been one of quiet struggle for equal rights inside Israel. Though as a group their efforts have nearly always been nonviolent (Hareven, 2002), they experienced two quite significant further traumas at the hands of the Israeli military. The first of these occurred on March 30, 1976. Protesting the state's expropriation of Arab lands, which had continued unabated since 1948, organized groups of Palestinian citizens in several locales came together (and have every year since) in the event known as "Land Day." That fateful day was met with a state response that resulted in numerous Arab deaths.

In October of 2000, just after the initiation of the second Palestinian *intifada*, Palestinian citizens organized protests in the north of Israel. These protests were met with a harsh Israeli military response, resulting in the death of 12 young Arab citizens, one of whom was a politically active alumnus of Seeds of Peace. In bitter irony, he was struck down while wearing his green Seeds of Peace T-shirt. The "October events," as they are commonly called, represented a major trauma for the Palestinian citizens of Israel (Eqeiq, 2002), a moment at which their helplessness and existential insecurity were once again highlighted and proven salient to a new generation of youth (Rabinowitz & Abu-Baker, 2005).

The story of the Palestinian Israelis is thus, like the story of the Palestinians, a tragedy. Yet its tragic slope is somehow not quite as accentuated as that of the

Palestinian master narrative, for daily life for the Palestinian Israelis does not compare to daily life in continued military occupation. The Palestinian Israelis today tend to live in towns and villages entirely separate from Jewish citizens, or within larger cities in segregated neighborhoods. But they move freely throughout Israel, and many of them work with Jewish Israelis. Relative to the Palestinians in the territories, the Palestinian Israelis have benefited economically from being Israeli citizens, and their quality of life is generally much higher than that of Palestinians in the occupied territories (Ghanem, 2002). They do not, however, possess equal rights compared to their fellow Jewish citizens of the state and thus experience discrimination and marginalization as a minority group whose identity continues to be, for Jewish Israelis, "the enemy" (e.g., Canetti-Nisim, Ariely, & Halperin, 2008).

Formally, we can identify an immediate similarity between the Palestinian master narrative and that of the Palestinian Israelis: the trauma of 1948. The beginning of the story is characterized by the seemingly mythical harmony of life in Palestine before 1948. The ethos was peaceful, and the stories of family celebrations reveal the ability of cultural expression before Israel. Israel, then, is a major *disruption* in the story of the Palestinian Israelis (Rabinowitz & Abu-Baker, 2005; Sa'di & Abu-Lughod, 2007; Tessler & Grant, 1998), just as it is for Palestinians in the occupied territories. 1948 and its immediate aftermath are therefore tragic in the Palestinian-Israeli story, but the story is not without some measure of recovery, and it is in this formal ascent that the master narrative begins to diverge from that of the Palestinians in the occupied territories.

With time, and perhaps with some level of resignation, the master narrative ascends and stabilizes, as the Palestinian Israelis adjust to being citizens in a new state. The two further disruptions in the master narrative represent Land Day of 1976 and October of 2000. Although these are by no means the only events during which the Palestinian Israelis have attempted to protest and struggle against the perceived injustices of the Israeli state and been met with a violent response, they are the most central events in the contemporary Palestinian-Israeli consciousness. Yet, despite these disruptions, the narrative continues to stabilize, albeit never to a level comparable to pre-1948.

The master narrative of Palestinian-Israeli identity describes a story with several key themes. I will highlight three of these themes, though there is a high degree of interrelationship among them. First, the theme of *discrimination* and *subordination* is central to the master narrative, rooted in their minority status and their identity as Arab citizens who are, for a number of reasons, considered "threatening" to Israel (Canetti-Nisim et al., 2008). Second, because of this unique minority status, Palestinian Israelis undergo a most complex identity development process in which they must somehow reconcile their disparate civic and cultural identities as Israeli citizens who are Palestinian. The master narrative is anchored in this *liminal* place of necessary *hyphenation*—this need to reconcile the radically divergent allegiances and affiliations prescribed by a civic identity and a cultural identity at war with one another. This state of hyphenation is thus characterized by a *double marginality*—an existence that is marginal both within the context of one's civic life as an Israeli citizen and one's cultural life as a Palestinian, considered at least in some sense "Israelized." Finally, and once again connected to their sense of collective identity itself, Palestinian Israelis experience *existential insecurity*, rooted in their experiences with the Jewish majority. I will briefly detail these three themes—discrimination and subordination, hyphenation and double marginality, and existential insecurity—in greater detail, reviewing the vast amount of scholarship on the Palestinian Israelis that has emerged, particularly beginning in the 1990s with the work of sociologists like Sammy Smooha, anthropologists like Dan Rabinowitz, political scientists like As'ad Ghanem, Ilan Peleg, and Ahmad Sa'di, and social psychologists like Nadim Rouhana.

Theme 1: Discrimination and Subordination

According to a number of political scientists and sociologists who have examined the Israeli political system, Israel is best characterized as an "ethnic" democracy (Smooha, 2002), an "ethnically hegemonic" democracy (Peleg, 2004), or an "illiberal" democracy (Sa'di, 2002). Although the Israeli Proclamation of Independence (State of Israel, 1948/2001) promises to "uphold the full social and political equality of all its citizens, without distinction of religion, race, or sex" (pp. 82–83), it defines Israel as an ethnic Jewish state and, as such, inherently privileges Jewish over Arab citizens.

Smooha (2002) argues that this kind of political system is best described as an "ethnic democracy." *Liberal* democracy, represented by nations such as France, is characterized by the equal treatment of all citizens, and the state attempts not to recognize "ethnicity" institutionally. In *consociational* democracy, the state recognizes ethnic groups and institutionalizes systems to reduce conflict among groups through power sharing. Smooha (2002) suggests Belgium and Switzerland as examples, but we may also consider Lebanon as an example. In contrast to these two types of democracies, an *ethnic* democracy is one in which a single ethnic group claims a territory as its homeland, and "national" or "ethnic" identity is considered distinct from "civic" identity. That is, one can be a citizen while belonging to an ethnic group distinct from the one in ideological control of the state. An ethnic democracy relies upon a pri-mordial notion of national identity (Suny, 2001) and therefore identifies non-citizens of the state who are members of the ethnic group as part of the ethnic "nation" (i.e., members of the nation either live in the state or in a diaspora).

Israel represents the archetypal ethnic democracy, although Smooha (2002) argues that other states are assuming this model (e.g., Estonia and Slovakia). Although the political system is democratic, nonmembers of the *ethnic* nation do not receive the same rights as members, which creates a citizenship hierarchy. Indeed, Peleg (2004) argues that Israel is best understood as an ethnically hegemonic democracy. Through a number of calculated measures, including the massive expropriation of land undertaken by the new Israeli state after 1948, the Palestinian citizens currently own only 3.5% of the land in Israel, although they comprise approximately 18% of the population (Peleg, 2004).

Systematic discrimination against Israel's Arab citizens has been well documented, particularly with regard to land expropriation (Elrazik, Amin, & Davis, 1978; Lustick, 1980; Peleg, 2004; Rabinowitz & Abu-Baker, 2005; Tessler & Grant, 1998), unequal resource allocation compared to Jewish communities (Ghanem, 2002; Hareven, 2002; Peleg, 2004; Rabinowitz & Abu-Baker, 2005), inequalities in education and economic attainment (Abu-Saad, 2004; Al-Haj, 2002; Hareven, 2002; Lustick, 1980; Peleg, 2004; Pinson, 2007; Rabinowitz & Abu-Baker, 2005; Rouhana, 1997; Sa'di, 2002; Tessler & Grant, 1998), differential treatment in the justice system (Peleg, 2004; Sa'di, 2002, 2004), and exclusion from influential aspects of government (Ghanem, 2002; Ghanem & Rouhana, 2001; Hareven, 2002; Louër, 2007; Peleg, 2004; Rabinowitz & Abu-Baker, 2005; Rouhana, 1997, 2006; Rouhana & Sultany, 2003; Sa'di, 2002, 2004; Tessler & Grant, 1998). Sociologists and political scientists have documented that these disparities are not, as some might prefer to suggest, rooted in "cultural" differences between Jews and Arabs. Rather, there is ample evidence that the state supports conditions in which the Arabs are guaranteed a lesser social position.

According to Peleg (2004), Israel is best understood politically as an *exclusivist*, rather than an *accommodationist*, regime. Exclusivist regimes inherently create hegemony, either through majority or minority rule of a population. Israel is an example of an exclusivist regime with a majority hegemony, whereas Saddam Hussein's Iraq could be considered an exclusivist regime with a minority hegemony (though Iraq, of course, did not have a democratic political system). The hegemonic nature of Israel, which influences all of its state institutions and their preferential treatment of Jews over Arabs, gives it the distinction of being an "illiberal" democracy (Peleg, 2004; Sa'di, 2002).

The Palestinian citizens of Israel thus, like any minority group living in a political system that is institutionally hegemonic, experience discrimination in a number of basic routine life events. They are accorded the status of "second class" citizens as they engage with their Jewish fellow citizens, stared at for speaking Arabic on the street (a sight I witnessed firsthand on several occasions), passed up for jobs, implicitly denied jobs from employers advertising for applicants "after army" only (the Arabs are prohibited from serving in the IDF). They are the victims of what Johan Galtung (1969) calls *structural violence*—violence that is "built into the [social] structure and shows up as unequal power and consequently as unequal life chances" (p. 171). The interesting question for our present purpose is how this experience of structural violence impacts identity and, more broadly, the psychological development of young Palestinian Israelis. The personal narratives of youth offer a key window into the subjectivity of subordination.

Theme 2: Hyphenation and "Double Marginality"

Social scientists have long sought to consider the impact of subordinate status on both individual psychological development and on social interaction. Erik Erikson, the famous psychologist and "father" of identity as a scholarly (and popular) topic, argued that individuals who belong to oppressed groups are likely to develop a sense of *negative* identity that internalizes an element of self-hatred. More contemporary theorists and researchers talk about this phenomenon as *internalized oppression*—a phenomenon that appears to exist in group members oppressed on the basis of factors such as race, ethnicity, or sexual orientation.

Psychologists working in the context of colonialism and postcolonialism have also written extensively about the ways in which oppressed groups often come to internalize a sense of inferiority. Classic formulations by Aimé Césaire (1955/1972), Albert Memmi (1965), and Frantz Fanon (1952/1967) emphasized the way in which the inherent hegemony of colonialism created the *psychological* roles of "colonizer" and "colonized." Among the colonized, internalized inferiority was viewed as inevitable as individuals confronted a matrix of social identity in which the colonizer—his language, style, and skin color—existed at the nexus of power. Far from relegated to history, the psychological consequences of colonialism remain deeply relevant and have continued to frame a major concern for psychologists (e.g., David, 2008; David & Okazaki, 2006; Okazaki, David, & Abelman, 2008).

The negotiation of a hyphenated self is, therefore, not a value-neutral enterprise for Palestinian-Israeli youth. Rather, the two "weights" of the hyphen

(Zaal et al., 2007) bring with them powerful implications for individual mobility within a context of subordination (e.g., Golash-Boza, 2006). Though the
question of whether Israel can appropriately be considered a colonial power on
par with Britain, France, or Spain brings us to a place of unnecessary distrac-
tion (so far as this book is concerned; see Rodinson, 1973), it remains relevant
to recognize that Israel's Palestinian citizens were native, indigenous inhabitants of a land that came to be ruled largely by immigrants who possessed a
distinct language and culture.

The politics of a hyphenated self have consequences not solely for individual psychology, though. Erving Goffman's (1963) classic theory of stigma
directs our attention to the psychological consequences of subordination as
they are manifest in social interaction. Individuals who possess a stigma—"an
attribute that is deeply discrediting" (Goffman, 1963, p. 3)—must artfully
manage the consequences of what Goffman calls a *spoiled* identity. In Israel, an
Arab identity is an inferior, stigmatized identity, and therefore a significantly
discrediting personal characteristic. Regardless of the fluency of one's Hebrew,
once an Arabic accent is detected in an Arab–Jewish encounter, the interaction
is characterized by *stigma* for the Palestinian Israeli. Palestinian Israelis must
constantly manage the possibility of discreditation once their Arab identity is
detected, thereby engaging in a process of what Goffman (1963) calls *information control.*

Conditions of hegemonic relations such as those that characterize the
social and political ecology of Israel naturally set up an identity matrix in which
stigma thrives. (Incidentally, the Mizrahim share this stigma with the Arabs to
some extent, though they are redeemed by their Jewish identity and hence
belonging to the ethnic nation.) The Arabs provide for the Jews a perfect mirror
image, their differential identity status as members of the *losing* (though still
threatening) group supplying a necessary contrast that casts the Jewish-Israeli
identity as *the* positive identity (Rabinowitz, 2002). As Erikson (1968) so eloquently stated, "Our God-given identities often live off the degradation of
others" (p. 299).

The boundaries of hyphenation are thus not politically neutral for
Palestinian Israelis, and the ways in which they are negotiated are intimately
linked to questions of power and status in Israeli society. And Palestinian Israelis
are, in a profound sense, locked into an impossible place of hyphenation—
a place from which accentuation of one "side" of the hyphen over the other can
be deeply discrediting. This state of hyphenation has been discussed largely in
terms of the negotiation of one's *civic* (i.e., citizenship) identity with *national* or
cultural identity as Palestinians (Suleiman, 2002a, 2002b; Suleiman & Beit-
Hallahmi, 1997). That the two national identities that each side of this hyphen

indicates are locked in a bitter, intractable conflict creates a status of *double marginality* for the Palestinian Israelis. If they accentuate the *Palestinian* side of the hyphen, they risk further subordination and discrimination in Israeli society; if they accentuate the *Israeli* side of the hyphen, they risk being construed as "collaborators" against their Palestinian brethren in the occupied territories, not just by the Palestinians themselves but also throughout the Arab world. (It is noteworthy that their Israeli passport automatically denies them entry to most of the Arab world.)

The politics of hyphenation possess consequences not only for individual psychology and social interaction. Rather, the process of identity negotiation is tied intimately to the discourse of the state and its political *response* to identification among its Arab citizens. As already noted, there was a deliberate attempt to erase the *Palestinian* identity from those who remained inside the borders of Israel after 1948 through the discursive construction of the term "Israeli Arab" (Rabinowitz & Abu-Baker, 2005). The evidence suggests that this project was, by and large, a major success for the Jewish state—at least for a certain generation of its Arab citizens.

In Peres and Yuval-Davis' (1969) study of Palestinian citizens just prior to the 1967 Arab-Israeli War, the majority of participants ranked their self-categorization preferences as follows: (1) Israeli, (2) Israeli-Arab, (3) Arab, (4) Palestinian, and (5) Muslim or Christian. In their follow-up after the war, the ordering had changed significantly: (1) Arab, (2) Muslim or Christian, (3) Israeli-Arab, (4) Palestinian, and (5) Israeli. In 1975, only 12% of the population preferred either the term "Israeli-Palestinian" or "Palestinian-Israeli"; by 1987 the figure had increased to 40% (Smooha, 1988). And it continues to increase since the second *intifada* and the events of October 2000 (Rabinowitz & Abu-Baker, 2005).

Suleiman and his colleagues have proposed a bidimensional model of identity among Palestinian Israelis in which their national-cultural and civic identities are considered entirely separate (Suleiman, 2002b; Suleiman & Beit-Hallahmi, 1997). Their findings revealed that Palestinian Israelis rate their Palestinian cultural identity as more salient than their Israeli civic identity and evaluate their civic identity negatively in terms of political and social dimensions.

Compositionally, then, the Palestinian Israelis have undergone a process of growing national consciousness since the rupture of 1948, in which out of fear, intimidation, and helplessness, they surrendered not just their land (and, in some cases, their homes) but also their identities. Under a restrictive military administration, they came to identify with their new Israeli civic identities, perhaps because of the success of Israel's systematic program of thwarting the rebirth of Palestinian nationalism among them (Rabinowitz & Abu-Baker, 2005). But after the military administration, their integration into Israel's society was somehow rendered permanently incomplete. The hostility of the majority, coupled with the eventual realization that their status was not going to improve dramatically under Israel's hegemonic democracy, perhaps served to revitalize their desire for connection with the *ideological*, not just *cultural*, expression of their Palestinian identities. The generation Rabinowitz and Abu-Baker (2005) label "Survivors"—those who witnessed firsthand the terrible losses of 1948—gave way to a generation who sought to impact the Israeli political system from within.

The sociologist Sammy Smooha (1988) declared the existence of a "new Arab" identity in Israel—of one who successfully integrates multiple identities and is both bilingual and bicultural. In his study with Arab students at the Hebrew University of Jerusalem (conducted prior to the second *intifada* and the October 2000 events), Brian Schiff (2003) collected life story narratives and examined the balance of multiple affiliations and multicultural interaction that characterized these students' lives. Arguing for the primacy of social relationships in the life story, Schiff suggested that it was the uneven power dynamic between Jews and Arabs that served to complicate the identities of Arab students. As Arab students enter into a context in which they are no longer segregated from Jews, as Kashua's protagonist reflects upon in his twelfth-grade experience, they undergo a complex process of making decisions about "identity talk"—the way in which they will engage with their Jewish peers around issues of collective identity. Schiff's (2003) study reveals that Arab citizens, by virtue of their spoiled identities, must go through a delicate process of information control (Goffman, 1963) in order to minimize conflict and personal discrimination based on stigma.

The most interesting and relevant finding in Schiff's (2003) study for our own purposes is the great *variability* in the life story narratives of his Arab interviewees. Ibrahim, for example, "lives" the Palestinian narrative, having appropriated a discourse of dissent and resistance into his own life story. Amjad's story displays significant confusion in his own collective identity, not sure whether to fully embrace the Palestinian narrative or to continue the struggle for legitimacy within Israel.

The responses of Israel's Palestinian citizens to their liminal status is anything but monolithic, as Schiff's (2003) study affirms. In other words, Schiff's (2003) study reveals the extent to which young Palestinian Israelis negotiate the process of hyphenation in ways that reveal different strategies, characterized by the political context of stigma and the ongoing larger Arab–Israeli (and Israeli–Palestinian) conflict. While anthropologists and sociologists seek to reveal larger generational patterns in processes of Palestinian-Israeli identity development—and very usefully document these patterns (e.g., Rabinowitz & Abu-Baker, 2005; Smooha, 1988)—psychologists like Schiff seek to explore the often unpredictable and improvisational ways in which individuals negotiate the boundaries of hyphenation. My own research agenda is very much on par with Schiff's ambition to document individual processes in the larger socio-political context of discrimination, subordination, and political violence.

The politics of hyphenation has, since 2000, entered a new phase of generational consciousness for Palestinian citizens of Israel. The symbolic death of the peace process, with the failure of the Camp David summit in 2000 and the outbreak of the second *intifada*, marks a turning point in the master narrative of Palestinian-Israeli identity. The perception of continued neglect of minority rights, symbolized most tragically in the October 2000 events, in addition to the continued occupation of the Palestinian territories, has created a new political and historical context for Palestinian-Israeli identity development.

This new consciousness of hyphenation seems most characterized by the accentuation of their Palestinian cultural identities and, subsequently, a new challenge to the ethnic hegemony of the Jewish state (Peleg, 2004). This "Stand Tall" generation seems to have abandoned the assimilationist project of a prior generation in favor of a strong call for equal rights and social justice (Rabinowitz & Abu-Baker, 2005). Yet, while these large-scale collective patterns appear to ring true in surveys and the visible political mobilization of a new generation, less discussed, acknowledged, and debated are the individual processes of identity negotiation that characterize the "Stand Tall" generation. Thus, we know little about individual stories of struggle and success with the reconciliation of a hyphenated identity. The voices of youth have been notably absent, as social scientists have, in many ways, *presumed* the internalization of a new master narrative of Palestinian-Israeli identity, rather than query the process of individual engagement with this new narrative.

The idea of an identity *configuration* provides a useful heuristic to query the process of hyphenation for Palestinian-Israeli youth. Israeli psychologist Elli Schachter (2004) calls upon Erikson's (1959) original formulation of identity as an "evolving configuration" to argue that identity assumes a particular structure that relies upon our ability to reconcile divergent discourses and identifications in the process of development. Schachter's (2005) case study of Gil, an Orthodox Jewish Israeli, focused on his ability to reconcile his professional focus on science with his religious orthodoxy—two discourses that, in fact, pose formidable conflicts at the surface. Schachter suggests that it is a hallmark of human resilience in the face of multiple, disparate discourses to be able to construct a workable configuration of identity. In keeping with my view of identity as a text rendered through the construction of a personal narrative, I see our ability to access configurations of identity through narrative. In other words, the life story provides an essential window into the process of constructing this workable identity configuration—a window into the creativity, improvisation, and resilience that characterizes lives in conflict.

Applying Schachter's (2004) theory of identity configurations to the Palestinian Israelis, we can identify at least four possible configurations that might manifest in the personal narratives of youth. First, as predicted by much of the recent social science literature on the "Stand Tall" generation (e.g., Rabinowitz & Abu-Baker, 2005), we might expect Palestinian-Israeli youth to accentuate their Palestinian cultural identities as they traverse the discursive terrain of hyphenation. Second, as Smooha's (1999) pre-*intifada* work suggested, we might see an accentuation of Israeli civic identity among youth, seeking perhaps to elevate their perceived status within Israeli society by deliberately minimizing their perceived allegiance to the Palestinians. This kind of strategy of *individual mobility* can frequently occur among members of low-status groups (Tajfel & Turner, 1986). Third, the narratives of youth might be characterized by significant conflict as a consequence of hyphenation. That is, the double marginality inherent in the hyphenated identity of Palestinian Israelis might result in a considerable amount of fragmentation within their personal narratives. Finally, we might expect among some youth a kind of "metacognition" about their hyphenated identities. Their narratives might be characterized by life immediately *at* the hyphen, where they seek to transcend the tension of polarization within the self by recognizing the benefits, rather than the burdens, of hyphenation.

Hyphenation and its accompanying double marginality thus represent a key theme in the master narrative of Palestinian-Israeli identity. Young Palestinian citizens of Israel traverse the politics of identity hyphenation in the course of their development, making important decisions for their own life stories. Yet we know little about the *lived experience* of hyphenation for Palestinian Israelis—a gap in our knowledge that I seek to address (admittedly only as an initial, limited inquiry) in this chapter. To specifically probe the individual's momentary negotiation of hyphenation, I will use the concept of identity configuration.

Theme 3: Existential Insecurity

As I have already suggested, discrimination and subordination—whether explicit or implicit in state institutions, allocation of resources, or life course possibilities for Israel's Palestinian citizens—represent forms of *structural* violence (Galtung, 1969). In contrast to *direct* violence, in which there is a clear perpetrator who inflicts some harm, structural violence is not committed by a single individual against another but rather by the social structure itself. In other words, structural violence speaks to institutional forms of oppression, discrimination, and social injustice for certain groups in a society.

The theme of existential insecurity in the Palestinian-Israeli master narrative speaks to the other two forms of violence that may befall this group. First, connected again to the status of hyphenation, Palestinian Israelis experience the effects of *cultural* violence when the state and its institutions (e.g., the educational system) seek to eradicate their Palestinian cultural identities and memories. Galtung (1990) defines cultural violence as "those aspects of culture, the symbolic sphere of our existence... that can be used to justify or legitimize direct or structural violence" (p. 291). By seeking to construct a historical and political discourse in which the notion of Palestinian identity (and cultural memory) is erased, the Israeli state practices cultural violence on its Arab citizens. Second, Palestinian Israelis experience the effects of *direct* violence—perpetrated by state actors such as the IDF or the police—when they have attempted to protest the actions of the state, either with regard to their own subordination or to the violence perpetrated against Palestinians in the occupied territories.

Existential insecurity is thus symbolic, referring to the systematic attempt to eradicate the Palestinian cultural identity and memory of Israel's Arab citizens, through discursive tactics such as relabeling, as well as through the state-controlled and monitored educational system that fails to educate youth about Palestinian history and culture prior to the establishment of Israel in 1948 (Abu-Saad, 2004; Rabinowitz & Abu-Baker, 2005). But the trope of existential insecurity is also rooted in the very real experience with defenselessness at the mercy of the state and its security institutions (Rabinowitz & Abu-Baker, 2005).

Since its creation in 1948, the Israeli state has adhered to a policy of separation, control, and subordination for its Arab citizens. Fear and intimidation motivated many in the generation of Survivors to conform to the state's expectations, by assuming the new identity label "Israeli Arab" and avoiding political discourse associated with Palestinian liberation or independence. The state's attempt to eradicate a Palestinian cultural identity among its Arab citizens was systematic, most readily apparent in the educational system (Abu-Saad, 2004). In his comparative study of Arab and Jewish education in Israel, Al-Haj (2002) concluded that Arab education can legitimately be considered "multicultural," whereas Jewish education cannot. While the Jewish curriculum contains a comprehensive section on Jewish national consciousness, there is no parallel section for Arab youth. In fact, much of the Arab curriculum emphasizes the significance of Jewish contributions and identity while referring only to a diffuse "Arab" identity. There is no reference, really, to a distinct Palestinian culture and identity.

This feature of the Israeli educational system is hardly surprising. For Israel, Palestinian identity is inherently threatening, given that it represents the rival nationalism for control of the territory once known as Palestine (e.g., Cannetti-Nisim et al., 2008). So it makes sense that its formerly "Palestinian" citizens ought to be *resocialized*, their identities reformulated so as to minimize the possibility of existential threat to the state and its Jewish national identity. Rabinowitz and Abu-Baker (2005) argue that a growing consciousness of the state's attempt to reconstruct the identities of Palestinian citizens characterizes the Stand Tall generation of contemporary youth.

The state's attempts at identity restructuring through labeling might highlight existential insecurity among youth with political and historical sensitivities about the Palestinian-Israeli experience. Drawing on the idea of dual-identity development (or identity *hyphenation*), Smooha (1999) argues that Israel's Palestinian citizens undergo two parallel socialization processes, what he calls "Israelization" and "Palestinization." While he argues that Palestinization has increased significantly since the 1967 war, what is most striking about Smooha's (1999) findings is the extent to which Israelization appears to have occurred among the Palestinian Israelis. The systematic increase in cultural indicators of Israelization (Table 5.1) reveals its success.

The survey results in this table reveal a general pattern of Israelization among the Palestinian citizens, with increases in Hebrew language use and fluency, acceptance of Israel as a Jewish state, and acceptance of the Israeli

TABLE 5.1 Indicators of Israelization among Arab citizens of Israel, 1976–1995 (percent).

	1976	1980	1985	1988	1995
Speak Hebrew	62.3	69.9	68.8	74.2	80.8
Read Hebrew newspapers	27.1	42.4	49.8	53.1	65.4
Accept Israel's right to exist as a Jewish-Zionist state	*	*	37.9	36.8	64.6
Regard Israel's flag as representing themselves	*	*	*	*	71.3
Define self as Palestinian, Palestinian Arab	32.9	25.7	29.2	27.1	10.3
Define self as Israeli, Israeli Arab, Arab	54.7	45.4	32.1	33.2	53.6

Adapted from Smooha (1999).
(*) Indicates question was not asked.

identity label as some component of identity (although note that "Arab" was also considered in this same question, which complicates interpretation of the results). Smooha's data also demonstrate a powerful decrease in self-definition as Palestinian. All of this suggests the success of Israelization and the gradual eradication of a strong Palestinian consciousness among the Arab citizens prior to the second *intifada*. But it is important to note that these data do not extend beyond 1995 and thus do not include the period of the second *intifada* and the responses of the Stand Tall generation, who would have been too young to participate in Smooha's surveys in the 1990s. (Their members were born during the first *intifada*.) It is also important to bear in mind the historical context of the 1990s as a time when the possibility of genuine peace with the Palestinians and the fulfillment of Palestinian national identity at last seemed to be emerging, which may have impacted these indicators.

Caveats aside, the data do suggest that Israelization is a process that indeed occurs among the Palestinian citizens and that the state's systematic program of identity restructuring was, by and large, successful until 2000. The period of the second *intifada* and the sentiments of the Stand Tall generation suggest a new Palestinian cultural consciousness and the recognition of the state's attempts to block the development of this consciousness among its Palestinian citizens (Rabinowitz & Abu-Baker, 2005). The reclamation of the Palestinian identity label is telling enough.

Attempts at Israelization through state institutions such as the educational system speak to more symbolic existential threats, as they suggest a desire to erase the Palestinian cultural identity of Israel's Arab citizens. Such forms of existential threat represent cultural violence against Palestinian Israelis in that they use the ideology of the state and its powerful institutions to control the identity development process. In keeping with Althusser's (1971) classic notion of the *ideological state apparatus*, such attempts seek to control the *meaning* of identity and of the social categories that are deemed to be significant in a given society (see also Bourdieu, 1984). In seeking to construct a particular narrative of history—inculcated through the educational system itself—the Israeli state apparatus contributes to the surveillance of its Arab citizens, whose hyphen-ated identities represent a constant threat to Jewish hegemony (Peleg, 2004).

Beyond discourse and attempts at resocialization through cultural violence, the state has used force to threaten the existential security of its Palestinian citizens, thus also participating in acts of direct violence. The brutal responses to Arab demonstrations have served to convince them of their own fragile existence. This realization has taken its most recent form following the October 2000 events. Amal Eqeiq (2002), a Palestinian-Israeli scholar of comparative literature, characterized the response of her own community in Taybeh as decidedly "posttraumatic." She argues that the October events served to create a deep feeling of insecurity among Israel's Arab citizens and a sense that they were no longer welcome in Israeli society.

This period was characterized by a number of clashes between Jews and Arabs in Israel, with police response generally favoring the Jewish communities and penalizing the Arabs (Rabinowitz & Abu-Baker, 2005; Slone, 2003). Most poignantly, Eqeiq (2002) refers to the Arab community's inability to recover from the October trauma as connected to the "unresolved ongoing trauma of the Arab Palestinian as a minority in Israel" (p. 12). The October events are, according to Eqeiq, just another chapter in the "tragic and traumatic history" of the Palestinian Israelis.

Summary

The Palestinian-Israeli master narrative is characterized, at its core, by the tragic rupture of 1948 and its consequences for a particular politics of identity with powerful social, psychological, and economic ramifications. Yet, unlike the Palestinian master narrative, the fact that Palestinian Israelis were subject to a *regime* of *hyphenation* alters the course of the master narrative and forces a thematic divergence between these two groups of Palestinians.

Rooted in the social science literature on the Palestinian Israelis, I suggested that the master narrative of this group contains three primary themes, all of which are in many ways closely interrelated. Given Israel's inherent status as an ethnic democracy in which Jewish hegemony is inscribed in the foundational documents of the state (Peleg, 2004; Smooha, 2002), the Palestinian citizens are subject to structural violence that alters their life course possibilities and places them on a trajectory of subordination. Their hyphenated identities create a state of double marginality in which they must delicately manage their dual affiliations—affiliations that serve to discredit them in both Jewish-Israeli and Palestinian societies, as well as the larger Arab world. They suffer from both cultural and direct violence at the hands of the Israeli state and its educational and security institutions, constantly suspect and under surveillance.

While charting the course of this master narrative has, in many ways, represented a major focus of scholarship on the Palestinian Israelis, less attention has been devoted to querying individual processes of identity negotiation and navigation in a social ecology of subordination and insecurity. The limited work that has been done occurred prior to the second *intifada*, in a radically different political context (e.g., Schiff, 2003). Thus, my central aim—and indeed my intended contribution—in the remainder of this chapter is to illustrate the strategies young Palestinian Israelis use to traverse the terrain of identity hyphenation. Using the same basic interpretive and idiographic approach to understanding—and documenting—lives in context, I present three life story narratives of youth in their entirety, examining the elements of the master narrative that they either appropriate or repudiate. In allowing the space for *voice* among these youths, I hope to counter the history of *silencing* that has characterized this unique group (McLean, 2008), inhabiting a liminal place of hyphenation in a region whose identity politics confer life, death, and the anxiety of existential uncertainty.

The Stories of Youth

The stories of Jibril, Rania, and Sami reveal the ways in which youth of the Stand Tall generation are negotiating the process of identity development in the midst of a new phase of internal conflict between Jews and Arabs. Collected between 2003 and 2004, these life stories possess little temporal distance from the October events, and the place of these events and of the second *intifada* more generally figures prominently in my analysis. The presentation of only three life stories—necessary more for the maintenance of a reasonable book length than for the absence of other interesting cases for presentation and analysis—is admittedly incomplete in its ability to reveal anything comprehensive about the relationship between the master narrative and the identity development of contemporary youth. I trust the reader will appreciate a consideration of these life stories as exemplars of the numerous other stories collected, more of which will be discussed in Chapter 7.

As in Chapters 3 and 4, my analysis of life stories is guided by techniques of formal and thematic analysis in narrative studies (e.g., Lieblich et al., 1998), yet influenced more by idiographic or person-centered approaches (e.g., Gregg, 2007; Josselson, 1996). As my outline of the master narrative reveals, this analysis was guided by a commitment to capturing the narrative *content* of hyphenation and its implications for identification with the master narrative. Thus, my analysis centered on (a) the appropriation of the three key master narrative themes identified, and, relatedly, (b) the current configuration of identity in terms of the discursive *navigation* of hyphenation.

"I am Israeli First": The Story of Jibril

A 15-year-old heavyset Muslim boy with glasses and an inviting smile, Jibril is from Taybeh, an Arab city close to the West Bank in what is known in Israel as "the Triangle." He narrated his life story to me for the first time in the placid woods of Maine, far removed from the routine sounds of Apache helicopters conducting an operation in the nearby West Bank city of Tulkarm, in the summer of 2003. His narrative reveals the extraordinary complexity that consumes the identity development of Palestinian-Israeli youth.

Formally, Jibril's narrative appears to discard the tragic, if ultimately redeemed, form of the Palestinian-Israeli master narrative in favor of a more traditional redemptive, descent-and-gain pattern (Lieblich et al., 1998; McAdams, 2006). The formal properties of his narrative thus more closely replicate that of his Jewish-Israeli, rather than Palestinian, peers.

Jibril begins his life story by telling me that his family has always lived in Taybeh. There are no stories of disruption and dislocation, just a linear account in which his life is now in continuity with that of his extended family. It could easily be the case that Jibril's family did indeed experience relatively less dislocation and disruption compared to other Palestinians in 1948, for Taybeh was a preexisting village that survived the war.

His life-line begins to ascend with the move to a new, nicer home in Taybeh. It continues its ascent to the following year, as Jibril is selected as a "talented" student at his school. The first descent in his life story occurs at the death of his grandfather in 1997. In 1999, he switches schools and recalls this transition as a positive one in which he made new friends. The final descent in his narrative is a significant one: the start of the second Palestinian *intifada* in 2000. Jibril identifies this moment as a turning point in his life story, for its significant impact on his life course possibilities:

> The start of the *intifada* in 2000, this was really terrible for my life because, you know, before the *intifada* my family and I would go to the West Bank. And we could go to the restaurants, and to buy clothes and vegetables. And this stopped. If you remember in October, Arab Israelis were killed because they were part of some brotherhood of Palestinians living in Israel. So Arabs start to make a demonstration, and the Israeli soldiers killed 13 of them, and this was terrible. Fortunately, in my town nobody was killed.

In identifying the start of the second *intifada* and the October events as a clear turning point, Jibril's life story becomes infused with the *existential insecurity* of the master narrative. But fundamentally for Jibril, this turning point marked a shift in Jewish–Arab relations in Israel—a shift that profoundly impacted his life course:

> Before the *intifada*, we would go to the Jewish cities. There was freedom. But since the *intifada*, the people in the Jewish cities do not accept Arabs.

They think all Arabs are terrorists. So when we went to this Jewish city, about 15 people attacked us, my family. Fortunately, there was a police car there, and they stopped them. And after the *intifada*, the relationship between Arabs and Jews changed so much. Before the *intifada*, the Jews would go to the West Bank to eat or shop.

Before the *intifada*, people from the West Bank would come through the checkpoints, and nobody would talk to them. They were just going to work. Now the police won't let people from the West Bank work in Israel. The relationship between Arabs has changed too, because some people say we should say we're Palestinian, they're our brothers, these kinds of things. Others think we can't, that this is not a good idea.

From a place of (perhaps imagined) harmony before the *intifada* and the October events, Jewish–Arab relations in Israel are now, according to Jibril's narrative, characterized by a deep distrust of the Arabs *and* acts of direct violence at the hands of the Jewish majority and the state institutions. In addition, Jibril views the *intifada* as creating tensions among Arabs in Israeli society, with divergent perspectives on identity management and political response strategies.

As a major historical turning point in the conflict itself, the second *intifada* indeed altered the relational possibilities between Arabs and Jews, both inside Israel and between Israel and Palestine. From Israel's occupation of the territories captured in 1967 until the implementation of the Oslo accords, movement was essentially open between Israel and the occupied territories. The IDF was not deployed *within* the territories, as it is today, but along strategic points along the borders with Lebanon, Syria, Jordan, and Egypt (Rabinowitz & Abu-Baker, 2005). What this openness meant was a high degree of interaction between Palestinian citizens and noncitizens in the occupied territories, despite some tension between the "'48 Arabs" (i.e., Palestinian Israelis) and the "'67 Arabs" (i.e., Palestinians in the occupied territories), who saw the Palestinian citizens as resigning themselves to Israeli rule. This openness began to reduce during the Oslo period, when Rabinowitz and Abu-Baker (2005) argue the actual *military* occupation of the territories began in earnest, with the infusion of the IDF inside of them, closely monitoring and restricting movement.

For Jibril, who relished the opportunity to visit Palestinian communities in the West Bank as a child, the *intifada* permanently ended his interaction with noncitizen Palestinians. But its relational impact seems even more profound for Jibril in the way in which it impacted his treatment in Israel as an Arab. His family's existential security has now even been threatened as they have attempted to visit a Jewish city. This spike in intergroup conflict has, it seems, served to polarize Jewish and Palestinian Israelis to levels previously unimaginable—and tragic—to Jibril. A particularly upsetting post-*intifada* experience occurred when Jibril and his father attended a soccer game:

> The crowds in the soccer games, they curse. After the *intifada*, they started to curse Arab players. They're Arab players from Israel! After the *intifada*, they start to make bad songs about the Arab players, cursing them. They say things like "terrorist." This was really hard. All these people from Likud, they start to say "Death for Arabs!" ... This is hard for the Arabs and the Jews.

The *intifada* thus marks a turning point for Jibril in his integration of another key theme in the master narrative—discrimination and subordination. After the *intifada*, Arab citizens are subject to new levels of discrimination that are likely rooted in suspicion and insecurity among Jewish Israelis themselves (Canetti-Nisim et al., 2008). In other words, Jewish and Arab citizens are locked in an interdependent state of existential insecurity—Jews might discriminate against Arabs out of fear of their loyalty (Canetti-Nisim et al., 2008), and Arabs might become less loyal to the state because of their subordination (Rabinowitz & Abu-Baker, 2005). This state of mutual insecurity creates unique challenges in the identity development of young Palestinian citizens of Israel like Jibril.

The most obvious path to probe the navigation of hyphenation among Palestinian-Israeli youth is to discuss identity labels. The present choice of identity labels provides a window into the immediate process of hyphenation and specifies a current configuration of identity. For the youth in this study, it is important to note that their participation in intergroup contact makes this issue all the more significant as they narrate their life stories to me. In other words, the fact that they are about to, or are just beginning to, engage in contact with Jewish Israelis and Palestinians from the occupied territories *primes* the significance of hyphenation in such a way that they must make decisions about identity labels. Capturing these preliminary efforts to construct an identity configuration was precisely my aim.

Just as he is beginning intergroup contact, Jibril describes his identity as follows:

> My identity is Arab-Israeli. I am Israeli first; I have no question about this. I live in Israel. Israel is my country. I'm proud of being Israeli, and I'm proud of my country. When an Arab Israeli says, "I'm Palestinian," it's because somebody has told them, "You are a Palestinian living in Israel. You must remember your brothers who have been killed," or

something like this. And this happened with me, in the first day of camp. Somebody came and asked me, "Who are you?" I said, "I'm Jibril, I'm from Israel. I'm Arab." He said, "How can you say you're from Israel!? You're a Palestinian!" I said, "No. I'm Israeli!" He said to me, "You forgot your brothers, you forgot what the Jews did to us." These kinds of things, this doesn't help make peace. This makes it harder!

At this moment of life story narration, Jibril chooses to accentuate his Israeli civic identity and to see that as, in fact, his national identity. He does not identify with Palestinian identity at all and views attempts to make him do so as manipulative. Rather, he sees himself as a legitimate member of Israeli society, with little reference to his differential rights or status as an Arab citizen, except in reference to the post-*intifada* changes in relations between Jews and Arabs.

Jibril's narrative offers a fascinating case of a young Palestinian citizen who struggles to fully reconcile a hyphenated self. Rather than reconcile fully the inherent conflict at the hyphen, he abandons one side of his identity entirely. Curiously, it is his Palestinian cultural identity that is discarded. As I have related Jibril's story time and time again to both Israeli and Palestinian colleagues, they have been both surprised and skeptical, as if somehow a young man like Jibril could not possibly exist. Before I offer some of my field-informed insights into why Jibril's narrative is not all that surprising to me, which we will see is intimately connected to the *local* context of Taybeh, let me offer some examples of how Jibril's choice to embrace an Israeli identity colors some of his impressions of critical events in his life. In particular, Jibril's account of the history of the Israeli–Palestinian conflict and of the origins of the second *intifada* reveal a closer proximity to the Jewish-Israeli master narrative of these events.

Recall that the Jewish-Israeli master narrative frames the Zionist conquest of Palestine as a *progressive* endeavor (e.g., Hess, 1862/1997). Jewish control of the land liberated its economic possibilities and, subsequently, its stature in the world order. Jibril has internalized this basic narrative when he discusses the origins of the conflict:

Because the Jews came to Palestine at that time, it was the start of the conflict. It was the twentieth century. The Jews built the country, but the Arabs didn't accept what the Jews said. So there was a war between the Arabs and the Jews, and the Jews won. But there were six Arab countries against the Jews, and the Jews won! ...[The conflict,] it's not between Jews and Arabs. It's between *Israelis* and *some* Arabs—not all Arabs. Because I'm Arab, and they don't have a problem with me. I'm not involved.

Jibril has internalized the Zionist narrative of "developing" the land, along with Arab rejection as the basis for the prolonged armed conflict, although his identification of Jewish immigration to Palestine as the ultimate catalyst of the conflict is more consistent with the Palestinian narrative. He seeks to distance himself from the Palestinian idea of liberation and resistance, constructing for himself an identity clearly distinct from the Arabs who struggle against Israel.

In general, Jibril's narrative can be viewed as a great distance from that of the Palestinian master narrative in its ideological and interpretive content regarding the conflict. He essentializes Palestinian education as, at base, education to fight against Israel—a common form of delegitimization among Jewish Israelis (Oren & Bar-Tal, 2007). In describing his own education in Israel, he says,

> I learn about Islam, and the French Revolution, and the Holocaust. So I think the Jews just don't want to teach about what happened here in Israel, cause they would have to say something against the Palestinians, and they can't. So they just avoid teaching about our history here.

> The [school] books don't have anything about the conflict. The Hebrew book has stories about peace between Muslims and Jews. But they don't have things like this in Palestine. They're taught to be against Israel. They learn really bad things about Israel. Everybody there is against Israel. The European Union gave Palestine money to make new books, but they were really bad books. All their books are about war, and against Israel.... Teaching hate for Israelis will not help. We don't learn anything against Arabs in the Israeli schools.... I don't know why the Arabs do it against the Jews.

In Jibril's personal narrative of his own education, the state-sponsored curriculum is presented as benevolent and avoiding the conflict and Palestinian history only to ensure that anti-Arab sentiment is not expressed. Rather than interpret this omission as part of the systematic attempt to reduce the salience (or even existence) of a Palestinian identity among its Arab citizens (Bar-Gal, 1994), Jibril sees the neglect of these subjects as entirely legitimate, and not equally met among Palestinians. Unlike Israelis, in Jibril's view, Palestinians are taught to hate, and it is this hate that reproduces the conflict.

Nowhere is Jibril's internalization of the Jewish-Israeli narrative of the conflict more readily apparent than in his characterization of the second *intifada*'s commencement. Recall that the *intifada* represents the most significant turning point in Jibril's life story. It has disrupted his narrative, infusing it with a negative tone and with new painful constraints on his life experience.

Even attending the soccer match is an opportunity for anti-Arab discrimination for Jibril. Rather than view the discrimination he now receives as a continuation of Israel's systematic subordination of its Arab citizens (Abu-Saad, 2004), as the Palestinian-Israeli master narrative would have encouraged him to do, Jibril sees the discrimination he faces as an Arab as a result of the Palestinian *intifada*. And the blame for his hardship falls squarely on the Palestinians as a result.

In speaking about the origins of the *intifada*, he says,

> It's what the Palestinians say, because Ariel Sharon entered al-Aqsa Mosque. But a lot of Jews enter the Mosque, so why exactly this man? They say because he is a killer. He killed a lot of Arabs or something like this. But they were just waiting for something to start the *intifada*—the terror organization, I think. Because if there is no war, there is no work for the terror organization.

Interestingly, instead of viewing the impetus for the *intifada* through the prism of the Palestinian narrative, Jibril appears to have internalized the Jewish-Israeli perspective on the start of the *intifada* as a coordinated effort among the "terror organizations." The very fact that he has appropriated the discourse of "terrorism" to describe Palestinian resistance reveals how distant his narrative is from the Palestinian master narrative in its construction.

The disruption of the *intifada* was thus, in Jibril's view, instigated by the Palestinians. It has had disastrous consequences for the way in which Jewish Israelis now view him as an Arab. Describing the nadir in his life story, he says,

> The *intifada*, because before we came here in the airport, they treated me different from the Jewish kids. All the Arabs, they searched our bags, put them through the machine, asked us a lot of questions. Why? Because of the *intifada*, because they think that Arab Israelis are going to do something bad. I'm not really sad about this. They do it because the airplane must be secure. So that's OK that they check me. But the *intifada* is a really bad thing that happened in my life.... I see on the news the *intifada* is dying—they write it in Arabic. I feel good, that it's dying.

Jibril interprets the discrimination he receives at the airport because of his Arab identity as both legitimate and a response to Palestinian terrorism. It is in his mind, entirely justifiable. In this way, through these narrative interpretations of his life events as an Arab citizen, Jibril appropriates the dominant Jewish-Israeli discourse on the conflict.

Jibril's life story narrative demonstrates the key dilemma of Palestinian-Israeli identity. The form of his narrative fails to resemble that of the master narrative (admittedly constructed largely by social scientists, most of whom examine large-scale patterns rather than individual experience) and assumes more of the classic descent-and-gain pattern of Jewish-Israeli youth. Naturally, the experience of the *intifada* and its impact on his life story are quite significant, given the increase in anti-Arab discrimination it has caused him. Yet the way in which Jibril interprets his experience of discrimination is closely connected to an internalization of the *Jewish-Israeli* master narrative, rather than that of the Palestinian Israelis. His experience with discrimination is more attributable in his mind to the Palestinians in the occupied territories and their aggression against Israel, his home country. Jibril, it seems, has been fully "Israelized."

I believe there are many ways to interpret Jibril's current identity configuration, characterized by the surprising challenge it presents to the social science literature on the Palestinian Israelis since the second *intifada*. Perhaps most simply, Jibril's narrative demonstrates a very common strategy employed by members of low-status groups: *individual mobility*. In their classic formulation of social identity theory, Tajfel and Turner (1986) present a number of strategies that members of low-status groups use to elevate their status. While many individuals use strategies that aim to enhance the positive distinctiveness of the low-status social identity (e.g., social creativity or social competition), some individuals try to *leave* the low-status group and "pass" for a member of the high-status group. Tajfel and Turner (1986) call this strategy *individual mobility*, and this understanding of intergroup relations offers an interpretation of Jibril's narrative. He chooses to accentuate his Israeli civic identity in the midst of an ongoing, intractable conflict in which his Palestinian cultural identity constructs him as an enemy in the eyes of the state. If he can construct himself as loyal to the state—by accentuating his civic identity and essentially abandoning his cultural identity—the extent to which his Palestinian identity is a "spoiler" in his life experience might be minimized. Thus, Jibril's current identity configuration is consistent with social psychological theory on status hierarchies and social change.

Some insights from my fieldwork in Israel also provide some interpretive ease to the case of Jibril. One of the first things that struck me about my good friend and colleague Yasmine, who also happens to be a Palestinian citizen from Taybeh, was her adept skill at identity adaptation. Far from someone ideologically polarized or divisive, she possessed an incredibly "accommodating" identity. There was no doubt that she was Arab, but she traversed Israel's highways on a daily basis, coming into contact with Jewish Israelis with great frequency. She had a perfect command of both Arabic and Hebrew, as well as English and Spanish, and had a unique way of making Jews, Arabs, Americans—whomever—totally comfortable. She seemed to fit Smooha's (1988) notion of the "new Arab" in Israel, one for whom a genuine multi-cultural identity thrived.

While there is much about my dear friend and colleague that is unique to her infinitely generous personality, there is also something unique about her city of origin, the home city of Jibril as well: Taybeh. I discovered this on a number of my field visits to Israel in 2004 and 2005. When I asked one of my Seeds of Peace colleagues at one point why so many Arab participants seem to hail from Taybeh, she explained that the Israeli government had always preferred Taybeh's students to others because of their greater expressed affiliation with an Israeli identity and their criticism of the Palestinians. Suddenly Jibril's story began to make more sense when contextualizing it in a local identity narrative.

The residents of Taybeh are culturally Palestinian, and the city itself, as I described in Chapter 2, resembles a West Bank city much more than any other city in Israel. But in Taybeh, parents encourage their children not to talk about politics. Their memories of the Israeli *Shabak* (secret service) remain from the early years of the state and the military administration in their community. Many adults commute outside of Taybeh for work and for university, to places throughout Israel. Even one young man I stayed with on one of my field trips there was a student at a university in Ariel—a massive West Bank settlement. How ironic, I thought, for a Palestinian citizen of Israel to be attending that school. But in the "integrational" context of Taybeh, whose inhabitants long to be included in an Israeli identity and do not mourn the loss of Palestine in anything other than nostalgia, such activity is not so surprising.

The content of Jibril's story, then, ought to be considered in relation to his local developmental context. Taybeh is a city that has seen little protest and little direct disruption in the course of the conflict. It is a town without painful stories of loss and suffering. It is, if you will, a very peaceful place, and a place whose inhabitants prefer to stay out of trouble and live their lives. Do not be misled by my characterization, though. This inclination toward passivity when it comes to the conflict, both within and outside of Israel, is resented among many of Taybeh's youth, and they deal with this resentment in different ways.

Let us conclude Jibril's story by noting that his narrative is far from fully scripted. We will return to it, as I did, one year after his participation at Seeds of Peace. But now, as he embarks on this adventure in intergroup contact, he has deeply internalized a narrative that fuses his civic and national identities into one harmonious Israeli identity. His Arab identity is problematic only insofar as the Palestinians polarize the Jewish-Israeli public. The form, content, and ideological setting of his life story reveals considerable divergence from the master narrative of Palestinian-Israeli identity, and there are in fact more connections between his personal narrative and the Jewish-Israeli master narrative. But ultimately, Jibril is a young man who craves peaceful coexistence. His ideological setting may favor the interpretation of events promulgated in the Jewish-Israeli discourse, yet it is hardly unsympathetic to the Palestinians.

"I Had a War with Myself": The Story of Rania

Now abundantly clear based on the narratives considered thus far in the book, one of the most striking features of Israeli and Palestinian life stories is the extent to which they reveal the significance of *local* identity. The local context of the city or village, kibbutz or moshav, seems to bring with it a distinct ideological context in both Israel and Palestine. Typically, the influence of local identity on youth is not all consuming, narratively speaking. We have seen that Jewish Israelis and Palestinians from a number of diverse local contexts in fact share much with one another and with the particular master narrative of their group. Jibril's life story and its initially surprising ideological content are uninterpretable without knowing something of Taybeh and its inhabitants. In his case, as in many others, we witness the value of an approach that combines interviewing and fieldwork to access a complete window into the lives of youth.

Rania's story offers an excellent contrast to Jibril's and highlights the salience of local identity for Palestinian-Israeli youth. While some traditionally "mixed" cities like Haifa and Jaffa (now essentially subsumed by Tel Aviv) continue to have significant Arab populations, two geographic regions in Israel are known for the denseness of their Arab population: the Triangle, of which Taybeh is a part, and the Galilee, in the north of the country. The Galilee consists of villages and cities that remained intact in 1948, their inhabitants "rebranded" Israelis overnight. The Galilee remains to this day an area with a majority Arab population.

The Galilee, and Rania's small village in particular, was in fact a focal point of the dissent that occurred in October 2000, with a major protest. It is not surprising, then, that Rania's narrative conforms more closely to what Rabinowitz and Abu-Baker (2005) refer to as the "Stand Tall" generation of Palestinian Israelis. She is a proud Palestinian, struggling to transform Israel from a "Jewish state" to a "state of its citizens"—from an *ethnic* democracy to a genuinely *liberal* democracy.

Narrated to me for the first time at age 14, Rania's life story begins with stability and achieves a healthy ascent with her graduation from one school and transition to another. It is a time of great happiness and success for Rania:

> It was really great, because I feel I'm growing. Going to another school, it's a new experience for me. I got the highest marks in my class, even though I'm the youngest. I'll go to a high school now in another village, for a better school.

Rania's achievements create in her a sense of personal growth and gain. She feels rewarded to now attend a better school and to advance herself academically.

For members of the Stand Tall generation, the October 2000 events represent a defining moment and likely contributed to the resurgence of a collective Palestinian consciousness (Rabinowitz & Abu-Baker, 2005). Rania's engagement with the October events offers the nadir of her life story:

> It started with a demonstration, and that's when my cousin was killed. From my home, you could see everything, mountains of people. I didn't see anyone get shot, but I heard them. The first one was a guy in the village, dead immediately. Then we heard another shot. We thought it was someone else, and then we realized that it was my cousin. When the demonstration started, I just had this strange feeling that something bad's gonna happen. When I saw the policemen and the soldiers, I was convinced that something bad was gonna happen, and it happened.

The trauma of the October events and the death of her cousin represent a key turning point in her personal narrative—from the innocence of childhood and the *insulation* of her life story to the recognition of existential insecurity for her group. In other words, the trauma of the October events, while deeply *personal* for Rania, is also central to the development of her *social* identity as a Palestinian Israeli, for she narrates the collective threat of direct violence from the state. Coping with the trauma by channeling her narrative toward meaningful activity—action that would serve the cause of her cousin, a staunch supporter of coexistence through dialogue—Rania's life story takes its strength in tone from the events of October. In collective trauma, she finds the source of collective identity as a Palestinian Israeli. The ability to fulfill her mission—to continue her cousin's legacy and, therefore, his very identity—results in the ascent of her life-line, with her acceptance to Seeds of Peace.

As the master narrative of Palestinian-Israeli identity would suggest, then, the October events are indeed *the* formative events of a new generation of youth, politicized and mobilized toward securing and defending their rights as a minority whose existence is threatened. The political action and collective mobilization of the Stand Tall generation toward some purposive end requires a specific method of dual-identity reconciliation: the powerful identification with their Palestinian national identity, and their resistance to "Israelization." Jibril stands out as the ultimate counterexample, a young man so convinced of his belonging to the Jewish state. Rania, on the other hand, is an archetypal member of the Stand Tall generation.

Coming to Seeds of Peace and at last being given the *choice* to self-label the way she wants, rather than fear consequences of that act, Rania describes the dilemma she faced:

> I have a great connection with the Israelis. I live with them; I have an Israeli passport.... I also have a great connection with the Palestinians, because, you know, we are originally from Israel—the Palestinians. So in this camp I say that I'm Palestinian, but when I travel everywhere I say I'm Israeli.
>
> It's the only place I can do it safely, to call myself a Palestinian.... I had a war with myself. To make peace, you have to go to war with yourself. And I made it, and I think I made the right choice.... I am with the Palestinians. I understand how they feel.... Even if I say I'm from Israel, I can't lie to my heart, to say I'm not Palestinian. So I made that choice, to say I'm Palestinian.

At the time of narrating her life story to me, at age 14, in the serene woods of Maine, far from the social structure that subordinates her, Rania is at last free to go through the struggle of self-identification. And, more importantly, owing to the new social structure in which she finds herself, she possesses the agency to come to her own decision about that self-identification and to implement it in her discourse with others. She has struggled, yet she believes "in her heart" that her true identity is Palestinian; her connection to Israel is official but ultimately meaningless in her own budding national consciousness. Excluded, marginalized, threatened, assaulted, and collectively traumatized, the Stand Tall generation reveals Israel's success at cultivating a new generation of youth who do not see themselves as part of the state (Rabinowitz & Abu-Baker, 2005). Rania's narrative offers an excellent example of this phenomenon.

In its form, Rania's life story assumes a descent-and-gain pattern that resembles the master narrative of Palestinian-Israeli identity only more recently, with the impact of the *intifada* period most integrated. In its content, Rania's narrative reveals positive gains, yet it is haunted by the great nadir of her cousin's death. Her posttraumatic response, though, is one that restores meaning to her story. Her cousin, the martyr, lives on through her and her social practice. She seeks to emulate him and, in this way, to preserve his memory and restore his own narrative of peaceful struggle.

The ideological setting of Rania's life story is thus consistent with the ideological setting of the master narrative: the struggle for justice and equal rights for Arabs within Israel. She does not speak of "liberating" the whole of Palestine, for such liberation is viewed within the Palestinian-Israeli narrative as futile, given Israel's demonstrated military superiority (Rabinowitz & Abu-Baker, 2005). Rather, she speaks of a two-state solution:

> I think in this region there are two peoples. There must be two states, and one future for them. That's the only way to come to peace.... The *intifada* is about the Palestinians wanting their own land and their own state, 'cause they have the right to have their own country. They don't have the right to leave their village.... There are all these tanks and guns, and every day there is someone who is killed.

In her narrative, Rania expresses support for the Palestinians in the occupied territories and their cause of national liberation, yet she believes that Israel will continue to exist. She argues for the infeasibility of a one-state solution.

Rania's narrative offers a stark contrast to Jibril's in its appropriation of a master narrative of Palestinian-Israeli identity thematically organized on an axis of subordination, insecurity, and the negotiation of hyphenation through an accentuation of Palestinian identity. Her current identity configuration is characterized by the high salience of her Palestinian identity, coupled with an acknowledgment, but low salience, of her Israeli civic identity. The fact that she describes her own process of self-identification at camp as a "war" with herself (in fact appropriating a sentiment expressed by a former participant) speaks to the challenges of identity hyphenation for young Palestinian Israelis.

Rania is a young member of a new generation of Palestinian Israelis, one for whom a master narrative anchored in discrimination and subordination, existential insecurity, and the politics of identity hyphenation is salient. It is a generation whose Palestinian identity has become accentuated out of a sense of collective necessity, to ensure the continuation of its existence (Rabinowitz & Abu-Baker, 2005). It is a generation that resists Israel's systematic attempts at identity restructuring. It is a generation of whom Rania is a part, but Jibril is not—yet.

"I Am Divided Between the Two": The Story of Sami

Though it fails to figure prominently—or at all, really—in their life stories, it is noteworthy that Jibril and Rania are both Muslim. Both identify their families as generally nonobservant. The Palestinian Israelis in small cities and villages tend, by and large, to be Muslim. Palestinian-Israeli Christians, by contrast, tend to inhabit the larger cities of Nazareth and Haifa. Sami, a 16-year-old Christian Arab, is from Haifa, well-known in Israel for its designation as "the city of coexistence."

Jews and Arabs do indeed jointly inhabit Haifa, though the city remains quite segregated, both residentially and commercially. As it turns out, though, Sami is someone whose family has defied the structural constraints of voluntary segregation and chosen to "desegregate" themselves. They live in a predominantly Jewish neighborhood. In discussing his contact with Jews, Sami relates the ways in which this experience has impacted his life:

> I've never had any close Jewish friends, because of the environment. The
> place, the neighborhood that I lived in when I was young was mostly
> Arab. I moved to this house in the seventh grade, and here it is exactly
> the opposite. Most of the neighborhood is Jewish, except for a few Arab
> students.... I'm not allowed to hang out on the street here, so I keep
> going back to my old neighborhood, with my old friends.

During one of my visits to Sami's welcoming home, his mother related stories of their struggles with Jewish neighbors, even though they have good relations with most of them. She recalled an incident in which her neighbor had a death in the family, and she visited to pay her respects. The neighbor was most grateful, but her adult children, who live on a West Bank settlement, refused to even acknowledge her presence in the home. Sami's mother was incredibly offended, feeling a deep sense of existential insecurity in the moment.

Though relations with Jews may be unpredictable for the Arab citizens of Haifa like Sami and his family, such relations do nevertheless occur, which makes these Palestinian Israelis a unique group. Palestinian citizens like Jibril and Rania rarely encounter Jews as children or adolescents. Only when the inhabitants of places like Taybeh go to university or to work in Jewish cities like Netanya or Tel Aviv do they finally engage in regular social interactions with Jews. Such is not the case for Haifa's Arab residents, no matter how separate their lives may be from the Jewish residents. These lives necessarily intersect, and it is difficult to live one's life in complete segregation from the "other."

Even though the cosmopolitanism of Haifa's bustling (ironically named) Arab commercial street, Ben-Gurion, seems to resemble the Arab cosmopolitanism of Ramallah, it feels closer to what I perceive as a European cosmopolitanism than a distinctly Arab one. Once again, we must consider the significance of local identity. Haifa's Arab residents are quite diverse, though there are a large number of Christians in the city. But given the level of economic development of the city, they are by and large doing well relative to their peers in the villages, and certainly relative to Palestinians in the occupied territories. They are, generally speaking, a people who are more interested in living a peaceful life than in sacrificing themselves in the name of "liberation." Bear in mind that many of Haifa's contemporary Arabs are descendants of those Palestinians who chose (or were permitted) to remain in 1948.

Arab culture in Haifa, then, should be considered for what it is: cosmopolitan and gazing Westward. There are elite private schools, and families vacation in Europe. They are connected to the West in part out of their assumption of the Israeli identity, as their passports are not welcome in much of the Arab and Muslim world to this very day. Sami's story must be contextualized in this way: as a young Haifa resident, whose family is financially secure and seeks for him a life of great success, measured mostly in educational and economic terms.

It should come as little surprise then that Sami's life story is, to date, a narrative of progress. As he begins his narrative, he says,

> As I remember it, I was happy most of the time, so it was all up. And then as I got to, I first went to school, so things got steady. Life took a regular path. It doesn't have many changes, and here it was the first tough thing in my life. And then it picks up again.

The narrative tone of Sami's story is, at base, very positive. He interprets his life as characterized primarily by happiness up to this point, taking a "regular path."

Sami's story begins with gradual ascent and stability, disrupted by an accident in childhood. A frightening time in his life, and a time in which he was suddenly made aware of his own mortality, Sami describes it as follows: "When I was a kid we were driving down the hill, and a bus hit us and pulled us.... Life didn't go back like it was before, after the accident."

His childhood car accident serves as the nadir in Sami's life story, and it is an event he is loath to revisit emotionally. The remaining peaks and valleys in his story relate to school transitions and adjustments, all of which Sami has ultimately mastered. In describing his general attitude toward life's necessary transitions, he says, "I got used to the changes in life. A person needs to adjust more quickly, and this is what I learned."

The form of Sami's narrative is best characterized as *progressive*, with a descent-and-gain pattern. Formally, there is little connection between Sami's life story and the master narrative of Palestinian-Israeli identity. Sami has no stories of great tragic loss, and no stories of subordination emerge unsolicited in his narrative. Even in its content, then, Sami's story seems to contain little, if any, internalization of the major themes of the Palestinian-Israeli master narrative.

Events related to the conflict are, like many Jewish-Israeli life stories, absent in the spontaneous narration of Sami's story. With probing, some emerge but are clearly tangential to the daily experience of Sami's adolescent life. That is, the conflict has little tangible impact on his life, which is again perhaps particular to the social and political ecology of Haifa, as well as his level of economic advantage.

When asked directly about any perceptions of discrimination in Israel based on his Arab identity, Sami says,

> I think that if I'm going to be discriminated against, I still don't feel it. Like my parents tell me that when you go to the university, they have a certain percentage of Arabs in every course. They don't allow more, even if you are qualified.... I think that the state of Israel doesn't consider me as a full citizen, let's say, it will prefer to have a Jewish citizen more than an Arab-Israeli citizen. But until now, I don't feel it.

For Sami, anti-Arab discrimination is more of a hypothesis than a lived experience. He has lived nothing of it, and it has only been internalized in his consciousness through discourse—the discourse of his family, who seek to prepare him for an adult life of subordination.

On my last visit to Haifa, the subject of Sami's career came up while we were all enjoying predinner drinks and discussion. (The fact that Sami's family is Christian meant that dinner was always preceded by aperitifs and accompanied by wine.) While Sami at this point expresses an interest in technology, his mother says to me, "He should be a doctor, shouldn't he?" I note that medicine is certainly a noble profession and confess that my own father was in fact a physician. But Sami's mother has another justification for her suggestion: "If he is a doctor, they cannot discriminate against him for being Arab. It's too noble of a profession, and it's too difficult to become a doctor. Once he has become a doctor, they will have no choice but to accept him."

Sami's family, it turns out, has gone to great lengths to shield him from discrimination as a child. They have enrolled him in the best private schools in Haifa for Arabs, and they do not permit him to associate in their predominantly Jewish neighborhood. Sami has yet to fully engage with the Jewish majority, living for the moment in comfortable segregation from them. His parents prepare him for what they consider to be the inevitable: his experience of discrimination upon the more complete engagement with mainstream Israeli society as an adult.

Yet perhaps more than just physical segregation protects Sami for the time being. His life story presents an ideological setting that is tolerable in Israeli society. It is not polarizing or divisive; it does not call for the illegitimacy of

Zionism or the destruction of Israel. It does not even highlight the tragic conditions of either the Palestinians in the occupied territories or the Arabs in Israel to any considerable length. The recent tragedy in the Palestinian-Israeli narrative—the October events—is not even referenced by Sami.

Let us consider that all too common identity predicament for Israel's Palestinian citizens—the choice of an identity label. Sami has only begun this process of identity negotiation as a 16-year-old, but for now, he says,

> I feel some kind of connection [to the Palestinians], but it doesn't necessarily mean that I support their actions. I am part of this people, this nation.

Q: Which nation?

> The Palestinian *and* the Israeli. I don't belong to one part. I am divided between the two. When they reach a point when they can achieve peace, I will be whole. Then I won't need to keep struggling with myself. I'm not connected to this side or that. This gives me an inner conflict.

Q: So what identity label do you prefer?

> I guess Arab Israeli, because I live in Israel, and I am a Palestinian. To that question, when I think about it twice, I think I would prefer to be called Palestinian-Israeli or Israeli-Palestinian. Maybe that can be achieved after peace.

This excerpt from Sami's narrative reveals the current conflict within himself over the hyphenation of identity. This conflict, which extends beyond labels and infuses his entire narrative and his interpretive frame of political events, is intimately connected to the larger conflict between Israel and the Palestinians in the occupied territories. It is, as Sami relates, preventing a complete integration of his identities—a sense of wholeness. As scholars have noted, the Arab–Jewish conflict inside of Israel cannot begin to fully be addressed until Israel is at peace with her Arab neighbors, and with the Palestinians *outside* of Israel proper (Tessler & Grant, 1998).

For now, we ought to recognize that Sami, like all of the youths whose narratives I have examined thus far, is only beginning a process of identity development. His narrative is in its earliest stages of formation. Thus, his current identity configuration is but a window into the process of conflict and consolidation necessitated by the hyphenated nature of Palestinian-Israeli identity. In this telling of his life story, Sami recognizes some connection to

Palestinians in the occupied territories, nationally and culturally, yet he does not fully approve of their actions against his home state of Israel. The ideological setting of his life story, as revealed in his discussion of the history of the conflict and his thoughts on its current phase, suggests a closer identification with Jewish Israelis than with Palestinians. His own historical narrative of the conflict illustrates:

> The conflict began with the Balfour Declaration, when the British promised the Jews to give them Palestine. And the Palestinians who were living here didn't know. And, actually, I remember my grandparents telling me that even before that, Jews used to live here side by side with the Palestinians, sharing bathrooms and having one bathroom for two apartments in the old houses.... And then, after the Balfour Declaration, after the British occupation, the Jews started coming from all over the world. They came here and settled here and this was the starting of the Independence War in 1948. Then a lot of Palestinians fled out of the country, including some of my family members.... And some of the Palestinians stayed here, in their homes, and some went to the West Bank because, and when the Israelis, when the Jews came here, they started building the country. And that's how some Arab Israelis got here. They didn't flee to some other place. Like me and my family.... And then we had the '67 war, when Egypt, Syria and Jordan, I think, attacked, at once, Israel. Israel had to defend the territory and some of them they have taken them, territories from the other countries.

At first glance, this brief historical narrative is certainly accurate enough in its basic accounting of actual events, especially for an adolescent for whom the subject is avoided in formal educational contexts. (Recall that the state-approved curriculum, even for private schools, deliberately excludes direct education about the history of the conflict.) Yet, as we begin to consider Sami's account in its interpretive frame—that is, the particular ways in which these historical events are assembled into a coherent narrative—we can begin to see his internalization of a perspective more in line with a Jewish-Israeli, rather than a Palestinian, perspective on the conflict.

First, Sami traces the origins of the conflict not to *the Jews* or to Zionism (which, incidentally, is not mentioned at all in his narrative), but rather to *the British*. Rather than see the British as a "tool" for Zionist colonialism, as the Palestinian narrative does (e.g., Arafat, 1974/2001), Sami sees the British as largely responsible for mass Jewish immigration. Note, however, that absent in Sami's narrative is any mention of Jewish persecution and suffering in Europe, so he has not fully internalized that narrative but has instead adopted a more "in-between" stance. In addition, his narrative does suggest that British policy was meant to benefit Western powers, alluding to elements of the Palestinian master narrative.

Although we see a glimpse of the Palestinian narrative of harmony among Jews, Muslims, and Christians before Zionism, as Sami recalls his grandparents' account, he refers to 1948 as the "War for Independence"—a label that is rejected in the Palestinian narrative in favor of *al-Nakba*, the "Catastrophe" (Sa'di & Abu-Lughod, 2007). Referring to 1948, Sami also describes Arabs as "fleeing" Palestine, without any suggestion that their evacuation may have been forced by Jews (Morris, 1987). The Palestinian narrative insists that the refugees were violently expelled from Palestine, whereas the Israeli narrative insists that they left willingly (Abdel-Nour, 2004; Jawad, 2006).

Perhaps most surprisingly, Sami's account of the 1967 war between Israel and her Arab neighbors represents the Jewish-Israeli narrative. In that war, Israel destroyed the capabilities of Egypt, Syria, and Jordan preemptively in response to its perception of their intent and preparation for war (Smith, 2001). The actual historical events of this war are, for our purposes, irrelevant. What is relevant is the narrative constructed by individuals *about* those events, and for Sami to describe the 1967 war as a "defensive" war on Israel's part, in specific response to an attack by the neighboring Arab states, reveals his identification with a historical narrative of the conflict closer to that of Jewish Israelis than of Palestinians.

In terms of the most current phase of the conflict—the second *intifada*— Sami's narrative reveals the internal conflict created by his hyphenated identity. On the one hand, he sympathizes with the Palestinians. On the other, he is radically opposed to suicide bombing. Describing the origins of the second *intifada*, he says,

> I think that it was started when the Israeli prime minister—or, he was the defense minister—entered al-Aqsa, and the Muslims didn't agree to that. So they started with the *intifada*. That wasn't the only reason—they were in poverty, their economic situation was getting bad, and it was getting worse, so they didn't have other things to do. It was the only solution. So they started sending suicide bombers to Israel.

As he begins his narrative of the current context of conflict, suddenly Sami seems more aligned with the Palestinians. Jewish Israelis and pro-Israel advocates tend to argue that the *intifada* was entirely coordinated and planned to coincide with the failure of Camp David, so as to elicit more sympathy for the Palestinians and, hopefully, get them an even better deal than what Prime Minister Ehud Barak had offered (e.g., Dershowitz, 2003; see Bar-Tal, 2004b).

But Sami does not make this argument. He does acknowledge that, while Sharon's visit to the Temple Mount may have been the catalyst, the *intifada* has its origins in the economic suffering of the Palestinians (see Roy, 2004).

While Sami identifies the emergence of the *intifada* in the structure of Israel's occupation (Gordon, 2008a, 2008b), with all of its economic consequences (Roy, 2004), he does not support the tactics of the uprising. Yet he is able to fuse both Israeli and Palestinian perspectives on suicide bombers into his own account, thus providing evidence of interpretive *integration* in his current identity configuration:

> Suicide bombers, I think they undergo a mind wash, brainwash. Yeah, they get into a very bad situation. Their family, some members of the family are dead during this conflict, so they feel like they have no choice. They feel like they can't do anything else, so they decide to sacrifice their life. But it's not exactly a sacrifice, because when someone sacrifices something, he does it to benefit other people, and I don't see they are benefiting the Palestinian people as they come here and kill innocent civilians. So Israel needs to strike back, more strongly. This is also a circle of violence.

Interestingly, Sami's narrative of suicide bombing integrates both Israeli and Palestinian discourse. Characterizing the bombers as "brainwashed" is consistent with the Israeli narrative, which positions the bomber as a tool of the larger "terrorist infrastructure" committed to Israel's annihilation. Also, the notion that the tactic of suicide bombing does little to actually *help* the Palestinians—the idea of its futility and its misguidedness—is characteristic of the mainstream Israeli interpretation. Sami does, however, identify the motive to become a bomber in the economic and existential insecurity of the occupation (Gordon, 2008a, 2008b; Roy, 2004), which suggests a level of identification with the Palestinian narrative. In his fusion of interpretive stances, he has constructed a narrative that legitimizes both, providing a pragmatic, integrated narrative of mutual acknowledgment.

Ideologically, then, Sami's identity appears to be more closely positioned with the discourse of the Jewish majority in Israel, yet his narrative reveals an affiliation with the Palestinians that creates a level of pragmatic integration. In his views on the conflict and its history, Sami appears to have internalized a largely Jewish-Israeli interpretive frame. But in his account of the second *intifada*, Sami demonstrates a higher level of narrative integration in his ability to consider disparate accounts and recognize their mutual legitimacy.

Sami's narrative must, like all of the narratives examined in this book, be viewed as a psychosocial project in its beginning stages. As he strives to organize his life events and ideological convictions into a story that possesses credibility and integrity, he is in the midst of confronting the consequences of a hyphenated identity. For the moment, his identity as an Israeli citizen is quite salient. Culturally, he recognizes his connection to the Palestinians, yet he has not integrated that connection into his personal narrative in such a way that influences its ideological setting with much significance. The stories of discrimination based on his Arab identity are nothing *more than* stories—abstract possibilities for his future life course. Prejudice is not, for him, readily perceptible in his lived experience, and so he feels a connection to the Jewish majority in which he is embedded and, in his mind, accepted as a legitimate member. To Sami, the Palestinian-Israeli master narrative is just an abstraction. It is a collection of stories and struggles that have little connection to his peaceful, pleasant life in Haifa. And so in Sami we see little, if any, identification with this master narrative.

Summary: The Cultural Psychology of Palestinian-Israeli Youth

The stories of Jibril, Rania, and Sami reveal one remarkably powerful and unifying theme in the Palestinian-Israeli master narrative: the need to traverse the challenging discursive and ideological terrain of identity hyphenation. Scholarship on the Palestinian Israelis, particularly beginning in the 1990s, has presented a fairly linear account of a shifting master narrative for this subordinated minority in Israel—from the injustice of "Israelization" to the reclamation of a Palestinian national and cultural identity (e.g., Rabinowitz & Abu-Baker, 2005; Rouhana, 1997). Yet what the narratives of contemporary youth reveal quite strikingly is that Palestinian Israelis do not undergo a fully linear process of identity development. Rather, they are embedded in a context of circulating *conversations* about identity, discourses that are polyphonic and far from monolithic. These discourses are deeply connected to social and political issues that comprise a given context for Israel's young Palestinian citizens—issues that link to the history of family and local community as much as the larger Palestinian populace in Israel, the occupied territories, the refugee camps, and the diaspora.

The negotiation of a hyphenated identity, with its differential "weights" and "tugs" at various moments, reveals the connection of narrative identity development to a process of *narrative engagement* (Hammack, 2008; Hammack & Cohler, 2009). The idea of narrative engagement is deceptively simple, even as it challenges received notions of human development as a linear process. Narrative engagement describes the process of confrontation with multiple storylines that young people encounter as they begin to make their identities through social practice and life story construction. As a conceptual idea, narrative engagement speaks powerfully to the Palestinian Israelis, confronted with multiple and often conflicting discourses of history and identity. The recognition of a *polyphonic* master narrative—one that is in a dynamic state of tension and negotiation, rather than simply appropriated by a nonagentic actor—allows for an interpretation of the fault lines among the stories of Sami, Rania, and Jibril.

An inhabitant of a social ecology still scarred from the legacy of military administration and convinced of its relative privilege in the Jewish, rather than Palestinian, state, Jibril sees a trajectory of success in the embrace of his civic identity as an Israeli. Aware of his historical and cultural connection to the Palestinians, he favors a life course as an Israeli citizen and constructs his own personal narrative to "fit" within the acceptable identity discourse of its Jewish majority. In social psychological terms, Jibril favors the strategy of *individual mobility* as a response to the subordination of his minority status.

By contrast, Rania's narrative is emblematic of the "Stand Tall" generation described by Rabinowitz and Abu-Baker (2005). Her rejection of the pressures of "Israelization" and her staunch accentuation of a Palestinian national identity, over and above her Israeli civic identity, provides clear evidence of the historical identity process that has come to be described as "normative" for contemporary Palestinian Israelis (e.g., Rouhana, 1997). Yet the clear *distinction* between the narratives of Rania and Jibril reveals the problematic nature of applying a monolithic, linear master narrative to *all* the members of a group, for such an account fails to recognize the *agency* individuals possess (always bound by a larger matrix of power and hegemony) to appropriate discourse into their own personal narratives.

In other words, the Palestinian Israelis provide another important layer of theorizing the relationship among culture, power, and identity, for the politics of hyphenation and their uniquely "liminal" status positions them in a place of "double marginality" from which they will undoubtedly utilize diverse strategies for narrative identity development. The narratives of youth examined here reveal the attempt to establish an ideological setting for the life story through the *engagement with* and *appropriation of* a particular discourse of identity encountered within one's social ecology of development.

The general statement we might make about the cultural psychology of Palestinian-Israeli youth is that it is characterized by this fundamental process of identity negotiation and reconciliation. The narratives of Jibril, Rania, and Sami present their identities as entirely static, as any kind of empirical data necessarily does. Considered more for their implications for developmental *process*, these narratives suggest that Palestinian-Israeli youth are actively making decisions about how to negotiate the disparate discourse to which they are exposed in their identity development. As I present longitudinal data on the life story development of these and other youths in Chapter 7, we will begin to be able to better query narrative identity development as a process, rather than a static product, of human development.

PART III

Interventions

"Each person you know about and can affect is someone to whom you have responsibilities: to say this is just to affirm the very idea of morality. The challenge, then, is to take minds and hearts formed over the long millennia of living in local troops and equip them with ideas and institutions that will allow us to live together as the global tribe we have become."

—Kwame Anthony Appiah, *Cosmopolitanism: Ethics in a World of Strangers* (2006), p. xiii

6

Peace and the Politics of Contact: A Brief History

Contact: The Allure and Challenge

Although I have known him for a year, it is my first visit to Ali's home in East Jerusalem. It is the summer of 2004, and the fighting of the *intifada* has calmed, however tenuously. Compared to the homes of other Palestinians, and Israelis as well, Ali's is quite impressive. It is spacious and clean, with bedrooms for each of the children and several bathrooms. The living room is massive, with a big-screen TV and several luxuriant sofas. As he takes me on the tour of his home, we pass the kitchen, where our feast of a lunch is being prepared not by Ali's mother but by the family's servant, to whom I offer my hand before I realize the impropriety of the gesture. She turns to her work, as I withdraw it, somewhat embarrassed by my sudden amnesia on the rules of Palestinian culture.

Minutes later, I am in Ali's room, which contains a full-size bed, desk, computer, weight-lifting machine, and posters of Eminem, 50 Cent, and Britney Spears. Ali is anxious to show me his collection of pirated DVDs, burned from the Internet. He is also anxious to show me the contents of a particular folder on his computer—the folder that contains scores of images of death and destruction since the second *intifada*. "Remember when

I met you last summer, I told you there was so much to see here. I wanna show you now, what we, the Palestinians, go through." A 30-minute prelude to our follow-up interview, to be conducted 1 year after his participation in Hands of Peace and 2 years after his participation in Seeds of Peace, it utterly confused me that Ali could continue to be so ideologically polarized in his thinking, so determined to "prove" his identity to me as a Palestinian, and to maintain a fervent anti-Israel stance, even after his experiences in these programs. And yet the more I considered our knowledge of the social psychology of intergroup contact, as well as the unique context of Israeli–Palestinian relations, the less elusive his postcontact behavior and identity became to me.

The contact hypothesis offers an incredibly appealing idea to the cosmopolitan liberal pluralist—the individual who, like Gordon Allport in his time and both Kwame Anthony Appiah and John Wallach (founder of Seeds of Peace) in our own time, possesses a genuine sensibility for human coexistence through mutual recognition and ongoing conversation. Originating in the social psychology of the postwar United States, as the Civil Rights Movement began to brew and the immorality and injustice of institutionalized racism became increasingly recognized in American liberal discourse, the contact hypothesis seems deceptively simple. Allport (1954), who is typically credited with its original articulation, argued that contact between groups could, *under certain conditions*, reduce the prejudice within individuals that secures the maintenance of intergroup conflict.

Social psychologists Tom Pettigrew, once a student of Allport's and a distinguished scholar of race relations in the United States, and Linda Tropp recently examined over 500 studies of contact between groups in conflict to put contact theory to test. They discovered that, overall, contact appeared to reduce prejudice, suggesting that contact can indeed be a very positive force for improving intergroup relations (Pettigrew & Tropp, 2006). However, not all efforts are so successful. There are clearly situations in which contact may, in fact, produce negative consequences or fail to reduce prejudice, and there is a need to study such encounters (Pettigrew, 2008a).

To understand how contact might not produce its desired, ideal effects—to make sense of Ali's steadfast polarization 1 year postcontact—we need to consider the contact hypothesis more fully. In particular, we must consider its application in the particular context of the Israeli–Palestinian conflict, to query both whether this application is appropriate and whether the anticipated consequences of contact are even reasonable in the midst of an ongoing intractable conflict. In other words, we must take the contact hypothesis from its grounding in some universal (but American-produced) conception of mind and society to the particular world inhabited by Palestinians and Israelis. In so doing,

I will interrogate the very idea of contact as a product of a distinctly American folk psychology of intergroup relations.

First, though, let us consider the idea of contact in greater depth by returning to Allport's original text. The excerpt from Allport's (1954) seminal volume that specifies the hypothetical conditions by which intergroup contact is deemed "effective" is, like the idea of contact itself, deceptively simple:

> Prejudice ... may be reduced by equal status contact between majority and minority groups in the pursuit of common goals. The effect is greatly enhanced if this contact is sanctioned by institutional supports (i.e., by law, custom or local atmosphere), and provided it is of a sort that leads to the perception of common interests and common humanity between members of the two groups. (p. 281)

From these two sentences, social psychologists have extracted four basic "principles" of effective intergroup contact, although the conditions for "optimal" intergroup contact have essentially become a catalog of conditions unattainable in any authentic social setting (Dixon et al., 2005). These four key conditions are: (1) equal status between groups in the encounter; (2) an active pursuit of common goals; (3) facilitation of cooperation, rather than competition, between groups; and (4) external support for the aims of intergroup contact.

Translation from the idealistic laboratory analogue to the real-world context of improving interethnic relations almost immediately called the contact hypothesis into question (Amir, 1969). A cursory consideration of Allport's original conditions suggests that the contact hypothesis appears problematic in the context of the Israeli–Palestinian conflict. First, the asymmetrical status of Israelis and Palestinians makes the first condition seemingly insurmountable. Although efforts to create symmetry of power in the intergroup encounter are, in fact, successful in many cases in Israel (using frequency of participation as a measure; see Maoz, 2004a, 2006), the structural reality of asymmetry is unyielding, revealing such a power equilibrium as largely ephemeral (Rouhana, 2004; Rouhana & Fiske, 1995; Rouhana & Korper, 1996, 1997).

The second and third conditions specified by the original hypothesis are also problematic, given that the Israeli–Palestinian conflict is at base a *competition of identities*. It stands to reason that engineering contact toward the pursuit of some common goal, and in some cooperative way, would be quite difficult, since it does not serve the interests of either group in their efforts to "win" the conflict through securing the legitimacy of their national identity. In other words, the zero-sum, intractable nature of the conflict makes it difficult to envision cooperation, given that Israelis and Palestinians are in a fierce competition over political and territorial control *and* exclusive claims to legitimacy

(Bar-Tal, 1998b, 2007). Yet such a statement fails to consider the possibility of revising the end goal, and thus deflating the zero-sum nature of the conflict. Although the official position of Israelis and Palestinians may not as yet endorse such a revision (though one might argue that a two-state solution is inherently a revision of the original goals of the rival nationalisms; see Kelman, 1978), certainly many individuals on both sides of the conflict do.

It is the fourth and final condition specified by Allport's original hypothesis that appears the most problematic, for it specifies the need for cultural and institutional support of intergroup contact. While institutional support certainly exists in both Israeli and Palestinian societies in some measure (recall that both governments officially support Seeds of Peace and select participants for the program), whether or not the *culture* of these two societies indeed supports the identity transcendence that contact may seek is questionable. At base, the practices of Israelis and Palestinians are themselves rooted in the existence of conflict, with compulsory army service, resistance fighting, fences and walls, segregation and polarization.

In spite of the somewhat obvious challenges of applying the contact hypothesis to intergroup relations in Israel and Palestine, there has indeed been a rich and exhaustive effort to use this social psychological strategy to support efforts at peacebuilding. In the rest of this chapter, I will provide a brief history of the contact hypothesis and its application in Israel and Palestine since 1948, attempting to situate the two American programs examined in this study within the context of other projects and the broader idea of contact as a worthwhile enterprise for young Israelis and Palestinians. This review will, I hope, provide the reader with the necessary frame with which to interpret the narratives of youth collected after contact, which I will present in the next chapter.

I frame my review of Israeli–Palestinian coexistence programs within the larger history of the idea that produced them—the idea of peacebuilding from the "bottom up" through interventions designed to alter individual psychology, to transform "prejudiced personalities" to "tolerant personalities" (Allport, 1954) and, in the process, activate a mass *psychological* movement for social change. To fully comprehend this idea, we need to turn to the historical context of its origination in social psychology.

The Pathology of Prejudice

In an early articulation of the concept of *ethnocentrism*, the American sociologist William Graham Sumner (1906) defined it as "[the] view of things in which one's own group is the center of everything, and all others are scaled and rated with reference to it" (pp. 27–28). He goes on to say that "ethnocentrism leads a people to exaggerate and intensify everything in their own folkways which is peculiar and which differentiates them from others. It therefore strengthens the folkways" (p. 28). In other words, as a form of what psychologists would call *prejudice*, ethnocentrism entails the internalization of attitudes associated with cultural superiority. The question for psychologists has been how and why such attitudes come to exist in the mind and, consequently, how they might be eliminated or reduced.

The earliest work in group psychology was captivated by the idea of a "collective mind"—the notion that, when an individual becomes part of a group, he or she loses any sense of personal subjectivity or agency. This view is well articulated in three classics of early social psychology: Gustave Le Bon's (1895/1969) *The Crowd: A Study of the Popular Mind*, William McDougall's (1921) *The Group Mind*, and Sigmund Freud's (1921/1959) *Group Psychology and the Analysis of the Ego*. These early texts are united in their focus on the way in which a collective psyche can emerge in social situations to obstruct the free will of individuals.

Given its origins in Western intellectual thought, this early scholarship tended to assume a dark view of collective consciousness or behavior. In other words, these early thinkers all clearly privilege the idea of a rational individual agent, whose ability to function at the height of reason is thwarted by the group. For this reason, Taylor and Moghaddam (1994) refer to this school of thought as the "irrationalist" view within social psychology. Simply put, groups are bad, and individuals are good.

The subfield of "intergroup relations" within social psychology emerged from these earlier schools of thought in the mid–twentieth century United States with a central intellectual question: How can individuals become motivated by their group membership to engage in mass collective violence? Not far from this question was another: How can members of a majority come to "hate" members of a minority so much as to be complicit in a genocide?

Obviously, these questions were motivated by the sociopolitical context of World War II and, more precisely, the Holocaust in which Nazi Germany attempted to annihilate entire groups, the most numerous of which were Jews. The line of thought that developed, consistent with the irrationalist model, was that only a *pathology of personality* could motivate individuals to engage in such violence.

Freud (1921/1959) argued that individuals become members of an "obedient herd" by forging an identification with the leader of the group. They must come to identify with the leader, seeing him or her as their own *ego ideal*, internalizing the norms, mores, and rhetoric of the leader. Consistent with his psychosexual theory of development and his structural theory of mind, Freud viewed this process as connected to individual libidinal impulses and instincts. Libidinal (love) psychic energy is directed toward the group, translating into loyalty, commitment, and the willingness for personal sacrifice. Freud suggests that the individual ego becomes blindsided by the ego ideal, as represented in the leader to which the identification is formed.

The most important implication of Freud's theory, especially when contrasted with theories of intergroup conflict that would follow, is that hostility between groups serves a primary psychological *function* for an in-group. The ability to distinguish between in-group and out-group—and thus to distinctly *feel* a commitment to some group—produces in-group harmony and cohesion and the displacement of aggression from in-group members to a clearly defined out-group. As Freud suggests, this psychological function might be considered "primal" or fundamental in that it can clearly be linked to strategies for individual survival in harsh environments of the past. In other words, there might be an *evolutionary* reason for such a social psychology. Another key implication of Freud's theory, and one that would become all the more relevant as World War II approached, is that there are definitive *roles* within groups—most notably, the role of the leader—and these roles are requisites for the basic functioning of groups.

As I have suggested, there are some significant critiques that can be levied upon the irrationalist view of groups. First, the tendency to place group psychology in a place of "primitive" consciousness relative to individual psychology speaks to an underlying bias toward individualism among Western social scientists. In other words, individual reason is privileged over emotion, as well as over collective experience, which may be reflective of an intellectual bias (see Moghaddam, 1987). This tendency to privilege individual subjectivity and agency also leads to a general lack of acknowledgment of the *material* basis of intergroup conflict. Thus, such theories tend to overlook the role of a larger social structure, or of power differentials between groups, in producing antagonism or competition. The work of thinkers like Freud, Le Bon, and McDougall seems heavily connected to a Eurocentric Enlightenment narrative of identity, in which individual *liberty* represents psychological freedom from the "savagery" of collective identity. Although there is recognition of the psychological *function* groups appear to serve, there is little emphasis on the psychological benefits of group membership or collective identity—a position that now seems to come from a place of identity *privilege*, where there is little need for collective mobilization for social justice, for example.

As World War II came to a close and the extent of the Holocaust became known, social psychologists in the United States sought an explanation for how such horrors could be willingly committed. Theodore Adorno, the German sociologist and critical theorist of the Frankfurt School, collaborated with a team of researchers at the University of California, Berkeley, to construct what would become known as *authoritarian personality theory* (Adorno et al., 1950). Their central task: to understand how prejudice in general, and anti-Semitism in particular, could become so pervasive and so efficiently translated into direct violence against an entire group.

Adorno and his colleagues (1950) assumed that personality and culture were entirely intertwined and that "the political, economic, and social convictions of an individual often form a broad and coherent pattern, as if bound together by a 'mentality' or a 'spirit'..." (p. 1). Thus, they were aligned with a particular school of thought in the twentieth century, typically associated with psychological anthropology, that examined concepts of "national character" and the ways in which members of a nation were bound to a basic personality configuration that differentiated them from others (e.g., Benedict, 1946). Such studies are now typically discredited for their tendency to reify and essentialize groups, as well as their use in justifying colonial projects (see Neiburg & Goldman, 1998).

Interestingly, though, the conclusions of Adorno and colleagues privilege individual psychology over the cultural context in which prejudice is produced. Based on a number of studies reported in their seminal volume, Adorno and colleagues (1950) argue that conflict and large-scale collective violence such as witnessed in the atrocities of World War II can be explained at the level of individual psychology. More specifically, the origins of violent conflict between groups can be explained in terms of a pathology of personality:

> A basically hierarchical, authoritarian, exploitative parent-child
> relationship is apt to carry over into a power-oriented, exploitatively
> dependent attitude toward one's sex partner and one's God and may well
> culminate in a political philosophy and social outlook which has no room
> for anything but a desperate clinging to what appears to be strong and a
> disdainful rejection of whatever is relegated to the bottom. (p. 971)

The problem of the "potentially fascistic individual" (Adorno et al., 1950, p. 1) that Adorno and colleagues sought to examine can, they argue based on their numerous studies, be reduced to a particular parent–child relationship. This destructive relationship, in turn, results in the formation of a particular personality or character structure that then ultimately leads the individual toward a path of domination and violence.

A comprehensive review or critique of authoritarian personality theory is far beyond my aims here. What is most key for our purposes in this chapter is to understand the evolution of thought within social psychology that eventually led to the formulation of the contact hypothesis. In order for scholars to consider the idea of contact as a solution to conflict, the reliance on a notion of conflict as rooted in a state of pathology had to be challenged.

The Normative Psychology of Prejudice

Just as individuals are always embedded within a particular "political, economic, and social" context that informs their personality development, as Adorno and colleagues (1950) suggested, so too are scholars prey to the "spirit" of their times as they formulate their theories. Thus, it makes sense that, given the backdrop of the Holocaust and the need to address the pervasiveness of anti-Semitism, Adorno and colleagues would come to a view more in line with the irrationalist perspective within social psychology. It seemed unthinkable to imagine anything "rational" or "normative" about the prejudice that developed within Nazi Germany to justify collective violence against Jews and other groups.

Yet Gordon Allport brought a new perspective on the idea of prejudice. Unlike Adorno and his colleagues, Allport had no personal connection to the atrocities of World War II. Many social scientists—including Adorno, Freud, and Kurt Lewin—were forced to flee Europe because of either their political stance or their Jewish identities (or both). Allport, however, was an American personality and social psychologist spared from the personal horrors of World War II. As opposed to the anti-Semitism and genocide of Europe, it was the distinctly American context of racial segregation and discrimination that motivated Allport to study prejudice and to develop the contact hypothesis. His work can in many ways be viewed as signaling an important transition for psychologists away from a focus on the individual mind—and its potential for pathology—to a more integrated view of personality and social structure (e.g., Allport, 1961).

One of Allport's key contributions to the psychology of prejudice was to argue for its *normative*, expectable manifestation *in contexts of segregation*. In other words, for Allport, prejudice begins with a problem in the structure of a society: the physical separation of groups and their subsequent inability to engage with one another in basic daily contact, to get to know one another as distinct individuals rather than simply members of an out-group.

While Allport's theory of prejudice placed its ultimate antecedent in the social structure, rather than the mind of an individual, his idealism for prejudice reduction through contact suggested a bottom-up (i.e., individual-driven) theory of social change. That is, though he argued that, in order for race relations to improve in the United States, institutionalized segregation needed to end, he believed in the power of psychological interventions to contribute to the process of social change. In this way, he was guilty of the same intellectual bias as Freud and other members of the irrationalist school: he viewed individual reason as "superior" to collective mobilization. This bias toward individualism in his thought led him to recommend interventions focused on changing individual personalities, rather than the unjust social structures that produced those personalities themselves. I will return to this critique of contact in the next two chapters because it is so central to understanding why youths like Ali are unable to sustain the major psychological transformations that do indeed occur during contact.

The idea that prejudice is a normal psychological phenomenon, as opposed to some pathology of personality, was an intellectual breakthrough and liberated social psychology from a need to view social phenomena as rooted in clinical concerns. This breakthrough opened an intellectual path for a new theoretical approach to conflict: realistic conflict theory (e.g., Sherif, 1958).

Muzafer Sherif (1958), a Turkish-American psychologist, argued that conflicts between groups are best understood as *real, materially based conflicts of interest*. When groups are competing over resources, such as food, water, land, money, and the like, their members will develop hostile attitudes toward members of the other group. Thus, for Sherif and his colleagues, prejudice is a naturally occurring in-group bias that is rooted in material conflicts. The psychology of prejudice is an epiphenomenon to the physical and social structural context that *demands* conflict.

Sherif and his colleagues conducted a now-famous field experiment at the Robbers Cave State Park in Oklahoma in which they tested these ideas about conflict and concluded that it was possible to reduce conflict by altering the *functional* relationship between groups (Sherif et al., 1961). In other words, they found that simple contact interventions were ineffective. In fact, contact between the groups seemed to exacerbate intergroup hostility and even violence. Conflict was reduced only when the experimenters altered the relation between groups by introducing the need for cooperation to achieve *superordinate goals* (e.g., fixing the camp's communal water supply).

Sherif took the social psychology of conflict in an important new direction in two ways very relevant to Israeli–Palestinian relations. First, he, like Allport, assumed that conflict begins with a problem in the environment in which individuals are embedded, rather than in any fundamental pathology within an individual mind. The psychology of prejudice thus becomes an *effect* of or a *correlation* with a particular material condition—in Allport's case, segregation;

in Sherif's, competition over resources. Second, he suggested that, in order to reduce conflict, mere contact between group members is insufficient. Rather, the nature of the relationship between groups must itself be altered so that the original conditions that produced prejudice are eliminated.

Given that Israelis and Palestinians are involved in a fierce competition precisely over material resources—the land, water, and the economy (see Wasserstein, 2003)—the relevance of realistic conflict theory is obvious. The social-structural basis of Israeli–Palestinian relations is characterized by both segregation and a real conflict of material interests, and it stands to reason that the ultimate resolution to the conflict will require, as Sherif would argue, a dramatic change in the functional nature of this relationship. But before we consider the implications of Sherif's idea of superordinate goals for the contact situation between Israelis and Palestinians, we must consider another key development in the history of social psychology—the emergence of social identity theory.

From Personality to Identity

Two interrelated intellectual problems plague the early social psychological theories of conflict and intergroup relations I have thus far presented. The first problem, which I have already indicated, concerns the Enlightenment-based tendency to privilege individual psychology over group psychology, thus producing a crude picture of the individual as basically *contaminated* by his or her group membership. The second problem, which I suspect may be derivative from the first, concerns the lack of attention to *relative power* between groups.

Let me clarify this second point: It is not that theorists like Allport and Sherif do not recognize asymmetry between groups; Allport's work in particular is very clear about White racial hegemony in the United States. The problem is that the kinds of interventions specified—for Allport, an intervention designed to reduce stereotypes and prejudice by promoting acquaintanceship; for Sherif, an intervention designed to alter the functional relationship between groups—rely on the ability to *neutralize* power. That is, rather than acknowledge the effects of power asymmetry and the way in which it might influence attempts at intervention, both models essentially try to "play" with power in a way that is not possible in the real world—a world in which social structure and hierarchies exist and can be impervious to change, absent some form of *political* intervention.

A theoretical approach that began to address these critiques was developed in the 1970s and 1980s in the United Kingdom by Henri Tajfel and his colleagues. The approach came to be called *social identity theory*. It is useful to think about the emergence of social identity theory in relation to the broader context of social psychology in the 1970s. In an important article published in 1987 in the *American Psychologist,* Fathali Moghaddam contextualizes social identity theory in his exploration of "psychology in the three worlds." He argues that most psychological knowledge had been produced in the "first world" of North American psychology (and more specifically, in the United States), with its bias toward an individualistic, agentic model of the person (see also Markus & Kitayama, 1991; Shweder & Bourne, 1982), which Moghaddam suggests is connected to "United Statesian" capitalist ideology.

According to Moghaddam (1987), psychological knowledge produced in the "second world" includes research from the (now former) Soviet Union and other countries in Europe and the "developed" world. In this case, concepts and paradigms were often imported from the United States but discovered to be either irrelevant or problematic when applied to a different population. (I will shortly connect this story within social psychology more generally to the development of contact programs in Israel itself.) Most centrally, investigators increasingly recognized the need for a broader research paradigm that was not so heavily biased toward the individual rational agent. There was a need for a paradigm that could recognize the significance of the collective in less pejorative terms than originally postulated by Freud and his contemporaries.

It was in this broader historical context within social psychology that Henri Tajfel, a Jew who had escaped the Holocaust by fleeing to the UK, developed social identity theory. Tajfel aimed to develop a distinctly European social psychology that would focus on issues of collective identity and power relations among groups (e.g., Tajfel, 1978, 1981, 1982a, 1982b; Tajfel & Turner, 1979, 1986). He argued that American theories of conflict were primarily focused on *interpersonal,* rather than *intergroup,* relations. He was also critical of realistic conflict theory's tendency to view in-group identification as an epiphenomenon of the material world and not as central to the production and reproduction of conflict. Tajfel did not deny the significance of the material world, or of the social structure. In fact, matters of social structure were key to his analysis of intergroup relations beyond the laboratory. Rather, he argued for the significance of the social psychological process of *identification* with the group in the larger context of conflict.

Tajfel's theory was both *cognitive* and *social structural* in that he viewed groups as *social categories:* "cognitive tools that segment, classify, and order the social environment, and thus enable the individual to undertake many forms of social action" (Tajfel & Turner, 1986, pp. 15–16). Tajfel and his colleague Joseph Turner go on to say, in their classic essay, that social categories "provide a system of orientation for *self-reference*: they create and define the individual's place in society" (p. 16). As we organize the world, one of our central tasks is to make sense of social categories and *to identify the place of those categories within a larger matrix of possible social identities*. In other words, social categories are never neutral features of social cognition. Rather, they are *evaluative* and are thus connected to some emotional response.

It was in this vein that Tajfel and Turner came to their classic definition of social identity as "those aspects of an individual's self-image that derive from the social categories to which he perceives himself as belonging" (p. 16). They assumed that individuals would naturally seek to enhance the *positive distinctiveness* of their social identities, and that social identities are differentially valued within a given social order, producing differential conditions of "prestige" and power within an intergroup encounter. Thus, in the social world, self-evaluation always occurs with reference to one's social identity, and behavior is a function of the need to attain or maintain a positive social identity.

The basic assumption of social identity theory—that individuals in an intergroup situation will seek to attain or maintain a sense of positive differentiation relative to an out-group—has been unequivocally demonstrated in countless laboratory experiments using the "minimal group" paradigm (e.g., Tajfel, 1978, 1981). This paradigm is characterized by *assignment* to a particular social identity (e.g., "overestimators" vs. "underestimators"). Thus, in the context of *artificial* social identities, evidence of strong in-group bias is robust, which suggests that in the context of the real world, where extremely *meaningful* social categories abound, this effect will likely be even more pronounced.

What was key to the work of Tajfel and his colleagues was their discovery that, in a direct blow to realistic conflict theory, competition over resources was not necessary to produce significant intergroup conflict. Rather, all that was needed was the *perception of distinct social identities*—of belonging to different groups. In other words, identity itself seemed to play a central role in the very creation of conflict.

Consistent with the movement toward depathologizing prejudice, Tajfel and colleagues clearly demonstrated the *normative* occurrence of in-group bias—what they saw as the laboratory analogue to real-world ethnocentrism (Tajfel & Turner, 1979, 1986). Social identity theory, though, sought to move concepts of *identity* and *power* to the forefront of analysis of intergroup relations, demonstrating the inherent need for group distinctiveness that occurs in an intergroup setting. The implications, of course, are that (a) social identity, rather than individual identity (or personality), is the dominant force in intergroup contact; and (b) interventions that only seek to address individual identity (or personality), without attention to the power relations or the structural configuration that produces power asymmetries, will likely fail to address long-term improvement in intergroup relations.

Social identity theory challenges the bottom-up view of social change that underlies the contact hypothesis. The target for social identity theorists is not individual psychological change. Many would likely argue that such change is ephemeral at best. Rather, many social psychologists operating from the social identity theory tradition would likely suggest that the *meaning* and *value* placed on various social categories—Black or White, gay or straight, Israeli or Palestinian—must be a target for social change if we want to see a change in intergroup relations. While the link between individuals and social categories is of course dynamic and coconstitutive, individuals are themselves embedded within a matrix of social identities and cannot challenge the social structure it constructs in the absence of collective action.

Identity and the Cultural Psychology of Contact

I have thus far presented a historical narrative of the social psychological idea of contact as a means to reduce prejudice and conflict. As the reader can discern, my narrative seeks to recognize the unique contribution of major theorists and schools of thought, while also critiquing the assumptions upon which the work has been produced. Before I link this narrative to the field of Israeli–Palestinian contact programs itself, it is important for me to articulate my own theoretical stance toward contact.

I view contact through the lens of a narrative psychology that privileges both *discourse* and *practice*, and through the lens of a social psychology that emphasizes the way in which identities are *made* through social interaction. As I outlined extensively in Chapter 1, my approach seeks to integrate ideas from across the social sciences to articulate a view of culture and identity as coconstitutive, dynamic, and grounded in the practical activity that makes up our everyday lives. I view this approach as firmly rooted in several traditions associated with *cultural psychology*—from Shweder's (1990) concern with the mutual constitution of culture and psyche to Bruner's (1990) vision of a cultural psychology concerned with the meaning we narrate about our actions and Vygotsky's (1978) conviction that development occurs through mediated social activity.

Contact between groups thus provides an opportunity to generate new possibilities for social practice—possibilities for "improvisations" (Holland et al., 1998) that defy the expected and prescribed rules of social interaction for groups in conflict. In other words, I view contact as a potentially transformative—even potentially *subversive*—activity. For groups in intractable conflict like

Israelis and Palestinians, contact brings with it significant risks; it can be a transgressive act, a site to cultivate resistance and to repudiate a social order that benefits from the maintenance of antagonism.

At minimum, contact forms part of the many social acts that might make up a personal narrative and, potentially, a narrative that disrupts the reproduction of conflict. I view contact, then, as one of many sites of *narrative engagement* for Palestinian and Israeli youth. As a context for the confrontation of contradictory master narratives—and their consequences in the personal narratives of out-group members—contact offers a new venue for identity development, a place to experiment with identity.

But, in keeping with social identity theory, contact does not occur absent its own social structure. That is, the contact setting—from its physical location to its curriculum, its characters and customs—has its own *cultural* psychology. There are, thus, cultural *models* of contact that bring with them a set of assumptions about individuals and groups, the path to social change, and the possibilities of a life course. These models are also linked to different traditions within social psychology. The distinctly "American" cultural model of contact, devised as it was to confront the problem of ethnocentrism and interracial prejudice, relies upon a vision of the individual rational actor who can transcend the more "primitive" social allegiances that entangle him or her in a polarized web of intergroup relations. Here we see both the influence of American individualism (Bellah, Madsen, Sullivan, Swidler, & Tipton, 1985) and its concomitant denial of the significance of social identity. From this model of a hierarchical relationship between *personal* identity and *social* identity, with the faith in the individual's ability to transcend the "group mind," comes also a view of social change from the bottom up—that is, a faith in the power of individual psychological change to play a significant role in the process of social change. And finally, we see in this model a particular faith in *youth* to produce this change, a confidence in the wisdom of the young to repudiate a previous social order. As I have argued in Chapter 2 and elsewhere (Hammack, 2009), this is the cultural model that underlies both Seeds of Peace and Hands of Peace.

I will reserve further discussion of other potential cultural models of contact for the next two chapters, as we consider the postcontact narratives of youth in depth. For now, it is sufficient to recognize that, while I view contact as a site of potential transformative activity, I also believe that, like the enterprise of peace education or multicultural education more generally (Bekerman, 2002, 2005, 2007, 2009b; Bekerman & Maoz, 2005), contact might actually contribute, paradoxically, to the reproduction of conflict. Thus, my own view of contact seeks to moderate the tendency toward both individualism and idealism that characterizes the traditional social psychological perspective. My emphasis on contact as a site of narrative engagement and experimentation with identity allows for the possibility of multiple psychological processes and outcomes.

The Idea of Israeli–Palestinian Contact

If there were a key concept that best summarizes the relationship between Israelis and Palestinians since 1948, it would certainly be *separation* (Bargal, 1990). Given that the impetus for 1948—the Israelis' "independence" and the Palestinians' "catastrophe"—involved the direct contestation over control of the land, and concurrently a direct competition over the legitimacy of rival nationalist movements in Mandate Palestine, it stands to reason that Israeli–Palestinian relations in 1948 were characterized by separation. My purpose here is not to review the history that frames the segregation of Jews and Arabs in Palestine; that is a task that has been diligently undertaken by historians (e.g., Morris, 2001; Smith, 2001; Tessler, 1994).

I begin the story of Israeli–Palestinian contact efforts with the decisive moment that in a sense *created* the contemporary context for understanding "Israeli" and "Palestinian" as categories of social identity, for 1948 represents a clear turning point in the discursive construction of these categories of *national* identity. Not surprisingly, given the ultimate *institutionalization* of segregation that 1948 produced (recall that Palestinian citizens of Israel were ruled by a military administration until 1966; Tessler & Grant, 1998), the idea of contact was not really on the horizon for Israeli–Palestinian relations in the 1950s and 1960s.

It was not until the 1970s, following the end of the military administration in Palestinian communities in Israel and the 1967 war and subsequent occupation of the Palestinian territories, that contact between Jews and Arabs began in earnest. Official organizations designed to promote contact were born, such as Neve Shalom/Wahat-al-Salaam and Givaat Haviva (see Abu-Nimer, 1999). Part of the impetus for these efforts was the increasing economic integration between Jews and Arabs. For example, many West Bank Palestinians began to gain employment in factories in Israel, which brought them together with Jewish Israelis.

The Israeli psychologist Yehuda Amir, whose 1969 review and critique of the original contact hypothesis was in part instigated by his observations about Israeli society and Israeli–Palestinian relations, conducted a number of studies in the 1970s on Arabs and Jews who worked together in industry in Israel. Obviously these contexts for intergroup contact were not the organized, peace-building initiatives, with formal curricula, that would later follow. But they were nonetheless opportunities for interpersonal acquaintanceship, consistent with the contact hypothesis. Amir and his team of researchers found that contact did indeed seem to influence attitudes toward out-group members, but they suggested that the power asymmetry between Jews and Arabs presented challenges for the Arabs to adopt genuinely positive attitudes toward Jews (Amir, Bizman, Ben-Ari, & Rivner, 1980; Amir, Ben-Ari, Bizman, & Rivner, 1982). Their studies importantly initiated, at least within social psychological studies of Israeli–Palestinian relations, a consideration of how relative status and power asymmetry influences possibilities for Jewish–Arab relations.

One of my aims in this review of Israeli–Palestinian contact efforts is to identify the underlying scholarship, particularly within social psychology, that informs them. Interestingly, although the findings of Amir and colleagues represent a better conceptual fit with social identity theory, they did not rely on this theoretical orientation for their analysis or interpretations. Rather, they appeared to be in dialogue with Allport, Sherif, and other American psychologists working within the general framework of prejudice and intergroup contact.

Beginning in the 1970s, a team of Americans led by Harvard social psychologist Herbert Kelman began to conduct a number of "problem-solving" workshops with influential Israelis and Palestinians—politicians and community leaders in the region (e.g., Cohen, Kelman, Miller, & Smith, 1977; Kelman & Cohen, 1976; Kelman, 1997, 2008). Rooted in a more pragmatic frame, the goal of these workshops was not to work toward major social psychological change through interpersonal acquaintanceship, as the original contact hypothesis prescribed. Rather, Kelman and his colleagues sought to foster an analytic, problem-solving approach to concrete issues that produce conflict between groups. And, even more important, they sought to maintain the focus of the workshops as sites of inter*group*, rather than inter*personal*, contact, thus seeking not to threaten salient social identities (see Kelman, 1993).

As opposed to social psychologists such as Allport, Kelman's primary intellectual influence was John Burton, a conflict resolution scholar known for his work on the theory of "human needs" (e.g., need for security, need for identity) implicated in conflict (e.g., Burton, 1988, 1990a, 1990b; see also Christie, 1997). Kelman (2008) also identifies social psychologist Morton Deutsch, whose work has centered on fundamental group processes in conflict and cooperation (e.g., Deutsch, 1973, 1977, 2002; Deutsch & Coleman, 2000), as a major influence in the design and implementation of these workshops. Thus, Kelman's approach indirectly challenged the significance of the contact hypothesis, particularly with its early emphasis on individual personality and social cognition, for social change. That Kelman and his colleagues focused their work entirely on *influential* Palestinian and Israeli *adults* is quite significant, for it reflects a more "top-down" approach to peace building in which power brokers in conflicting societies are targets for intervention. This approach stands in marked contrast to the more grassroots, "people-to-people" approach that characterizes the vast majority of contact efforts between Israelis and Palestinians (Maoz, 2004b)—efforts that are more often also targeted to youth, based on the assumption that youth, rather than the adults who educate them, are the appropriate targets for intervention (Bekerman, 2005).

The workshops that Kelman and colleagues conducted through the 1980s and early 1990s probably paved the way for the Oslo accords by preparing influential Israeli and Palestinian leaders to make pragmatic compromises (see Kelman, 1982, 1995, 1997, 2008). And, consistent with Amir's recognition of the need to include relative status in the analysis of Israeli–Palestinian relations, the interactive problem-solving workshops increasingly involved an analysis of power asymmetry between Jews and Arabs (Rouhana, 1995a, 1995b; Rouhana & Korper, 1996, 1997). Interestingly, though, the intellectual framework of the approach never advanced beyond Burton's original inspiration, and the opportunity to integrate social identity theory, and thus more of an approach that *integrated* social and cognitive levels of analysis, was never undertaken.

In the 1980s, as formal contact efforts began to flourish in Israel, Hebrew University psychologist David Bargal developed and studied a series of conflict management workshops at Neve Shalom/Wahat-al-Salaam. Bargal and his colleague Haviva Bar sought to integrate Kurt Lewin's theoretical approach to group dynamics in their work with Jewish and Arab youth (see Bargal, 1990; Bargal & Bar, 1992; see also Bargal, 2008). Consistent with the contribution of Amir and colleagues, Bargal (1990) argued that mere contact between Jews and Arabs was insufficient to significantly reduce conflict in and of itself. Calling upon Lewin's (1951) general "field theory" approach, in which the social, historical, and political context is fully considered, Bargal (1990) argues that Jews and Arabs in Israel cannot engage in equal-status contact because of the social structure that privileges Jews. Again appropriating an important Lewinian concept, Bargal (1990) argues that Jews and Arabs require "reeducation" rather than "contact of an intimate nature" (p. 186) if they are to assume a role in social change to improve intergroup relations. In other words, the problem of conflict is not located within individual minds or the lack of opportunity for interpersonal interaction. Rather, conflict is a problem of society, of the "life space" (Lewin, 1951) that Jews and Arabs inhabit, and it is only through their own reeducation to see the injustice of this situation that they might become motivated to participate in *action* for social change. Bargal (1990) thus viewed intergroup workshops as sites to "not only evaluate social practice but also to advance it" (p. 188).

Bargal took care to note that, like Allport, Lewin developed his framework in the United States, largely in response to interracial relations, but also to matters of anti-Semitism and Jewish identity. As the critical approach undertaken at Neve Shalom/Wahat-al-Salaam would evolve in the 1990s and 2000s, this recognition would become increasingly important. And as contact interventions and efforts at coexistence education increased exponentially in the post-Oslo years, program organizers increasingly looked away from American models of contact toward Tajfel's distinctly "European" approach (Moghaddam, 1987).

In the history of Israeli–Palestinian relations, the Oslo accords represented a true watershed moment—an absolute breakthrough in the stalemate of mutual existential denial that characterized relations since 1948. With the mutual recognition of legitimacy, including the official recognition of the State of Israel by the PLO and the recognition of the legitimacy of Palestinian autonomy by Israel, came the institutional support needed to design contact interventions and peace education more generally. Thus, the 1990s initiated a veritable explosion of programs and research on contact and coexistence. It was in the optimism of this era that Seeds of Peace was born (Wallach, 2000).

While the Oslo accords certainly initiated a major change in Israeli–Palestinian relations, from mutual existential *denial* to at least a bare minimum of recognition, the absence of a *comprehensive* agreement that did not delay issues (e.g., the Palestinian refugee problem or the borders of a Palestinian state; the status of Jewish settlements in the occupied territories) would seem to fix Israeli–Palestinian relations in a permanent liminal state. In other words, because Oslo policy only *initiated*, but did not complete, a process of mutual national recognition, it has created an uncomfortable situation of in-between status for Israeli–Palestinian relations. Thus, the severity of conflict has ebbed and waned fairly consistently from 1993 to the present, and both societies are characterized by conflicting internal discourse about the legitimacy of the other (as I discussed in Chapters 3 and 4). The general outcome of this liminal, ambivalent peace "process" seems to have been a gradual erosion in confidence in a two-state solution (e.g., Abunimah, 2007; Tilley, 2005).

This unique historical moment in Israeli–Palestinian relations—from absolute mutual denial to a kind of quasi-recognition—that began with the Oslo accords created space for contact interventions that could satisfy that evasive condition of institutional support. That is, with the leaders of both groups now at least recognizing a momentum toward mutual recognition and peace, contact could be sanctioned by both parties, and their support for such efforts could be held up as evidence of their desire for peace. Based on his origin story for the program, Seeds of Peace founder John Wallach seems to have capitalized on this motivation for leaders to support the program by proposing to both Israeli and Palestinian leaders that they cooperate by selecting their own participants (Wallach, 2000).

Thus, Seeds of Peace was part of a concerted effort in the 1990s to develop peace education and contact programs that would work to prepare the general population for an ultimate and definitive peace. In developing its curriculum, as I outlined in Chapter 2, Seeds of Peace seems to have blended classic assumptions of the contact hypothesis and an explicit bottom-up theory of social change with the premises of a social psychological approach that developed around the same time—common in-group identity theory (e.g., Gaertner et al., 1993). Hands of Peace would later adopt the same basic model, closely associated with efforts in multicultural education.

In Israel, though, a different story was brewing. By the 1990s, the leaders of Neve Shalom/Wahat-al-Salaam had begun to fully repudiate an approach to contact based on the original contact hypothesis, or on the "human relations" school of thought that grew out of it and was imported to contexts like Israel (e.g., Lakin, Lomranz, & Lieberman, 1969). They moved a step further toward embracing social identity theory in their practice and developed a distinct approach based on the model.

Focusing on the conflict *within* Israel between Jewish and Palestinian citizens, the leaders of the School for Peace at Neve Shalom/Wahat-al-Salaam during this period argued that only an encounter that emphasizes some of the core principles of social identity theory—the notion that individuals serve primarily as group representatives in the encounter, the expectation that contact will actually enhance the salience of national identity, the assumption that power cannot be neutralized and thus must be acknowledged—can effectively contribute to social change (Halabi & Sonnenschein, 2004a). Rather than seek to effect individual psychological change toward prejudice reduction, their model aims to expose the social-structural underpinnings of conflict in issues like unequal access to resources. Thus, they aim to motivate individuals to work for change within the structural configuration that creates the conditions of conflict, rather than seek to build cross-group friendships.

In her recent review of 20 years of contact efforts between Jews and Palestinians in Israel, Israeli social psychologist Ifat Maoz (in press) proposed a typology for such programs. She suggests that the *coexistence* model, which continues to be the dominant model, relies on the basic premise of prejudice reduction through interpersonal acquaintanceship promulgated by the original contact hypothesis. The *joint projects* model, which has more of a basis in ideas related to realistic conflict theory, seeks to transform intergroup relations through superordinate or common activities that generally avoid discussion of conflict or power asymmetry. The *confrontational* model corresponds to the approach ultimately adopted at the School for Peace. Rooted in social identity theory, it involves a direct discussion of collective processes, structural asymmetries, and political positions that maintain the conflict. The fourth and final model she identifies—the *narrative* approach—seeks to blend an emphasis on the personal and collective through the use of storytelling.

The growing recognition of the structural origins of conflict realized by the emergence of the confrontational model (and hence the more limited role for contact and coexistence education) has become a hallmark of scholarship since the late 1990s. Bar-Tal (2004a) argues that education for coexistence is most effective in contexts of ethnocentrism, such as the United States and parts of Europe, rather than intractable intergroup conflict. Education can play only a minimal role, he argues, in such contexts since they require a negotiated settlement and since a society's members must be educated for possible war while a conflict is active.

In examining peace education efforts in Israel (and education more generally), Hebrew University scholar Zvi Bekerman has revealed the way in which they have only served to reify concepts of national identity that themselves represent a core cause of the current conflict (e.g., Bekerman, 2001, 2002, 2007, 2009a, 2009b, 2009c; Bekerman & Horenczyk, 2004; Bekerman & Maoz, 2005; Bekerman & Silverman, 2003). That is, the Israeli–Palestinian conflict is in large part rooted in the rival national movements of Zionism and Palestinian nationalism that grew out of the nineteenth century, when concepts of national identity (such as in Germany) were constructed in exclusive, essentialized terms that actually promoted collective violence. In an increasingly "postnational," globalized, and interconnected world, this tendency to promote static conceptions of "culture" and "identity" in peace education seems problematic for its likely role in *maintaining*, rather than challenging, the status quo. Bekerman (2005) suggests that the "problem" in conflict-ridden societies like Israel does not seem to be *children* who require peace education. Rather, his extensive study of integrated schools in Israel suggests that it is the adults who educate them who seem to serve as guardians of reified notions of nation, culture, and identity that maintains conflict (see also Bekerman, Zembylas, & McGlynn, 2009).

Thus, as critical perspectives on the idea of contact itself have multiplied (e.g., Connolly, 2000; Dixon et al., 2005), increasingly questioning its grounding in an American cultural model of intergroup relations (Hammack, 2009), so too have scholars in Israel and Palestine begun to critically evaluate contact efforts and their role in possibly perpetuating the status quo. As I will explore at greater length in Chapter 8, a critical approach to contact and peace education does not negate its utility, suggesting, for example, that it is simply futile to engage in such efforts. Rather, the central need for an evolving critical conception of Israeli–Palestinian contact is to move from this mode of *reproductive* contact— that is, contact that seems to do little more than reproduce the narrative conditions of conflict—toward *transformative* contact that can contribute to social action within Israeli and Palestinian societies.

Contact, Narrative, and Identity

My aim in this chapter has been to construct a narrative that contextualizes the intervention efforts I examined in this study of Israeli and Palestinian youth. I sought to outline, in broad strokes, the history of the contact hypothesis and its grounding in an American context of interracial relations. I suggested that, as the cultural grounding of the contact hypothesis has been increasingly interrogated, the notion that conflict is primarily a product of individual personality development has been contested. An integrated approach that recognizes the social structural origins of conflict and their consequences for social cognition and intergroup behavior was developed by Henri Tajfel and his colleagues in the UK as an alternative to this original emphasis on personality. In my brief review of Israeli–Palestinian contact, I suggested that the history of those efforts actually runs parallel to this intellectual history within social psychology. The growing influence of social identity theory among practitioners of intergroup encounters in Israel provides evidence of this parallel history (e.g., Halabi & Sonnenschein, 2004a, 2004b; Suleiman, 2004a, 2004b).

Though this contextualization of contact is vital to our interpretation of the consequences of contact I will present in the next chapter, it has brought us to a level of abstraction that is distant from the voices of Israelis and Palestinians who actually live such experiences. Thus, my focus on narrative outcomes of contact—that is, the shifts in life story construction that occur, or do not occur, 1 or more years postcontact—attempts to restore this sense of voice and thus to try to make sense of the lived experience of youth using the tools of social science discourse.

As I outlined in Chapter 1, I view identity as an *ideologically* derived index of the self in social context, made manifest through the construction of a personal narrative or life story, and formulated, rehearsed, and realized through social interaction and practice. Thus, in my analysis of contact between Israeli and Palestinian youth, the central measure of outcome is the life story narrated I or more years postcontact. Just as it was in Chapters 3, 4, and 5, the form, thematic content, and ideological setting of that narrative represent the focus of my analysis. And in relying upon an idiographic, person-centered approach to making sense of each personal narrative, I can formulate interpretations about the consequences of contact based on my ethnographic and interview data. It is important to note that I am not seeking to make causal claims about the particular contact interventions themselves for the development of a single life story. Such a goal would require a systematic experimental and longitudinal design, which was entirely impossible in the context of this kind of naturalistic inquiry. Rather, I examine each case through the interpretive lens of a social practice theory of identity—an approach that seeks to consider the ways in which mediated social activities such as the contact experience might (or might not) generate new cycles of practice. A narrative approach provides me with access to the discursive resources youth draw upon in making meaning of their own participation in such social activity (Bruner, 1990).

Thus, the central question I examine in the next chapter concerns *change* in the narration of the life story for Israeli and Palestinian youth. To integrate social psychological theories and conceptions of contact and its cognitive consequences, I explore two possible narrative outcomes specified by the theories: *transcendence* and *accentuation*. These outcomes provide us with a discourse to understand the identity processes that occur for youth who engage in contact, while simultaneously revealing the extent to which particular interventions achieve their underlying aims. Through the voices of youth, we come to theorize the role that particular interventions appear to serve in the larger process of social change or maintenance of the status quo.

7

Restorying Self and Other: An American Experiment

The Synagogue and the Mosque

Aya is sitting on the curb outside the synagogue crying. Aiesha, a Palestinian-Israeli staff member at Hands of Peace, is trying to console her. It has been a long day—a long week, in fact. Aya came to Chicago from Ramallah, the cosmopolitan Palestinian city in the West Bank. As I watch her and Aiesha, I am reminded of my first journey to her home, 2 months prior. Her home is on the outskirts of the city. My colleague Khaled and I went by taxi to meet her and her family. I recall sipping warm mint tea, scanning the photographs on the wall of Aya's home, my eyes suddenly locking on the picture of her father shaking hands with Yasser Arafat. The photo looks very dated, I thought, perhaps from the 1980s. As Aya and I sit to conduct our interview, a voice calls from the kitchen, and a hand extends out from the carefully covered door, with a plate of fruit. It is Aya's mother, who I never meet. I recall the big smile on Aya's face as we discuss her upcoming trip to the United States—her first there. Her father smiles approvingly, proud of his daughter's contributions to her nation. He and Khaled recede into the living room as Aya and I begin our interview.

Tonight the smile from Aya's face has been replaced by tears, as she cries to Aiesha in Arabic, "What the hell am I doing here?!" There is a flag of Israel just inside the door, hanging on the synagogue's bulletin board. In the course of the program, it is Friday night of the first week and the end of a day in which the participants have attended religious services at a mosque and are now to attend services at a synagogue. Sunday they will do the same at a Christian church—the progressive one that anchors (and provides considerable funding for) the program in the local community.

Two years later, I am sitting on the steps of a large mosque in the Chicago suburbs with Aaron and Shay, two Jewish-Israeli participants in Hands of Peace in the summer of 2006—the summer of Israel's war with Hezbollah in Lebanon. The boys have left the mosque in a fury because the imam's sermon has turned to the war and harshly admonished Israel's behavior, imploring those in the mosque to not sit idle while such injustice occurs in the world. Aaron and Shay, and most of the other Israelis, interpret this sermon as a threat to their nation—it primes that common perception of existential insecurity among Israelis that has, this week for these youths, been largely forgotten in the safe confines of the American suburbs. As we sit on the steps of the mosque, while latecomers eye us curiously, the boys launch into several diatribes about "radical Islam" and the fundamentally violent nature of Muslims and Arabs.

Obviously, youths like Aya, Aaron, and Shay are, in these instances, under-going a significant degree of psychological challenge. At this point in the contact program, they are confronted with an *institution* they associate with the conflict. While they have spent the first week largely in dialogue and program rituals designed to promote a process of decategorization—the reduction of out-group stereotypes and prejudice through coming to see the diversity that actually exists within a group—attendance at religious services seems to jolt them back to a place of reality, back to a recognition of the clear *distinctions* that divide them as groups.

Recall from Chapter 2 that the primary aim of both Seeds of Peace and Hands of Peace is to activate a psychological process of *recategorization*—of coming to recategorize self and other in a higher level of category inclusive-ness, such as the new common identity of a "Seed," or simply a "human being." The point here, consistent with social psychological theories developed in the 1990s designed to address issues of pluralism and multiculturalism (e.g., Gaertner et al., 1993), is for the youth to recognize their "unity in diver-sity," to borrow a ubiquitous phrase from multicultural education. Attendance at the religious services is a part of this intended process. The rationale is that, if young people can witness in a safe and secure setting that everyone has a religion that promotes peace and intergroup harmony, they will come to see more commonality, rather than difference, between them. In other words, if they can come to *transcend* the narrowness of their own singular identity and come to see the world as a pluralistic place, with a diversity of identities and rituals, they will develop a *consciousness for coexistence*, and, hence, an outlook oriented toward peace, rather than war.

As the stories from my fieldwork suggest, though, this process is not necessarily so simple or linear for youth. In this chapter, I will explore the personal narratives of youth collected after their participation in these programs in order to understand the role that contact seems to assume in their identity development. It is important to note that, of course, contact is not the only meaningful experience with the conflict any of them will have had in the years following their participation. Thus, we can never attribute *causality* of a particular identity configuration or life story narrative to contact itself. We can, however, *interpret* the life stories of youth in reference to this contact experience and, in the process, theorize its psychological consequences.

In the remainder of this chapter, I will examine the narratives of youth according to a basic taxonomy that conforms to social psychological theories of intergroup contact, as well as the aims of both contact programs. *Identity transcendence* is characterized by a reduction in the salience of in-group identity and the assumption of a common in-group identity that is inclusive of the out-group. I will refer to identity transcendence as a categorical outcome, although I believe it is risky to speak of identity "outcomes" in this context, for identity is an ongoing construction across the life course (Cohler, 1982). A transcendent identity narrative is one that is no longer a slave to the master narrative of in-group identity that maintains the conflict. It is a cosmopolitan narrative of mutual legitimization and responsibility.

Identity accentuation, by contrast, is characterized by polarization. That is, it describes a high salience of in-group social identity, typically simultaneous with continued delegitimization of out-group identity. Conformity to a master narrative of in-group social identity is common in a state of identity accentuation. A narrative characterized by identity accentuation is an anti-cosmopolitan narrative, in that the singularity of one's identity is highlighted for its claims to legitimacy and recognition. Simply put, an accentuated identity postcontact is one that is likely to maintain (or perhaps even exacerbate) the conflict.

Identity Transcendence

In his 1999 essay, Herbert Kelman argues that the key to resolving the Israeli–Palestinian conflict lies in the development of a transcendent identity for the two peoples. Israelis and Palestinians, in his view, must come to transcend the condition of negative interdependence inherent in their polarized, irreconcilable narratives of history and identity. They must come to view their histories and identities as irreversibly intertwined; they must come to recognize that they share a common fate as peoples who cannot be so easily "disengaged" from each other. This transcendent identity must not threaten the particularity of each national identity, but it must be cultivated in order to recognize the potential for positive interdependence between Palestinians and Israelis.

Kelman's thesis parallels the tenets of common in-group identity theory and the notion of recategorization. Israelis and Palestinians must, in his view, come to recognize the higher level of category inclusiveness that exists between them. They must fashion new social identities that recognize the legitimacy of the other in such a way as to reduce the potential in-group identity threat that transcendence commands.

The idea of recategorization and identity transcendence is incredibly alluring for those who seek coexistence between Israelis and Palestinians. It offers an optimistic, deceptively simple solution to what has become an intractable problem. As I argued in Chapter 2, both Seeds of Peace and Hands of Peace are founded on the premise of contact as a mechanism of identity transformation. That the primary social psychological "press" of the programs is for a recategorization of identity, and therefore the transcendence of identity polarization, is readily apparent in the culture of these programs, with their rituals and social structures. Yet the empirical question remains: To what extent does identity transcendence indeed occur, and how is it manifest in the narratives of youth?

Before I present three life stories that demonstrate the outcome of identity transcendence, let me more precisely elaborate upon its meaning. It seems inconceivable to speak of the transcendence of identity, particularly during adolescence, when a coherent sense of identity is only in its nascence. So when I speak of identity transcendence, I do not refer to such a totalizing kind of phenomenon. Rather, I mean by the term an apparent cognitive ability to consider the existence, legitimacy, and identity needs of the out-group. Identity transcendence is visible in the emerging life story narrative with the recognition of the out-group and its existential needs. It also refers to a willingness to challenge the master narrative of in-group social identity. Although a transcendent identity suggests an in-group identity critique, or at least a *willingness* for critique, by no means does it suggest an abandonment of in-group ideology. The individual with a transcendent identity has, rather, discovered a way to integrate both in-group and out-group into the life story narrative in such a way that does not threaten the in-group and his or her identification with it.

Very concretely, we can speak of a reduction in the salience of in-group identity, or at least in the salience and identification with the polarizing components of the in-group master narrative, when we speak of identity transcendence.

Let us now consider three life stories that reveal the outcome of identity transcendence: the stories of Liat, Laila, and Noa. I wish to immediately draw attention to the reader that these three stories are, most notably, the stories of young women. Second, I wish to note that two of these young women (Liat and Noa) are Jewish Israeli and one is Palestinian Israeli (Laila). These demographic considerations are significant, though I will reserve a discussion of why the life stories of males and of Palestinians from the occupied territories seem to rarely display this identity outcome.

"I Had Never Even Spoken to an Arab": The Story of Liat

Liat is a 16-year-old blonde-haired, blue-eyed Jewish Israeli from Ashkelon, the largest Israeli city in close proximity to the Gaza Strip in the south, on the Mediterranean Sea. Like many in the multicultural "melting pot" of Israel, Liat was born outside of the country, in South Africa. Liat's family immigrated to Israel when she was 10 years old because, as she describes it, "my father is a Zionist." Her extended family, with origins in Lithuania and Russia, is now dispersed across the globe, in South Africa and Australia. Only their tiny branch of the extended family chose to settle in Israel.

Liat's narrative at age 16, like most Israeli youths in this study, closely conforms to the master narrative of Jewish-Israeli identity in its form. It is a story of descent and gain, of valleys and peaks, of challenges and triumphs. The ultimate gain for Liat thus far in her life has indeed been her participation in Seeds of Peace—an experience that both enabled Liat to examine her identity and to witness the possibility of identity transcendence.

Narrating her life story to me 1 year after her participation in Seeds of Peace, Liat expresses concerns about Zionism, which she connects to the difficulties she felt upon the family's immigration to Israel:

> My life in South Africa, everything was great. I had many friends. I went to a Jewish school.... I don't know, it was just great. And moving to Israel, it was really exciting at the beginning. But it was a different country. I didn't really fit in cause it took me 3 years to learn the language.... I had a few close friends here and there, mostly English speakers, not really Israelis.... Even till this moment, my best friends are Lithuanian and Russian. I don't know what it is with the Israelis. I don't really connect with them.

I'm now in Israel, and I know it's the state *of* the Jews. It doesn't mean it has to be the state just *for* the Jews. It *is* the state of the Jews—Israel. Everyone calls it Israel, not Palestine or something. But it's not about Jews *only* or something. It's not realistic at all.

Liat claims to have never "felt" fully Israeli. She refers to Israelis in the third person to this day, 6 years after her family's arrival. The move to Israel is the nadir in her life story, for its challenges to her identity. The language in particular is a source of identity dissonance for Liat. She yearns for an inclusive Israeli state, one in which she, and the non-Jewish inhabitants of the land, will feel a part.

Yet as Liat arrived at Seeds of Peace, suddenly her in-group social identity was primed, and she reports a strong feeling of connection to the other Israelis at the camp. She describes the cognitive process she underwent, from her own salient self-categorization to decategorization of the other and recategorization of self:

> Before Seeds, I couldn't connect with Israelis. Then suddenly with Seeds, the people I am obviously most connected with is the Israelis. And then those people became my *really* good friends, not like my friends in Ashkelon. That's why the first 2 weeks, the Israelis just stay with the Israelis. Then the last week of camp, we started interacting with the other countries, and it was fine, cause then we were one big group.... It didn't happen right away at camp, but pretty soon I ended up making friends with Arabs and Palestinians, and it ended up totally changing my life. After camp, my views about everything had changed so radically. I suddenly became the defender of Arabs in front of my family and friends.... The history of the hatred of the Jews has been forever, from the Germans to these and that, and now it's with the Arabs, what we're doing to them.... I just became so much more aware of what's really going on—the injustices. And making friends—I mean, *real* friends— from the other side, it totally changed me. Now when something happens in the West Bank, I worry. I think, what if my friend is hurt?

> And this whole year was just great cause I stayed in touch with all the friends I met, not only the Israelis but the Palestinians too. I go twice a month to Jerusalem or to Haifa for Seeds of Peace.... Camp is like a dream. It's our second home. We were so happy!

In this important excerpt from Liat's life story, a number of significant psychological processes related to her participation in Seeds of Peace emerge. First, the initial experience of intergroup contact primes a process of salient categorization in which Liat comes to identify more closely with her in-group social identity as a Jewish Israeli—an identity which she had previously felt somewhat unidentified with. Contact gradually activates a process of decategorization of the out-group, as Liat professes to befriend Palestinians and to begin to see them as distinct individuals. Consistent with Pettigrew's (1997, 1998) reformulation of the contact hypothesis, the development of cross-group friendship appears to be the key mechanism of psychological transformation. Such a mechanism reveals the significance of social relationships in the construction of self (e.g., Gergen, 1994). Ultimately, as Liat's account of her own process of participation reveals, recategorization of self and other occurred, and she came to view herself as deeply connected to the Palestinians, united in the common identity of a "Seed." Continued social practice in the program back home has enabled Liat to continue to develop this transcendent identity in a safe and supportive context.

Yet the end of this particular portion of Liat's narrative, in which she proclaims that "Camp is like a dream!", reveals the problematic nature of identity transcendence, for the context in which it has begun to develop is ultimately a false reality, a place of utopian coexistence. But for now, 1 year after her initial participation, Liat is able to practice her new social identity as a "Seed." In accordance with common in-group identity theory, being a Seed seems to represent for Liat an identity supplement—a superordinate level of categorization in which both Israelis and Palestinians can comfortably coexist. Her new identity contains empathy for the out-group, rooted in the friendships she developed in the context of participation at camp, and it is sustained through active social practice, such as presentations about Arabs that she makes in Jewish schools in Israel, attempting to educate Jewish Israelis about coexistence.

Liat's life story reveals the possibility of identity transcendence as an outcome of contact with Palestinians. In her narrative, she acknowledges her own psychological process of identity transformation, which culminates in the recategorization of both in-group and out-group into a new, common identity. Yet Liat's story raises a number of questions about this process. To what extent is her ability to undergo a process of recategorization related to her already low level of in-group identity salience prior to participation? How sustainable is her identity transcendence should the opportunity for social practice, such as reductions in follow-up services for Seeds of Peace, diminish? As a temporary window into the development of an identity, the collection of a life story at a particular time and place is always constrained by the ever-evolving forces of history. Yet Liat's narrative suggests great possibility for contact between Israelis and Palestinians.

"I Have Been Changed a Lot": The Story of Laila

A 16-year-old vivacious Muslim from Taybeh, Laila is a Palestinian citizen of Israel. Motivated by her interest in politics, but also by the thrill of a trip to the United States, Laila identifies participation in Seeds of Peace as the peak experience of her narrative. With the birth of her political consciousness, which she claims to occur around age 11, Laila's life story begins its great formal ascent. Even as the second *intifada* begins, when Laila is 14, this ascent continues, as the political happenings motivate her to become active in her community:

> I didn't have any interest in political things till I was 11. From 11 to 14, I became very interested, in the *intifada* and in the history of Palestine. And Israel, but more Palestine.... Actually, when I was 9 and Rabin died, I became really interested in the Israeli government. And I was really sad when he died because he really wanted peace.... When I was 14, the *intifada* began. And I started being interested more and more in the situation and more in the history and what it is about.

The social ecology of Laila's development is saturated with political events, which awaken a passion for politics and history in Laila in early adolescence. Like many Jewish-Israeli youth of her generation, she mourns the loss of Yitzhak Rabin (see Raviv, Raviv, Sadeh, & Silberstein, 1998; Raviv, Sadeh, Raviv, Silberstein, & Diver, 2000), his death a defining moment in the tragic course of the conflict but also a motivating factor in the birth of Laila's political consciousness. Considered in its totality, Laila's story is a basic narrative of progress and ascent, her life experience culminating in her participation at Seeds of Peace.

Laila's experience at Seeds of Peace represents both a peak experience and a turning point in her life story. She describes the major transformation that occurred in her ideological perspective by referring to her views on the use of suicide bombing:

> My grandma was telling me stories about how they lived before '48, their traditions, the songs they were hearing, their houses, how they left their houses. She told me a story about a family that was eating, and they told them to get out from their houses. They were eating a family dinner, so they got out. And the food was still warm. So the new Jewish family entered the house, saw the food, sat and started eating! When I heard this story, I cried a lot. How is *that*—that people left their houses and others who have nothing to do with those houses just come in?!
>
> And I had these opinions—these political opinions—about the suicide bombers, after the terrible situation was going on.... I really was agreeing

with all the suicide bombing and the things they were doing in the
Jewish cities. I really agreed with them. Kill! I don't care! They're doing
the same! They kill babies, they kill women and men in Gaza and in the
territories, so I don't care.

Laila begins her narrative of the way in which Seeds of Peace has impacted her
political beliefs with a family story of the *Nakba*—a story, which, regardless of
its veracity, carries tremendous symbolism for the relationship between Israeli
and Palestinian identities. Laila's internalization of this story, along with the
many stories of Palestinian suffering she has seen or heard since the outbreak
of the *intifada*, has created within her a sense of solidarity with the use of
suicide bombers to harm Israelis. Conforming to the Palestinian master narrative in her ideological commitments, Laila once viewed suicide bombing as
a legitimate form of resistance to Israeli occupation. But with her participation
at Seeds of Peace, those commitments have been reconfigured.

The turning point for Laila at Seeds of Peace results in a reversal of ideological setting for the life story, but it is also interpreted by her as a transformation from a "prejudiced" to a "logical" individual.

> Before I came to Seeds of Peace, I had a lot of racist ideas. After Seeds
> of Peace, I have been changed a lot. I *really* agreed with the suicide
> bombings, like my family and like most of the Arabs in Israel. But after
> Seeds of Peace, I totally disagreed. Because, you know, I don't see any
> human thing in the suicide bombing. And I don't think this is the kind
> of *jihad* that Islam talks about. And suicide bombing gives the world the
> reason to take Islam in the wrong way, to misunderstand Islam. So I
> totally disagree with it now. And after I had a lot of friends, *Jewish* friends,
> after Seeds of Peace, I would see the news and I kept thinking, how
> would that be if a Jewish friend of mine would die in a suicide bombing?
> How would I respond? Everyone can be hurt. Even me, I'm an Arab
> Israeli, but I can be hurt by a suicide bomber. So I've been changed a lot,
> and I have to say that after ... Seeds of Peace.

> I didn't care whether it was logical or not, I just *hated* the Jewish, you
> know. This *hatred*, I just couldn't change it. After Seeds of Peace,
> I realized, when you understand someone, you can like him. So when
> I respected them and when I played with them in Color Games and had
> this coexistence with them, ate with them, and slept next to each other, it
> changed it a bit, you know.

A key component of Laila's identification with the Palestinian master
narrative—the legitimate use of violence as a means of resistance and

liberation—has vanished as a consequence of her participation in Seeds of Peace. Again, as for Liat, the primary mechanism of transformation appears to be the development of cross-group friendships, which provoke a sense of empathy and an ability to see the perspective of the other, considered to be an indication of higher moral development (Kohlberg, 1976; Piaget, 1932; see also Batson et al., 1997; DeTurk, 2001; Galinsky & Moskowitz, 2000). The other, in some ways, becomes part of the self (Aron, Aron, Tudor, & Nelson, 1991), as the polarization of in-group identity is transcended.

Laila's story to this point suggests a process of personalization and decategorization of the out-group, and her self-reported ideological change fits well with classic perspectives on intergroup relations that emphasize interventions in individual personality development to reduce prejudice (e.g., Allport, 1954). Laila herself presents a contrast between two social ecologies, one that promotes "hatred" and one that promotes "logic." Not surprisingly, the former is Israel/Palestine, the latter, Seeds of Peace. So while decategorization appears to be a significant social psychological process in Laila's life story transformation, it is ultimately the process of *re*categorization that serves to instill identity transcendence in Laila's narrative:

> Seeds of Peace gives the opportunity and the freedom for everyone to express himself. In the end, there's a kind of impact that Seeds of Peace has.... I don't know how it happens, but I think it's about learning to be logical. Here, it's not about disagreeing, and who's right and who's wrong. It's about learning to be logical and being human. Humanity is the most important thing in Seeds.

Laila attributes the impact of the program to the development of a "logical," presumably more rational and less emotional, perspective on the conflict. But she also acknowledges the significance of the recognition of a higher level of category inclusiveness for both Israelis and Palestinians—that of human being. The notion of "common humanity," so central to the culture of Seeds of Peace, provides a clear category to which all participants can achieve a sense of belonging.

Yet the strength of a common in-group identity extends beyond Laila's simple claim that "humanity is the most important thing in Seeds." Laila reports a process of identity assumption, of full acculturation to the Seeds identity, in her life story narrative:

> Yeah, there's a lot of equality at Seeds of Peace. That makes you feel really comfortable. Discrimination is not bred here. You can find it maybe in the house, in the family, everywhere. I feel as a young girl I am

discriminated against because I'm young. But not ... at Seeds of Peace,
I don't think anyone [at Seeds of Peace] feels discriminated against....
Because even the clothes, everyone has the same! And the bunks, the
showers, the coexistence, even the schedule, it's equal. Everything.
Everyone has to do the things they have to do. Everyone gets the rights
that they're supposed to get, which makes us all feel really comfortable to
be [at camp] and talk with others. [At Seeds of Peace], if I'm talking with
someone who's Jewish or Palestinian, it doesn't matter. I don't care if he's
Palestinian. I don't look at him *as* a Palestinian. And I don't look at him
as an Israeli. I just look at him as a *Seed*. I see the green T-shirt in front
of me, and that's what I care about.

The most important part of my identity is being a Seed, but at the same
time being Muslim, because they're connected somehow.... The first
thing really is being a Seed. I so *feel* Seed in being everything I am.
Being a Muslim, I still feel Seed.

The sense of equality and absence of discrimination that Laila experiences at
camp reveals the extent to which the program is successful in satisfying the
condition of an equal-status encounter. For Laila, a member of the Arab minority in a Jewish state, this sense of equality is euphoric. It is symbolically realized
in the camp uniform, but for Laila, it has a deeper psychological impact. The
homogenizing effect of recategorization allows Laila to view her peers as united
in a common identity as "Seeds." This process of recategorization is both cognitive and emotional, as Laila reports to "feel Seed." Yet Laila is quite clear that
this new common identity does not replace her other social identities: she
remains a Muslim, an Arab, a Palestinian citizen of Israel. But "feeling Seed"
influences these other identities. In this way, recategorization and the assumption of a nonthreatening superordinate identity indeed seems to characterize
Laila's process of identity transformation.

In expressing her view on how the conflict might indeed be resolved,
Laila reveals the new, transcendent ideological setting of her life story:

I think the Israelis have to give freedom to the Palestinians. The refugees,
if they want to go back, to be able to go back. It's their land. But the
Israelis can't leave their land, which is what the Palestinians want. They
can't. This is the reality. I just want to feel that both sides will live, and
just stop the killings, stop the bloodshed, stop all these stupid things
that's going on. Just let the Palestinians feel freedom, at least smell the
freedom. So they can be in their homes without thinking right now the
roof might crash over my head. And also so the Israelis won't be afraid to

leave their houses. There are so many people who are afraid. Even me and my sister, we'll be afraid to take the bus! Or even be next to the bus! I would really like to have this day, when people will not be afraid to leave their houses, and not be afraid to say what they think, to not lie to ourselves. Just the right to live, this is what both groups need. Living in safety.

Although obviously quite sympathetic to the Palestinian desire for independence and self-determination, Laila nonetheless expresses a genuine understanding of the security concerns for Israelis. Her narrative reveals her support for the legitimacy of both Israelis and Palestinians, with their seemingly intractable ideological perspectives. The solution to the conflict, in Laila's transcendent vision, is one in which the needs of both groups—needs for both existential security and mutual recognition—are fully realized. She has accomplished this ambitious task within herself; she has reconciled these disparate needs within her own narrative, at least for the time being. In her desire to extend this reconciliation beyond herself and her own personal narrative, she has in the year since camp sought to influence friends and family members.

One of the implicit premises of intergroup contact is that the newly tolerant and unprejudiced individual will positively contribute to conflict and prejudice reduction simply by sharing his or her experience with family or friends. This "extended contact effect," whereby knowledge that an in-group member has out-group friends in and of itself causes positive intergroup attitudes, has been empirically demonstrated in experimental and survey research (e.g., Wright, Aron, McLaughlin-Volpe, & Ropp, 1997). In the context of Seeds of Peace, there is an explicit desire to see the youth participants share the possibility of coexistence in their home communities and to, as a consequence, perhaps create a web of ever-expanding transcendent identities.

In her life story, Laila directly discusses her own efforts to contribute to this aim of the program:

Actually, I faced a difficult reality back at home.... I understand that *I* am the one who changed, not my family, not the situation back here.... So when I went back home, I expressed to my family and friends that I disagreed with suicide bombing. But they disagreed and supported suicide bombing. I went back home, and I tried to change them and to convince them that it's not good, that it's hurting people, you could be hurt and I could be hurt. Everyone can be hurt. The suicide bomber—when he gets into a mall—he doesn't care if there's an Arab Israeli or a baby or a woman. He just wants to do it, you know. But they were not convinced at all. So I had this really, really big problem of convincing them, and successfully I could. My family right now, they totally disagree with suicide bombing. When I spoke with my parents and told them about my experience here and my opinions, what my reactions were to the news. You know how they would react to the news of a suicide bombing? They would say, "Oh great! How many killed? Only two? Oh no." I was like, oh my God, is this my family? I don't know, it was just really weird. It's like, where's the humanity of my family? They really love me, and they're a really warm family, but I still felt so far away from them somehow. But when you tell someone your experience here, I mean in detail, about how it was you slept together and lived together and ate together, and how I expressed myself as an Arab Israeli, they were kind of proud of me. Even though I'm young, they were interested to hear more, and I have a lot of things to tell them, even though I'm young. I've had an experience that they haven't.... I feel that I did something, and I feel really good about it.

Just as Liat became the defender of Arabs in the face of her friends' racist jokes, Laila has charged herself with the defense of the common humanity of the Jews. She believes that her experience at Seeds of Peace not only provides her with a distinctive identity within her family, as a young woman having gone through an emotionally challenging experience independently, but also has enabled her to argue for the immorality of suicide bombing in a compelling and credible way. She claims ultimately to have had an impact on her family's thinking—to have reduced their ardent support for suicide bombing at least partially.

Laila's identity transcendence and awakening to the possibility of thinking of Israelis and Palestinians in terms of their common humanity are central to her personal narrative of progress. As she acknowledges, her primary social identity is, for the moment, being a Seed. Her narrative is thus told to present a coherent account of how that identity came to be, and how it offers her the opportunity to contribute positively to her social ecology of development. As a Palestinian Israeli, already a member of a group "predisposed" to integrate the existential and ideological legitimacy of both sides, Laila's postprogram narrative is perhaps more expectable. "Becoming a Seed" has provided Laila with the identity coherence she has never been able to achieve as a Palestinian Israeli, trapped in a liminal state of existence. Adopting the language and ideology of her new identity as a Seed, Laila reveals the possibility of identity transcendence. We will return to her story again, to trace its evolution over time. But for now, let us return to a familiar character in our story of Israeli–Palestinian coexistence.

"Maybe They Are the Victim, the Real Victim": The Story of Noa

I returned to the Gilboa in the summer of 2005 to interview Noa and other youth from the area. Recall that in 2004, prior to her participation in Hands of Peace, Noa's life story offered a classic account of descent and gain, closely mirroring the Jewish-Israeli master narrative. Yet in the salience of her local identity as a child of the kibbutz, and therefore a true "pioneer," Noa resisted some of the most ideologically polarizing aspects of the master narrative. Owing largely to her family and the stories of her brothers' army service, Noa was quite sympathetic to the Palestinians before having ever met one. She identified as "left-wing," and her solution to the stalemate of the conflict was for Israel to simply return all lands occupied following the 1967 war. About this point, she seemed to possess little uncertainty. The key to peace was with Israel and the bold action of complete withdrawal, not with the Palestinians.

The contents of her precontact narrative were thus already suggestive of a kind of identity transcendence—a recognition of the existence and legitimacy of the out-group and its own narrative, an open critique of one's own in-group narrative and its likely contribution to the maintenance of conflict. But regardless of the openness apparent in Noa's precontact narrative, as I observed her in the early stages of participation in 2004, there was no question that contact forced her to more closely connect with her in-group identity as a Jewish Israeli. In dialogue sessions, she often became the passionate defender of the Israeli interpretation of history, with its emphasis on the constant rejection of a Jewish state by the Arabs. Yet 1 year later, Noa has crafted a narrative that fully integrates the contact experience, and she has, like Liat and Laila, assumed a new identity "supplement" through her participation in Hands of Peace.

In her 2005 interview, the experiential content that characterizes Noa's story has changed very little since 2004. The first descent in her life story still represents the divorce of her parents; the ascent, her recovery and recognition that she has the social skills to find support from peers, rather than her family. The peak of her narrative consists of the last year, when her sense of self-confidence has been at its highest. The peak experience of her story—last year's Purim celebration—is a Jewish holiday, which, as Noa describes it, is "such a happy holiday because someone tried to kill all the Jews and we won." The holiday commemorates the rescue of Persian Jews from the threat of extermination in ancient times.

What is most significant for our consideration of the role of Hands of Peace in Noa's narrative identity development is that she identifies her participation in the program as a major turning point in her life story:

> Every time I think about something big that happened in my life, or a big thing that changed my way of thinking, I think of Hands of Peace.... I

used to think of myself that I'm not a person who's really good at
listening and being quiet. In Hands of Peace, I just listened, I learned to
listen. And I know that just hearing a lot of things you haven't heard
before and listening to the stories, it wasn't so comfortable and nice to
listen to. So I got to think a lot with myself, about myself. I think it
changed me in a way. I learned how to listen and let other people talk
and not saying all the time what I'm thinking and what's my opinion,
because sometimes this isn't the most important thing.

For Noa, the turning point is most connected to a shift in self-perception
through the acquisition of new skills—listening skills—that she identifies as
beneficial. The storytelling process that occurred in the program seems to have
greatly impacted her sense of self and her understanding of the conflict, consistent with other such efforts (e.g., Albeck, Adwan, & Bar-On, 2002; Bar-On,
2006; Bar-On & Kassem, 2004; Litvak-Hirsch, 2006).

Though already an "open" person, based on her precontact narrative, Noa
underwent a process of challenge in which, initially at least, she had difficulty
listening to and accepting the stories of her Palestinian peers:

I remember Aya, she was telling a story about her friend that got killed by
a soldier at a party or something. And first of all, I thought, What? In a
party? What are you talking about? People in my army don't just come to
parties and kill innocent people! But when I saw her reaction as she told
the story, I realized it had to be real. She couldn't be lying or making it
up. When she started crying, I knew it was real. It was hard to listen to
someone talking about her friend that died. She just said that she lost
a friend. And I felt sorry for her as a friend and, in a way, ashamed.

Noa initially struggles with the challenge to her sense of in-group identity that
stories of Palestinians like Aya, who have lived their entire lives under Israeli
military occupation, create. Though she initially rejects, or at least questions,
the veracity of such accounts, in her empathy with Aya's emotional response
Noa finds the importance of being able to listen and fully process these stories.
Though they may create a sense of shame in her, for the suffering of the out-
group at the hands of members of her own in-group, Noa accepts this difficult
emotional place for both herself and for Aya, and she does not "retreat" to identity polarization. Her response is transcendent in that, in the moment, she
recognizes the common humanity of both herself and of Aya, and she legitimizes Aya's narrative, even as this legitimacy threatens to destabilize her own
identity.

Yet we must recall that Noa entered the program already questioning the
master narrative of her in-group. She was already exposed to the suffering of

Palestinians in the occupied territories through the stories of her brothers whose army service took them there, and into the homes of Palestinians. So for Noa, the path to recategorization was destined to be a short one. Hearing the stories of Palestinians with this preconception of their legitimacy facilitated the path to identity transcendence that had already begun in Noa before she had even met a Palestinian:

> With Aya, she said these experiences she had made her hate all Jews, and this was very difficult for her, but even in Hands of Peace she couldn't say that she didn't hate or blame all the Jews. And I thought to myself, I don't feel that way about Arabs or Palestinians. That's when I realized she feels that way maybe because she suffered the most. She had the biggest loss, much bigger than any of mine. She was the closest. She was closer to the conflict. She was closer to death.

Noa attributes Aya's hatred of Jews to her experience of life under Israeli occupation, rather than to some inherent and unshakeable prejudice. Israel's existential security is threatened by its military occupation of the Palestinians, not by the "natural" attitude of the Palestinians toward Jews, in Noa's view. Noa identifies the power asymmetry between Israelis and Palestinians, with all of its social structural consequences (Gordon, 2008a, 2008b; Rouhana, 2004), as the root cause of Palestinian sentiment toward Israelis.

This identification of power asymmetry and in-group responsibility is consistent with a left-wing political ideology in Israel—an ideology that calls for an end to the Israeli occupation of the Palestinian territories. Hands of Peace has pushed Noa to identify even more strongly with this left-wing ideology:

> Hands of Peace made me definitely more left-wing. I was in the left wing when I came to Hands of Peace, but it makes me more extreme. Hearing all those stories of the Palestinians and Arab-Israeli kids and I thought, OK, I'm right. They are more right than me. Their stories are more like, I remember being there, in the dialogue session we used to say to them, you're not the only victim because our soldiers get killed and our innocent people get killed all the time. But then, after hearing all their stories, I thought, maybe they are the victim, the real victim. Maybe they suffer more than we do. I came there and I thought that they might suffer more than we do, but after Hands of Peace, I knew that for sure.

Acknowledging that she entered the program with a willingness to accept the legitimacy of Palestinian stories and thus to transcend her own national identity to some extent, Noa reveals her process of coming to view the Palestinians as the "real victim" in the conflict. She has come to reject the notion that the

Israelis suffer just as much at the hands of Palestinians. Once again, she identifies the occupation, and hence Israel, as the root cause of the current suffering of both groups. She is able to cast a critical gaze toward herself, and to her
own in-group.

The extent to which Hands of Peace, in fact, "caused" Noa to undergo this
level of identity transcendence is difficult to discern. Noa may have continued
along the ideological trajectory that her precontact narrative already suggested.
But the experience of Hands of Peace has provided Noa with the "evidence" of
her ideological convictions through the stories of her Palestinian peers. Her
advice to future Hands of Peace participants: "The most important, try to listen,
because you're gonna hear lots of things you never heard before. You're gonna
learn a lot."

That at age 15 Noa's life story narrative reveals, in its ideological setting,
a measure of identity transcendence is hardly surprising. The seeds of transcendence were apparent at age 14, and Noa comes from a left-wing family and
local community critical of Israel's policies toward the Palestinians. Hands of
Peace can probably best be considered a "facilitator" of the ideological trajectory of Noa's narrative. The experience of contact, while it certainly created
moments in which Noa agrees she felt the need to "defend Israel," ultimately
may have increased her level of sympathy for the out-group, for Noa is keenly
aware of the power asymmetry that infuses Israeli–Palestinian relations.
Viewing herself as a member of the more powerful group—a group that ultimately can control the outcome of the conflict—she is prepared to sacrifice that
power for peace.

Summary: The Problem of Transcendence

The stories of Liat, Laila, and Noa reveal narratives of transcendence through
recategorization of self and other. In all three cases, the absence of identity
polarization in the life story narrative 1 year after intergroup contact is attributable to at least some extent to the willingness to accept the legitimacy of the
out-group narrative. With the recognition of the legitimacy of the out-group
and its narrative necessarily comes a transcendence of the rigid master narrative, with its tendency to reproduce a status quo of conflict. All three young
women have come to reject the most polarizing aspects of their respective
master narratives—that Israel's need for security outweighs the Palestinians'
need for self-determination (in Noa's and Liat's case); that suicide bombing
is a legitimate form of resistance (in Laila's case); that the out-group is somehow less "civilized," and therefore less human, than the in-group (in all three
cases).

Particularly in the cases of Liat and Laila, the experience of contact has resulted in the assumption of a superordinate identity as a "Seed." They have internalized what I earlier referred to as a "third narrative," the narrative of coexistence, with all of its ritualistic mythology tied to the camp culture itself. It does not seem to be coincidental that, although Hands of Peace participants like Noa reveal a measure of identity transcendence and have undergone a cognitive process of recategorization, the indoctrination of a superordinate identity seems less powerful for Hands of Peace participants. Recall that Hands of Peace does not occur in the context of a carefully manipulated isolated camp, but rather in the real-world setting of suburban Chicago. While it does indeed seek to construct a kind of culture in which recategorization will occur, it does so perhaps less dramatically than Seeds of Peace.

If the optimistic outcome of transcendence seems somehow fragile and untenable to the reader, I would suggest that he or she has come to appreciate the psychological depth of intergroup conflict, and perhaps of the Israeli–Palestinian conflict in particular, and to not be easily swayed by the possibility of coexistence. The reader surely has also kept in mind that the outcome of identity transcendence seems to rely on the political psychology of demography. The absence of young men (of all groups) and of Palestinians from the occupied territories is striking here, yet not incredibly surprising if we consider three interrelated factors: (1) the threat of identity transcendence to nationalism, by encouraging individuals to reduce the salience of their national identities; (2) the fragility and insecurity of national identity in the context of Israel and Palestine (e.g., Pettigrew, 2003); and (3) the common connection between masculinity and nationalism, whereby men have historically served to protect, promote, and violently expand the nation-state (Nagel, 1998).

If we recall that the Israeli–Palestinian conflict is a site of contested national identities (Kelman, 1978), still unresolved, then we must consider that those individuals whose transcendence would be too destabilizing, too threatening to the outcome of the contest, are destined to remain in a state of identity polarization—or perhaps, to become only further polarized by contact. It makes sense that, for young men, the need to identify with the master narrative is simply too powerful to be thwarted. Were they to relinquish their ideological adherence to the in-group, the power dynamics of the conflict could be destabilized. It also makes sense that we would witness no examples of identity transcendence for Palestinians from the occupied territories, for recall that in this contest of identities, they continue to be the losers. As such, they approach the experience of contact with a particular aim: to argue for the legitimacy of their national identity, still unrealized in the achievement of territorial sovereignty (Maoz, 2000a). With this end still unaccomplished, the Palestinians cannot so easily transcend the narrative that makes them so unique, for their distinction as a group—their identity—is what is most at stake for them. To put it in social psychological terms, Israelis and Palestinians possess divergent levels of *optimal distinctiveness* (Brewer, 1991), since there is divergence in the recognition and fulfillment of their respective national identities.

But regardless of the sources of variability in identity transcendence as a narrative outcome of contact, we must also query our own—and the programs'—expectation of such an outcome. Even though Kelman (1999b) suggests the need for identity transcendence at the structural level in order for a genuine, sustainable resolution to be secured, the design of his interactive problem-solving workshops with high-status Israeli and Palestinian leaders reveals the limitations of transcendence at the individual psychological level (e.g., Kelman, 1993, 1997). Kelman's work has focused on the building of coalitions among influential Israelis and Palestinians, but he argues that these coalitions must necessarily be "uneasy" ones, and it is this important observation that reveals the key problem with identity transcendence.

The reality of the conflict is a reality of polarization between groups. It is a reality of division, separation, insulation, and "unengagement." The problem with intergroup contact in a new reality, with a new system of power and categorization, is that, if an individual group member denies this inherent state of identity polarization and too readily engages in a recategorization process, his or her credibility as a member of that group diminishes. In other words, if the "coalition," as Kelman (1993) calls it, becomes too strong, its effectiveness is lost.

If group members sacrifice their in-group credibility for a cohesive coalition among participants, if they indeed recategorize too rapidly and allow that superordinate identity to overshadow the commitments of their distinct social identities, they sacrifice their political effectiveness upon reentry to the context of conflict (Kelman, 1993). Participants in such endeavors in intergroup contact must not "become so strongly bonded to each other that they jeopardize their relationship with their own national communities" (Kelman, 1993, p. 254), for the goal of such encounters ought not be the construction of an entirely new social identity, lacking in any national or geographic fulfillment. Rather, as Kelman and others whose focus is increasingly on an approach to contact grounded in the structural reality of the conflict (e.g., Halabi & Sonnenschein, 2004b; Suleiman, 2004b) contend, the outcome of such encounters must be consonant with the possibility of mutual identity recognition. With this idea in mind—this inherent problem with the *demand* of identity transcendence—we consider another, far more common outcome of participation: identity accentuation.

Identity Accentuation

I have already characterized the Israeli–Palestinian conflict as a problem of polarized identities, of negatively interdependent historical narratives, and of asymmetrical power dynamics. Tracing the origins of intractability to the mutual perception of existential insecurity, the Israeli–Palestinian conflict is maintained through the reproduction of narratives, the polarizing elements of which are accentuated (e.g., Bar-Tal, 2007; Hammack, 2008; Kelman, 2007; Rouhana & Bar-Tal, 1998). Such is the condition of the "narrative stalemate" of Israeli–Palestinian relations.

The social psychology of identity is characterized by the need to balance competing needs for integration and differentiation of the social ecology into the self-narrative (Adams & Marshall, 1996), all the while achieving some level of optimal distinctiveness within a given social identity or between social identities (Brewer, 1991). Contact between groups in conflict may lead to a process of recategorization that does not threaten this need for optimal distinctiveness (Brewer, 1996), but contact can also contribute to greater polarization between groups (e.g., Hewstone & Brown, 1986; Tajfel & Turner, 1986). The psychological mechanism of this process of increased identification and polarization, which I will call *identity accentuation*, is likely a combination of affective and cognitive factors, such as the emotional salience of group belongingness (see Baumeister & Leary, 1995), the collective emotional experience of conflict (e.g., Bar-Tal, Halperin, & de Rivera, 2007; Halperin, 2008), enhanced self-esteem (Tajfel & Turner, 1979), or simply the fundamental cognitive need to *categorize* self and other (Allport, 1954; Brewer, 1991), and in that process to fulfill some basic human function for creating cohesion in the social ecology or "life space" (Lewin, 1951). If identity is a fundamental process of human development in its own right—a psychological need that, in fact, drives development in some way—then the idea of categorization as an epiphenomenon of mere existence seems credible.

Precisely by constructing a social context in which identity is primed, the experience of contact between Israelis and Palestinians necessarily activates the need for narrative exploration. As an outcome of this process, identity accentuation refers to an increase in the salience of identification with the in-group and its master narrative. It represents, for the most part, the ultimate antithesis to the desired outcome of these American-based programs, with their underlying ideology of cosmopolitanism. And yet, that contact can result in this kind of identity response has long been known in social psychology, as I discussed in Chapter 6. Contact can increase the perception of identity threat, through the *pressures* of both decategorization and recategorization. With this threat may emerge, particularly during adolescence when an individual is only beginning to reconcile the relationship between self and society (Erikson, 1968), a kind of identity defense that restores coherence to the life story.

If we accept the premise that contact is inherently challenging and potentially threatening to the in-group narrative of identity with which all youth are called to identify, the outcome of *increased* polarization, of a *greater* accentuation of in-group identity (and therefore the distinctiveness of social identities), becomes comprehensible. I will present three stories that suggest a process of identity accentuation following contact. As their voices have thus far been silent in this chapter, let us begin with consideration of a Palestinian from the occupied territories.

The Fatalist: The Story of Mohammed

In my field notes, I came to describe Mohammed and his family as fiercely anti-ideological. Unlike my experiences with many families in the West Bank, Mohammed's East Jerusalemite family seemed to avoid discussions of politics at every turn. Secular Muslims, they are the model of a family whose members have been deeply impacted by the forces of globalization. Decidedly middle class, they all speak near-flawless English, among other languages besides Arabic and Hebrew, routinely surf the Internet, and have an adult daughter living in the United States with a family of her own. Mohammed, like Ali, has countless pirated DVDs of American films, downloaded from the Web. He listens to American pop, rap, and hip hop, in addition to Arabic pop from Lebanon, Egypt, and the Gulf. The family is just as likely to watch an American film on their satellite TV—without subtitles, since they claim the English is always mistranslated into Arabic—as they are to watch the Arabic version of *American Idol*, featuring competitors from throughout the Arab world.

Like many Jerusalemite families, whose national identities have been obscured by their exclusion from both Israeli citizenship (recall that they were granted permanent residency status after Israel's internationally unrecognized annexation of East Jerusalem following the 1967 war) and the auspices of the Palestinian Authority, which has no jurisdiction over Jerusalem, Mohammed's family lives a liminal existence, residing somehow between identities (Turner, 1967; van Gennep, 1960)—even more so than the Palestinian Israelis. Their Jerusalemite identity, which confers upon them a kind of "structural invisibility" or ambiguity (Turner, 1967), limits the degree to which they see themselves as "fully Palestinian." I considered this problem in Chapter 4 with the narrative of Ali. I will offer a very concrete example from my field observations with Mohammed's family that reveals the extent of their identity ambiguity.

I tended to take copious field notes about my meals in Israel and Palestine, not simply for the hope of somehow replicating some of the cuisine upon my return home, but also because distinctions in my meals seemed to provide important data about my research "subjects." In Qadas, the food was always either far too salty or far too sweet for my tastes. In this small village of desperation, was this tendency connected to the extremes of the place, or simply the need for stimulation that seemed to characterize the eternal eventlessness of the place? It was interesting that, at the home of Ofra in Haifa, her mother expressed no interest in preparing food from her native country of India, even though she herself grew up there and did not immigrate to Israel until she was an adolescent. Was her need to make food that was distinctly "Israeli" (I will always recall her delicious, massive "Israeli breakfast," which she would serve to me with such pride) a reflection of her need to express an Israeli identity, and to, like so many Mizrahi immigrants to Israel, reveal her commitment to an Israeli identity through the rejection of her former cultural practices? Such questions invariably arose over the simple act of consuming a meal in Israel or Palestine.

For a deeper window into Mohammed's identity, consider my own breakfast experience in his household. While I do not recall receiving any breakfast other than fresh hummus, *labne* (a yogurt dip), *zatar* (a thyme spice mixture), bread, olives, eggs, and an assortment of homemade pickles while residing with my host families in the West Bank, my breakfast at Mohammed's home revealed the complexity of his family's cultural location. While my first morning I was typically offered *labne*, pickles, *zatar*, and bread, most mornings I was offered corn flakes and Nescafé. Based on my field experience, few Palestinian homes in the West Bank possess an accessible supply of Nescafé. Rich, cardamom-infused Arabic coffee, served in a small espresso cup, was the only form of coffee I consumed in the West Bank. Yet every Israeli family with whom I stayed would customarily offer me Nescafé in the morning. Some Israeli families would offer me cereal for breakfast, but such a breakfast was still uncommon. But in general, the infusion of Palestinian, Israeli, and American customs into the family breakfast at Mohammed's home, I believe, says much about the family's sense of identity.

Mohammed's family is a subject of middle-class globalization, and as such naturally exudes a kind of cosmopolitanism—a predisposition for conversation across sites of difference. Mohammed's family members typically expressed a great openness to the world as a result. Unlike in the West Bank, where in homes I would be subject to routine diatribes on the occupation, Zionism, and resistance, Mohammed's family only seemed to seek a stable economic place in the world—a place to be comfortable and content, a cultural context conducive to an unburdened existence. Mohammed's mother and two older brothers, all of whom served as important models for Mohammed (his parents were divorced, and his father was fairly estranged from the family), were always very clear with me in their desire to avoid political discourse in the home, or in life in general for that matter. It is in this decidedly anti-ideological context that the ideological setting of Mohammed's life story was beginning to form.

In the summer of 2005, 2 years after participating in Seeds of Peace and 1 year after participating in Hands of Peace, Mohammed narrated his life story to me, the view of East Jerusalem in the background outside his home, sights of the separation barrier visible in the distance. True to the Palestinian master narrative, Mohammed's narrative takes the form of a tragedy.

Mohammed's narrative ascends only during his period of professed social unconsciousness, and its tragic descent begins as problems within his family become unavoidable:

> I was born in 1988, I was like a kid that didn't understand nothing at all, so everyone was giving me attention, growing up, in my family. So everything was like happy and normal.... Then when I was like 8 years old, I start to really understand that there's like school and I have to study, there are a lot of things going on in life.... And the family had tough times at that time, when I was 8 years old, my parents started having problems, and they got divorced.... I was always depressed with changes in my family.

The euphoria of childhood, in which Mohammed's life centered on himself and his own pleasures, ends dramatically with the family disruption of divorce. Organizing his life story into chapters, Mohammed describes the trajectory of this early period with the chapter titles "Being Born in the Family," "Living in Childhood," and "Realizing Things: The Family Problem."

Mohammed's transition into early adolescence occurs at the commencement of the second *intifada*, and his story takes a series of interesting turns as a consequence. Describing that period and the emergence of his political consciousness, Mohammed professes confusion about what his role in the conflict ought to be:

> At that time, I started thinking, "Should I do something, or should I not? Should I just stay here?" So pretty much I kept on talking to my mom about it and she said, "If you want to do something, you'll only ruin your life." So I just stayed here and watched. It's bigger than all of us. It's out of each one of our power. So this wasn't like any other teenage life.

The *intifada* created a crisis for Mohammed's identity. Was he to be a fighter, a protester, a helper? Ultimately, his identity as a *fatalist*, someone deeply committed to the belief that much of life lies beyond his control, emerged in response to this crisis. Unwilling to participate in the political action of the *intifada*, he chose instead to become an audience member to it.

But Mohammed did indeed take action—a kind of action atypical of young Palestinians at the time. He chose to participate in Seeds of Peace. For him, it represented a way of "doing something" about the situation. Two years after this experience, now at age 16, Mohammed offers this account:

> And then by chance I went to Seeds of Peace, deciding that I'm meeting Israelis. And the thing is, I wasn't like changing, or like I accept them or anything, or what they say, it's like, I feel *more* like I'm the real owner of this land. I understand why they say what they say, but even, I was like *more* Palestinian when I came back—I *felt* more Palestinian. So I just came back, new, fresh Palestinian...
>
> Like being in dialogue with them, seeing them and knowing that a lot of them really don't care...When I hear them say things, and I was like, nothing's gonna change. There's no hope.... Also if you convince some of them, they'll be back here and remix with their society and it won't stay. So I was like, nothing's gonna change. Nothing like Seeds of Peace will help. So I just stay focused, and never, like, give up something because you are the legitimate owner of this land.
>
> So now we're living here, at this time, in the conflict. I don't know, I'm trying to avoid remembering that I'm in conflict. It's like I want life to like go on, seriously, and reach the best point I can in life, and live my life.... I know that people are suffering.... I always say, "A day will come and everything will be like the way it should be from the beginning"— we'll have our land back, our country back. And if not, the end of the world will come soon, and people will be judged for what they did. That's it, I'm just living here...

The experience of intergroup contact has, in Mohammed's interpretation, served to *enhance* his solidarity with a Palestinian identity. In his narrative, contact appears to have facilitated his differentiation of self and other: "It doesn't really matter if we agree or not, but it's like each other was raised in a different way of life, and each one should be different because we are in a conflict. So we won't agree on everything; it's impossible."

According to his present narrative, contact has increased Mohammed's identification with the Palestinian master narrative, with its focus on the significance of the land and its liberation. Mohammed now delegitimizes the

Israeli narrative entirely, having become convinced of the legitimacy of the Palestinian narrative and its basis in ultimate truth. Interestingly, though, there is some suggestion that Mohammed has a more nuanced appreciation for intergroup dialogue between Israelis and Palestinians, claiming to "understand why they say what they say." In other words, though he has come to an insular view of "truth," he seems to understand the basic need for group members to defend their own master narratives, thus suggesting a certain level of self-consciousness about identity.

Coming together with other Palestinians from the West Bank during Seeds of Peace, and having to navigate a rejecting reintegration home, let us not dismiss the possibility that Mohammed's need to identify so thoroughly with the Palestinian master narrative may be connected to his need to "prove" his identity, to himself and to others. Mohammed in fact identifies the nadir of his life story as his return home from the United States after participating in Seeds of Peace:

> I don't know, coming back from the USA and from Seeds, trying to put it in the spot, where most of the people say you did something wrong. That was the lowest point for me in my life. 'Cause sometimes I thought, "Yeah, it was wrong." Here I'm living with Jews, I have no other choice. But there I went willing and chose to live with them. But it was like, I had to do something, I thought. There were no choices.

> When people gave me a hard time for it, I was like, well, I tried something for myself. I wasn't brainwashed—I'm more Palestinian, I figured out that there's a difference, that's obvious. They have their own truth, their own books, their own history that they wrote themselves.... It was for my good, I gave a strong idea about the Palestinian people. I didn't send a wrong message. I told them we're a people whose land was occupied, we're sent out, we're forced out of the country, forced to do that. And we are people who want education, want to read, want to live a peaceful life, and that's not happening now. So I don't think I did something wrong. I wasn't there for having fun and forgetting the main things. I'm Palestinian, everybody's gonna look at me as Palestinian.... So I gave a good message, and whether it was wrong or right, I think for me, it helps me a lot, realizing more things and working on my personality.

Mohammed's participation at Seeds of Peace creates an identity "crisis" for him, for his society views this action as "conspirational" in nature. The only acceptable form of narrative integration for such an experience is thus to frame its purpose as (a) faithfully representing the Palestinian cause, and (b) securing his own connection to his Palestinian identity. Mohammed's participation has fulfilled both of these aims, according to his current narrative.

Are Mohammed's new, stronger commitments to the Palestinian master narrative motivated by a sense of guilt about participation in contact, or by a feeling that, like Ali, because of his privileged Jerusalemite identity, he is, in fact, "less Palestinian" than his West Bank peers? When we deal with the retrospection of narrative, we can do no more than speculate about the deep psychological motives for ideological identifications and commitments. Without question, Mohammed's "globalized," Jerusalemite identity makes him a prime candidate for identity accentuation during adolescence. His need to manage the distinctiveness of his personal identity, so that it is consonant with a perceived normative Palestinian life course, seems to be primed by the experience of intergroup contact. But contact with Israelis—who have been represented in Palestinian collective consciousness as dark enemies in their quest for self-determination—is psychologically dissonant for Palestinians. In order to make meaning of their will to partake in such an endeavor, they must, it would seem, construct an acceptable narrative that secures their place as "legitimate" Palestinians doing their part for the liberation of the Palestinian nation. In Kelman's (1993) framework, they must not develop *too* close of a coalition with Israelis, for that would reduce their credibility as members of their own national group (a credibility perhaps already shaky for Jerusalemite Palestinians).

I call Mohammed the "Fatalist" precisely because of the attitude of resignation he espouses in this and other parts of his life story. Mohammed's narrative emphasizes a level of powerlessness as a Palestinian, with no citizenship in a sovereign state he can readily claim as culturally and historically salient. He frames the events of the world as beyond his control, and even more so, as beyond *everyone's* control. He has internalized a skeptical, fatalistic view of the world and of political events in particular, believing instead that "one day, everything will be as it should." What I had initially mistaken for a kind of anti-ideological stance in Mohammed and his family was, in fact, an extraordinary degree of fatalism, which extended even to a boycott of Palestinian Authority elections, not out of protest but simply because, as Mohammed's mother told me, "It's fixed; it's already been decided."

Seeds of Peace, then, seems to be associated with the accentuation of Mohammed's Palestinian identity and the cultivation of a deep sense of distinction between this identity and an Israeli one. Contact has contributed to the polarization between himself and his Israeli peers. It has affirmed the story of his in-group as the just and accurate story of the conflict, in accordance with the Palestinian master narrative. Mohammed now frames the Israeli narrative as a work of fiction, a falsehood constructed only for the psychological benefit of its citizens. Most significantly, contact has appeared to provide Mohammed with an acceptable *role* that contributes to the Palestinian cause; it has provided him with a relatively safe outlet for social practice as a Palestinian, to become connected to his identity and to express that commitment. In this way, Seeds of Peace offers a set of practices for Mohammed during his adolescence that he can meaningfully identify as valuable to his own identity development, even as it seems to affect his identity in ways counter to the program's intent.

Mohammed's experience with contact appears to contribute to his ability to differentiate between identities and to make the existence of his identity as a Palestinian fully known. Given the power asymmetry of the conflict (Maoz, 2000b; Rouhana, 2004), perhaps this kind of outcome is the most realistic possibility for Israeli and Palestinian youth. As practitioners at the School for Peace in Israel have argued, perhaps the need for Israelis to fully accept the legitimacy of Palestinian identity must *precede* the kind of mutual acceptance that so many of these programs benevolently pursue (Halabi & Sonnenschein, 2004a, 2004b; Nadler, 2004; Suleiman, 2004b). I will consider this idea further in Chapter 8, but for now we must recognize that for Mohammed, like virtually all Palestinian youths in this study, identity accentuation appears to be the most psychologically manageable narrative outcome of contact with Israelis. To make meaning of their experience, they must somehow integrate it with the collective narrative of liberation and identity fulfillment that consumes Palestinian discourse and, in the process, dispute claims that their coalition with Israelis might render them "collaborators."

The aims of these American-based programs may not, in fact, conform well to the reality of the conflict, with its unique system of structural relations. I will consider this notion quite thoroughly in Chapter 8, but for the moment let us acknowledge that contact has only seemed to contribute to further polarization in Mohammed's identity. It has enhanced the salience of his in-group identity as a Palestinian; it has accentuated this social identity above all other aspects of his identity. It has not "decategorized" or "recategorized," for Mohammed has resisted those "presses" of the Seeds of Peace experience. It has, rather, enabled him to more readily see the ideological distinctions between Palestinians and Israelis. It has exposed him to the very basis of the conflict, its origins in the actual distinction between identities and narratives of the past, present, and future.

Fatalism is not, for Mohammed, an idiosyncratic personality characteristic. It is, rather, an interpretive tool that allows him to confront the challenge of his Palestinian identity in a way that is psychologically manageable. In his narrative of the present, of his current project of self-development, Mohammed is trying to manage the uncertainty of his life as a Palestinian, and he is attempting to integrate his sense of fatalism with his aspirations for a good life:

> It's like, nowadays, I'm trying to change myself. I don't want to put obstacles in my way—those are already thrown in, being a Palestinian. It's like really hard, not so easy as everyone thinks. So I'm trying to avoid everything, avoid thinking and avoid worrying. ...And like the current situation, it's no way I can stay here. And nothing's gonna change for a while. I'm not waiting for anything to change in the meantime, and I don't know if it's gonna change or not. You got yourself and you got to live your life on your own and like live as if there's nothing going on.

> The biggest challenge in my life is being a better person. I work on myself being a better person, so strong as to face all of these difficulties and pass through all these obstacles that are thrown in the way just because of one reason, which is my nationality. This is a challenge. I want to be better, because of that. This is not going to make me less than any other person. This has to make me better.

Having come to fully embrace his Palestinian identity, with all its existential challenges, Mohammed's life project now centers on the need to channel the experience of oppression and subordination into personal and collective strength. He refuses to allow his national identity to limit life's possibilities. Although his identity constructs obstacles and challenges—the greatest challenge of his life, in fact, greater than the traumatic rupture of his family with the divorce of his parents—Mohammed seeks to maneuver around them. He actively uses the tool of an evolving personal narrative to do so.

Mohammed is a 16-year-old secular Muslim from East Jerusalem. He is the subject of a globalized world, and his cultural practices reveal his desire to be a part of that cosmopolitan world. But he cannot escape the accentuation of his social identity, for it is a source of existential threat and ontological insecurity (Giddens, 1991). His ability to fully embrace the idea of a cosmopolitan worldview is limited by the liminality of his national identity. And he cannot come to legitimize the Israeli narrative of identity in the absence of his own identity fulfillment, for the universal recognition of Palestine as a distinct nation remains elusive, along with the status of his native city of Jerusalem. Is it at all surprising, given the psychological dynamics of the conflict and of Palestinian identity, that for youth like Mohammed the transcendence of identity represents the ultimate threat to the realization of Palestine as a recognizable national entity? Recognition and ontological security probably need to precede the possibility of transcendence, which makes Mohammed's identity accentuation and perception of intergroup differentiation not only a comprehensible outcome, but also perhaps the most "realistic" of any possible identity outcome.

The Settler: Revisiting the Story of Roai

I will now return to a familiar character in our story of Israeli and Palestinian youth, to the story of Roai, the Mizrahi Israeli from a West Bank settlement. Like Mohammed, Roai is a subject of globalization. The son of immigrants from Iraq and Morocco, Roai and his family have embraced the liberal cosmopolitan values of the West. He is well traveled in Europe and North America; he feverishly consumes American films and pop music. He spends each evening chatting on MSN with friends from around the globe. Roai is someone genuinely interested in intercultural conversation. For this reason, like Mohammed, Roai seems a fitting candidate for intergroup contact.

At age 16, his precontact narrative revealed a measure of ideological confusion, as he strived to integrate his support for the idea of Palestinian statehood with his emphasis on Israel's need for both security and a Jewish majority. His recognition of the legitimacy of Palestinian identity was conditional upon their abandonment of the violent tactics that consumed their struggle for independence. A compromise was only possible if the Palestinians were able to make the first move, to reject the use of violence against Israelis and to dismantle the "terrorist" organizations inside of the occupied territories.

When I first met Roai, he was 2 years shy of his compulsory military service and still in the process of solidifying his ideological commitments. Recall that he was exposed to two distinct ideological realities: the "extremism" of his home community on the settlement, in which the idea of a Palestinian identity was essentially rejected, and the left-wing sentiments of his peers at a liberal elite secondary school in Jerusalem, whose anti-settlement ideology delegitimized Roai's very existence. Ideologically, then, Roai's narrative was set in a very unstable place; it possessed the potential to be pulled one way or another.

Like many Jewish-Israeli participants in Hands of Peace and Seeds of Peace, Roai was distressed during contact by the destabilization of the power dynamics that frame the conflict at home. In his immediate postcontact interview, he reported feeling a sense of identity insecurity as a consequence of participation:

> First of all, I felt like the program was somehow not equal, that somehow the Palestinians were more powerful, and we heard so much of only their suffering and not *our* suffering as Israelis. What surprised me most about the program, talking with Palestinians, is the facts. I mean, I know

facts, and they know facts, but it's not the same facts. They're changing the facts! I know the facts! I believe Israelis don't change the facts. They want the world to see the Israelis as bad people, but I know that what they say is not true. Like in Lebanon, they say Sharon ordered the Sabra and Shatila massacres, and it's not true!... I didn't change my mind about anything listening to the Palestinians, but it was interesting.

Roai's experience of contact is characterized by the perception of an all-out assault on the legitimacy of his own group's narrative. In defense, he seems now unwilling to acknowledge the potential legitimacy of the Palestinian historical narrative, instead suggesting that only the Israeli narrative represents actual "facts." Rather than recognize the relative or interpretive nature of history and identity, as the program may have sought, Roai has become hardened to the idea of absolute historical truth and the exclusive accuracy and legitimacy of his group's narrative. In addition, he sees the psychosocial pull of the program toward a common identity as a threat to his Israeli identity. The notion of a common identity may be too threatening to the identity distinctiveness youth seem to *need* to assert, probably because neither Israelis nor Palestinians possess a sense of security about the sustenance of their national identities.

One year after his experience in contact with Palestinians and Palestinian Israelis, Roai's life story has retained its basic form. His narrative continues to follow the basic redemptive, descent-and-gain pattern of the master narrative of Jewish-Israeli identity. His remains a story of resilience in spite of significant challenge and adversity. The peak experience of his story remains his pre-*intifada* travel to the United States, where his observations of a different cultural reality revealed the possibility of an unthreatened existence. The great nadir in his narrative, his father's untimely death in 2002, is salient, but his recovery from this trauma reinforces his sense of personal resilience.

Ideologically, Roai's narrative is now infused with a deeper sense of loyalty to his national identity, his experience in contact having provided him with a more "realistic" vision of the Palestinian narrative:

[Contact] was really different from what I expected because of [the] opinions [of the Palestinians and Palestinian Israelis].... I thought they were very militaristic. I thought that there were things that they don't think, only the old people think about. But after I came to Hands of Peace, I realized that even the young people get education to think and to do what the old people tell them.... It's not very realistic to think that old people forgot. My reality has totally changed. In some ways it was disappointing, but you should see the reality. You shouldn't see something else.

Roai was surprised to hear the stories and the political views of the Arabs at Hands of Peace because they seemed only to support the negative stereotypes about them he had grown up with. He had assumed that Palestinians of *his* generation had moved on and were basically ready to compromise for peace. His disappointment at the realization that young Palestinians seem just as ideologically rigid as he was led to expect influences the development of his own political views—from a place of possible transcendence to one of greater polarization.

At age 17, Roai now explicitly identifies as "right-wing." His willingness to recognize Palestinian identity and its fulfillment in territorial sovereignty remains conditional upon Israel's security, and he is reluctant to meet some of the most basic demands of the Palestinian position:

> I think that we should solve the problem in a way in which we shouldn't give up on our security.... We need to fight about it, and send soldiers and do something, that's the way we will do it. There's no other way to do it.

> I think they should get a country of their own. The Palestinians should get a country of their own, not all the territories we have now, but the majority of them. And we should remove all the settlements from the area, but some of them should remain. I don't think they should have a capital city in Jerusalem. That's not what I think. And the right of return, I don't think they'll get it. Actually I am sure they won't get it, because ever since 1948 when we give up something, they also need to do it.

Even though he identifies as right-wing, Roai would probably best be considered "center-right" or even perhaps "center" or "center-left" in the realm of Israeli politics. His willingness to grant Palestinian independence in a "majority" of the occupied territories distinguishes him ideologically from most in the right wing. Yet Roai's conditional acceptance of the legitimacy of Palestinian aspirations—which, by and large, has remained constant in his narrative over the course of the year—continues to be infused with a discourse of classic Orientalism.

Roai's personal narrative of success, in spite of formidable struggle, mirrors the master narrative of Jewish-Israeli identity closely and contributes to his belief in the exceptionalism of Israel as a nation. When asked to identify a film that has impacted him significantly, Roai does not hesitate to nominate *Forrest Gump*:

> If you think about it, it's a really good movie that proves that you can, even when people think you're an idiot, you can do great things if you believe in yourself. If you want something so much, you can

get it.... It shows the life of a person that, when he traveled, nobody liked him. He was raised just by his mother, and people thought he was an idiot. And when you watch the movie, you see his life story, after the army, what he did in his life. And you see he was a really successful man, even though people thought he was an idiot. He always wanted success and to do what he believed in.

Roai's identification with this film and its protagonist reflects his own desire for success and resilience in spite of tragedy. Other influential stories, such as those passed down from Roai's family, all center on this theme of success and strength in the face of obstacles:

> The story of my grandmother, when they moved to Israel, that had a big effect on me. One of them lived in Morocco and one of them lived in northern Iraq, in Kurdistan. When they moved to Israel it was really difficult, they didn't have a lot of money, they were newcomers, they didn't know the language. And they treated my parents very well. And even though they didn't have all the money and the education, they did a great job and all of them are very successful.

Finally, Roai identifies the story of the Jewish people as a significant source of strength in his own life story narrative:

> Being Jewish, I think it is really special than other religions in the world. [We] are a really small group of people, and I've seen that even though we have a lot of problems, as the world is going on, today we are still strong.

Roai's identification with a narrative of success and resilience, along with his belief in Israeli exceptionalism, is critical to understanding the ideological setting of his current life story, with its foundation in an Orientalist conception of the Palestinians.

The internalization of Orientalism is problematic for Israeli–Palestinian relations in an intergroup encounter because it interferes with the possibility of power redistribution. It allows the relationship between "occupier" and "occupied" to be inevitably reproduced (see Halperin, Bar-Tal, Sharvit, Rosler, & Raviv, 2010; Rosler, Bar-Tal, Sharvit, Halperin, & Raviv, 2009):

> The source of the conflict is the land. They think it is their land, and we think it's our land.... But we brought development to the area. We built the country. That's the problem. We built the country in our territories, and now they want it back.

The brevity of Roai's admitted Orientalism or delegitimization of the Palestinians in our interview was striking to me, particularly since he spoke quite candidly

about his view of the inferiority of Arabs during my stay in his home. One evening after dinner, we had a long discussion about politics. The Palestinians had
just elected Mahmoud Abbas as the new president of the Palestinian Authority,
and Roai and I were watching the election report on television:

> I say give them their country. Give them the West Bank and Gaza—not
> all of it, but most, and none of Jerusalem. They will destroy themselves
> anyway. The Arabs, they're a disorganized people, a naturally violent
> culture. So why should we still be taking care of them all these years?
> Just give them a country, and we'll see how they can handle it.

Roai's views on the Arabs are most clearly infused with an Orientalist frame in
these informal conversations we have during my stay with his family. They take
him outside of the positioning he is seeking to achieve in the interview setting
and provide a much "thicker" description of his current narrative. During my
stay in his home, he takes great care to tell me how loathsome Arabic music is,
and how Israel would be much better off without any Arabs at all. When I
query him about some of the educated Arabs he befriended at Hands of Peace,
he says, "Those Arabs weren't representative, they were exceptions."

In the absence of viewing out-group members as representative, a process
of decategorization is largely impossible (Hewstone & Brown, 1986). And
without an initial process of decategorization, recategorization is unlikely. In
other words, if individuals do not see members of the out-group as representative, they cannot break down their stereotypes of the content of the category.
If they cannot break down those stereotypes in the first place, they cannot
"rebuild" the meaning of the category. Hence Roai's interpretation of his
Palestinian interlocutors as "exceptions" to the general rule about the category
"Palestinian" or "Arab" serves no end toward improving intergroup relations. It
provides a narrative mechanism to justify the *reproduction* of the conflict and
continued violence.

Ideologically, then, it seems that Hands of Peace has done little to alter the
trajectory of Roai's life story. He suggests that his participation was primarily
"useful" in his acquisition of information about the out-group and its ideological perspective:

> I realized their reality is not my reality, and what they think is not what
> I think. I think that's the effect Hands of Peace had on me. It's very hard
> to tell them, "Why do you think like that?" Maybe it's the right way for
> you, then they hear what I have to say about that. That's the process.

Roai's experience is more consistent with the *mutual intergroup differentiation*
model that characterizes the School for Peace approach in Israel (Halabi &
Sonnenschein, 2004a, 2004b; Hewstone & Brown, 1986) than with the

common in-group identity model that characterizes the underlying philosophy and curriculum of Hands of Peace. Like Mohammed, intergroup contact has facilitated Roai's ability to differentiate self from other through hearing the stories and ideological perspectives of the out-group. It has, in this way, facilitated the consolidation of his own ideological identifications into a coherent narrative.

What is most problematic about Roai's consolidation is that it has only reinforced his own identity polarization. His experience in intergroup contact has legitimized the need for psychological distance from the Palestinians, for theirs is a story of consistent failure in the face of struggle, in marked contrast to the story of Roai and his people. His is a story of progress, theirs a story of regress. And so Roai's exposure to the stories of his Palestinian and Palestinian-Israeli peers seems only to have reinforced his need for in-group insulation. Most important, though, Roai does not believe his own ideological perspective, and his expressed psychological needs as a Jewish Israeli, has been fully legitimized by the out-group:

> Like the right of return. They really believe in the right of return! They don't think it's impossible. When you describe the reality to these people about the right of return, they don't see where is the problem. They don't understand that this is *our* land, and this is the country of the Jewish people. They don't seem to recognize that Israel is a country. They believe that, in some way, they will rule this land and we will go out of here.

> With Hands of Peace, I didn't like change my political opinions or anything, but I got more information about what they think.... And especially the Arab Israelis. I thought that the Arab Israelis, that they feel like an Israeli, that they belong in this country. But when I came to Hands of Peace I realized they feel more Palestinian than Israeli. They support, totally, with their brothers, the Palestinians, instead of the Israelis. And they are here just because in some ways it's better to be an Arab Israeli, a "Palestinian Israeli"—that's what they call themselves— instead of a Palestinian. They have more rights, they have more opportunities to be successful, and they're just using Israel as a tool for their life. It was a big shock.

Contact has provided Roai with useful information about the out-group. It has reinforced his perceived need for his own kind of identity polarization. He finds the Palestinian insistence on the right of return for the refugees—a fundamental and seemingly unshakeable demand in the Palestinian ideological position—extremely threatening to Israel. The inability of the Palestinians to recognize the demographic consequences of Israel's acceptance of such an agreement—that Israel would, out of necessity to remain a legitimate democracy, cease to be a distinctly Jewish state if the refugees should return—seems to heighten Roai's collective existential insecurity. It seems to demonstrate to him that the Palestinians continue to deny the legitimate existence of a Jewish state in what was Palestine. The "information" that Roai obtained through contact has contributed to a process of intergroup differentiation, perhaps most of all in his view of the Palestinian Israelis.

Roai's narrative account of contact is strikingly similar to Mohammed's. The experience has provided him with the opportunity to fully differentiate his identity from that of the out-group. It has highlighted the distinctions between himself and the Palestinians. It has placed him in a position of in-group defense, which has served to align him even more closely to the Jewish-Israeli master narrative. Roai experienced contact as "interesting" in this end but also very threatening, for the program's attempt to engineer a common identity was a source of great resistance for him. Roai preferred to remain inside the "reality" of Israeli–Palestinian relations and to use the opportunity to develop a strong identification with his own in-group narrative, thus contributing to the reproduction of conflict. Considering the narratives of Roai and Mohammed together, the stalemate of narratives between Israelis and Palestinians becomes quite lucid. To meet the ideological needs of the out-group threatens the *existence* of one's in-group identity, and the absence of secure narratives seems to limit the potential outcomes of contact and to facilitate the reproduction of the conflict's identity dynamics.

The New Palestinian: Revisiting the Story of Jibril

"My identity is Arab Israeli. I am Israeli first; I have no question about this. I live in Israel. Israel is my country. I'm proud of being Israeli, and I'm proud of my country." These were the words of Jibril describing his identity when I first interviewed him, at age 15 in the summer of 2003 at the start of Seeds of Peace. The experience of contact had created a crisis for Jibril, an affable young man whose integrity was transparent in his handshake and warm smile. Was he Palestinian? Was he Israeli? These were questions generally avoided in his family and his local community of Taybeh. But at Seeds of Peace, they commanded a resolution.

The Palestinian citizens of Israel indeed undergo a unique process of identity development. As I considered at length in Chapter 5, Palestinian Israelis must reconcile their Israeli civic identities with their cultural identities as Palestinians, all the while negotiating a master narrative that highlights their

experiences with loss, discrimination, and subordination. Contemporary scholars of Palestinian-Israeli identity tend to view the way in which Palestinian
Israelis traverse this challenging process in a highly linear form, historically
speaking (e.g., Rabinowitz & Abu-Baker, 2005). They tend to see the increasing
collective accentuation of their Palestinian cultural identity and the rejection of
their Israeli identity—a consequence of their disempowerment and inequality
within the state's institutions—as an indicator of gradual reidentification with
a Palestinian identity. But Jibril's story challenged that notion by revealing that
Palestinian-Israeli youth may, in fact, prefer to accentuate their Israeli identities at different times and places in their life course. The hyphenated identity
status of Palestinian Israelis suggests that they undergo a far more complex
and individual process of identity reconciliation than many scholars seem to
suggest.

The extent of "Israelization" readily apparent in Jibril's narrative at age 15
revealed his preferred way of reconciliation at that particular moment, and it
infused the entire content of his life story, from its form (which resembled the
Jewish-Israeli master narrative much more than the Palestinian-Israeli) to its
ideological setting. Regarding ideology, recall that Jibril, like his Jewish-Israeli
peers, tended to view the central problem in the current phase of the conflict as
Palestinian "terror." The Israeli occupation was certainly problematic according to Jibril's narrative, but it was Palestinian action that had increased the
fighting to its current level of intractability. Palestinian action was to blame for
the new levels of daily suffering for ordinary Palestinians, and Palestinian
action was responsible for changing Jibril's life, for increasing the Jews' hostility toward Arabs, for preventing Jibril and his family from visiting the shops
and restaurants of Tulkarm. Ironically, Palestinian action—or, more accurately,
Jibril's interpretation of that action—complicated Jibril's ability to identify with
Palestinian culture, for it now prevented him from associating with Palestinians
in the occupied territories. The polarization of Palestinians and Israelis during
the second *intifada* transformed identity for Palestinian Israelis like Jibril from
a process of developmental complexity to a zero-sum affair. The accentuation
of the distinction between identities that has occurred since the start of the
second *intifada* suggests that Palestinian Israelis might no longer comfortably
ontologically reside in the center of these poles but might instead have to make
an uncompromising choice.

If Jibril's narrative at age 15 revealed the salience of his Israeli identity, at
the start of his experience with intergroup contact, how did this experience
seem to impact his process of identity development? Jibril narrated his life
story to me again at age 16, 1 year after his participation at Seeds of Peace.
As we sat in his house in Taybeh, I saw before me a very different looking

young man. At age 15, Jibril was confident but uncomfortably stocky in build. At age 16, his shoulders had broadened, he had gained several inches in height, and he had lost much of his previously stocky frame. As he narrated his life story to me once again, with the memory of his first lingering in my mind, as it had for virtually the entire year that separated our meetings, I realized that far more than Jibril's appearance had changed.

Jibril's story retained its descent-and-gain form, with Seeds of Peace now representing the peak experience in his narrative. For Jibril, contact served as an opportunity for personal gain through identity exploration. In fact, for Jibril and other Palestinian Israelis, contact with Jewish Israelis and with Palestinians seems to activate a process of identity *discovery* in which they might come to accentuate their Palestinian cultural identities *over and above* their Israeli civic identities. The cultural significance and salience of their Palestinian identities becomes readily apparent, while they come to question and challenge the extent to which they truly are "Israeli." This process of identity discovery is particularly apparent in Jibril's narrative 1 year after contact.

Jibril's life story, with its peaks and valleys, represents a narrative of highs and lows, of the inherent challenges and successes of life's uncontrollable events. Speaking of his experience at Seeds of Peace, Jibril immediately reflects on how this event shaped his own identity consciousness:

> I think after Seeds of Peace, I feel now I understand where I am on the map in this conflict. I know now how the Jews think about me, and how do the Palestinians think about me. After the camp, I know how to work with people from Palestine and also Jews.

> I know I'm in the middle because sometimes I am driven to Palestine and I belong to Israel, and I'm in a big dilemma what to do. And at Seeds of Peace, I come to realize how I want to think, and what I want to do. And also at Seeds of Peace, Seeds of Peace gives us more self-confidence to talk, to share our opinions...

> I still feel confused sometimes,... but now I understand that I'm Palestinian, and how important that is. After I came together with everyone involved, Palestinians, Israelis, and other Arab Israelis like me, I realize I'm more Palestinian than Israeli. The Palestinians understand me, and I understand them. I side with them cause I'm Palestinian, and now I have a better sense of that.

Like Mohammed and Roai, the experience of intergroup contact has facilitated a process of mutual intergroup differentiation for Jibril. His categorization of self and other(s) has proceeded from a place of abstraction to concrete perception. The identities of the conflict have now become fully cognized for him, and hence differentiated. He also has now come to locate himself within this matrix of categories; he has come to understand his own identity in a way that possesses both meaning and security. His identity commitment has shifted from "Israeli" to "middle" or, perhaps, "Palestinian."

Jibril identifies the motivating factor in this identity formation process for him as, at least in part, the acceptance he received from Palestinians versus the rejection he perceives from Jewish Israelis. Two experiences from his current life story narrative are illustrative. Reflecting on a meeting of Seeds of Peace participants with Palestinian Authority officials in Ramallah in the past year, Jibril describes his experience with Palestinians:

> I went to the seminar in Ramallah, and I wanted the Palestinians to know me. There was me and like two other people from Taybeh, and like three other Arab Israelis. There, I felt like I was Palestinian. Each one there welcomed us, and we were with Arafat. Somebody told Arafat that there were five people from Israel there, like Arab Israelis, so he said, "You are with us, we are with you." I felt the Palestinian with me, and the Palestinians support me. How do I support them? And it was a good thing, somebody to support you, that's a good thing.... A man there said, "We will stand with you,... you will be our people in Israel." So we support them and they support us.... At the Palestinian seminar, I felt I am more Palestinian because they stand with me and they support me, so after Seeds of Peace I feel more Palestinian than Israeli.

> You know, the Palestinians, I want the feeling. I can't sing the Israeli anthem because it doesn't belong to me. I can't have the Israeli flag. Also, I cannot have the Palestinian flag. So you know this is a bad thing—to feel like you don't belong to anybody. So in the Palestinian seminar, I feel like I belong.

From individuals in authority, Jibril perceives support for his unique identity among Palestinians. In contrast to some of his experiences at camp, in which the Palestinians assailed him for even identifying as "Israeli" in any way, Jibril perceives complete acceptance—and support—from the PA officials whom he meets in Ramallah. This experiences stands in contrast to his perception of rejection from Jewish Israelis:

> There was a Knesset member who said that in a few years the Arabs will be transferred from Israel. There is no one in Palestine saying that thing about the Jews! It was Jews saying this about Arab Israelis. This makes

me feel separated from the Israelis. If I said in the news, I want to kick all the Jews out in the sea, everybody will be against me, but if one of them says like this, nothing happens.

Exposure to political discourse that advocates the transfer of Arabs from Israel obviously induces a perception of vulnerability, insecurity, and inferiority for the Palestinian citizens. This feeling of rejection, of discrimination, has become more salient in Jibril's postcontact narrative, and it has been planted in the narrative by actual experiences with discrimination. (It is noteworthy that the Knesset member about whom Jibril speaks, Avigdor Lieberman, ascended to power as Foreign Minister in the 2009 election that brought Benjamin Netanyahu back as Prime Minister.)

The perception of discrimination and subordination, so salient in the Palestinian-Israeli master narrative, seems to contribute significantly to Jibril's deaccentuation of his Israeli identity. Given that Jibril's precontact narrative did indeed contain many references to discrimination, it is not so much that he has experienced *more* discrimination in the year after contact. Rather, his postcontact narrative suggests a heightened *sensitivity* to discrimination and subordination, now each such incident reminding him that, in spite of his attempt to "pass" as an Israeli, he will never be fully accepted in the Jewish state. Jibril's return to Israel from the United States illustrates:

I find I am discriminated against as an Arab, that Jews look at me as not part of their country. Like in the airport when we left New York, they told each Jew in security, "Just go, go." Just me, because I am Arab, he stopped me for like 10 minutes.... They asked me lots of questions, "What did you do in the U.S.? What did you do in the camp?" ... It made me feel like they don't want me in the country cause I'm Arab.... I am part of the country! I'm Israeli, why are they doing this to me?

While the debate on racial and ethnic "profiling" in the United States seems to have been silenced since 9/11, there is plentiful evidence that such practices of surveillance and suspicion possess psychological consequences for the target (e.g., Zaal et al., 2007). The experience of being "singled out" in contexts such as the airport serves to "discredit" identity through a process of stigmatization (Goffman, 1963). The individuals *not* being singled out for additional security are done so by nature of their nonthreatening identity. To be considered a threat among one's own society is to possess a delegitimized social identity, and what appears initially to be a benign instance of marginalization can likely sensitize the individual to an expansive network of subordination, discrimination, and rejection. The encounter at the airport is thus anything but benign for Jibril. It is symbolic of the structure of social identities in Israel, and it is a reminder of the extent to which his identity is discreditable within the context of his own society.

We can view the change in Jibril's narrative from age 15 to 16 in at least two ways. First, we can identify the change in his own sense of self-categorization from "Israeli" to "Palestinian" as connected to the experience of intergroup contact. As hypothesized by the mutual intergroup differentiation (MID) model (Hewstone & Brown, 1986), and supported by some of the most basic premises of social identity theory (e.g., Tajfel, 1981), contact has resulted in the ability of Jibril to clearly differentiate among groups implicated in the conflict. In this process of mutual intergroup differentiation, Jibril has come to locate himself. This process is by no means complete for Jibril, as his life story continues to be in a process of only initial construction. But now, at age 16, he has come to a new place of identity reconciliation as a consequence of contact: he has come to see himself as "more Palestinian"; he has come to "feel" more Palestinian. He seems to have undergone no process of "decategorization" or "recategorization." Rather, he has differentiated among the categories of self and other that are cognitively relevant to his own identity. He has undergone a process of *subcategorization* (see Brewer, 1996). In this cognitive process, he has been motivated by his perceived acceptance among Palestinians and his perceived rejection among Jewish Israelis, affectively nesting within him a "feeling" of affiliation with the Palestinians.

I suggested that this process seems to have occurred within Jibril "as a consequence" of contact, but that is really an impossible claim to make, for field research such as this can do nothing to "control" the host of other variables that likely has led Jibril's narrative to possess its current form and content. This acknowledgment leads me to the second view I believe we must take when considering the development of identity among Palestinian-Israeli youth. It is perhaps the increasing understanding of, experience with, and sensitivity to discrimination and subordination that begins to fully activate an identification with the Palestinian-Israeli master narrative of identity. And so, in the year following contact, Jibril's admitted increase in sensitivity to such experiences likely contributes to his growing discontent with an Israeli civic identity. For him, there is an alternative narrative with which he can identify, one in which his identity is infused with the legitimacy, fidelity, and credibility it seems so robbed of in the daily experience of majority–minority relations in Israel.

So at age 16 we see the nascence of a new identity for Jibril, his narrative having taken new turns as the experiential possibilities of his life have multiplied. Though we cannot isolate the precise "impact" of contact on his developing narrative, we can discern its place in his process of identity development. For Jibril, contact appears to have offered an opportunity for identity discovery through intergroup differentiation. He came to ascribe meaning to the social identities "Israeli" and "Palestinian," thereby attempting to situate his own fragile and discreditable identity as a minority in the Jewish state within some comfortable place of ideological compromise. But such idealism proved untenable for Jibril's narrative. Ultimately, he came to view his own identity as unequally valued by Jewish Israelis and Palestinians, the former identifying him as symbolic of their own existential threat (e.g., Canetti-Nisim et al., 2008), the latter accepting him and providing him with a sense of legitimacy and value. This process of identity discovery is thus incredibly complex and has its basis in the need to make meaning of his own lived experience, to construct an account that is coherent, credible, and empowering. To accept his devalued and discreditable status in Israeli society as an "end" to identity is simply impossible for Jibril, as it is for most Palestinian Israelis in this study. Such resignation lacks any kind of coherent identity that is simultaneously empowering.

To what extent is Jibril's postcontact experience similar to that of other Palestinian Israelis? In my analysis of the postcontact narratives of youth in this study, I discovered three basic patterns of outcome among the Palestinian Israelis (Hammack, 2010). The first pattern is well illustrated by Jibril's story and involves accentuation of one's Palestinian cultural identity over and above Israeli civic identity. Youths like Rania, whose story was presented in Chapter 5, who seemed to enter the contact situation already accentuating a Palestinian identity, tended to narrate stories across time points that were remarkably similar. These youth displayed a kind of *temporal stability* in their personal narratives. The form, thematic content, and ideological setting of their life stories did not indicate much change in the year following contact, and contact itself seems to have been a relatively uneventful part of their narrative (at least as far as their identity development is concerned). A third pattern I call *life at the hyphen*, in which the narratives of youth reveal an active attempt to fix one's narrative somewhat uncomfortably between Israeli and Palestinian. Sami's postcontact narrative suggested this outcome. Life at the hyphen was characterized by an active and ongoing negotiation between conflict and integration of disparate identities for these youth.

More than Jewish Israelis or Palestinians, Palestinian-Israeli youth reveal diverse strategies of identity negotiation, in large part because of the inherent hyphenation of their identities and their liminal status. At minimum, though, it was clear to me that contact can and often does serve as a critical site for identity development among this unique group. Confronted for the first time with members of the rival national identities that, in fact, create the state of hyphenation that characterizes Palestinian-Israeli existence, youth respond in ways that reflect an active process of narrative engagement. They are confronted with several possibilities for life-story-making, several possibilities for interpretation and discourse, and they undergo a process that is as dynamic as their inherent hyphenated status would suggest.

From Transcendence to Accentuation: An Analysis of Two Narratives Over Time

I have presented the outcomes of transcendence and accentuation as if they were somehow independent, as if perhaps different individuals, by virtue of their level of "readiness" or their particular value orientations (Sagiv & Schwartz, 1995), simply reacted differently to the experience of contact. But this kind of outcome pattern is too simple and suggests too much of a binary. In actuality, my fieldwork suggested that many youth undergo processes of both transcendence and accentuation over time, as they weave the experience of contact into their life story narratives. They experiment with different strategies to integrate the contact experience and to make meaning of it.

Much to the delight of the programs themselves, many youth do indeed display all the signs of recategorization immediately postcontact. They speak of their common humanity, and of the possibility of peaceful coexistence realized through this encounter. Yet, as the immediacy of their experience—far removed from the actual social and political ecology of the conflict—fades and they resume the rituals of their daily lives, youth struggle to maintain these changes in how they think about self and other, in-group and out-group.

As Kelman (1993) argues, if the recategorization of self and other conflicts too much with what is socially and culturally acceptable in their societies, it will prove untenable. The delicate balance lies in forming a coalition with members of the out-group without sacrificing the distinctiveness of one's in-group identity. But such is not the psychosocial "press" of these programs, as I have already suggested in Chapter 2. Recategorization is their ultimate social psychological aim. Getting participants to think beyond categorical visions of identity is central to their methods. So it is useful to consider two cases familiar to us to consider the *process* of identity change that often occurs after contact, from initial transcendence to ultimate accentuation.

The Cosmopolitan: Revisiting the Story of Ayelet

The path to identity accentuation as an outcome of contact can be a rather simple trajectory, such as that of Mohammed and Roai, or it can be a more complex and unpredictable one, as the story of Ayelet reveals. Recall that Ayelet is from Tel Aviv, the cosmopolitan center of Israel, and that her precontact narrative followed a classic pattern of descent and gain. The conflict had barely touched her life and did not enter her life story unsolicited. Ideologically, she displayed a remarkable level of ambivalence at age 16. On the one hand, her narrative revealed already a degree of identity transcendence in her willingness to assume a very critical stance toward her in-group. On the other, she did not recognize the need for a Palestinian state, as she viewed Arabs with an extraordinary level of homogeneity.

During Hands of Peace, Ayelet underwent a significant process of identity exploration. She immediately identified with the stories of her Palestinian peers, having been, in her view, sheltered from knowledge of the actions that her government had taken against them. At one point during the program, she said to Israa, a West Bank Palestinian who had become her best friend in the program,

> I can't believe my people are doing to you what was done to us. We didn't learn anything from the Holocaust, and it's wrong. When I go home, I'm gonna make a change for you guys.

During contact, Ayelet came to view the behavior of her in-group with disdain and vowed to engage in action that would work to improve the lives of Palestinians. Her immediate postcontact interview reveals a significant degree of identity transcendence:

> When I go home, I wanna tell everyone about all the Arab friends I made, and what amazing people they are, and how they're just like us. There's no difference really between Jews and Arabs. Everybody should come to this program to realize this. Listening to all of the stories of the Arabs, it made me realize why they do those things [like bombings]. I realize if I go to the army, it'll be just so I can see what it's like, what happens in the army—but not to give a hand for the war against the Palestinians. I will change anything that my leaders in the army will think of, like slapping an Arab just because he's an Arab. What's *that* about? I don't care to stand up to my commanders and talk freely. They might be commanders, but they might be foolish too. If I go to the army, it'll be to change it, to be more human. We are all human beings.... Growing up in Israel, I always knew there was a war, and suicide bombings, but I never understood the reason. Now, listening to the Palestinians, I realized my country is totally wrong. It's nothing to be ashamed of, to admit you're wrong. It takes a lot of courage and maturity. Now I see the whole picture, and now I understand myself and I'm proud of myself.

Through intergroup friendship (Pettigrew, 1998), Ayelet has undergone a significant process of out-group decategorization. The lack of content she once possessed about Palestinian identity is now gone, and she has come to "unlearn" much of her received knowledge about the Palestinians, her own in-group, and the conflict in general. But her psychological process of transformation does not appear to stop there. She demonstrates a clear process of recategorization in her claim that "there's no difference really between Jews and Arabs." She has come to see Jews and Arabs, Israelis and Palestinians, as united in a common identity. She has *integrated*, rather than differentiated, the identities of Israelis and Palestinians into a new narrative of coexistence. It is precisely this outcome—of coming to see the other as deeply human and, at base, more alike than different from oneself—that these programs seek to elicit, implicitly if not always explicitly.

Ayelet's immediate postcontact narrative suggests an identity outcome seemingly quite divergent from that of Mohammed or Roai. It seems, rather, more like the classic identity transcendence displayed by Liat and Laila. Ayelet has come to view the Palestinian narrative with legitimacy, and, in fact, perhaps a higher degree of legitimacy than her own in-group. That is, she has come to question the Israeli narrative and appears to identify the crux of the conflict as a problem of Israel's treatment of the Palestinians, not, as others like Roai argue, a problem of Palestinian unwillingness to recognize the legitimacy of a Jewish state. And perhaps most crucially, she vows to engage in social practice that will work toward a reduction in conflict.

Immediately after her experience at Hands of Peace, Ayelet's precontact ideological ambivalence would seem to have vanished. She has now become ardently left-wing, identifying the root cause of the conflict's intractability in the policies of her own in-group. But let us consider for a moment Roai's perspective on Hands of Peace, and his view of its most problematic feature:

> The problem with the program is that, when you come back and end this program, you are going back to reality, and your reality is not the way it was in the program. The biggest problem is taking us out of Israel, and I think this is the main difference, in the reality of the program versus the reality in Israel. To be with the Palestinians inside a bubble, you know things and you remember things but in some way you can't hear things that are going on. But we're not touching. So when you're back here, you forget about things. The environment [in the program] is really kind and peaceful. You think in another way there than here.

One year after his experience in contact, Roai reflects on the differential reality of the program versus Israel/Palestine, and he suggests that one's cognition and behavior are entirely dependent on the unique social ecology of the program itself. His insight is significant, as it speaks to the salience of context in cognition.

With this idea in mind—this "problem," as Roai calls it—let us return to Ayelet's story. Despite her insistence that she intended to actively work for social change in Israel, Ayelet failed to attend a single follow-up meeting organized by the program in the year following her participation. She also did not participate in the online listserv that provided a forum for program participants to communicate. In the summer of 2005, I almost failed to secure a follow-up interview with her, as she struggled to balance her social calendar with our meeting. In the challenge of setting up our interview, I sensed a kind of avoidance, perhaps with the memory of her identity transcendence lingering in her consciousness. The content of her life story, narrated to me at age 17 in a trendy Tel Aviv café on a hot summer night, suggested a motivation for such avoidance.

Formally, Ayelet's life story has changed very little in the past year. It is initially a narrative of stability punctuated by periods of descent, all of which relate to the discord between her parents, who divorced when Ayelet was quite young. It is, in this form, a story of descent and gain, mirroring the tone and form of the Jewish-Israeli master narrative. But Ayelet's story now contains a formidable spike over the past year, in which she describes great progress in her life story. The progress of the last year is, for Ayelet, connected to gains in self-confidence with peers and romantic relationships:

> This is the period of time that I got out and getting used to stuff and now eleventh grade is always starting to be up.... I feel like since I became 17, I totally changed. Every year I'm getting older and bigger and more mature. And I'm having a love this year. I have a boyfriend. It's great. We were like best friends for like 2 1/2 years and somewhere he came up with the opinion that he's in love with me, and I was like, damn it, me too.... Yeah, and we decided that that's it, and he's a surfer, and he's a great surfer. He surfs amazingly, and he knows a lot, he's twenty something, he's 25.... And now I'm very happy. My school is getting better and better everyday. I'm getting amazing grades that I never thought I would be able to.... I'm making my dreams come true, basically.

This small portion of Ayelet's narrative reveals her story as infused with the positive tone of cumulative gain. She sees her life on an ever-ascending slope, which is connected to her ability to master life's challenges (e.g., her parents' divorce) through individual successes in work and love, in school and relationships.

Absent from Ayelet's narrative at age 17 is any integration whatsoever of her experience in contact with Palestinians and Palestinian Israelis at Hands of Peace. The event fails to receive even the most minor of places in her life story, until I query its absence:

> As a Jewish-Israeli girl who, all her life, been here, my bubble burst last summer. You know, you get out sometimes abroad, but growing up in Israel, I grew up and am still growing up in a place where you don't get much of Arabs around.
>
> I know that we're not angels and … that we have bad things we do. But they have so much stuff that we did bad to them, and I heard so many things that I think I would never hear. And the whole picture, I didn't know where I live. I mean, all my life, I've been in Israel and don't even know what Israel means. I didn't know what Ramallah means. I didn't know what the West Bank or West Jerusalem means. It didn't say anything to me—I mean, it's a name, of a place, that's it, I didn't know who's coming from there.
>
> Israa and Sylvia mostly changed my mind toward a new point of view of life to me, how it feels to be an Arab, in a small way, just to understand that. As much as I was on their side, I felt like we are the same, it's the same blood.

In this initial narrative of contact, Ayelet begins by acknowledging the segregation of her social ecology—that as a Jew she rarely interacts with an Arab. She has also retained a degree of transcendence in her willingness to view the actions of her in-group critically and in her view that she and her Palestinian peers share "the same blood." Finally, Ayelet identifies intergroup differentiation as an outcome of contact. Once obscure names of places, the meaning of local identities now possesses a level of familiarity for her—places like Ramallah and the West Bank in particular. The "bubble" of her local Tel Aviv identity, with its insular brand of cosmopolitanism, began to fade as Ayelet's knowledge of other identities increased.

As evident from her own initial omission of the experience of contact from her life story, Ayelet continues to struggle to integrate the experience into a coherent personal narrative. The ideological setting of her life story, once riddled with ambivalence but a clear willingness to consider the Palestinian perspective, has now proceeded from a place of transcendence immediately postcontact to one of increased confusion and, ultimately, in-group accentuation.

That is, while at first *decreasing* the psychological distance between in-group and out-group for Ayelet, contact seems to have ultimately resulted in a further degree of identity polarization, as indicated by the ideological commitments she now espouses:

> I came back so confused. I didn't know which side to pick and what is my opinion.... And there are so many pluses on taking the other side but so many minuses, and I can't give up on my minuses.

> When I got back, I told my friends what all the Palestinians had said, and they said to me there's no way it could all be true. Like what they said about the checkpoints and what goes on there, the injustices, or other stuff that goes on in the West Bank with the army and stuff, it's just not true. I think they were just exaggerating it.

> I've been, my country, my people have been through the Holocaust, the most horrible thing ever. Israel is a place that nobody can ever touch us again and do what Hitler did. As much as I want to understand them, I can't give up my country. I can't give up Jerusalem. As much as I don't live there and I don't really go to the Wall and everything and don't pray and I'm not that religious.

> Basically, I feel confusion. You want to be a friend with them, but there are so many things that they don't let you be friendly with them because they want too much.

Ayelet's initial attempts to transform her new transcendent identity into action upon her return to Israel were met with skepticism from her peers. As someone who has come to rely on her peers, rather than her family, for emotional support and a sense of self-confidence and coherence, Ayelet is perhaps particularly susceptible to such negative responses. But the reaction of her peers has engendered a sense of ideological confusion. On the one hand, she wants so badly to see beyond the frame of the Jewish-Israeli master narrative. On the other, she "can't give up" her national identity to realize such transcendence.

Herein lies the dilemma that I refer to as a "narrative stalemate": to transcend identity polarization is inexorably linked to a sacrifice in nationalism, an acknowledgment of the social construction of national identity, and a willingness to script a new national narrative in the interest of conflict resolution. But to ask for such a rescripting of collective narrative during adolescence is to betray the most fundamental understanding of the cultural psychology of youth and its functional role in social stasis and change. In a state of perceived collective identity threat, a state of ontological insecurity and existential anxiety, youth likely perceive the reproduction of social identity as essential to the survival of the group. And so in considering the evolution of Ayelet's personal narrative, we can readily witness the challenge of identity transcendence for youth and the call to narrative *reproduction*, rather than *repudiation*.

Considering the ideological setting of Ayelet's life story at age 17, the salience of in-group identity is palpable:

> We need to live equally, quietly with them, next to each other. They don't need a country. We need to kill all the extremely, extremely right-wing Arabs that want to kill all the Jews. Yeah, if those people seriously didn't exist, probably the peace will be here. ... If the Palestinians want to stay here, that's a problem, because you need to find a territory to put them. You can't cut from Israel anything. She's small enough.

> The West Bank, I don't know, it's places that don't mean anything to me. But probably there are Jews in Israel who it's important to. I live in Tel Aviv, I don't even relate to those places. But probably there are Jews that are related to those places.

Once willing to relinquish half of Jerusalem for peace, Ayelet now opposes a two-state solution to the conflict. She has a vision of "Greater Israel" that could potentially involve some "Palestinian territory," should they "want to stay." She sees the absence of peace as connected to Arab "extremists" rather than as she had just after contact, when she identified the actions of her own in-group and the occupation of Palestinian territory as the fundamental obstacle to peace. Though she personally feels no connection to the occupied territories or necessarily to the idea of Greater Israel, her increased affiliation with her in-group and the master narrative of Jewish-Israeli identity seems to influence her unwillingness to accept a two-state solution. Though her local Tel Aviv identity remains most salient, she now feels the need to ideologically position herself according to the (potential) desires of others in her in-group. Hence, the occupied territories may hold no significance for her personally, but because they matter to *other* Jewish Israelis, she feels the need to retain Israel's control of them.

When we consider the evolution of Ayelet's life story, the accentuation of her social identity is quite striking. In the absence of any comparison group of nonparticipants, we cannot say with any certainty that contact has in fact "caused" this gradual process of increasing identification with the in-group. Such a process may indeed characterize the identity development process of Israeli and Palestinian adolescents regardless of the experience of contact. But the social psychology of intergroup contact suggests that such an outcome is indeed possible, if not highly probable, following contact. In particular, with the formidable discrepancy between the culture of the programs and their recategorizing agenda and the reality of identity polarization in Israel and Palestine, a crisis is created for youth who participate in such encounters. Are they to resist recategorization, as Mohammed and Roai do, and undergo a process of intergroup differentiation, increasing in-group identity salience? Or are they to be taken with the allure of identity transcendence, as Ayelet was, only to face a crisis of identity upon their return home? Before I comment further on the generalizability of these kinds of outcomes, let us consider a second case by revisiting the narrative of another familiar character in our story.

The Realist: Revisiting the Story of Laila

When Laila narrated her life story to me 1 year after Seeds of Peace, I was struck by the seeming success of the program's attempts at recategorization. It was one of my first postcontact interviews, and the experience of collecting that life story left me with a tremendous sense of optimism. I had yet to realize that Laila's narrative of transcendence, the inculcation of her new "Seed" identity supplement, would be relatively uncommon for youth in my study. I also had yet to realize just how ephemeral that particular narrative would be for her.

I met Laila again in the summer of 2004, in her home in Taybeh. She was now 17 years old and had grown in inches and poise. Laila possessed an eloquent grace that made her such an exceptional representative of the Palestinian Israelis. Two years after her initial experience in contact, the tone and form of Laila's narrative had shifted considerably. At age 16, hers was a narrative of great progress, with its perpetual ascent. She had, in her view, overcome the polarizing temptation of "hatred" for the Jews and had now embraced a narrative of coexistence based on shared humanity. But now at age 17, the great possibility realized in her identity transcendence had faded from her personal narrative.

In 2004, when Laila narrated her life story to me at age 17, the *intifada* was raging, which had severely compromised the ability of Seeds of Peace to run a comprehensive and inclusive follow-up program. The political trajectory seemed to be operating against the current for youths like Laila, who had embraced the narrative of peaceful coexistence. Laila describes the crisis that this situation created for her:

> This year is really hard for me, for all the Seeds, for all the people, the citizens, the Arabs, Palestinians, Jews, it's really hard. It's kind of depressing for us. The last 4 months, or maybe more, I'm so hopeless, and I don't believe in Seeds of Peace anymore.

> I thought about Seeds of Peace and my experience, and I thought about the situation, and I had this point where I realized the situation and the reality is much harder and much stronger than Seeds of Peace.... The influence of the reality is much stronger than the influence of Seeds of Peace.... We are seeing things, seeing facts on TV, in radio, in Internet, but Seeds of Peace, it's just words you learned at camp.... I really regret the idea that I was in Seeds of Peace, but the thing is I just felt that it's going nowhere. I was really depressed and hopeless.

While once "being Seed" influenced every aspect of her identity, now her "Seed" identity is a source of shame, frustration, depression, and hopelessness. Laila now views her experience at camp as a venture in fantasy, its culture far too removed from the reality of conflict that characterizes Israeli–Palestinian relations.

For Laila, the eventual rejection of her Seeds identity is connected to the inability of that identity to effect any meaningful change in the conflict or in her own social ecology:

> I couldn't change anything. I just went to camp, and I returned from camp and it's, everything is just for nothing, politically. I mean, I know it affected me personally. I met so many intelligent people, and it affected my language, lots of things. And my social things, but it's still, the political thing is not going anywhere.

As I have suggested, American-based contact programs link individual psychological change to potential political transformation. Because they privilege the power of individual agency over social structure, they assume that social change can occur from the "bottom up." That is, they possess and promulgate a model of the person as politically powerful. In this excerpt of her narrative, Laila is struggling precisely to integrate this underlying mythology of the program with her lived experience as a political actor in the conflict. While she recognizes the individual psychological change of the contact experience, she is disenchanted with the ability to translate that change to some kind of political action. Contact has not, it turns out, provided her with the tools to work for social and political change, and the unforgiving structure of intractable conflict has conspired against Laila's initial vision of identity transcendence for Israelis and Palestinians.

With her rejection of a Seeds identity comes the return of Laila's "hatred" for the Jews—a sentiment that had so dramatically been eradicated after her experience in contact with Jewish Israelis:

> I watched this program about the checkpoints, and this year and last year, and what they're doing to the citizens, us, the Palestinians. I felt, you know, I'm still Palestinian. I can't just not feel anything. I feel hatred. Not to my friends, which is weird, not to my Jewish friends, because I know this is not their fault, but to the Jews.... When I watch TV and I see how they treat people so unhuman, I just feel this kind of "Oh my God, I just want to kill this soldier." Just like this. I feel this hatred inside. But not all the Jews. You know what I mean? *Those* Jews.

The fact that Laila's "hatred" fails to extend to her Jewish friends suggests that personalization and decategorization have indeed had a lasting impact on Laila. She now views the out-group with greater heterogeneity, although she clearly continues to struggle to uphold that view in her everyday cognition.

As another shift in the ideological setting of her life story, consider Laila's current attitude toward suicide bombing. Recall that she had, after Seeds of Peace, entirely reversed her moral and ideological perspective on the practice of suicide bombing and had even successfully convinced friends and family of its problematic nature. Now, 2 years after contact, her narrative has shifted once again:

> I know that suicide bombing is not good, but it's the only way they have. Yeah, I mean, what way do they have to react? If you are a Palestinian and you don't have an army and you don't have a government, and you just want to defend yourself, how can you defend yourself? I'm just asking, how can you? I'm trying to think sometimes, how can Palestinians defend themselves, after the killing of their, this hopeless life they have. I just think about that.... *Jihad* is good. I mean, it's better if it won't be, but *jihad* is not bad for our religion. *Jihad* is to kill the one who came to take your land, the one who came to take your money, if you have money, to take your honor. By defending those things, you have to defend yourself by killing him.

Once viewing suicide bombing as "totally wrong," Laila has now internalized the classic Palestinian narrative of moral justification for the bombings—that they are acts of desperation, symbolic of Palestinian hopelessness, committed because they represent the "only way" of "defense" against Israel.

But Laila's identity is a subject of great complexity, for she is a Palestinian citizen of Israel, existentially fixated in a liminal position between Israel and Palestine. That she has internalized some of the "Islamist" discourse of contemporary Palestinian struggle is hardly surprising; contact has enabled her interaction with Palestinians from the occupied territories—something previously impossible. So she is, as her identity would suggest, ideologically divided within herself. The assumption of the Seeds identity helped to resolve the crisis of her Palestinian-Israeli identity by offering a third narrative that was inclusive of all—including her. But now that she has lost confidence in the viability of this identity, she must come to a new resolution within herself of her hyphenated identity:

> You have just to manage the conflict in yourself, that there are two
> things—the reality and Seeds of Peace.... And the conflict in myself,
> I still have two conflicts, my self, between the conflict and Seeds of Peace,
> and the conflict that I am living in, as an Arab Israeli, as a Palestinian.

> You know I thank God that I have a better life than anyone in Palestine.
> But I still sometimes feel that, how come I don't have a country? I don't
> feel that I have a country. I don't feel like I belong right here, although it
> is my land. I feel like I belong to my land when I sit with my grandpa. He
> just tells me about all the things, the stories. I feel some belonging to this
> land, but not to this country. Walking in the malls and the streets, and
> everyone is just staring at you, because you are Arab, it's so different.

> I don't know, I'm so confused, you know. About the situation, about
> myself, about my identity. Palestinians, Israelis, my city, my country.

The inability of her Seeds identity to resolve the conflict of her hyphenated identity has, for Laila, activated a renewed identity crisis. She struggles to reconcile her Israeli and Palestinian identities, which creates significant ideological confusion in her present life story. She feels entirely disconnected from her Israeli identity, and yet she does not want to live the Palestinian experience:

> They're not my society, the Jews. We are different societies right here, the
> Arabs and the Jews. And I cannot think of myself as one of their society
> because they won't take me, they won't accept me.

Like Jibril, Laila identifies the source of her identity confusion as rooted in the discreditability of her Arab identity within Israel. Hers is a stigmatized identity in an ethnic Jewish state (Peleg, 2004; Rabinowitz, 2001b; Rouhana, 1997), and her current narrative reveals the internal struggle she is waging to reconcile the consequences of this experience.

Laila's path from transcendence to accentuation of her Palestinian identity illuminates the relationship between the social structure of conflict and youth experience. The reversal in ideological setting of Laila's story, from polarization to transcendence, relied upon her internalization of the Seeds of Peace narrative—a narrative of liberal cosmopolitan coexistence. As a Palestinian Israeli, Laila was able to embrace this new narrative as a means to reconcile her own inevitable identity crisis as an Arab citizen of the Jewish state. The internalization of this narrative specified a particular life course for Laila: one in which social practice tied to a cosmopolitan ideology might in fact affect the course of the conflict, her own identity transcendence expanding like a web across the region.

Yet 2 years beyond contact, Laila has come to identify the limits of a cosmopolitan narrative in the reality of the conflict. She has become a realist, if a confused one. Contact has, at this point in her evolving personal narrative, only contributed to her identity confusion, creating another crisis for her to reconcile. She has come to see the extent to which Seeds of Peace diverges in its culture from the reality of the conflict. With this revelation comes the rejection of the third narrative, now dubbed "just words" by Laila.

Discourse in the absence of viable social practice to sustain it is, as exemplified by Laila's narrative, ephemeral at best. While youths such as Roai identify the instability of the narrative of coexistence and essentially reject it immediately, youths like Laila undergo a challenging process of gradual acknowledgment of the untenable nature of this narrative. They proceed from transcendence and all of its great possibilities gradually to a place of compulsory accentuation, for conflict commands conformity to a master narrative, for security and solidarity. Palestinian Israelis, perceiving themselves rejected from the Israeli master narrative, like both Laila and Jibril, come to accentuate their Palestinian identities over time.

Conclusion: Contact and Identity

Let me now briefly summarize the findings reported in this chapter and reserve a more substantive discussion of their implications for Chapter 8. This chapter addressed my second overarching research question on the cultural psychology of Israeli and Palestinian youth: What role does intergroup contact appear to assume in the development of a personal narrative? Quite simply, does it seem to strengthen or weaken the likelihood of master narrative reproduction?

Does such an *unusual* form of social practice create new possibilities for narrative understanding between young Israelis and Palestinians, or does it rather simply reproduce the narrative stalemate of the conflict, as many other peace education efforts appear to do (e.g., Bekerman, 2002, 2005, 2009b, 2009c)?

Through the lens of personal narratives, I sought to address these important questions about conflict, identity, and youth. I considered the identity outcomes of participation in American-based coexistence programs—sites at which a new social structure and accompanying narrative were presented to youth. Though I speak of "outcomes," it is important to reiterate that my framework for understanding and studying identity is more dynamic than this discourse would suggest. My consideration of multiple tellings of the life story, coupled with my numerous observations in fieldwork, allowed me to consider identity as a *process*. Thus, the narratives I have presented here are but momentary windows into the identity development of contemporary Palestinian and Israeli youth. Yet I believe an empirical account of these narratives provides us with vital data on the lived experience of conflict and the possibilities of intergroup contact for conflict transformation (or reproduction).

In the course of my fieldwork, characterized by immersion into the lives of young Israelis and Palestinians who undergo contact, I came to recognize the idea of intergroup contact as both incredibly alluring and cosmopolitan in its foundational ideology. With its origins in the American context of racial discrimination, contact is rooted in the desire to transform cultural realities—racism, intolerance, prejudice, conflict—through a dialogue of identities. For Israelis and Palestinians, this dialogue is framed within the context of formidable existential insecurity and identity nonrecognition (Pettigrew, 2003). This *vulnerability* of identity, then, seems to place limits on the ability of American-based programs to achieve their goals for identity transcendence.

Influenced by classic perspectives on intergroup contact and multicultural education, both Seeds of Peace and Hands of Peace seek to elicit processes of decategorization and recategorization through the design of their programs. This distinctly *American* approach finds itself uncomfortably transported across cultures (Abu-Nimer, 1999; Halabi & Sonnenschein, 2004a), as the findings reported in this chapter suggest, for conflict's inevitable identity polarization prevents such cognitive processes from having any lasting effect. Such intervention strategies may be useful in the cultural context of ethnocentrism and racism, *concurrent with political and social structural transformation*, as they were in the United States, but they appear to have limited value in the context of intractable conflict (Bar-Tal, 2004a).

The narratives of youth examined in this study indeed reveal that identity transcendence is an attainable end for such programs, but it is untenable in the actual cultural context of conflict. So such a recategorized identity begins to fade over time, as it did for Laila or for Ayelet, as youth come to deeply internalize the in-group narrative of identity. In this process, the programs come to represent sites of identity "essentialization" (Bekerman et al., 2009; Helman, 2002) in which youth only affirm stereotypes in their defense of in-group narratives. While "dialogic moments" (Steinberg & Bar-On, 2002) certainly occur in both programs I studied, they cannot seem to be sustained in the life story narratives of youth. The "discourse of nation" (Bekerman, 2002) proves extremely resistant to subversion. Consistent with social psychological theory, contact in this case seems to elicit a powerful process of *mutual intergroup differentiation* (Hewstone & Brown, 1986), whereby youth come to differentiate among the identities implicated in the conflict, and in that process to locate themselves within a particular master narrative. This process is apparent in the postcontact narratives of Mohammed, Roai, Jibril, Ayelet, and Laila.

As I alluded to, and as we will consider at greater length in the next chapter, the outcome of mutual differentiation ought not to be viewed as a "failure," although it is not necessarily the desired outcome of these programs. A sustainable resolution to the Israeli–Palestinian conflict will likely require as a psychological *prerequisite* the perceived security of identities, and a dialogue between secure identities may be a more fitting aim for such programs (Nadler, 2004). The process of intergroup contact may facilitate the growth of knowledge in group distinctiveness, thereby instilling the realization of a need for mutual identity recognition and fulfillment. If the conflict has indeed represented a clash of competing national movements in which each group has sought to delegitimize the national identity of the other, then perhaps contact as a means of cultivating an awareness of and appreciation for identity distinctiveness represents a useful contribution to the long quest for resolution and reconciliation between Palestinians and Israelis.

PART IV

Possibilities

"The philosophers have only *interpreted* the world, in various ways; the point, however, is to *change* it."
—Karl Marx, *Theses on Feuerbach* (1888/1978, p. 145)

"Scientists, like other mortals, cannot help but be motivated by their own personal values."
—Gordon W. Allport, *The Nature of Prejudice* (1954, p. 516)

"The research needed for social practice is a type of action research, a comparative research on the conditions and effects of various forms of social action, and research leading to social action. Research that produces nothing but books will not suffice."
—Kurt Lewin, "Action Research and Minority Problems" (1946), p. 35

8

Peace, Justice, and the Politics of Identity: Toward a New Praxis

A Virtual Dialogue

Malak, Palestinian Muslim female (August 11, 2006):
Hi everybody, I hope that all of you are OK and safe. As you
know the situation now is very difficult. During this war
there was Qana, and other massacres, and there is no word
that can express the pictures that I have seen. It's a very
shameful situation to kill all these innocent people.... All the
people in Palestine now are talking about Hezbollah and are
on their side, because they saw the Israeli army targeting
children under 10 years old, but the other side is targeting
soldiers. How can we change? How can we create a better
situation?

Orli, Jewish Israeli female (August 11, 2006): Hi everyone!
How are you all? I can't even describe how much I miss you!
It's so weird to go back to Israel. I feel like I woke up to a
new reality, a dark reality. It's so hard to wake up in the
morning from a radio that reports about soldiers and people
who got killed from both sides. It's so hard to have all these
nightmares every day.... I want to do something.

Walid, Palestinian Muslim male (August 14): Hey guys, how are you? I hope everybody is doing well and everything is going well too. Israel is a terrorist state. Israel is trying just to hit the civilians, that's what I see everyday in the news. I did not see for one time that IDF killed one struggler from Hezbollah. Israel is just killing the civilians, the innocent people. They are not killing anybody from Hezbollah and they did not stop. They know that they are killing innocent people and they just continue in killing them and I'm wondering why they are doing this.... The legend that the Israeli army can't be defeated has been ended by Hezbollah. Hezbollah showed the world that they can defend their land.

Ariel, Jewish Israeli male (August 14): Walid, if Israel wishes to defeat an enemy, it won't take a month nor a year, it'll take two hours or less.... I'm just tired of the fact that it's really comfortable to blame it all on the Jews.... It makes me frustrated that we are fighting a barbarian enemy. It's the twenty-first century! I mean, look, we declared a cease-fire, and they see it as a victory. Israel will not be silent this time. It's time to stand tall. Ariel, Proud ISRAEL.

In the summer of 2006, the fourth annual Hands of Peace coexistence program commenced amid the backdrop of a brutal war between Israel and Hezbollah. As youth from Palestine and Israel arrived in Chicago, they left behind families taking up temporary dwellings in basement bomb shelters, seeking refuge from the daily barrage of Hezbollah's Qassam rockets into northern Israel. Somewhat surprisingly, during the 2 weeks of intensive dialogue and social interaction that had come to characterize this experiment in identity "restructuring," the topic of Lebanon hardly came up at all. As the youth assimilated into a new reality in the quiet, comfortable, and expansive suburbs of Chicago—a reality in which the security of everyday life was anything but threatened—they gradually removed themselves from the psychological reality of war and conflict.

As I observed the process that this group of participants underwent in contact with representatives of their national enemy, what struck me most was the extent to which these youth, unlike the youth of other years of my fieldwork, resisted the program's press for identity recategorization. Yet even as the war back home seemed to enhance their resistance to the assumption of a common identity, they came to attach themselves emotionally to the cosmopolitan idea of coexistence. They cried the same tears as every other cohort I had witnessed on the final day of the program. They swore to not forget one another, or the new set of values they had embraced in Chicago. Upon their return home, they came to long for the reality of Hands of Peace, for its possible authenticity. Their return to Israel and to Palestine was exceedingly traumatic, perhaps more so than in previous years for the "nightmare," as Orli calls it, to which they were returning.

The above email exchange occurred soon after their departure from Chicago. While the exchange may have begun with expressions of the emotional trauma they were experiencing—the trauma of losing the social ecology of peace and mutual recognition that Hands of Peace had succeeded in providing for 2 weeks—it soon returned to ideology, and the discourse of the conflict came to consume the sentiments of youth just as rapidly as the context of coexistence seemed to liberate them from ideological insulation. Renewed exposure to their own national discourse, with its particular interpretive frame of the events of the Israel–Hezbollah war, seemed to bring them back to a place of psychological distance from one another imperceptible just a week before, as their parting of ways was accompanied with the tears and hugs that characterize the feeling of collective accomplishment.

And so Walid, who had become a close friend to Ariel, in spite of the antagonism between their peoples, now describes Israel as a "terrorist state" and seems to revel in what he perceives as a formidable humiliation for the IDF in this war. Ariel, for his part, must reclaim a sense of power that psychologically ensures his own existential security, expressed in his proclamation that it is time for Israel to "stand tall." And the cycle of identity polarization—characterized by a stalemate of stories, a competition over the *interpretation* of events—ensures its pernicious survival into another generation. The jockeying of power that consumes the mutual antagonism between Israelis and Palestinians, both of whom seek mutual identity recognition and national self-fulfillment, sustains itself through the ideologies of a new generation of youth, one for whom the contest of identities has been played out once again through uprisings and wars, the experience of collective loss, and the tangible insecurity of daily existence.

I began this chapter, the conclusion of this book, with a record of this virtual dialogue to demonstrate just how rapidly the success of identity recategorization can be eradicated through the structural reality of conflict and the absence of peaceful coexistence. That youth are so vulnerable to the lure of ideology and so consumed with reproducing a national narrative, absent its unshakeable security, is apparent in even this small exchange. In effect, a return to the context of conflict is a return to the lure of identity polarization, for polarization guarantees a level of in-group solidarity so comforting to youth in the midst of war and conflict. Working for peace, then, *through* identity is problematic, for it envisions individuals as all-powerful agents of change who can, through a transformation in social cognition, come to repudiate a status quo of identity politics. The mind would seem to be *subject* to this regime of social categorization, and a revolution against it would seem to require far more than the interpersonal acquaintanceship that contact affords.

But is the situation quite so simple? To think of minds solely as *products* of the material or structural reality would seem to betray any kind of possibility for human agency, which we know both intuitively and empirically is simply not the case (Silbereisen, Best, & Haase, 2007; Stetsenko, 2007). Political change requires the expression of agency; it thrives on possibilities for new social practices that develop in the gaps within an existing social structure. My view of human development, then, is fundamentally rooted in a cultural psychological approach that privileges the ability of *activity* to transform the mind (e.g., Rogoff, Baker-Senett, Lacasa, & Goldsmith, 1995; Stetsenko, 2008; Stetsenko & Arievitch, 2004; Vygotsky, 1978). Yet the very activity in which we can engage is the product of historical cycles of practice—the history of minds at work. Hence, we produce social reality just as social reality produces us. This is the fundamental thesis of *mutual constitution* (Shweder, 1990) and the underlying axiom of *dialectical materialism* that links mind and society in a reciprocal historical process (Marx, 1973; Vygotsky, 1978; see also Vianna & Stetsenko, 2006).

As I conclude this book, I want to bring together these theoretical ideas about the relationship between individual minds and the societies in which they are embedded with a practical prescription for *praxis* that might speak to the needs for peace, justice, and mutual recognition that Israelis and Palestinians both require. I speak of *praxis* as the linking of theory to action and the shift from interpretation to social change, in the tradition of scholars like Karl Marx (1888/1978), Paulo Freire (1970), and George Lukács (1971) (for review, see Bodemann, 1978; Ostereicher, 1975). In this chapter, I will explore the implications of this research for possibilities of new praxis, in both the discipline of psychology and the practice of peace education. In so doing, I will offer further critical interrogation of the American model of intervention, deconstructing some of its problematic assumptions about mind and society. My aim in this interrogation should not be interpreted as destructive, for I myself have invested years as a peace education practitioner in these programs. Rather, I aim to offer a constructive critique that challenges underlying assumptions but offers hypotheses for reconceptualized interventions.

I began the research reported in this book in 2003, at the peak of the second Palestinian *intifada*. While so many seemingly incredible historical events have unfolded since then—the loss of both Yasser Arafat and Ariel Sharon in the political arena, the de facto end of the *intifada*, the ascendance of

Hamas as a political party, the Israeli disengagement from Gaza, and most recently, the return of Benjamin Netanyahu to power in Israel—it seems that so little has changed in the structural reality of the conflict. The Palestinian territories remain occupied by Israel. The Palestinian Authority remains a quasi-governmental body, and an increasingly impotent one at that. Israelis continue to feel very much alone in the Middle East, a people whose existence is at stake, all the more perceptible with the inability to defeat Hezbollah or Hamas using military might, as well as threats of nuclear arms development in Iran. Jews and Arabs continue to view one another, generally speaking, with fear, suspicion, and a deep hostility. Indeed, the impasse between Palestine and Israel seems so immune from intervention. It is, as I have suggested, characterized by a stalemate of narratives.

Ambitious Arguments

In this concluding chapter, I want to make a series of arguments that link to the theoretical questions about culture and identity I articulated in Chapter 1, and I want to leave the reader with a clear sense of my own current thinking on the problem of Israeli–Palestinian coexistence and efforts to advocate for peace and mutual recognition. First, I want to return to what was, for me, a driving intellectual question in this research—the question of human *variability*, psychological *distinction*, and the *particularity* of human development across time and place. The reader immersed in the discipline of psychology will recognize the revolutionary nature of this kind of concern, for mine is not a search for the universals of the mental life but rather of what makes individual minds *different* from one another (Shweder, 2003). In short, I assume that people inhabit diverse ecologies of development, and that this diversity possesses profound implications for psychological life.

But recall that mine is not a static, reified view of the relationship between culture and identity. I do not view individuals as *either* producers *or* products of a given social ecology. Rather, I see a dynamic relationship between person and culture, mind and society, such that I believe the set of practices we inherit has a profound influence on the way we see ourselves. Yet we *engage* with and in those practices in such a way as to potentially *redefine* them. This, I believe, is the psychological cycle of history, fixed in simultaneous states of stasis and change, harmony and tension.

The view of culture and identity I charted in Chapter 1 and sought to illustrate throughout the book is one that privileges *language* and *discourse* as orienting frameworks for identity development. Consistent with narrative psychology,

I posited that we craft personal narratives that anchor our existence in space, place, and time and provide us with a vocabulary to make sense of our social reality. Following Vygotsky's (1978) framework, we internalize *social speech* to create an inner voice that possesses credibility in some context of development. My central argument about the relationship between *master* and *personal* narratives of identity, illustrated in Chapters 3, 4, and 5, sought precisely to chart out what this kind of theory of human development might look like when we consider the *specificity* of a particular context—in this case, the context of intractable conflict.

Thus, the first argument I wish to revisit and to summarize in this chapter centers on the lived experience commanded by a particular "sociopsychological infrastructure" of conflict (Bar-Tal, 2007). The narratives of youth illustrate strategies of *narrative engagement* that position themselves as social actors within a particular matrix of identity politics. Thus, they are not exclusively reproducers of a master narrative but rather reflect its evolution, its contradictions, and its points of tension and contestation in an active social environment.

The second argument I seek to elaborate upon in this chapter brings us importantly away from the nexus of "high theory" in academic accounts to the practical consequences of conflict for attempts at intervention. In other words, my second core argument attempts to deal with social change and how particular social psychological interventions do or do not work for peace and social justice. I will thus offer a pragmatic but critical assessment of the American project of cosmopolitanism with which the two programs I examined seem so consumed.

Finally, seeking to fuse pragmatism and intellectualism, I will develop an argument about the role of psychology as a discipline in contributing to the eradication of injustice, the illumination of oppression, and the promotion of positive human development for all. My intent here might initially sound overly idealistic, but I do not mean to suggest that psychology can or will offer some kind of prescription for the alleviation of human suffering. I am not so naïve—anymore. Rather, I simply want to suggest that, in order for psychology to contribute to larger conversations about the relationship among politics, society, and individual subjectivity, the core of the discipline needs to acknowledge the limitations of methodological and theoretical insulation. I immodestly suggest that the work described in this book, by seeking to transcend the boundaries of academic disciplines and their methodological territories, offers an example of the kind of scholarly endeavor that at least attempts to initiate both "bigger" questions that concern other scholars in the social sciences and humanities and "smaller" questions that deal with a concrete social problem. In other words, I want to suggest that the approach I have taken in this book and in my research more broadly can offer at least some model of scholarly inquiry that seeks to blend pragmatism with theory development, in conversation with a number of ideas generated from several disciplines, and toward social action for change. In this way, I seek to destruct artificial boundaries both *among disciplines of scholarly inquiry* and *between research and meaningful social practice for social change.*

The reader will have to determine the credibility of any of these ambitious arguments, which no doubt will derive from his or her own engagement with the series of narratives I have constructed in this book—narratives to make sense of the lived experience of conflict and of intergroup contact. This particular engagement with my interpretive stance is itself dialogic, and the reader brings with him or her a series of identities that bear upon his or her own interpretations—as a psychologist, an anthropologist, a philosopher, a peace activist, a Palestinian, an American, a Jew. I do not claim any monopolies on interpretation; that would represent a betrayal of the "interpretive turn" within the social sciences (Rabinow & Sullivan, 1987). I only claim that my participation in various communities—peace communities in Israel and Palestine, liberal and progressive activists in Chicago, groups suffering from oppression and subordination in the United States because of race, ethnicity, or sexual identity—has provided me with a unique lens through which to interpret Israeli and Palestinian life stories within their context of insecurity and intractable conflict, as well as a unique lens through which to interpret the set of practices that have come to be associated with my professional identity as a psychological scientist.

My conclusion to the book is thus organized to elaborate upon these three main achievements for which I had aimed in writing. I will first say more about the psychological consequences of conflict for the construction of a life story narrative in adolescence, linking the findings of my research to the larger literature on the context of conflict and its "sociopsychological infrastructure" (Bar-Tal, 2007). Second, I will elaborate upon my argument about American intervention in the conflict, making connections among my conclusions, other social psychological theory and research, and the growing critical approach to contact being pioneered in Israel. Finally, I will say more about the vitality of the kind of critical, cultural psychological approach I have employed here, linking it to similar efforts among scholars to use the tools of psychology in the service of *liberation* and exposure of an unjust status quo, thus claiming psychology as an emancipatory social science that can illuminate the connection between context and mind, society and the individual—not in some theoretically neutral way but as a force for social change. Though some may view this intellectual ambition as ideological, in supposed opposition to the "neutral" empiricism of psychology's underlying philosophy of science, I would argue that such an approach merely helps to *expose* the ideological underpinnings of the discipline that are always already present, veiled behind the discourse of science (Parker, 2007; Prilleltensky, 1994, 1997). In arguing for a psychology that is inexorably intertwined with politics, and a politics of identity in particular, I suggest that the production of knowledge is and always will be a political enterprise. The point, I believe, is to produce transformative knowledge that can liberate, rather than oppress (Sampson, 1993).

Thus, my aim is to advance a new *praxis* both for "psychological" intervention in intractable conflict *and* for psychological science in general. I want to argue that we need new ways of linking research and action on major social problems, such as intergroup conflict. But before advancing too far with this line of thought, which is perhaps mostly of interest to readers enmeshed in the discipline of psychology, let us return to the narratives of young Israelis and Palestinians for concluding reflections and interpretations.

Narrative and the Psychological Infrastructure of Conflict

It is a hot summer afternoon in Jerusalem. Mohammed and I are standing on the balcony of my modest hostel room in the Old City, the sounds of church bells and the call to prayer of the mosque echoing in the soundscape of this most unique city. He is smoking a cigarette. We have both had a long day.

Earlier in the afternoon, we were in a taxi together in Ramallah. It is the summer of 2007, just after the bitterly polarizing civil war between Fatah and Hamas in the Gaza Strip. Hamas emerged victorious there, assuming control of the territory, splintering the unity and coherence of the Palestinian movement for national liberation that Arafat had once been able to, however delicately, keep together. On the West Bank, Fatah maintains its supremacy, and Hamas is spoken of either in whispers (to avoid suspicion) or furious outbursts (to announce derision).

Just below the rearview mirror of the taxi was a glossy postcard featuring three men: Gamel Abdel Nasser, the former president of Egypt and quintessential Arab nationalist of the postcolonial Middle East, Yasser Arafat, and Saddam Hussein. As we stand on the balcony of my dilapidated hostel room, I am reminded of that postcard and begin to engage with Mohammed about it. With very little probing on my part, Mohammed launches into a monologue on these three men:

> The Arabs need these kind of leaders, strong men. This is why I admire
> Hitler. I think he had a good idea. Whoever wasn't loyal to Germany, they

should die. I believe in this; it's a good way of thinking. This is why
Saddam was good, and why Iraq is a mess now. You need strong leaders.
The Arabs need these kinds of leaders.

As I listen to Mohammed's monologue about leadership and the virtues of
Hitler, I reflect upon Palestine during this last of my travels to the region.
Mohammed's sentiments, no doubt inspired by the violent *intra*group conflict
that has just taken place in Gaza, seem to speak to the larger tensions of the
Muslim Middle East, lived within the conflict between Hamas and Fatah in
Palestine—the fundamental underlying tension between the secular nationalism of postcolonial figures like Nasser, Arafat, and Hussein, and the religious
nationalism of Hamas, Hezbollah, and Iran. These larger ideological conflicts
are lived in the daily experience of youths like Mohammed.

But it is Mohammed's reference to Hitler that naturally grabs my attention
at the moment of utterance, almost punching me in the gut, for the villain that
Hitler represents in the master narrative to which I have been so thoroughly
immersed. Yet I see Mohammed's need to appropriate this discourse—and to
call upon this particular historical figure—as a psychological consequence of
the collective weakness and insecurity he perceives, only magnified by the display of Palestinian fragmentation and disarray of the civil war in Gaza. In my
view, Mohammed's engagement with this discourse reflects his position within
the larger sociopsychological "infrastructure" of conflict that provides meaning
to his lived experience.

To illustrate the consequences of inhabiting this infrastructure, let us for a
moment consider the consequences of a permanent departure from it. Let us
return to the story of Ali, the young Palestinian Muslim who passionately
argued for the liberation of the whole of Palestine through violent means of
resistance. Recall that, in spite of the ideological setting of Ali's narrative in the
religious nationalism of Hamas, Ali came from a wealthy, secular, and cosmopolitan Palestinian family, and that he himself was quite secular. Determined
to secure a strong education for their son, coupled with his own desire to get
some distance from the "depressing" life of military occupation, as he himself
described it, Ali's parents sent him abroad for university study. He and I
remained in contact to a limited extent during that period, but I had not seen
him since he left the region.

Later that night, with Mohammed's surprising invocation of Hitler still
fresh in my mind, we are eating dinner out in the small strip of Palestinian
restaurants in East Jerusalem. We run into Ali, who is in fact back in Jerusalem,
visiting his family during the summer holiday from university. He and I engage
in discussion about his studies and his life outside of Palestine (he attends

university in a large cosmopolitan city in North America). His appearance has changed considerably since we last met. He has gained weight and lost much of his "boyish" energy, along with the feverish enthusiasm he once would bring to the telling of his life story narrative. Now he is far more mellow, subdued, and seemingly content. He no longer speaks English with even a slight Arabic accent.

Inevitably my conversation with Ali turns to the violence in Gaza, as it has with virtually every Palestinian on this trip:

> I can't believe what those Hamas idiots are doing in Gaza. I can't believe what they've done to us, to our movement. They're fucking crazy, man! They're, like, totally impractical. They say they won't honor any of the previous peace agreements! They say they won't recognize Israel, what kind of bullshit is that?! Thank God there is still some sense here and that Fatah and the international community is standing up to those bastards!

As much as the violence of his speech toward Israelis and his embrace of political Islam once challenged my view of context and identity, now this significant shift in Ali's ideological setting once again challenged my assumptions about narrative identity development and its continuity. Rather than see narrative as a fundamental anchor for self-consistency, I needed to come to see it as an interpretive frame for meaning making that could quite easily shift with the discursive and political currents of a time and place, as had clearly happened for Ali.

I relate these encounters with Mohammed and Ali not to highlight Palestinian identity, for the principles of culture, narrative, and identity pertain just as much (though with their own particularities, of course) to Jewish and Palestinian Israelis. My point in presenting these encounters from my field research is to illustrate what I view to be one of the major conclusions of this research: *the power of context in general, and the psychological infrastructure of conflict in particular, to shape narrative identity development*. The key difference— actually, one of the only differences—between Mohammed and Ali is that Ali has departed the context of conflict. They are both now secular nationalists, in terms of the ideological settings of their life stories, but Mohammed remains firmly anchored in the proximal context of conflict, and the possibilities for any kind of narrative transformation are locked within the discursive infrastructure of conflict.

Israeli social psychologist Daniel Bar-Tal has written extensively about the psychological consequences of conflict (e.g., Bar-Tal, 1990b, 1993, 1998b, 2000, 2001, 2004b, 2007), and it is his terminology of the "sociopsychological infrastructure" (Bar-Tal, 2007) that I appropriate here to make sense of possibilities for youth identity development. He argues that individuals who inhabit contexts of intractable conflict develop a variety of psychological mechanisms to cope with conflict's inevitable consequences, such as fear and insecurity. In particular, individuals appropriate the "societal beliefs" that characterize the ethos of conflict—beliefs about security, legitimacy, and identity—and that essentially reproduce the stalemate of conflict, even as they provide a sense of security and solidarity so needed in contexts of existential threat.

Thus, the internalization of a master narrative fulfills vital *cognitive* and *emotional* needs in contexts of conflict. In my view, this process speaks to an alignment of thought and word with lived experience—not on an *individual* basis, but rather, a *collective* one. This process is consistent with Vygotsky's (1978) view of the internalization of *social* speech, and it illustrates the way in which mind and society are intertwined in the course of human development. To stay with Ali and the evolution of his life story, it is clear that the discourse he internalizes to make meaning of his own lived experience is grounded in a cluster of cognitions—a series of interpretations and sequences within some inner voice—that is then reified in his narration of a life story. It is precisely in this act of narrating his story to me that he constructs his identity in such a way as to align thought with word and individual experience with collective memory (see also Brockmeier, 2002). To accomplish this alignment, he calls not only upon his own individual memories of insecurity (e.g., during the first Gulf War) but also upon the collective memory of dispossession, collective violence, and injustice. And his appropriation is not affectively neutral. Rather, it is grounded in the experience of fear, anger, frustration, and other emotions that are not simply his own but are *shared* across a community in conflict (see Bar-Tal et al., 2007; Halperin, 2008).

I call upon Ali's case to illustrate the way in which my understanding of conflict as constructing a psychological infrastructure, as Bar-Tal (2007) calls it, influences the interpretation of individual life stories. Personal narratives reveal the substance of these basic social psychological processes so well articulated by scholars like Bar-Tal and Israeli political psychologist Eran Halperin, whose work focuses on the role of collective emotions in the context of conflict (e.g., Halperin, 2008; Halperin et al., 2008; Halperin, Canetti-Nisim, & Hirsch-Hoefler, 2009). I view this research, then, as offering empirical support—through the thick description of ethnography and personal narrative analysis—to theories of conflict and its psychological consequences.

I have framed this theoretical concern in terms of the reproduction or repudiation of master narratives of in-group identity—those "big" stories of a group that convey central messages about collective memory, emotion, and ideology—in the development of a personal narrative. In this analysis, presented in Chapters 3, 4, and 5, I have suggested that contemporary Israeli and Palestinian youth are indeed exposed to master narratives that carefully position them as antagonists. In fact, these master narratives are, as Kelman (1999b) argues, negatively interdependent, such that the legitimization of one narrative (e.g., 1948 as a "catastrophe" for the Palestinians) would seem to totally negate the other (e.g., 1948 as a "celebration of independence" for the Israelis). My analysis, however, revealed that these master narratives are not blindly internalized by youth but are, rather, sites of dynamic *engagement*. Understanding and interpreting the relation between master and personal narratives, I argue, requires a particular approach to the study of lives—one that fully contextualizes a life and does not rely *solely* on a single telling of the life story, or a single account provided in a self-report survey. Thus, my fusion of ethnographic and interview methods allowed me to analyze and interpret the personal narratives of youth in a manner that revealed the contradictions among thought, word, and lived experience, as youth begin to seek an alignment that provides coherence and meaning.

This analysis suggested that youth motivated to pursue intergroup contact—already a unique sample—seem to appropriate enough of their respective master narratives in their precontact life stories to suggest challenges for attempts at intervention. Yet the personal narratives of youth revealed clear fault lines within these "big" stories of the collective. In the case of both the Jewish Israelis and the Palestinians, it is clear that the Oslo accords, signed during the early childhood of all these youth, created a new discourse with which to understand identity and intergroup relations in the region. Thus, the ardent delegitimization that had so strongly characterized both master narratives—carefully reproduced in the materialization of discourse through artifacts like textbooks (Bar-Gal, 1994; Bar-Tal, 1998a)—had certainly entered into a new phase. This generation of youth is the first to reach adolescence with this major policy shift in place. Thus, it is interesting to see that they had, consistent with the *incomplete* nature of those accords, constructed narratives of *ambivalence* when it came to legitimizing the national aspirations of the other. On the one hand, Jewish Israelis acknowledged that the Palestinians need and deserve an independent state, and Palestinians acknowledged that the reclamation of all of Mandate Palestine was no longer a realistic or sensible goal. On the other hand, though, Jewish Israelis sought to maintain the current status hierarchy in which they assume the position of *occupier* (Halperin et al., 2010; Rosler et al., 2009) by framing their recognition in *conditional* terms. And Palestinians, clearly also exposed to the discourse of religious nationalism of groups like Hamas, at times suggested that, in fact, annihilation of the Jewish state was indeed a legitimate goal.

The narratives of youth thus provided an empirical account of the larger process of *narrative engagement* I have described here and in other areas of my research (e.g., Hammack & Cohler, 2009; Hammack, Thompson, & Pilecki, 2009). This process illustrates the way in which individual subjectivity is nested within discourses that are not neutral vis-à-vis forces like the state (e.g., Althusser, 1971). The security and the sustenance of the nation-state command conformity to a particular understanding of collective identity, and thus the stories that individuals construct are never rooted merely in individual psychological experience, or even just the experiences of the "microsystem" of a family (Bronfenbrenner, 1979). Rather, the structural reality of the state and its economic and political interests infuses the personal narratives of youth precisely by deploying discourses—whether through textbooks, media, political speeches, or the particular content of policies themselves (e.g., the Oslo accords)—that maintain those interests and reproduce a status quo. This reification of nationalist discourse occurs in peace education itself, with the dominance of models that rely upon a categorical approach to culture and identity (Bekerman, 2009b; Bekerman & Maoz, 2005).

However, to privilege structure over agency is, in my view, to overlook the countless empirical examples of resistance, revolution, and reconfiguration of the status quo that can occur through mobilization (see McAdam, 1982; Tilly, 2004). Thus, individuals do indeed possess some agency within a particular political and social order to resist the inculcation of some beliefs over others. Societies may vary in the proliferation of polyphonic political discourses (which is itself an important area for further inquiry), but it seems to me a guiding principle that individuals will always engage with the discourse of a social ecology in ways that contest just as much as they conform, for the world is anything but a static site of social reproduction.

In this study, Israeli and Palestinian youth clearly at times contested the received discourse of conflict and challenged the very infrastructure upon which conflict is so easily reproduced. Youths like Noa, for example, appropriated a particular *local* discourse that challenged the recent religious-nationalist incarnation of Zionism that would deny the Palestinians a state of their own. In spite of growing up in one of the most existentially insecure locales of the West Bank, Lubna repudiated the utility or legitimacy of resistance in arguing that the Palestinians needed to come to see themselves as utterly defeated and "move on." That multiple ecological systems of development (Bronfenbrenner, 1979) were clearly at play in influencing these and other life stories—the family, the local community, the particular school—reveals the importance of studying individuals and social contexts in ways that reveal the complexity and fluidity of processes of human development. No individual exists *solely* as a member of a national identity, regardless of how salient that social identity might be rendered by virtue of conflict. Rather, individuals inhabit multiple social identities simultaneously (Brewer, 2001; Sen, 2006, 2008), as Israelis or Palestinians, kibbutzniks or settlers, peace activists or freedom fighters, men or women. Identity is rich and fluid, not static and monolithic. Yet where agency ends and the power of structure begins is a murky line, which leads us to a consideration of power relations within and between societies.

Who controls the resources needed to sustain and enrich life? This question was fundamental to Marx's analysis of the psychological consequences of economic life (e.g., Marx, 1844/1978). The particular location of an individual within a larger matrix of social identities—some of which are closer to this site of control, or means of production—determines the possibilities for social and psychological life. This materialist thesis for the relation between mind and society seems just as applicable to understanding the relation between conflict and identity as it does to the issue of social class that Marx intended, for the fundamental underlying concern of a psychological materialism is, of course, power.

What I mean to suggest here is that it is impossible to study phenomena such as "culture," "identity," and "intergroup contact" without reference to the positioning of individuals within a broader matrix of power and domination. The implications of this thesis became more clear, I think, in Chapter 5, with my analysis of the life stories of young Palestinian Israelis. More even than Jewish Israelis and Palestinians from the occupied territories, Palestinian-Israeli youth challenged the notion of a simple relation between social structure and the individual, for these youth utilized multiple strategies to position or reposition themselves within a context of subordination. They constructed configurations of identity that reflected hyphenated selves, and their stories revealed choices about these positions, reflecting the kind of agency that is even available when one occupies a subordinate status. Thus, Jibril favored a strategy of individual mobility (Tajfel & Turner, 1986) to reconfigure his status position within Israeli society, while youths like Rania favored social competition (Tajfel & Turner, 1986) to directly challenge the hegemony of the Jewish majority (Peleg, 2004).

The narratives of youth thus provide a rich mirror with which to reflect back upon scholarship in fields of study that concern themselves less with individual voices—fields like sociology, political science, and anthropology—than with indicators of collective experience. In this way, my approach engages with theories of conflict and notions of "culture" that obscure, or perhaps even disparage, voices that reflect individual subjectivity. I believe that this approach complements theoretical attempts to link individual psychology to society, particularly Bar-Tal's prolific work on the sociopsychological foundations of intractable conflict. The narratives of youth reveal the processes he and other theoreticians posit about conflict's psychological consequences, while they also serve to anchor an analysis of conflict in recognition of the dialectical nature of mind and society.

The *cultural psychology* of Israeli and Palestinian youth, or of youth more generally in my view, is thus not characterized by some kind of essentialism or reductionism about psychological life. Context does not *dictate* a kind of mental patterning of thought, word, and action, but it does *prescribe* the discourse to which youth will be exposed as they develop an inner speech to organize thought, word, and action. Youth inherit this discourse, but they are also active participants in its reproduction or repudiation. Individuals will thus engage with this discourse in ways that both defy our expectations and adhere to a patterned sensibility.

This process reveals culture as not monologic but *dialogic*, not static but *dynamic*, and not neutral but immersed in the politics of power and identity. Culture is thus not a *noun* but a *verb*, not a "thing" to be analyzed and dissected but a set of embodied practices, accompanied by a set of utterances that provides meaning and coherence to an individual mind. As cycles of practice and their accompanying narratives multiply, our ability to infer (or to impose) a patterned sensibility begins to occur with interpretive ease. Yet when we listen to the voices of youth, or to individual voices in general, we can embrace the complexity and fluidity of culture and its basis not in some monolithic discourse but in a polyphonic account of lived experience.

I believe that the personal narratives of Israeli and Palestinian youth presented in this book suggest just such a way of thinking about culture and identity. Rather than think about culture as *merely* providing a vocabulary of the self (e.g., Markus & Kitayama, 1991; Shweder & Bourne, 1982), or as specifying a set of material practices (e.g., Gutierrez & Rogoff, 2003) or cognitive models (e.g., Holland & Quinn, 1987), or as a tool for subjugation and subordination (e.g., Gjerde, 2004), I believe we need to consider culture as all of the above. The task of cultural psychology is to document, but not to *reify*, particularity in mental life (Shweder, 2003). Yet in this particularity we might come to see the universality of processes of human development (Shweder & Sullivan, 1993), anchored in the need to make meaning of experience through an alignment of thought, word, and action. I believe that the concept of *narrative*, because it speaks both to social and personal discourse as actively lived and contested rather than simply *given*, offers a unifying framework for thinking about culture and identity. And, importantly, a focus on narrative mandates the provision of voice to the subjects of a study, thus challenging the silence that too often accompanies the data of social science research. This silence, in my view, conspires to hide the power of both human agency and the psychological consequences of subordination. Thus, a theory and method that allow for genuine human expression and that provide an opportunity for individuals to account for the basis of their own thoughts and actions better speak to the possibilities of a *transformative*, rather than a *reproductive*, social science.

Against Cosmopolitanism

As I have argued throughout this book, to consider the single narration of a life story as a finished "product" of human development is to fall prey to prior notions of identity as something to "achieve" (Erikson, 1959). A half-century after Erikson's pioneering work, and the many very static derivatives of his dynamic theory, we now have a better understanding of narrative identity as a *process* that occurs across the life course, taking winding turns and not always, or perhaps ever, following some predictable linear trajectory (e.g., McLean, Pasupathi, & Pals, 2007; Peacock & Holland, 1993). Ali's story is a simple case in point.

This study, therefore, was concerned not solely with the narration of a life story in adolescence, but rather with *how that narration might change over time* and *in relation to a particular new form of social practice*—intergroup contact. I argued in several places in the book that this project of contact, by virtue of the history of the very idea itself in American social psychology, is infused with an ideology of cosmopolitanism—the philosophical notion that, as individuals, we have a sense of mutual responsibility to coexist, and that individuals can indeed transcend the divisiveness of identity insularity and singularity (e.g., Appiah, 2005, 2006).

The cosmopolitan thesis is alluring, elegant, intuitive, and extremely self-satisfying. But is it really the "right" ideal for intergroup relations? Does embracing cosmopolitanism as an aim for, say, education in a pluralistic world, really work to right the wrongs of history that underlie so much conflict across the globe? Does cultivating a cosmopolitan consciousness, or a cosmopolitan code of identity ethics, address the grievances of groups in ways that reconfigure intergroup relations and work toward a more just world, in which power is distributed and hegemony challenged? As I summarize the argument about such an effort with Israeli and Palestinian youth that I have been developing throughout this book, I will suggest that the answer is a resounding "No."

Let me be clear that I am not trying to disrupt, dismantle, or refute cosmopolitanism as a *philosophical* subject of inquiry, for I confess to feeling that a cosmopolitan ethic has in fact shaped my own sense of identity and my particular outlook on the world. But as a philosophical, rather than a social-scientific, line of inquiry, cosmopolitanism sacrifices the real for the ideal—the actual for the imagined possible—and in so doing it constructs problematic visions for transforming intergroup relations on the ground. Because it seeks to venture from the idealism of human interaction to the actual realm of inter-group relations, cosmopolitanism opens itself up to an ideological critique. And, as I argue, it seeks to capture the imagination of human universalism at its best, thereby obscuring the very important lines of *distinction* across human communities—lines that have often been used to oppress and subordinate. In short, I will argue that the cosmopolitanism that infuses the American attempts to intervene in Israeli–Palestinian relations I examined in this research problematically obscures difference and the power asymmetries of conflict in favor of a *neutral* politics of identity, or at least a notion of identity transcendence that says more about American folk psychology than about the ways in which we might work toward social justice and a reduction of conflict in the world.

To begin to summarize this argument, it is necessary to, for a moment, become historians of nationalism and of Israel, Palestine, *and* the United States. Palestine and Israel are both products of, or perhaps more appropriately "victims" of, the primordialism that so consumed the age of nationalism, the era of postimperialism in which groups of people might at last come to deter-mine their own political and economic destinies, thereby gaining control over their own history (Geertz, 1963; Hobsbawm, 1990). Primordialism com-manded the construction and cultivation of narratives of identity that were emotionally compelling, narratives that imbued the concept of nationality with a quality of indefinite and identifiable historical lineage (Suny, 2001). Out of the global dissemination of this ideology emerged Zionism, itself a reaction to the painfully exclusionary national movements of nineteenth- and twentieth-century Europe (Mosse, 1978). From Zionism sprang Palestinian nationalism and the stalemate of stories—interpretations of history and collective memory—that characterizes the Israeli–Palestinian conflict.

While the United States—as a nation created out of the ideals and ideolo-gies of the Enlightenment—was perhaps less prey to primordialism, its history is one of racial and ethnic exclusion, with its shameful legacy of genocide and slavery (e.g., Adams, 1995; Feagin, 2001). Over the twentieth century, as the Israeli–Palestinian conflict came to a dramatic climax in 1948, and then again in 1967, the United States was struggling to write a new, coherent narrative that accommodated the realities of identity pluralism within its own borders. To reconfigure the American master narrative from a place of ethnocentrism (characterized by White privilege) and androcentrism, the national discourse needed to change—both legally and vernacularly. That is, there needed to be both *political* transformations, such as achieved by the famous *Brown v. Board of Education* decision in 1954, and *cultural* transformations, such as achieved by changes in possibilities for racially and sexually integrated social activities (e.g., school desegregation, women in the workplace).

Enter the contact hypothesis into American folk psychology, which gained prominence precisely in the year of the landmark *Brown* decision (Allport, 1954). The contact hypothesis, which emerged as the dominant social-psychological "solution" to problems of intergroup relations in the United States beginning in the 1940s and 1950s, is itself a product of an American master narrative of redemption (see McAdams, 2006), of a need for atonement of a deeply racist and ethnocentric past (and present). Thus, we must view the project of contact—particularly as it is practiced in the American-based programs I have studied here—as an integral part of *American* history, as an attempt to contribute to the reduction of prejudice that underlies negative intergroup relations. My point is that this national project is *distinct* from that of Israelis and Palestinians, whose forms of nationalism are more concerned with the politics of identity *recognition* than the management of identity *pluralism*.

Programs like Seeds of Peace and Hands of Peace, founded on the idealistic premises of the original contact hypothesis, are very much outgrowths of this cosmopolitan view of identity diversity that emerged through the multiculturalism movements of the 1970s and 1980s (see Hollinger, 2006; Verkuyten, 2007). Following a very appealing storyline, the notion is simply that, through exposure to diverse others, we might come to *value*, rather than to derogate, *distinction* over *sameness*. Yet in coming to assume this ideal value, we come to a universal moral respect for pluralism. Hence, through our appreciation for difference there can emerge a universal code of human ethics—an ethics of *cosmopolitanism* (Appiah, 2005, 2006). There can even emerge, in the postmodern confrontation with numerous, hybrid, and constantly mutating settings, the "protean" identity (Lifton, 1993)—a state of resilient coherence and adaptation in the midst of rapid fragmentation.

Both Seeds of Peace and Hands of Peace are best understood as experiments in the construction of cosmopolitan identities, protean forms of being and behaving that accommodate the distinction among identities. But the possibility of a cosmopolitan identity narrative relies upon the security of identity and the fulfillment of a coherent national identity, both of which have been largely denied Palestinians and Israelis. While cosmopolitanism does not negate a sense of national identity, it is rooted in at least the partial transcendence of in-group interest. It recognizes the legitimate value in "otherness," a phenomenon that would seem to rely upon a level of identity security and recognition.

The second major question that drove the research I describe in this book centered on the success of cosmopolitanism in practice. As I began this work, I found the thesis of cosmopolitanism, and its manifestation in these American-based ventures in intergroup contact, incredibly alluring. I was captivated by the possibility of psychological transformation that might occur through such contact. Yet as I collected the narratives of youth beyond their participation in these ventures—these experiments in identity intervention—I began to realize the limits of a cosmopolitan code of identity ethics, and the great idealism of the cosmopolitan thesis lay exposed before me.

When we consider the narratives of youth over time, as they come to integrate the experience of intergroup contact into their life stories, it is readily apparent that the need to identify fully with one's in-group and its master narrative of collective identity outweighs the ephemeral satisfaction of identity transcendence. Although I found many youths to narrate a script of identity transcendence, particularly immediately after contact, my longitudinal interviews revealed the challenge of maintaining such narratives over time. I came to see among many youths a kind of "reaction formation" (Freud, 1923/1962) to the threat of identity transcendence—a defensive process in which contact seemed to threaten their sense of identity so much that they felt compelled toward a highly polarized narrative. In these instances, it seemed to me that their coalition with the "other" had crossed a line (Kelman, 1993), as the emotional proximity to members of the out-group destabilized the master narrative to which they had been so thoroughly exposed and thus created too much dissonance in their life stories.

I explored these data extensively in Chapter 7, where I suggested that there is indeed variability in the narrative outcomes of contact but that the narratives of most youth were characterized by *identity accentuation* over time. That is, contact did not appear to achieve the long-term goal of *recategorization* of self and other into a new common group committed to peaceful coexistence—the primary psychological aim of both Hands of Peace and Seeds of Peace. A cosmopolitan, transcendent identity narrative, when it did occur, was largely ephemeral.

The social psychological process that seemed to best characterize the process of contact for these youth was not *recategorization* but rather *subcategorization* (Brewer, 1996; Hornsey & Hogg, 2000), or *mutual intergroup differentiation* (Hewstone & Brown, 1986). Contact afforded them the opportunity to fully recognize the distinctiveness of self and other, thereby providing youth with the *rationale* for identity polarization. What had once been only discourse *within* their own societies was now laid out plainly before them, as they confronted directly the stalemate of narratives between themselves and their national "enemy."

What we do not know from my research is the extent to which the intervention of intergroup contact is *more likely* to enhance the desire for identity accentuation over and above its "natural" level in the context of conflict. That is, does intergroup contact in fact *cause* a higher level of in-group identity accentuation than would have occurred absent such intervention? Alternatively, is identity accentuation a normative process of adolescent development in contexts of conflict? To answer these important questions, a comparative design with youth who do not participate in intergroup contact would, of course, be necessary.

But the problem is not identity polarization per se, for even absent intractable conflict we know that intergroup behavior is characterized by an accentuation of social identity (Tajfel & Turner, 1979, 1986). We can thus *expect* contact to lead to a process of mutual differentiation, and this process would not be problematic were it not for the persistence of conflict between groups. The problem, then, is not the social psychological *process* of identity accentuation as an outcome of contact; it is, rather, the *content* of Israeli and Palestinian identities themselves. The problem lies in the *inherent* stalemate of narratives that currently exists between Palestinians and Israelis. If any intervention is to be successful in genuinely effecting social change in this situation, it would seem to be an intervention in the *master narratives themselves.* What is needed, then, is perhaps not so much *individual* change but rather *structural* change (cf. Bekerman & Maoz, 2005).

The evidence I have presented in this book suggests that mutual differentiation comes to represent the dominant social-psychological process following contact between Palestinian and Israeli youth. In this process, reproduction of the identity conditions that maintain the conflict would seem to be ensured. Contact thus seems to serve a reproductive function for the "monologic" national identities in conflict (Bekerman, 2009b, 2009c; Bekerman & Maoz, 2005; Helman, 2002). In other words, even if an authentic dialogue occurs in contact, the long-term construction of identity appears to continue along a path of monologism— of reifying the status quo of polarized and negatively interdependent identity politics (Bekerman & Maoz, 2005; Hammack, 2006; Kelman, 1999b).

But it is useful, and most practical, to ask ourselves *why* this reproductive process occurs through contact. Perhaps more to the point, why do these American-based coexistence programs appear to fail in their missions to cultivate cosmopolitan identities over time? I will offer two very basic, and perhaps obvious, explanations. First, the programs fail to assume a sufficiently *intracultural* approach and rely largely on an American cultural model of adolescence and intergroup relations. Second, in their desire for political "neutrality," the programs fail to address issues of power asymmetry that deeply influence the dynamics of the Israeli–Palestinian conflict. In so doing, they inhibit the extent to which issues of structural reality can be acknowledged and addressed by youth.

These problematic features of American-based programs conspire to create profound dissonance for youth as they strive to integrate the contact experience into their life stories. Interrogation and dismantling of these problematic features might, I speculate, lead us toward a different kind of practice in peace education—one in which individuals are given the opportunity to see the structural constraints of their own agency and a mythology of all-power individualism is moderated by a prescription for practical activity in the interest of peace and justice.

American Intervention as a "Civilizing" Project

The primary factor that seems to limit the extent to which these American-based programs can fulfill their missions of identity recategorization centers on their misguided application of an American cultural model of intergroup relations and adolescence to their project (Hammack, 2009). At first, to levy such a criticism may sound somewhat nonsensical, for these programs are, after all, *American*. But in blindly applying notions of moral and psychological universalism, they adopt a set of problematic assumptions and inhibit their own possibilities for effecting social change.

The American interventions I have described in this book reveal a collision of narratives—not only the collision of Palestinian and Israeli national narratives of identity and history, but also the collision of those narratives with the American narrative of cosmopolitanism as a solution to intergroup conflict. Rather than see identity through the lens of an Israeli or a Palestinian, the designers of these interventions instead view identity through the lens of privilege. This lens of privilege is rooted in the positions of these programs in terms of class and race in the United States (though not among all organizers or staff members, of course), but it is also rooted more simply in the privilege of living in a conflict-free setting—a setting in which identity is not a source of immediate existential threat, as *is* the case for Israelis and Palestinians.

In their underlying faith in the viability of a cosmopolitan consciousness, these programs essentially *deny* the structural reality of Israel and Palestine, thereby erroneously applying an American context of intergroup relations— one in which *ethnocentrism*, rather than *intractable conflict* (Bar-Tal, 2004a), is the dominant problem—to a widely divergent context. I came to believe, based not just on interviews and ethnographic work with youth in Israel and Palestine but also on active participant observation in the organizations themselves, that the design of these programs spoke more to the moral needs and desires of the organizers than the youth whose lives they were attempting to transform. In their quest to instill a narrative of cosmopolitanism, the organizers of these programs were perhaps seeking to fulfill their own psychological needs to redeem themselves from the legacy of American racism, or to demonstrate how they believe our society has successfully overcome racism as normative. The development and implementation of these programs might have more to do, then, with the fulfillment of their own master narratives of redemption (McAdams, 2006) through cosmopolitanism.

To clarify my point, let me clearly state that I do not intend to somehow delegitimize the theses of either liberal pluralism or cosmopolitanism as mechanisms of multicultural accommodation. Nor do I refute the possibility of protean identities more generally as an individual response to globalization and postmodernity. Rather, what I mean to suggest is that the utility of political, legal, and social ideological systems such as those promulgated by these theses are context dependent. They require certain cultural preconditions, not the least of which is a deployment of discourse that identifies such a code of identity ethics as somehow desirable. The context of conflict, I would argue based on the findings of my research, does not produce such a discursive possibility with enough power to attract the youth of a society *en masse*. The inculcation of identities attuned to a cosmopolitan code of ethics requires a particular structural reality, one in which diversity in identity is both recognized and valued. But absent mutual recognition and the guarantee of identity security, how can we realistically expect to instill a cosmopolitan ideology among Israeli and Palestinian youth?

We ought also to note that, although I have used the term "liberal pluralism" almost synonymously with cosmopolitanism, the political philosophy described by Galston (2002), based on the ideas of Isaiah Berlin and others, is much more radical than cosmopolitanism. I think Galston (2002) expresses the true radicalism of liberal pluralism when he says, "To demand that every acceptable way of life reflect a conscious awareness of value pluralism is to affirm what value pluralism denies—the existence of a universally dominant value" (p. 53). Liberal pluralism is not meant to create a hierarchy of meaning in social, national, or political organization, for it recognizes at its core the legitimacy of plurality in the ways in which lives are culturally organized and lived.

Yet cosmopolitanism, as an ideological derivative of liberal political and moral philosophy, is a value-laden concept, for it privileges a distinct way of cultural being. To embrace liberal pluralism in all of its authenticity would destabilize the value hierarchy set up by cosmopolitanism, for as its own ideology, it recognizes its *absence* as problematic. That is, cosmopolitanism as posited by Appiah (2006) and as manifest in the practices of these American-based coexistence programs is framed as *the* solution to the problem of intergroup conflict and multicultural accommodation that characterizes our time. In this way, it is a betrayal of the tenets of liberal pluralism, for liberal pluralism seeks precisely to avoid a hierarchy of ideologies through its rejection of universalism in values.

It is beyond both my concern and my competence to extend this argument further. But I think it important to identify the distinction between cosmopolitanism and liberal pluralism as ideologies that mutually infuse the American project of psychological intervention in the identities of Israeli and Palestinian youth. Suffice it to say that the organizers of these programs view themselves as highly cosmopolitan endorsers of liberal pluralism, in spite of their seeming failure to fully embody what it is that such a commitment entails.

The cultural psychology of these American-based programs is thus itself characterized by a philosophical approach that is grounded in American folk models of conflict, intergroup relations, and the life course itself (e.g., a folk psychology of adolescence). To say more about the underlying view of conflict, it is clear that these programs believe that, while admittedly not exhaustive in scope, these interventions in individual personality and identity development can affect the course of the conflict and help to reconfigure intergroup relations between Israelis and Palestinians. Thus, they would seem to privilege *individual psychological change* in the cycle of social regeneration, just as an American folk psychology more generally privileges individual subjectivity over and above the collective (Markus & Kitayama, 1991). In their reliance on a theory of social change that relies primarily on individual psychological intervention, with little or no interest in or consideration for issues of social structural or political change, these programs are guilty of the same unrealistic aims of the classic contact hypothesis, challenged as it has been for its underlying individualism and its reliance on a set of "optimal" conditions that rarely exist in situations of intractable conflict (Dixon et al., 2005).

Hands of Peace and Seeds of Peace rely on an American narrative of intergroup relations, manifested in their faith in the idealism of the original contact hypothesis and the idea of cosmopolitanism, but they also rely on a distinctly American cultural model of *adolescence* itself. We can credit Erik Erikson and other scholars of the 1960s and 1970s with the elaboration and popularization of a model of adolescence that imbues this life course moment with prodigious power to change a social order (see also Keniston's work on "youth"; Keniston,

1971, 1972). I believe these scholars were right to describe youth as the psychosocial moment of cultural regeneration, yet the promulgation and popularization of such a model suggested that adolescents possessed unparalleled power to effect social change. The perspectives of these scholars were, of course, developed in a particular historical context in the United States—one in which the social order was indeed being questioned and, ultimately, repudiated by a generation of youth. So it made sense to fashion a theory of adolescence that accorded sufficient cultural power.

While I agree with the premise that youth is always and everywhere the moment at which a given social order is either reproduced or repudiated (e.g., Erikson, 1968), I would argue that the extent to which youth do or do not reproduce a given social order is not entirely within the realm of their own collective agency. I believe that the process of social reproduction that occurs in the case of Israelis and Palestinians, as evident in the narratives of youth subject to an intervention to specifically *prevent* just that reproduction, reveals the limits of agency in the context of conflict and existential threat.

Both Seeds of Peace and Hands of Peace promulgate visions of social change through the leadership of a new generation. They argue that "treaties are negotiated by governments; peace is made by people" (Seeds of Peace, 2010; see also Engstrom, 2009). Is this not a decidedly *American* (or perhaps Western, liberal) perspective on the way in which social change occurs? Does this not somehow suggest that governments "serve" their people—a particularly American premise? These American-based programs subscribe to a "bottom-up" theory of social change, but in so doing, they deny that adolescence itself might not be a universal moment of social and political upheaval. That is, they rely upon a particular model of youth inherited from an American narrative of history and politics.

I do not question that the context of conflict in which Israeli and Palestinian youth find themselves today is an utterly unacceptable and unjust social order. Intuitively, it makes sense that encouraging the revolution of youth might somehow represent the best chance for cracking the "sociopsychological infrastructure" of conflict. And yet we find in the revolution of Zionism itself, as well as that of Palestinian nationalism, not the ideologies of youth but of *adults*—individuals deeply dissatisfied with a given status quo, whether it be the anti-Semitic context of Europe or the occupation of Palestinian territory. Nationalist Israeli and Palestinian discourses have long been governed by powerful ruling elites, not by the whimsical rebellion of youth. In such a context, why ought we to expect youth to possess significant power for social change? Are the ideologies of both Israeli and Palestinian nationalism not *so entirely consumed* with instilling in youth the moral legitimacy of their struggles, whether through the IDF or the political youth movements of Fatah or Hamas, that they prove quite irresistible to youth? Are these master narratives not so *compelling* and *comforting* as to appeal directly to youth as they consolidate their ideological commitments?

Unfortunately, both Hands of Peace and Seeds of Peace, because of their assumption of a universal code of identity ethics, appear to be consumed with the project of American "missionary progressivism" (Shweder, 2004) that has come to infuse American foreign policy in the early twenty-first century. Quite benevolently, the missions of these programs are embedded in a discourse of American cosmopolitanism, one largely irrelevant to the context of the Israeli–Palestinian conflict. Furthermore, the reliance on youth to forge a revolution in the realm of identity betrays the idea of pluralism itself—that human development assumes a diversity of forms connected to local meanings and interpretations of group history and identity (Shweder, 2003). That the *process* of youth identity development is indeed universal, as some kind of transitional moment between the eccentricities of childhood and the demands of adulthood, is not what is at stake here. Rather, it is the idea of adolescence as somehow a period of inevitable rebellion—an idea that was refuted so long ago by Margaret Mead (1928) herself—that is most misdirected in this case, for Israeli and Palestinian youth seem to possess a *need* to conform to master narratives of identity, for the sustenance of those narratives is fragile and insecure.

The inability of these programs to "succeed" in the long term thus has much to do with their blind adoption of an American cultural model of both adolescence and intergroup relations. The unchallenged assumption that such a model applies to Israeli and Palestinian youth reveals the extent to which a discourse of *American* exceptionalism (McAdams, 2006) has perhaps been internalized by the organizers of these programs. The ideology of these programs themselves—indeed, the ideology of cosmopolitanism—seems somehow reflective of an ongoing "civilizing" project (Shweder, 2003), in which the West might somehow pass on its enlightened discovery of pluralism as an accommodation of cultural difference. But in this philosophical dilemma, these programs have conflated their own unique national narrative with that of Israel and Palestine, thereby blindsiding the structural distinctions among the United States, Israel, and Palestine.

The Problem of Power and Social Structure

Having argued that the American-based programs examined in this book are limited by their reliance on an uncritical folk psychology of both intergroup relations and youth, I want to now say more about the importance of addressing issues of power and social structure in any intervention that seeks to effect meaningful individual *and* social change. As I suggested in Chapter 6, research on both the social psychology of contact in general, and on Israeli–Palestinian contact in particular, has increasingly incorporated an analysis of power and social structure *and* an integration of these concepts into the interventions themselves. Simply put, contact efforts have recognized that politics underlies all aspects of human interaction, and that *there is no politically neutral place from which to intervene.*

In order to serve their own psychological and economic interests, these programs seem to deliberately avoid politics (an oxymoronic endeavor for an organization seeking to address political conflict), thereby reproducing the status quo of conflict itself. In their quest to "pass" as somehow politically "neutral," and thus to maximize their ability to receive financial support from a variety of sources, these programs ignore the structural realties of the Israeli–Palestinian conflict itself. Most notably, they neglect issues of power that exist in the conflict, thereby preventing youth from exploring ways in which they can realistically serve as agents of social change in their communities of origin.

Social psychological research on contact, however, suggests that interventions that fail to address issues of social structure—the origin of conflict itself, as Allport (1954) argued—cannot be effective. As Pettigrew (1986) notes in his critical review of the contact hypothesis, *"The use of intergroup contact as a means of alleviating conflict is largely dependent on the societal structure that patterns relations between the groups"* (p. 191, italics in original). Efforts at intergroup contact cannot avoid the social structure and power dynamics that characterize the *actual* context of intergroup relations (Brewer, 1996), which suggests the need for a model of intergroup contact that is grounded in a cultural approach.

As subjects of an experiment, participants in Hands of Peace and Seeds of Peace are encouraged to reduce the salience of their in-group identities, for the sake of mutual identity recognition and coexistence. But the seeds of identity *non*recognition run deep in Israel and Palestine, and mutual denial of identity is a source of empowerment for those who vie for control over this rather diminutive piece of the globe. In the case of Israel and Palestine, power is neither symmetrical between nor within the two respective societies, and the failure of these programs to take a critical stance toward the power dynamics that seem to contribute to the conflict's intractability inhibits the ability of youth to challenge (and thus to potentially rescript) master narratives of identity.

Israeli and Palestinian practitioners in the field of peace education and intergroup contact have increasingly embraced approaches that lean more toward both mutual differentiation and the exploration of power dynamics as end goals (e.g., Bekerman & Maoz, 2005; Halabi & Sonnenschein, 2004a,

2004b; Maoz, 2000a, 2000b, 2001; Rouhana, 2004; Suleiman, 2004a, 2004b), for a resolution to the conflict requires *at minimum* mutual identity recognition. Rather than rely on an American model developed for a different purpose—namely, racial integration—programs that bring Israeli and Palestinian youth together must directly confront the structural reality of a conflict rooted in needs for both security and the recognition of identity. In such an approach, recategorization would be eliminated as an aim for identity intervention and replaced by an emphasis on mutual intergroup differentiation. In other words, such efforts would take as their mission the strengthening of identity, for as identities are *advocated*, they might become *recognized*. They would abandon the unrealistic attempt to fashion a common identity of two very distinct peoples whose modern identities have not even had the chance for ontological security.

Beyond differentiation, though, youth must come to acknowledge the power dynamics that characterize the narrative stalemate of their identities. Quite simply, if Israelis and Palestinians are to *share* control of the land that was Mandate Palestine, they must recognize the need to create power symmetry between them. I do not think it at all taboo to recognize the power asymmetry that exists between the master narratives of Israelis and Palestinians, and Israeli scholars have not shied away from an empirical analysis of asymmetry (e.g., Gordon, 2008a, 2008b; Maoz, 2000b; Peleg, 2004). It is not the Israeli master narrative that must be rewritten, for it is already a story of success, however fragile.

Rather, the key to peace, or at least to a situation of intergroup contact in which the power asymmetry and structural inequality that characterize the conflict have been transformed, lies in a transformation of the Palestinian master narrative, from a story of resistance to one of realization. But the context of physical occupation prohibits the realization of a Palestinian identity that can ascribe meaning to the practice and fulfillment of a culture, rather than to the quest for liberation from domination. This recognition, so carefully *avoided* in both of these programs, is increasingly identified as essential by practitioners in Israel (e.g., Halabi & Sonnenschein, 2004a). The recognition of social structure and its relation to systems of conflict maintenance is simply a basic need for the experience of intergroup contact to carry sufficient experiential meaning that can be fully integrated into the personal narrative of identity.

The Meaning of Contact: Toward a Cultural Approach

What I hope the work described in this book most directly reveals is the importance of a cultural approach in research and practice on intergroup contact.

After decades of work on designing an "optimal" strategy for intergroup contact, practitioners are now presented with a list of utterly unattainable conditions to ensure "success" (Dixon et al., 2005). Rather than seek some kind of universal means to improve intergroup relations, it is probably more appropriate, though admittedly infinitely more cumbersome, to take a cultural approach that examines the *specificity* of the contact situation and sets *realistic* goals accordingly. I believe the evidence presented in this book supports such a reformulation of the practice of intergroup contact. What must be considered most prominently are the *meaning* of the contact situation and its level of threat to in-group identity.

In their significant review of over 50 years of research on the contact hypothesis, Dixon and his colleagues (2005) argue precisely for such an approach. Their paper, aptly subtitled "A Reality Check for the Contact Hypothesis," identifies the metatheoretical origins of the contact hypothesis in utopianism and individualism. As such, intervention in the process of individual cognition and behavior has long been the dominant emphasis of contact. The programs examined in my research are no exception to this traditional focus. In focusing primarily on the promotion of individual change, practitioners of intergroup contact have typically overlooked the reality of structural relations among groups and the political needs those relations achieve. They traditionally fail to consider the ways in which intergroup conflict is connected to the reproduction of a particular social order, with a particular power dynamic.

If the contact hypothesis is to remain viable, as Dixon et al. (2005) argue, it must transcend its metatheoretical reliance on a utopian notion of intergroup relations and instead embrace an approach that fuses the psychological, sociological, and political implications of intergroup contact. In the case of Seeds of Peace and Hands of Peace, if they are to evolve into sites of social interaction between Palestinians and Israelis that are politically "useful" in contributing to the eradication of conflict, they must also abandon the comforting narrative of the original contact hypothesis. They must instead engage more directly with the *actual* sociopolitical reality of Israeli–Palestinian relations. Were they to somehow refashion their missions, goals, ideologies, and rites of passage in such a way as to *facilitate*, rather than to *complicate*, integration of the experience of contact into the life story narrative, I would argue they would do a far greater service to the possibility of peace, for peace between Palestinians and Israelis must be grounded in the concrete reality of mutual recognition and the transformation from *negative* to *positive* interdependence (Kelman, 1999b). Such an end cannot be achieved through the "transcendence" of in-group identity; it is possible only with the rescripting of narratives whose existential viability relies on the negation of the other. This rescripting is itself entirely dependent on the structural reality of conflict.

If peace education relies on the mutual recognition of collective narratives (Salomon & Nevo, 2001), approaches to intergroup contact that embrace mutual differentiation as a possibility for eventual coexistence seem both beneficial and necessary. In fact, such approaches, which may emphasize the development of "cultural fluency" over identity decategorization or recategorization (Glazier, 2003), are more in line with the tenets of liberal pluralism, for they recognize the legitimacy of diversity in thought, feeling, and value—in the process of meaning making itself. A genuine pragmatism cannot emerge in Israeli–Palestinian relations before the fundamental task of mutual acknowledgment and recognition has occurred (Kelman, 1999a). As such, efforts at intergroup contact must resist the lure of cosmopolitanism and instead come to embrace the authenticity of liberal pluralism, with its grounding in the radicalism of pluralistic recognition.

In sum, I have argued, based on several years of fieldwork and interviews with Israeli and Palestinian youth who participate in coexistence programs, that the cosmopolitan foundations of American-based programs are misguided and, in fact, problematic. There is no evidence that these types of interventions actually contribute to conflict reduction, which calls into question the commitment of resources to such ventures, *absent a critical reformulation of their missions and goals.* Let me be clear that I support, as both a researcher and a practitioner, efforts to promote positive interpersonal acquaintanceship between young Israelis and Palestinians. And I would not necessarily claim that the current programs do more harm than good—such a claim requires a different kind of research design. What I question, though, is whether efforts that fail to address the social structural realities of conflict and privilege the power of individual psychological change really do much to work for social change. The narratives of youth examined after contact suggest that youth are challenged by the loss of credibility in their societies as a consequence of participation (see Kelman, 1993). It is not clear, then, that contact has instilled within them any clear guidance on their own role in conflict reduction.

My interpretations and conclusions in this research are obviously, and unabashedly, colored by my identity as a social scientist interested in more than mere description. Rather, as a scholar, practitioner, and peace activist, I believe I have a responsibility to challenge the status quo through my work—anchored as it is in the voices of youth. It is in this vein that I suggest that we must think more critically about contact, and about intervention in general, as well as the *identities of those who seek to intervene,* if we are to fulfill the liberatory potential of social science research.

What's Wrong With Identity?

One way to think about the response of identity accentuation, as I have suggested, is to see it as a reaction to the threat of recategorization. That is, young
Israelis and Palestinians, with their mutually insecure senses of collective
identity, might respond to the "press" of identity transcendence by shifting
further toward in-group accentuation. As Rouhana and Bar-Tal (1998) argue,
identity accentuation fulfills an important function for individual coping in
contexts of conflict. If feeling a strong sense of identity is psychologically *useful*
in conflict, then a threat to that sense might result in even greater accentuation
of in-group identity and, hence, polarization between groups.

But I think we can go a step further and ask ourselves why precisely identity transcendence would seem to be so valued in contemporary liberal political
philosophy and social psychology. In a way, it was precisely this impulse to
problematize identity that Henri Tajfel and his colleagues sought to dispel in
crafting social identity theory. What's wrong with identity, and why do we need
to transcend it?

To summarize some of the threads of this chapter, I think we can understand identity accentuation postcontact for at least three reasons. First, the
sociopolitical reality of conflict is one in which identity accentuation thrives.
The discourse of identity accentuation is extremely comforting in the context
of conflict, for it provides individuals with a sense of security, comfort, and
legitimacy generally lacking (Rouhana & Bar-Tal, 1998). Second, there is a
clear dissonance between the cultural context of the coexistence programs and
the sociopolitical reality of conflict into which youth are reimmersed postcontact. The reality of conflict is one in which it is very difficult to promote coexistence, for the *policies* to promote and support such efforts are largely absent
(Bar-Tal, 2004a). Finally, identity accentuation is simply a normal, empirically
documented outcome of contact, even in contexts of *minimal* identity salience
and conflict (Tajfel & Turner, 1979, 1986). In other words, having a strong,
positive sense of social identity is a necessary condition for social-psychological
life, and to the extent that contact *threatens* identity, it is bound to polarize
groups further.

Insights and empirical evidence from social identity theory lead us to question the desire for identity transcendence. While identity accentuation would
seem intuitively problematic for peace education—for its tendency to reify
notions of "nation" and "culture" (Bekerman, 2002, 2009b, 2009c; Bekerman
& Maoz, 2005)—there are clear benefits to identity accentuation, particularly in
contexts of conflict. Scholars of ethnic identity have revealed that a strong affiliation with the group is associated with enhanced self-esteem (e.g., Phinney, 1991).

The ideological commitment associated with identity accentuation appears to facilitate coping with political violence (Punamäki, 1996). Youth can often attribute great meaning to political violence through identity processes, which appears to again buffer them from the negative psychological consequences of conflict (Barber, 2001, 2008, 2009b).

Identity is thus a *positive* force in human development, particularly at the level of individual coping. But there are two obvious problems with identity accentuation. First, as a process, it clearly maintains the status quo of conflict. Second, it contributes to the general reification of concepts like *nation* and *culture*. Through this reification—this process of making indices of human difference seem somehow grounded in an intrinsic, enduring state of affairs—social orders are maintained and reproduced (Reicher, 2004; Reicher & Hopkins, 2001). Individuals thus come to enact the positions that maintain a particular status quo. In many cases, this process is not necessarily problematic, for a social order is not inherently oppressive or repressive. However, in contexts of war, conflict, and social injustice, such reproduction would seem to benefit those in power by reproducing the status quo.

This critical view of identity and its place in the reproduction of social orders is a natural outgrowth of poststructural accounts that question the very basis of social categories and received taxonomies (e.g., Foucault, 1978; Hall, 1996). This view recognizes subjectivity within a *regime* of identity that commands adherence. In the practice of this adherence, though, our very consciousness of self and other, and of thought, feeling, and word is produced. We become psychologically subject to the demands of identity, and this subjectivity is problematic for the endurance of conflict and social injustice.

As a scholar, I feel a particular affinity for this argument of identity as essentially a *burden*, not only because I believe in the veracity of its theoretical foundation but also because I have witnessed the psychological struggles of youth to reconcile their experiences with a received politics of identity. Yet, there is an underlying problem with this critique of identity that unsettles me. The critique of identity is similar to the larger account of conflict as an inherently *negative* force. I am led to ask myself, from whose perspective is conflict negative, and who benefits from a critique of identity?

These kinds of questions lead us directly into a challenging dialogue on the politics of identity. From the perspective of the subordinated, the oppressed, and the marginalized, identity is obviously a great force for struggle (Hurtado, 1989). The idea of identity, and its accompanying collective narrative, provides a vehicle for social mobilization in the service of fighting an unjust status quo (see Brewer & Silver, 2000). When a group vies for recognition or competes for a measure of legitimacy among human communities, identity can become a tool for justice, and conflict takes the form of a virtuous endeavor to right the wrongs and settle legitimate grievances (e.g., Konefal, 2003). Hence, a critique of identity, at least in some cases, would seem to benefit maintenance of the status quo, and more specifically groups with greater power.

Thus, I am suspicious of my instinct to problematize identity accentuation as an outcome of contact, for identity is central to the struggle for recognition and legitimacy that consumes the Israeli–Palestinian conflict. Do we not then undermine this struggle if we challenge its basis in identity? And given that *both* groups possess histories of subordination, it stands to reason that a deconstruction of identity is politically problematic. To argue that the Israeli and Palestinian master narratives are artifacts of the nationalist era, and hence of regressive attempts to codify identity within the order of the monolithic nation-state, is certainly historically accurate. But to stop at this critique is damaging for the real interests of Israelis and Palestinians, for both groups are entitled to a secure setting in which to engage in their own desired practices.

Identity accentuation thus can be viewed not solely as a *burden* in contexts of conflict but also as a *benefit*, particularly because it represents the struggles of groups for recognition and legitimacy as authentically and inevitably *lived within* the subjects of a social order. To capitalize on identity accentuation in peace education practice does not necessarily require a process of blind reification of social categories. Rather, it seems entirely plausible that contact can—and should—provide a site at which two polarized identities meet and, usually for the first time, become embodied in a challenging social interaction.

With a heightened consciousness of self and other, and a direct *confrontation* of narratives, it seems possible for individuals to begin to understand their own subjectivities in a critical light. That is, raising awareness of one's own role not as a *unique individual* (as the American model would prescribe) but as a *political actor*, whose personal narrative is inescapably linked to a collective narrative framed by a larger sociopsychological infrastructure (Bar-Tal, 2007), would seem to offer a greater contribution to both *social* and *psychological* change. Because such an approach does not shy away from matters of power, policy, and identity and, rather, seeks to facilitate a critical political consciousness, or *conscientização* (Freire, 1970), it would seem to speak to the need for structural change in Israeli–Palestinian relations.

My suggestions and arguments on the *positive* nature of identity in Israeli–Palestinian contact are closely connected to the approach developed at the School for Peace in Israel (see Halabi & Sonnenschein, 2004a). Their *confrontational* model seeks to exploit identity accentuation as a positive, particularly for Jewish Israelis who tend not to fully recognize or acknowledge their power and privilege (Maoz, in press). I do not intend to speculate further, as I believe there remains a need for much more research and practice to be developed around some of these ideas. It is the case that most efforts in Israel, the United States, and elsewhere continue to be framed within the narrow (and shallow) purviews of a model of contact that privileges interpersonal acquaintanceship and the avoidance of politics as a basic method (Maoz, in press).

I believe that we have a responsibility, as social scientists, peace education practitioners, and individuals simply committed to issues of peace and social justice, to develop and implement programs with serious and thoughtful theoretical bases—not focusing on our own needs but rather on the interests of young Israelis and Palestinians, who stand to benefit considerably from a political solution to their intractable conflict. Thus, I believe we must engage in a comprehensive and systematic program of *action* research (Lewin, 1946) that is inherently reflexive and grounded in *what works* to promote peace and justice in Israel and Palestine, as opposed to continuing to engage in efforts that are rooted in the interests of a particular party and that are essentially *reproductive* in relation to the status quo of conflict. What this kind of research and practice might look like remains somewhat of a mystery to me, for it is impossible to engage in such work outside of the scope of interests and a highly influential political reality. Thus, I think the best we can do is to embrace an aim of reflexive practice and action research that is mutually informative and that is always oriented toward the end goal of peace and justice for both Israelis and Palestinians.

Psychology and the Politics of a New Praxis: From Interpretation to Social Change

Undisciplining the Discipline

In the autumn of 2001, I sat across from a 12-year-old African American on the South Side of Chicago, interviewing him about his exposure to community violence. I was in charge at that time of a large, federally funded study of youth exposed to violence, and this extremely brief interview represented a small portion of our protocol. As he narrated some of the acts of violence he had witnessed in his life, I felt a strong sense of professional shame. Here I was, a White man from the North Side, living in the context of class and race privilege, collecting information from this young man to be "analyzed," ostensibly to eventually reveal the injustice of daily life on the South Side.

Regardless of the good intentions of the study (which I directed but had not designed), there was no doubt that youths like the one from whom I sat across that day did not stand to benefit from my activity as a researcher. I was essentially engaged in that all-too-common practice of "drive-by data collection" in which the researcher only *takes* from a community without actually *giving* something meaningful in return. It is precisely this model that the community psychology movement has repudiated (Nelson & Prilleltensky, 2005).

At that time in my life, I had come to view these common research practices in the social sciences as problematic for a number of reasons. First, they were not rooted in a rich and complex understanding of individual lives. The kind of study in which I was engaged did not involve any kind of "immersion" into the lives of these youth. Rather, the methodology relied entirely upon self-report. Thus, my one-on-one interview, lasting no more than 15 minutes, offered the only window into the way in which these youth were making meaning of the violence to which they were exposed. Second, the research was not concerned at all with the matter of social change. Too often, as I began to see it, was psychological research concerned solely with issues of "basic science"—seeking to determine and document how individuals respond to various situations, assuming a strong universalist stance about the mind.

If we, as social scientists who possess the tools of social and psychological analysis, only seek to document experience, are we not unwitting participants in the reproduction of injustice? Obviously, this is most apparent when we are studying issues that somehow bear upon social justice, such as the social and economic context of African-American youth in Chicago, or the political context of Israeli and Palestinian youth. But even when we study basic mental processes, such as perception, apart from the context in which those mental processes occur, are we not denying the significance of the social environment to shape thought, feeling, word, and action?

In my view, the discipline of psychology must reckon with its inherent underlying conservatism if it is to evolve beyond the twentieth-century quest for legitimacy among the sciences. If we continue to promulgate a vision of "psychic unity" (Shweder, 1990) and to design and implement studies based on that assumption, we deny both common sense and an enduring empirical record about the diversity of human life. As I conclude this book, I want to suggest that we abandon this vision of the mind as an information-processing mechanism, a model we largely inherited from behaviorism, and instead focus our lens on the coconstitution of mind and society, as many have strongly advocated before me (e.g., Bruner, 1990). To do so requires that we abandon two other aspects of our disciplinary practice: (1) our methodolatry about experimentation, and (2) our illusory vision of science and politics as mutually exclusive.

I suggest that we need to abandon these underlying visions of psychology as methodologically and ideologically "pure" if we are to amplify the voices of psychologists in interdisciplinary conversations about war, conflict, peace, genocide, and identity politics in general. Though the notion that the experimental method reveals some kind of ultimate "truth" about human nature has long been challenged (e.g., Moghaddam & Harré, 1982), the mainstream of the discipline continues to hold up experimentation as methodologically superior. Let me be very clear that, as a social scientist, I believe in the utility and the explanatory power of experimentation. Yet I also know that not all questions related to human action can be addressed within the narrow confines of a decontextualized laboratory experiment. For example, knowing that two groups respond differently to a spatial memory task does not necessarily tell you *why* specific individuals may have responded in the way they did. To get this kind of information, one must elicit *narratives* of individuals that develop some account of intentionality for their actions (Bruner, 1990). And it would help to know something of the history of each individual, for his or her process of intentional action does not occur apart from a particular life history.

My point here is not to argue that narrative methods, or ethnographic methods, or even qualitative methods in general, are superior to experimental methods in explanatory power. To make such a claim would simply seek to reclaim the authority of explanation that experimentalists often promulgate. Rather, I believe strongly in *methodological pluralism* and *reflexive social science*, in which the investigator does not claim a lack of position vis-à-vis the "object" of study. My interview on the South Side of Chicago with a young African-American man exists within the continued legacy of racism in the United States. That I may myself not be a racist is irrelevant, for my identity as a member of the dominant racial group influences the nature of our brief interaction. And I must not shy away from (or deny) the reflexivity of such an analysis. But to do so requires that I abandon illusory notions of "pure" science in psychology—notions that human thought and behavior can truly be isolated from a context of its elaboration.

Hence, psychology would greatly benefit from a de-emphasis on particular methods in favor of constructing particular research *questions* that address real problems of human living. Psychology can continue to (rightfully) lay claim to the individual as primary unit of analysis, and the mind as its primary object of study. But an openness to methodological pluralism means that we can ask more research questions that can be answered outside of the laboratory. I believe this shift in research practice, away from a methods-driven science and toward a problem-focused orientation, creates new challenges for our received paradigms. Yet it is precisely toward new paradigmatic formulations that we must look to address the unique problems we face in the twenty-first century.

By no means is my call here entirely original or novel. The emergence and popularity of approaches like participatory action research (PAR) is a good example (e.g., Brydon-Miller, 1997). Yet I believe that psychological scientists continue to operate within the hegemony of a positivist philosophy of science that privileges both quantification and experimentation (Burman, 1997). These acts of resistance in research practice will surely (and hopefully) have a cumulative effect on the discipline, and I can only hope that the work described in this book contributes to disruptions in the status quo of research practice in psychology. I believe this research represents a historical document, just like all social science research (Gergen, 1973), of the interpretive practice of a particular analyst (in this case, me), himself or herself the product of engagement with numerous frameworks and paradigms. That this work reveals, or exemplifies, a disruption within the discipline of psychology says much about the history (and politics) of knowledge production.

Rather than seek to carve a particular niche for social and cultural psychology, I have been more concerned with thinking about Israeli and Palestinian youth apart from the confines of particular disciplines. This approach naturally led me to consume not just studies in psychology, sociology, or education but also political speeches, poetry, and novels. As an "outsider" to the Israeli–Palestinian conflict, I would never claim the privilege of fully grasping the nature of in-group consciousness. Yet I believe the *undisciplined* nature of my inquiry opened my eyes to a fuller understanding of the experiences of Israelis and Palestinians. I did not think of those with whom I came into contact as "objects" of study. Rather, I considered them as subjects inhabiting a world very different from my own. Their subjectivity, though, could not be fragmented or broken into various bits and piece, for it represented a whole that could only be understood from the vantage point of a wide-angle lens. Hence, I was consumed with the project of documenting and interpreting the lived experience of Israeli and Palestinian youth with the lens of a psychologist, an anthropologist, a peace activist, a compassionate listener, a practical thinker, and a human being. I do not claim in this methodological practice some kind of identity transcendence of my own, for I acknowledge that my positioning (as, for example, an American male) was always already present. Rather, I suggest that the openness I brought to my analysis, though exhausting in its breadth, enhanced my ability to understand the complexity and contradictions of young Israelis and Palestinians.

In this book, I have sought to model a particular kind of methodological practice that is problem oriented, theoretically grounded, and highly informative about social psychological processes at work for young Israelis and Palestinians. I would be remiss were I not to acknowledge that this kind of

methodological practice is utterly exhausting and requires a significant investment of time and resources. Yet I complete this project with a sense of self-
satisfaction I did not possess following the study on Chicago's South Side.
I believe that I came to know my research participants as real people, living
daily lives in the best way they could at a time of significant political turmoil,
and that my ethnographic, idiographic method provided me with a unique lens
through which to interpret their lives. I was given access through this method
to their particular processes of meaning making, their attempts to carve out a
mental life consonant with the goals, values, and imagination of a particular
community. By seeking to understand not simply them as individuals but also
the communities in which they sought to anchor their life stories, I believe
I was afforded a remarkable opportunity to consider their engagement with
forms of social being. That is, by mapping out both the discourse to which they
are routinely exposed *and the personal, inner discourse* they construct to attain a
sense of purpose and coherence, I could gain access to the mutually constitu-
tive process of mind and society in all of its richness and complexity. That other
studies might also embrace this ambition, to see a model of possibility to tackle
the "big" questions that are too often dissected among the social science disciplines, yet never reconnected into a holistic vision of the socially embedded
individual actor, would be a gratifying end for me.

Politicizing Peace

I want to end this book by taking the reader back to my first night at the Seeds
of Peace Camp in rural Maine, to the dance and drum circle I observed after a
long day of training. The ritual by the campfire that night could not have been
better scripted for me, a budding peace psychologist, in terms of the crude
stereotypes of individuals engaged in this kind of work. I came over the course
of my fieldwork to see the efforts of most Americans with whom I came into
contact as problematic for at least two reasons. First, they typically imposed a
distinctly *American* cultural model, or vision, of what "peace" ought to be on a
context about which they knew far less than they perhaps should. That is, few
of the Americans with whom I worked had actually spent a great deal of time
(or any time at all, in fact) talking with Israelis and Palestinians on the ground,
in their homes, over a meal, or a cup of coffee. Rather, the Americans had an
idea they thought would work—an intuitive idea in their own, culturally shaped
consciousness. This idea was then imposed upon Israelis and Palestinians,
and my long-term narrative data reveal the psychological challenge that this
imposition created for their lives.

The Americans I worked with were also consumed with a kind of *depoliti-cization* of Israeli–Palestinian relations—a move that I came to identify as a major problem and a source of great dissonance for the youth who participate in these efforts. These features of American intervention seemed to conspire to present an alternative value system to Palestinian and Israeli youth—a system in which the politics of group interests are set aside in favor of a common humanism. It did not take me long to see the problem with this contradiction for Israeli and Palestinian youth, whose lives are consumed with the politics of competing interests. Though alluring, the appeal to a common humanity is simply not resonant for Israeli and Palestinian youth, for such abstraction does not erase the concrete boundaries of their segregated lives and their polarized narratives.

In this book, I have attempted to illustrate how the social structure of con-flict is lived and embodied in the minds of youth. I used a comparative analysis of *master* and *personal* narratives as my window into the coconstitutive nature of culture and identity. The personal narratives of youth revealed processes of meaning making and accounts of intentional action in the midst of ongoing existential insecurity. Examining the narratives of youth over time and in rela-tion to intergroup contact, I came to see the inevitability of identity polarization in conflict. With this window into how lives in conflict appear to develop over time, I have come to believe strongly in the social-structural basis of psycho-logical development. That is, I no longer hold the idealism I once did for inter-group contact, even though I acknowledge that contact between diverse groups, in general, is likely to be associated with lower levels of prejudice over time (Pettigrew & Tropp, 2006).

The issue for me is not whether contact "works" to reduce prejudice. No doubt that it does so in many settings (but not all). Rather, the issue for me concerns the thoughtfulness and precision of social-psychological efforts to contribute to peacebuilding. That is, I think we need to be critical of our own practice as social psychologists, peace educators, and conflict resolution spe-cialists. Perhaps foremost, we need to be honest about what it is we hope our practice to achieve, and we need to be specific about how we envision those achievements contributing to peace. Then, of course, we need to actually study the extent to which our practice is contributing to the peace-building process. This cycle of *action research* articulated by Kurt Lewin (1946) long ago offers a model of how scientists and practitioners must work together to achieve social change.

Though I am reluctant to formulate some grand prescription for the practice of peace education, coexistence programs, or conflict resolution, I do want to end this book with a few concentrated reflections on the role of such interventions in the path to peace. First, I believe we must accept the reality that what is most needed, and what will ultimately bring a "domino effect" in the realm of human psychology, is a political settlement. This political settlement must aim for structural equality between Israelis and Palestinians. (I am not so naïve as to suggest that structural equality can ever fully be achieved in any society, so I would suggest that an *ethic* of equality would be minimally necessary.) The separation of groups must become an exception rather than a rule, for separation is the fertile breeding ground of the stereotypes that justify conflict (Allport, 1954). Finally, both groups must come to acknowledge the narrative of the other, to recognize that each group's collective memory is a document of both "fact" and "fiction," just as all historical narratives are. This kind of metacognition about history and narrative can only have broad resonance in the context of existential security, so I recognize that its attainability is highly dependent on the nature of a political settlement first and foremost. Absent these basic structural changes, though, attempts at individual or small-group intervention are destined to have a minimal impact on peacebuilding at best.

Is it possible, though, to fashion a kind of intervention that seeks to raise individual *awareness* of the structural basis of Israeli–Palestinian antagonism? In other words, might we who are not politicians or political scientists work with individuals to instill a critical awareness of the structural obstacles to peace? This, I believe, is the aim of the School for Peace model that has developed in Israel (Halabi & Sonnenschein, 2004a). And though I am not inclined to assume that this model holds the "key" for those of us who continue to want to work directly with individuals in conflict, even absent a political settlement, I think that the emergence of this model represents an important disruption in the models that have come before it and continue to be widely used—models that were imported from U.S. social science (Maoz, in press). What is usefully disruptive about this model is that it does not run from politics. It does not deny the structural reality of the conflict. Rather, it confronts individuals with the reality of their own complicity in maintaining a status quo. It refutes the notion of individuals as rational agents of their own collective destiny in favor of an approach that recognizes the individual mind as a slave to social structure.

Having suggested that this kind of model seems to present a compelling alternative to the coexistence model upon which U.S. programs are based, let me acknowledge that there is much empirical work to be done on this model. Though its foundations in social identity theory are based on a high degree of empirical rigor, the model in practice has been better theorized than empirically studied. My own work is evolving to take on the question of how young people respond differently to this kind of model for intergroup dialogue, compared to a conflict resolution approach modeled upon contact theory. But what is key is that this model has developed "on the ground" in Israel and has not been imposed from abroad, which represents a significant first step in enhancing the cultural relevance of such interventions.

Peril and Promise in Israeli and Palestinian Lives

To conclude this book, I want to suggest that the window I have offered into young Israeli and Palestinian lives reveals both the peril and the promise of young lives in conflict. Too often we have pathologized youth in conflict zones (Barber, 2009a), interpreting their lives through the lens of trauma. The stories of young Israelis and Palestinians presented in this book do reveal the challenges they face growing up in the midst of conflict—dealing with the threat of existential insecurity in particular—but they also reveal the way in which youth *use* narrative to make meaning of their lives and construct a possible future. Key to their ability to construct these narratives is a faith in community. This faith entails the internalization of a discourse that provides the individual with a sense of fidelity and credibility, a process Erik Erikson (1968) once eloquently theorized. A fundamental part of this discourse, I have suggested, is the larger historical narrative of the group. An affinity with this narrative naturally provides the security youth need to construct resilient life stories. A faith in the group redeems the narratives of youth from the contamination of conflict, for conflict is rooted in mutual existential denial and delegitimization (Bar-Tal, 1990a).

In spite of the promise that this basic process of human meaning making, social cohesion, and resilience holds for positive human development, I cannot deny that my fieldwork revealed the great injustice of conflict for youth. That young people must inhabit a developmental setting characterized by the uncertainty of life and the possibility of collective annihilation is deeply unsettling, particularly when the details of an ultimate political settlement are so well known and accepted by a majority of both Israelis and Palestinians. I think the point for those of us troubled by the injustice of this context is not simply, as Marx would suggest, to *understand* it. Rather, the point is also to try to *change* this unjust context.

My view takes us out of the comfortable place of armchair academic analysis to one of educated activism. In this effort, I do not see a contradiction between science and values, or between description and action. Rather, I see a role for the production of transformative knowledge (Sampson, 1993) that can be exploited for the service of peace and social justice, just as the knowledge of science has historically been exploited to justify subordination and hegemony (Prilelltensky, 1989). To this end, I cannot claim to have fully realized what this kind of social scientific activism looks like, only that I know it is a necessary response to the tyranny of injustice, a tyranny that conspires to defeat human perseverance. It is perhaps the rich ability to make meaning, even in settings of injustice, that defeats this kind of tyranny. If so, it is to the voices of subjects that we must turn to inform the potential activism of social science research.

References

Abdeen, Z., Qasrawi, R., Nabil, S., & Shaheen, M. (2008). Psychological reactions to Israeli occupation: Findings from the national study of school-based screening in Palestine. *International Journal of Behavioral Development, 32*, 290–297.

Abdel-Khalek, A. M. (2004). Neither altruistic suicide, nor terrorism but martyrdom: A Muslim perspective. *Archives of Suicide Research, 8*, 99–113.

Abdel-Nour, F. (2004). Responsibility and national memory: Israel and the Palestinian refugee problem. *International Journal of Politics, Culture and Society, 17*(3), 339–363.

Abunimah, A. (2007). *One country: A bold proposal to end the Israeli-Palestinian impasse.* New York: Holt.

Abu-Nimer, M. (1999). *Dialogue, conflict resolution, and change: Arab-Jewish encounters in Israel.* Albany, NY: State University of New York Press.

Abu-Saad, I. (2004). Separate and unequal: The role of the state educational system in maintaining the subordination of Israel's Palestinian Arab citizens. *Social Identities, 10*(1), 101–127.

Adams, D. W. (1995). *Education for extinction: American Indians and the boarding school experience, 1875–1928.* Lawrence, KS: University Press of Kansas.

Adams, G. R., & Marshall, S. K. (1996). A developmental social psychology of identity: Understanding the person-in-context. *Journal of Adolescence, 19*, 429–442.

Adorno, T. W., Frenkel-Brunswik, E., Levinson, D. J., & Sanford, R. N. (1950). *The authoritarian personality.* New York: Harper & Brothers.

Albeck, J. H., Adwan, S., & Bar On, D. (2002). Dialogue groups: TRT's guidelines for working through intractable conflicts by personal storytelling. *Peace and Conflict: Journal of Peace Psychology, 8*(4), 301–322.

Al-Haj, M. (2002). Multiculturalism in deeply divided societies: The Israeli case. *International Journal of Intercultural Relations, 26*, 169–183.

Allen, L. (2006). The polyvalent politics of martyr commemorations in the Palestinian intifada. *History & Memory, 18*(2), 107–138.

Allport, G. W. (1924). The study of the undivided personality. *Journal of Abnormal Psychology and Social Psychology, 19*(2), 132–141.

Allport, G. W. (1937). *Personality: A psychological introduction.* New York: Holt.

Allport, G. W. (1954). *The nature of prejudice.* Reading, MA: Addison-Wesley.

Allport, G. W. (1961). Prejudice: Is it societal or personal? *Journal of Social Issues, 18*(2), 120–134.

Allport, G. W. (1962). The general and the unique in psychological science. *Journal of Personality, 30*(3), 405–422.

Allport, G. W. (1965). *Letters from Jenny.* San Diego, CA: Harcourt Brace Jovanovich.

Almog, O. (2000). *The Sabra: The creation of the new Jew* (H. Watzman, Trans.). Berkeley, CA: University of California Press.

Althusser, L. (1971). Ideology and ideological state apparatus: Notes towards an investigation. In *Lenin and philosophy and other essays* (pp. 85–126). New York: Monthly Review Press.

Amir, Y. (1969). Contact hypothesis in ethnic relations. *Psychological Bulletin, 71*(5), 319–342.

Amir, Y., Ben-Ari, R., Bizman, A., & Rivner, M. (1982). Objective versus subjective aspects of interpersonal relations between Jews and Arabs. *Journal of Conflict Resolution, 26*(3), 485–506.

Amir, Y., Bizman, A., Ben-Ari, R., & Rivner, M. (1980). Contact between Israelis and Arabs: A theoretical evaluation of effects. *Journal of Cross-Cultural Psychology, 11*(4), 426–443.

Anderson, B. (1983). *Imagined communities: Reflections on the origin and spread of nationalism.* New York: Verso.

Antonius, G. (1965). *The Arab awakening: The story of the Arab national movement.* New York: Capricorn. (Original work published 1938)

Aoudé, I. G. (2001). Maintaining culture, reclaiming identity: Palestinian lives in the diaspora. *Asian Studies Review, 25*(2), 153–167.

Appiah, K. A. (2005). *The ethics of identity.* Princeton, NJ: Princeton University Press.

Appiah, K. A. (2006). *Cosmopolitanism: Ethics in a world of strangers.* New York: Norton.

Arafat, Y. (2001). Address to the UN General Assembly (November 13, 1974) (E. W. Said, Trans.). In W. Laqueur & B. Rubin (Eds.), *The Israel-Arab reader* (6th revised ed., pp. 171–182). New York: Penguin. (Original work published 1974)

Arendt, H. (1973). *The origins of totalitarianism.* New York: Harvest.

Arnett, J. J. (2002). The psychology of globalization. *American Psychologist, 57*, 774–783.

Arnett, J. J. (2008). The neglected 95%: Why American psychology needs to become less American. *American Psychologist, 63*(7), 602–614.

Aron, A., Aron, E. N., Tudor, M., & Nelson, G. (1991). Close relationships as including other in the self. *Journal of Personality and Social Psychology, 60*(2), 241–253.

Avgar, A., Bronfenbrenner, U., & Henderson, C.R. (1977). Socialization practices of parents, teachers, and peers in Israel: Kibbutz, moshav, and city. *Child Development, 48*(4), 1219–1227.

Awwad, E. (2004). Broken lives: Loss and trauma in Palestinian-Israeli relations. *International Journal of Politics, Culture and Society, 17*(3), 405–414.

Baker, A., & Shalhoub-Kevorkian, N. (1999). Effects of political and military traumas on children: The Palestinian case. *Clinical Psychology Review, 19,* 935–950.

Bandura, A. (1997). *Self-efficacy: The exercise of control.* New York: Worth.

Barber, B. K. (1999a). Political violence, family relations, and Palestinian youth functioning. *Journal of Adolescent Research, 14,* 206–230.

Barber, B. K. (1999b). Youth experience in the Palestinian intifada: A case study in intensity, complexity, paradox, and competence. In M. Yates & J. Youniss (Eds.), *Roots of civic identity: International perspectives on community service and activism in youth* (pp. 178–204). New York: Cambridge University Press.

Barber, B. K. (2001). Political violence, social integration, and youth functioning: Palestinian youth from the Intifada. *Journal of Community Psychology, 29,* 259–280.

Barber, B. K. (2008). Contrasting portraits of war: Youths' varied experiences with political violence in Bosnia and Palestine. *International Journal of Behavioral Development, 32,* 298–309.

Barber, B. K. (2009a). Glimpsing the complexity of youth and political violence. In B. K. Barber (Ed.), *Adolescents and war: How youth deal with political violence* (pp. 3–32). New York: Oxford University Press.

Barber, B. K. (2009b). Making sense and no sense of war: Issues of identity and meaning in adolescents' experience with political conflict. In B. K. Barber (Ed.), *Adolescents and war: How youth deal with political violence* (pp. 281–311). New York: Oxford University Press.

Barber, B. K., Schluterman, J., Denny, E. S., & McCouch, R. J. (2006). Adolescents and political violence. In M. Fitzduff & C. Stout (Eds.), *The psychology of resolving global conflicts: From war to peace: Vol. 2: Group and social factors* (pp. 171–190). Westport, CT: Praeger Security International.

Bargal, D. (1990). Contact is not enough—The contribution of Lewinian theory to inter-group workshops involving Palestinian and Jewish youth in Israel. *International Journal of Group Tensions, 20,* 179–192.

Bargal, D. (2008). Group processes to reduce intergroup conflict: An additional example of a workshop for Arab and Jewish youth. *Small Group Research, 39*(1), 42–59.

Bargal, D., & Bar, H. (1992). A Lewinian approach to intergroup workshops for Arab-Palestinian and Jewish youth. *Journal of Social Issues, 48*(2), 139–154.

Bar-Gal, Y. (1993). Boundaries as a topic in geographic education. *Political Geography, 12*(5), 421–435.

Bar-Gal, Y. (1994). The image of the "Palestinian" in geography textbooks in Israel. *Journal of Geography, 93*(5), 224–232.

Bar-On, D. (2006). *Tell your life story: Creating dialogue among Jews and Germans, Israelis and Palestinians.* New York: Central European University Press.

Bar-On, D., & Kassem, F. (2004). Storytelling as a way to work through intractable conflicts: The German-Jewish experience and its relevance to the Palestinian-Israeli context. *Journal of Social Issues, 60*(2), 289–306.

Bar-Tal, D. (1989). Delegitimization: The extreme case of stereotyping and prejudice. In D. Bar-Tal, C. Graumann, A. W. Kruglanski, & W. Stroebe (Eds.), *Stereotyping and prejudice: Changing conceptions* (pp. 169–188). New York: Springer-Verlag.

Bar-Tal, D. (1990a). Causes and consequences of delegitimization: Models of conflict and ethnocentrism. *Journal of Social Issues, 46*(1), 65–81.

Bar-Tal, D. (1990b). Israeli-Palestinian conflict: A cognitive analysis. *International Journal of Intercultural Relations, 14,* 7–29.

Bar-Tal, D. (1993). Patriotism as fundamental beliefs of group members. *Politics and the Individual, 3*(2), 45–62.

Bar-Tal, D. (1996). Development of social categories and stereotypes in early childhood: The case of "the Arab" concept formation, stereotype and attitudes by Jewish children in Israel. *International Journal of Intercultural Relations, 20,* 341–370.

Bar-Tal, D. (1998a). The rocky road toward peace: Beliefs on conflict in Israeli textbooks. *Journal of Peace Research, 35*(6), 723–742.

Bar-Tal, D. (1998b). Societal beliefs in times of intractable conflict: The Israeli case. *International Journal of Conflict Management, 9*(1), 22–50.

Bar-Tal, D. (2000). *Shared beliefs in a society: Social psychological analysis.* Thousand Oaks, CA: Sage.

Bar-Tal, D. (2001). Why does fear override hope in societies engulfed by intractable conflict, as it does in the Israeli society? *Political Psychology, 22*(3), 601–627.

Bar-Tal, D. (2004a). Nature, rationale, and effectiveness of education for coexistence. *Journal of Social Issues, 60*(2), 253–272.

Bar-Tal, D. (2004b). The necessity of observing real life situations: Palestinian-Israeli violence as a laboratory for learning about social behaviour. *European Journal of Social Psychology, 34,* 677–701.

Bar-Tal, D. (2007). Sociopsychological foundations of intractable conflicts. *American Behavioral Scientist, 50*(11), 1430–1453.

Bar-Tal, D., & Antebi, D. (1992a). Beliefs about negative intentions of the world: A study of the Israeli siege mentality. *Political Psychology, 13*(4), 633–645.

Bar-Tal, D., & Antebi, D. (1992b). Siege mentality in Israel. *International Journal of Intercultural Relations, 16*(3), 251–275.

Bar-Tal, D., Halperin, E., & de Rivera, J. (2007). Collective emotions in conflict situations: Societal implications. *Journal of Social Issues, 63*(2), 441–460.

Bar-Tal, D., & Labin, D. (2001). The effect of a major event on stereotyping: Terrorist attacks in Israel and Israeli adolescents' perceptions of Palestinians, Jordanians and Arabs. *European Journal of Social Psychology, 31,* 265–280.

Bar-Tal, D., Raviv, A., Raviv, A., & Dgani-Hirsh, A. (2009). The influence of the ethos of conflict on Israeli Jews' interpretation of Jewish-Palestinian encounters. *Journal of Conflict Resolution, 53*(1), 94–118.

Bar-Tal, D., & Teichman, Y. (2005). *Stereotypes and prejudice in conflict: Representations of Arabs in Israeli Jewish society.* New York: Cambridge University Press.

Batson, C. D., Polycarpou, M. P., Harmon-Jones, E., Imhoff, H. J., Mitchener, E. C., Bednar, L. L., et al. (1997). Empathy and attitudes: Can feeling for a member of a stigmatized group improve feelings toward the group? *Journal of Personality and Social Psychology, 72*(1), 105–118.

Battin, M. P. (2004). The ethics of self-sacrifice: What's wrong with suicide bombing? *Archives of Suicide Research, 8,* 29–36.

Baumeister, R. F. (1987). How the self became a problem: A psychological review of historical research. *Journal of Personality and Social Psychology, 52*(1), 163–176.

Baumeister, R. F., & Leary, M. R. (1995). The need to belong: Desire for interpersonal attachments as a fundamental human motivation. *Psychological Bulletin, 117*(3), 497–529.

Bekerman, Z. (2001). Constructivist perspectives on language, identity, and culture: Implications for Jewish identity and the education of Jews. *Religious Education, 96*(4), 462–473.

Bekerman, Z. (2002). The discourse of nation and culture: Its impact on Palestinian-Jewish encounters in Israel. *International Journal of Intercultural Relations, 26,* 409–427.

Bekerman, Z. (2005). Are there children to educate for peace in conflict-ridden areas? A critical essay on peace and coexistence education. *Intercultural Education, 16*(3), 235–245.

Bekerman, Z. (2007). Rethinking intergroup encounters: Rescuing praxis from theory, activity from education, and peace/co-existence from identity and culture. *Journal of Peace Education, 4*(1), 21–37.

Bekerman, Z. (2009a). The complexities of teaching historical conflictual narratives in integrated Palestinian-Jewish schools in Israel. *International Review of Education, 55,* 235–250.

Bekerman, Z. (2009b). Identity versus peace: Identity wins. *Harvard Educational Review, 79*(1), 74–83.

Bekerman, Z. (2009c). Identity work in Palestinian-Jewish intergroup encounters: A cultural rhetorical analysis. *Journal of Multicultural Discourses, 4*(2), 205–219.

Bekerman, Z., & Horenczyk, G. (2004). Arab-Jewish bilingual coeducation in Israel: A long-term approach to intergroup conflict resolution. *Journal of Social Issues, 60*(2), 389–404.

Bekerman, Z., & Maoz, I. (2005). Troubles with identity: Obstacles to coexistence education in conflict ridden societies. *Identity: An International Journal of Theory and Research, 5*(4), 341–358.

Bekerman, Z., & Silverman, M. (2003). The corruption of culture and education by the nation state: The case of liberal Jews' discourse on Jewish continuity. *Journal of Modern Jewish Studies, 2*(1), 19–34.

Bekerman, Z., Zembylas, M., & McGlynn, C. (2009). Working toward the de-essentialization of identity categories in conflict and postconflict societies: Israel, Cyprus, and Northern Ireland. *Comparative Education Review, 53*(2), 213–234.

Bellah, R. N., Madsen, R., Sullivan, W. M., Swidler, A., & Tipton, S. M. (1985). *Habits of the heart: Individualism and commitment in American life.* Berkeley, CA: University of California Press.

Bem, D. J. (1983). Constructing a theory of the triple typology: Some (second) thoughts on nomothetic and idiographic approaches to personality. *Journal of Personality, 51*(3), 566–577.

Ben-Ari, E. (1998). *Mastering soldiers: Conflict, emotions, and the enemy in an Israeli military unit.* New York: Berghahn Books.

Benedict, R. (1934). *Patterns of culture.* Boston: Houghton Mifflin.

Benedict, R. (1946). *The chrysanthemum and the sword: Patterns of Japanese culture.* Boston: Houghton Mifflin.

Ben-Yehuda, N. (1995). *The Masada myth: Collective memory and mythmaking in Israel.* Madison, WI: University of Wisconsin Press.

Bilge, B., & Kaufman, G. (1983). Children of divorce and one-parent families: Cross-cultural perspectives. *Family Relations: Journal of Applied Family and Child Studies, 32*(1), 59–71.

Blumer, H. (1969). *Symbolic interactionism: Perspective and method.* Berkeley, CA: University of California Press.

Boas, F. (1928). *Anthropology and modern life.* New York: Norton.

Bodemann, Y. M. (1978). A problem of sociological praxis: The case for interventive observation in field work. *Theory and Society, 5*(3), 387–420.

Bourdieu, P. (1984). *Distinction: A social critique of the judgment of taste.* Cambridge, MA: Harvard University Press.

Brawer, A. Y. (1936). *Our homeland.* Tel Aviv, Israel: Dvir. (in Hebrew)

Brewer, M. B. (1991). The social self: On being the same and different at the same time. *Personality and Social Psychology Bulletin, 17*(5), 475–482.

Brewer, M. B. (1996). When contact is not enough: Social identity and intergroup cooperation. *International Journal of Intercultural Relations, 20,* 291–303.

Brewer, M. B. (2001). The many faces of social identity: Implications for political psychology. *Political Psychology, 22*(1), 115–125.

Brewer, M. B., & Miller, N. (1984). Beyond the contact hypothesis: Theoretical perspectives on desegregation. In N. Miller & M. B. Brewer (Eds.), *Groups in contact: The psychology of desegregation* (pp. 281–302). Orlando, FL: Academic Press.

Brewer, M. B., & Silver, M. D. (2000). Group distinctiveness, social identification, and collective mobilization. In S. Stryker, T. J. Owens & R. W. White (Eds.), *Self, identity, and social movements* (pp. 153–171). Minneapolis, MN: University of Minnesota Press.

Brockmeier, J. (2002). Remembering and forgetting: Narrative as cultural memory. *Culture & Psychology, 8*(1), 15–43.

Bronfenbrenner, U. (1979). *The ecology of human development: Experiments by nature and design.* Cambridge, MA: Harvard University Press.

Bruner, J. (1986). *Actual minds, possible worlds.* Cambridge, MA: Harvard University Press.

Bruner, J. (1990). *Acts of meaning.* Cambridge, MA: Harvard University Press.

Brydon-Miller, M. (1997). Participatory action research: Psychology and social change. *Journal of Social Issues, 53*(4), 657–666.

Bucaille, L. (2004). *Growing up Palestinian: Israeli occupation and the* Intifada *generation* (A. Roberts, Trans.). Princeton, NJ: Princeton University Press.

Burman, E. (1997). Minding the gap: Positivism, psychology, and the politics of qualitative methods. *Journal of Social Issues, 53*(4), 785–801.

Burton, J. W. (1988). Conflict resolution as a function of human needs. In R. A. Coate & J. A. Rosati (Eds.), *The power of human needs in world society* (pp. 187–204). Boulder, CO: Lynne-Rienner.

Burton, J. W. (Ed.). (1990a). *Conflict: Human needs theory.* New York: Palgrave Macmillan.

Burton, J. W. (1990b). *Conflict: Resolution and prevention.* New York: St. Martin's Press.

Canetti-Nisim, D., Ariely, G., & Halperin, E. (2008). Life, pocketbook, or culture: The role of perceived security threats in promoting exclusionist political attitudes toward minorities in Israel. *Political Research Quarterly, 61*(1), 90–103.

Caplan, N. (1999). Victimhood and identity: Psychological obstacles to Israeli reconciliation with the Palestinians. In K. Abdel-Malek & D. C. Jacobson (Eds.), *Israeli and Palestinian identities in history and literature* (pp. 63–86). New York: St. Martin's Press.

Cassaniti, J. (2006). Toward a cultural psychology of impermanence in Thailand. *Ethos, 34*(1), 58–88.

Césaire, A. (1972). *Discourse on colonialism* (J. Pinkham, Trans.). New York: Monthly Review Press. (Original work published 1955)

Charmaz, K. (2006). *Constructing grounded theory: A practical guide through qualitative analysis.* Thousand Oaks, CA: Sage.

Christie, D. J. (1997). Reducing direct and structural violence: The Human Needs Theory. *Peace and Conflict: Journal of Peace Psychology, 3*(4), 315–332.

Christison, K. (2001). *The wound of dispossession: Telling the Palestinian story.* Santa Fe, NM: Sunlit Hills Press.

Cohen, E. (1995). Israel as a post-Zionist society. In R. Wistrich & D. Ohana (Eds.), *The shaping of Israeli identity: Myth, memory and trauma* (pp. 203–214). London: Frank Cass.

Cohen, S. P., Kelman, H. C., Miller, F. D., & Smith, B. L. (1977). Evolving intergroup techniques for conflict resolution: An Israeli-Palestinian pilot workshop. *Journal of Social Issues, 33*(1), 165–189.

Cohler, B. J. (1982). Personal narrative and life course. In P. Baltes & O. G. Brim (Eds.), *Life span development and behavior* (Vol. 4, pp. 205–241). New York: Academic Press.

Cohler, B. J. (2007). *Writing desire: Sixty years of gay autobiography*. Madison, WI: University of Wisconsin Press.

Cole, M. (1996). *Cultural psychology: A once and future discipline*. Cambridge, MA: Harvard University Press.

Collins, J. (2004). *Occupied by memory: The* intifada *generation and the Palestinian state of emergency*. New York: New York University Press.

Connolly, P. (2000). What now for the contact hypothesis? Towards a new research agenda. *Race, Ethnicity and Education, 3*(2), 169–193.

Cooley, C. H. (1902). *Human nature and the social order*. New York: Scribners.

Cressey, P. G. (1983). A comparison of the roles of the "sociological stranger" and the "anonymous stranger" in field research. *Urban Life, 12*(1), 102–120. (Original work published 1927)

Dannefer, D. (1984). Adult development and social theory: A paradigmatic reappraisal. *American Sociological Review, 49*, 100–116.

Danziger, K. (1990). *Constructing the subject: Historical origins of psychological research*. New York: Cambridge University Press.

David, E. J. R. (2008). A colonial mentality model of depression for Filipino Americans. *Cultural Diversity and Ethnic Minority Psychology, 14*(2), 118–127.

David, E. J. R., & Okazaki, S. (2006). Colonial mentality: A review and recommendation for Filipino American psychology. *Cultural Diversity and Ethnic Minority Psychology, 12*(1), 1–16.

Dershowitz, A. (2003). *The case for Israel*. New York: Wiley.

DeTurk, S. (2001). Intercultural empathy: Myth, competency, or possibility for alliance building. *Communication Education, 50*(4), 374–384.

Deutsch, M. (1973). *The resolution of conflict: Constructive and destructive processes*. New Haven, CT: Yale University Press.

Deutsch, M. (1977). Recurrent themes in the study of social conflict. *Journal of Social Issues, 33*(1), 222–225.

Deutsch, M. (2002). Social psychology's contributions to the study of conflict resolution. *Negotiation Journal*, 307–320.

Deutsch, M., & Coleman, P. T. (Eds.). (2000). *The handbook of conflict resolution: Theory and practice*. San Francisco: Jossey-Bass.

Dilthey, W. (1976). The development of hermeneutics (H. Rickman, Trans.). In H. Rickman (Ed.), *W. Dilthey: Selected writings* (pp. 246–263). Cambridge, England: Cambridge University Press. (Original work published 1900)

Dilthey, W. (1988). *Introduction to the human sciences: An attempt to lay a foundation for the study of society and history* (R. J. Betanzos, Trans.). Detroit, MI: Wayne State University Press. (Original work published 1923)

Dixon, J., Durrheim, K., & Tredoux, C. (2005). Beyond the optimal contact strategy: A reality check for the contact hypothesis. *American Psychologist, 60*(7), 697–711.

Dor, D. (2003). All the news that fits: The Israeli media and the second intifada. *Palestine-Israel Journal of Politics, Economics, and Culture, 10*(2), 27–32.

Durkheim, E. (1982). *The rules of sociological method*. New York: Free Press. (Original work published 1895)

Eagleton, T. (2000). *The idea of culture*. Malden, MA: Blackwell.

Eccles, J. S. (2004). Schools, academic motivation, and stage-environment fit. In R. M. Lerner & L. Steinberg (Eds.), *Handbook of adolescent psychology* (2nd ed., pp. 125–153). Hoboken, NJ: Wiley.

Elbedour, S. (1998). Youth in crisis: The well-being of Middle Eastern youth and adolescents during war and peace. *Journal of Youth and Adolescence, 27*, 539–556.

Elbedour, S., Bastien, D. T., & Center, B. A. (1997). Identity formation in the shadow of conflict: Projective drawings by Palestinian and Israeli Arab children from the West Bank and Gaza. *Journal of Peace Research, 34*(2), 217–231.

Elbedour, S., Ten Bensel, R., & Maruyama, G. M. (1993). Children at risk: Psychological coping with war and conflict in the Middle East. *International Journal of Mental Health, 22*(3), 33–52.

Elrazik, A. A., Amin, R., & Davis, U. (1978). Problems of Palestinians in Israel: Land, work, education. *Journal of Palestine Studies, 7*(3), 31–54.

Emery, R. E. (1988). *Marriage, divorce, and children's adjustment*. Thousand Oaks, CA: Sage.

Engstrom, C. (2009). Promoting peace, yet sustaining conflict? A fantasy-theme analysis of Seeds of Peace publications. *Journal of Peace Education, 6*(1), 19–35.

Eqeiq, A. (2002, May). *Post-traumatic identity: The case of the Arab-Palestinian minority in Israel*. Paper presented at the Seventh International Cultural Studies Symposium, Izmir, Turkey.

Erikson, E. H. (1958). *Young man Luther: A study in psychoanalysis and history*. New York: Norton.

Erikson, E. H. (1959). *Identity and the life cycle*. New York: Norton.

Erikson, E. H. (1963). *Childhood and society* (2nd ed.). New York: Norton.

Erikson, E. H. (1968). *Identity: Youth and crisis*. New York: Norton.

Esposito, J. (Ed.). (1997). *Political Islam: Revolution, radicalism, or reform*. New York: Lynne Rienner.

Evans-Pritchard, E. E. (1976). *Witchcraft, oracles, and magic among the Azande*. New York: Oxford University Press. (Original work published 1937)

Fanon, F. (1967). *Black skin, white masks* (C. L. Markmann, Trans.). New York: Grove. (Original work published 1952)

Fanon, F. (2004). *The wretched of the earth* (R. Philcox, Trans.). New York: Grove. (Original work published 1961)

Fatah (2001). The seven points. In W. Laqueur & B. Rubin (Eds.), *The Israel-Arab reader* (6th revised ed., pp. 130–131). New York: Penguin. (Original work published 1969)

Feagin, J. R. (2001). *Racist America: Roots, current realities and future reparations*. New York: Routledge.

Feldman, J. (2008). *Above the death pits, beneath the flag: Youth voyages to Poland and the performance of Israeli national identity*. New York: Bergahn Books.

Fine, M., & Sirin, S. R. (2007). Theorizing hyphenated selves: Researching youth development in and across contentious political contexts. *Social and Personality Psychology Compass, 1*(1), 16–38.

Fine, M., & Weis, L. (1998). *The unknown city: Lives of poor and working-class young adults.* Boston: Beacon.

Finkelstein, N. G. (2003). *Image and reality of the Israel-Palestine conflict* (2nd ed.). New York: Verso.

Foucault, M. (1972). *The archeology of knowledge and the discourse on language* (A. M. S. Smith, Trans.). New York: Pantheon.

Foucault, M. (1978). *The history of sexuality. Volume 1: An introduction.* New York: Vintage.

Foucault, M. (1982). The subject and power. *Critical Inquiry, 8,* 777–795.

Fox, D., Prilleltensky, I., & Austin, S. (Eds.). (2009). *Critical psychology: An introduction* (2nd ed.). Thousand Oaks, CA: Sage.

Freire, P. (1970). *Pedagogy of the oppressed.* New York: Continuum.

Freud, S. (1959). *Group psychology and the analysis of the ego* (J. Strachey, Trans.). New York: Norton. (Original work published 1921)

Freud, S. (1962). *The ego and the id* (J. Strachey, Trans.). New York: Norton. (Original work published 1923)

Fukuda-Parr, S. (2004). Cultural freedom and human development today. *Daedalus, 133*(3), 37–45.

Gaertner, S. L., & Dovidio, J.F. (2000). *Reducing intergroup bias: The common ingroup identity model.* Philadelphia, PA: Psychology Press/Taylor & Francis.

Gaertner, S. L., Dovidio, J. F., Anastasio, P. A., Bachman, B. A., & Rust, M. C. (1993). The common ingroup identity model: Recategorization and the reduction of intergroup bias. *European Review of Social Psychology, 4,* 1–26.

Gaertner, S. L., Dovidio, J. F., & Bachman, B. A. (1996). Revisiting the contact hypothesis: The induction of a common ingroup identity. *International Journal of Intercultural Relations, 20,* 271–290.

Gaertner, S. L., Dovidio, J. F., Banker, B. S., Houlette, M., Johnson, K. M., & McGlynn, E. A. (2000). Reducing intergroup conflict: From superordinate goals to decategorization, recategorization, and mutual differentiation. *Group Dynamics: Theory, Research, and Practice, 4*(1), 98–114.

Gaertner, S. L., Dovidio, J. F., Nier, J. A., Ward, C. M., & Banker, B. S. (1999). Across cultural divides: The value of superordinate identity. In D. A. Prentice & D. T. Miller (Eds.), *Cultural divides: Understanding and overcoming group conflict* (pp. 173–212). New York: Russell Sage Foundation.

Gaertner, S. L., Rust, M. C., Dovidio, J. F., & Bachman, B. A. (1996). The contact hypothesis: The role of a common ingroup identity on reducing intergroup bias among majority and minority group members. In J. L. Nye & A. M. Brower (Eds.), *What's social about social cognition? Research on socially shared cognition in small groups* (pp. 230–260). Thousand Oaks, CA: Sage.

Galinsky, A. D., & Moskowitz, G. B. (2000). Perspective-taking: Decreasing stereotype expression, stereotype accessibility, and in-group favoritism. *Journal of Personality and Social Psychology, 78*(4), 708–724.

Galston, W. A. (2002). *Liberal pluralism: The implications of value pluralism for political theory and practice.* New York: Cambridge University Press.

Galton, F. (2004). *Essays in eugenics.* Honolulu, HI: University Press of the Pacific. (Original work published 1909)

Galtung, J. (1969). Violence, peace, and peace research. *Journal of Peace Research, 6*(3), 167–191.

Galtung, J. (1971). A structural theory of imperialism. *Journal of Peace Research, 8*(2), 81–117.

Galtung, J. (1990). Cultural violence. *Journal of Peace Research, 27*(3), 291–305.

Gamson, W. A., & Herzog, H. (1999). Living with contradictions: The taken-for-granted in Israeli political discourse. *Political Psychology, 20*(2), 247–266.

Garbarino, J., & Kostelny, K. (1996). The effects of political violence on Palestinian children's behavior problems: A risk accumulation model. *Child Development, 67*, 33–45.

Geertz, C. (1963). The integrative revolution: Primordial sentiments and civil politics in the new states. In C. Geertz (Ed.), *Old societies and new states* (pp. 105–157). New York: Free Press.

Geertz, C. (1973). *The interpretation of cultures.* New York: Basic Books.

Gergen, K. J. (1973). Social psychology as history. *Journal of Personality and Social Psychology, 26*(2), 309–320.

Gergen, K. J. (1994). *Realities and relationships: Soundings in social construction.* Cambridge, MA: Harvard University Press.

Gergen, K., & Gergen, M. (1983). Narratives of the self. In T. Sarbin & K. E. Scheibe (Eds.), *Studies in social identity* (pp. 245–273). New York: Praeger.

Ghanem, A. (2002). The Palestinians in Israel: Political orientation and aspirations. *International Journal of Intercultural Relations, 26*, 135–152.

Ghanem, A., & Rouhana, N. N. (2001). Citizenship and the parliamentary politics of minorities in ethnic states: The Palestinian citizens of Israel. *Nationalism and Ethnic Politics, 7*(4), 66–86.

Giacaman, R., Abu-Rmeileh, N. M. E., Husseini, A., Saab, H., & Boyce, W. (2007). Humiliation: The invisible trauma of war for Palestinian youth. *Public Health, 121*, 563–571.

Giddens, A. (1991). *Modernity and self-identity: Self and society in the late modern age.* Stanford, CA: Stanford University Press.

Giele, J. Z., & Elder, G. H. (Eds.). (1998). *Methods of life course research: Qualitative and quantitative approaches.* Thousand Oaks, CA: Sage.

Gilroy, P. (2000). *Against race: Imagining political culture beyond the color line.* Cambridge, MA: Belknap.

Gjerde, P. F. (2004). Culture, power, and experience: Toward a person-centered cultural psychology. *Human Development, 47*, 138–157.

Glaser, B. G., & Strauss, A. L. (1967). *The discovery of grounded theory: Strategies for qualitative research.* Chicago: Aldine.

Glazier, J. A. (2003). Developing cultural fluency: Arab and Jewish students engaging in one another's company. *Harvard Educational Review, 73*(2), 141–163.

Goffman, E. (1959). *The presentation of self in everyday life.* Garden City, NY: Doubleday Anchor.

Goffman, E. (1961). *Asylums: Essays on the social situation of mental patients and other inmates.* Garden City, NY: Anchor.

Goffman, E. (1963). *Stigma: Notes on the management of spoiled identity.* New York: Simon & Schuster.

Goffman, E. (1967). *Interaction ritual: Essays on face-to-face behavior.* New York: Pantheon.

Golan, G. (1997). Militarization and gender: The Israeli experience. *Women's Studies International Forum, 20,* 581–586.

Golash-Boza, T. (2006). Dropping the hyphen? Becoming Latino(a)-American through racialized assimilation. *Social Forces, 85*(1), 27–55.

Golda Meir scorns Soviets: Israeli premier explains stand on Big-4 talks, security. (1969, June 16). *Washington Post,* p. A1.

Gordon, N. (2008a). From colonization to separation: Exploring the structure of Israel's occupation. *Third World Quarterly, 29*(1), 25–44.

Gordon, N. (2008b). *Israel's occupation.* Berkeley, CA: University of California Press.

Gregg, G. S. (2005). *The Middle East: A cultural psychology.* New York: Oxford University Press.

Gregg, G. S. (2007). *Culture and identity in a Muslim society.* New York: Oxford University Press.

Grossman, D. (2003). *Death as a way of life: Israel ten years after Oslo* (H. Watzman, Trans.). New York: Farrar, Straus, and Giroux.

Gutierrez, K. D., & Rogoff, B. (2003). Cultural ways of learning: Individual traits or repertoires of practice. *Educational Researcher, 32*(5), 19–25.

Haj-Yahia, M. M. (2008). Political violence in retrospect: Its effect on the mental health of Palestinian adolescents. *International Journal of Behavioral Development, 32,* 283–289.

Halabi, R., & Sonnenschein, N. (2004a). Awareness, identity, and reality: The School for Peace approach (D. Reich, Trans.). In R. Halabi (Ed.), *Israeli and Palestinian identities in dialogue: The School for Peace approach* (pp. 47–58). New Brunswick, NJ: Rutgers University Press.

Halabi, R., & Sonnenschein, N. (2004b). The Jewish-Palestinian encounter in a time of crisis. *Journal of Social Issues, 60*(2), 373–388.

Hall, S. (1996). Introduction: Who needs "identity"? In S. Hall & P. du Gay (Eds.), *Questions of cultural identity* (pp. 1–17). Thousand Oaks, CA: Sage.

Halperin, E. (2008). Group-based hatred in intractable conflict in Israel. *Journal of Conflict Resolution, 52*(5), 713–736.

Halperin, E., Bar-Tal, D., Nets-Zehngut, R., & Drori, E. (2008). Emotions in conflict: Correlates of fear and hope in the Israeli-Jewish society. *Peace and Conflict: Journal of Peace Psychology, 14*(3), 233–258.

Halperin, E., Bar-Tal, D., Sharvit, K., Rosler, N., & Raviv, A. (2010). Socio-psychological implications for an occupying society: The case of Israel. *Journal of Peace Research, 47*(1), 59–70.

Halperin, E., Canetti-Nisim, D., & Hirsch-Hoefler, S. (2009). The central role of group-based hatred as an emotional antecedent of political intolerance: Evidence from Israel. *Political Psychology, 30*(1), 93–123.

Halpern, D. (1969). *The idea of the Jewish state* (2nd ed.). Cambridge, MA: Harvard University Press.

Hamas (2001). Charter. In W. Laqueur & B. Rubin (Eds.), *The Israel-Arab reader* (6th ed., pp. 341–348). New York: Penguin. (Original work published 1988)

Hammack, P. L. (2006). Identity, conflict, and coexistence: Life stories of Israeli and Palestinian adolescents. *Journal of Adolescent Research, 21*(4), 323–369.

Hammack, P. L. (2008). Narrative and the cultural psychology of identity. *Personality and Social Psychology Review, 12*(3), 222–247.

Hammack, P. L. (2009). The cultural psychology of American-based coexistence programs for Israeli and Palestinian youth. In C. McGlynn, M. Zembylas, Z. Bekerman, & T. Gallagher (Eds.), *Peace education in conflict and post-conflict societies: Comparative perspectives* (pp. 127–144). New York: Palgrave Macmillan.

Hammack, P. L. (2010). Narrating hyphenated selves: Intergroup contact and configurations of identity among young Palestinian citizens of Israel. *International Journal of Intercultural Relations, 34*(4), 368–385.

Hammack, P. L., & Cohler, B. J. (2009). Narrative engagement and sexual identity: An interdisciplinary approach to the study of sexual lives. In P. L. Hammack & B. J. Cohler (Eds.), *The story of sexual identity: Narrative perspectives on the gay and lesbian life course* (pp. 3–22). New York: Oxford University Press.

Hammack, P. L., Richards, M. H., Luo, Z., Edlynn, E. S., & Roy, K. (2004). Social support factors as moderators of community violence exposure among inner-city African-American young adolescents. *Journal of Clinical Child and Adolescent Psychology, 33*(3), 450–462.

Hammack, P. L., Thompson, E. M., & Pilecki, A. (2009). Configurations of identity among sexual minority youth: Context, desire, and narrative. *Journal of Youth and Adolescence, 38*, 867–883.

Hands of Peace (2006). Retrieved from www.hands-of-peace.org on January 15, 2006.

Hareven, A. (2002). Towards the year 2030: Can a civil society shared by Jews and Arabs evolve in Israel? *International Journal of Intercultural Relations, 26*, 153–168.

Harkabi, Y. (2001). Fatah's doctrine. In W. Laqueur & B. Rubin (Eds.), *The Israel-Arab reader* (6th ed., pp. 121–130). New York: Penguin. (Original work published 1968)

Harré, R., & van Langenhove, L. (1999). Introducing positioning theory. In R. Harré & L. van Langenhove (Eds.), *Positioning theory: Moral contexts of intentional action* (pp. 14–31). Oxford, UK: Blackwell.

Haslam, N. (2006). Dehumanization: An integrative review. *Personality and Social Psychology Review, 10*(3), 252–264.

Haslam, N., Loughnan, S., Reynolds, C., & Wilson, S. (2007). Dehumanization: A new perspective. *Social and Personality Psychology Compass, 1*(1), 409–422.

Helman, S. (2002). Monologic results of dialogue: Jewish-Palestinian encounter groups as sites of essentialization. *Identities: Global Studies in Culture and Power, 9,* 327–354.

Herek, G. M. (2006). Legal recognition of same-sex relationships in the United States: A social science perspective. *American Psychologist, 61*(6), 607–621.

Herriot, P. (2007). *Religious fundamentalism and social identity.* New York: Routledge.

Herzl, T. (1997). The Jewish State. In A. Hertzberg (Ed.), *The Zionist idea: A historical analysis and reader* (pp. 204–226). Philadelphia: Jewish Publication Society. (Original work published 1896)

Hess, M. (1997). Rome and Jerusalem. In A. Hertzberg (Ed.), *The Zionist idea: A historical analysis and reader* (pp. 119–139). Philadelphia: Jewish Publication Society. (Original work published 1862)

Hewstone, M., & Brown, R. (1986). Contact is not enough: An intergroup perspective on the "contact hypothesis." In M. Hewstone & R. Brown (Eds.), *Contact and conflict in intergroup encounters* (pp. 1–44). New York: Basil Blackwell.

Hobsbawm, E. J. (1990). *Nations and nationalism since 1780: Programme, myth, reality.* Cambridge, England: Cambridge University Press.

Hofman, J. E. (1970). The meaning of being a Jew in Israel: An analysis of ethnic identity. *Journal of Personality and Social Psychology, 15*(3), 196–202.

Holland, D., Lachicotte, W., Skinner, D., & Cain, C. (1998). *Identity and agency in cultural worlds.* Cambridge, MA: Harvard University Press.

Holland, D., & Quinn, N. (Eds.). (1987). *Cultural models in language and thought.* New York: Cambridge University Press.

Hollinger, D. A. (2006). *Postethnic America: Beyond multiculturalism* (Rev. ed.). New York: Basic Books.

Horenczyk, G., & Munayer, S. J. (2007). Acculturation orientations toward two majority groups: The case of Palestinian Arab Christian adolescents in Israel. *Journal of Cross-Cultural Psychology, 38*(1), 76–86.

Hornsey, M. J., & Hogg, M. A. (2000). Assimilation and diversity: An integrative model of subgroup relations. *Personality and Social Psychology Review, 4*(2), 143–156.

Hume, D. (2000). *A treatise of human nature.* New York: Oxford University Press. (Original work published 1739)

Hurtado, A. (1989). Relating to privilege: Seduction and rejection in the subordination of White women and women of Color. *Signs, 14*(4), 833–855.

Hurtado, A. (2003). *Voicing Chicana feminisms: Young women speak out on sexuality and identity.* New York: New York University Press.

Jacobson, D., & Bar-Tal, D. (1995). Structure of security beliefs among Israeli students. *Political Psychology, 16*(3), 567–590.

Jagodić, G. K. (2000). Is war a good or a bad thing? The attitudes of Croatian, Israeli, and Palestinian children toward war. *International Journal of Psychology, 35*(6), 241–257.

James, W. (1890). *The principles of psychology*. New York: Dover.

Jawad, S. A. (2006). The Arab and Palestinian narratives of the 1948 war. In R. I. Rotberg (Ed.), *Israeli and Palestinian narratives of conflict: History's double helix* (pp. 72–114). Bloomington, IN: Indiana University Press.

Josselson, R. (1996). *Revising herself: The story of women's identity from college to midlife*. New York: Oxford University Press.

Kaplan, D. (2006). *The men we loved: Male friendship and nationalism in Israeli culture*. New York: Berghahn Books.

Kashua, S. (2004). *Dancing Arabs* (M. Shlesinger, Trans.). New York: Grove.

Kelly, J. B. (2000). Children's adjustment in conflicted marriage and divorce: A decade review of research. *Journal of the American Academy of Child and Adolescent Psychiatry, 39*(8), 963–973.

Kelman, H. C. (1968). *A time to speak: On human values and social research*. San Francisco: Jossey-Bass.

Kelman, H. C. (1978). Israelis and Palestinians: Psychological prerequisites for mutual acceptance. *International Security, 3*(1), 162–186.

Kelman, H. C. (1982). Creating the conditions for Israeli-Palestinian negotiations. *Journal of Conflict Resolution, 26*(1), 39–75.

Kelman, H. C. (1993). Coalitions across conflict lines: The interplay of conflicts within and between the Israeli and Palestinian communities. In S. Worchel & J. A. Simpson (Eds.), *Conflict between people and groups: Causes, processes, and resolutions* (pp. 236–258). Chicago: Nelson-Hall.

Kelman, H. C. (1995). Contributions of an unofficial conflict resolution effort to the Israeli-Palestinian conflict. *Negotiation Journal, 11*, 19–27.

Kelman, H. C. (1997). Group processes in the resolution of international conflicts: Experiences from the Israeli-Palestinian case. *American Psychologist, 52*(3), 212–220.

Kelman, H. C. (1998). Israel in transition from Zionism to post-Zionism. *Annals of the American Academy of Political and Social Science, 555*, 46–61.

Kelman, H. C. (1999a). Building a sustainable peace: The limits of pragmatism in the Israeli-Palestinian negotiations. *Peace and Conflict: Journal of Peace Psychology, 5*(2), 101–115.

Kelman, H. C. (1999b). The interdependence of Israeli and Palestinian national identities: The role of the other in existential conflicts. *Journal of Social Issues, 55*, 581–600.

Kelman, H. C. (2007). The Israeli-Palestinian peace process and its vicissitudes: Insights from attitude theory. *American Psychologist, 62*(4), 287–303.

Kelman, H. C. (2008). Evaluating the contributions of interactive problem solving to the resolution of ethnonational conflicts. *Peace and Conflict: Journal of Peace Psychology, 14*(1), 29–60.

Kelman, H. C., & Cohen, S. P. (1976). The problem-solving workshop: A social-psychological contribution to the resolution of international conflicts. *Journal of Peace Research, 13*(2), 79–90.

Keniston, K. (1971). *Youth and dissent: The rise of a new opposition.* New York: Harcourt Brace Jovanovich.

Keniston, K. (1972). Youth: A "new" stage of life. In J. Cottle (Ed.), *The prospect of youth* (pp. 631–654). Boston: Little & Brown.

Khalidi, R. (1997). *Palestinian identity: The construction of modern national consciousness.* New York: Columbia University Press.

Kimmerling, B. (2001). *The invention and decline of Israeliness: State, society, and the military.* Berkeley, CA: University of California Press.

Kinnvall, C. (2004). Globalization and religious nationalism: Self, identity, and the search for ontological security. *Political Psychology, 25*(5), 741–767.

Kintz, B. L., Delprato, D. J., Mettee, D. R., Persons, C. E., & Schappe, R. H. (1965). The experimenter effect. *Psychological Bulletin, 63*(4), 223–232.

Kitayama, S., & Cohen, D. (Eds.). (2007). *Handbook of cultural psychology.* New York: Guilford.

Klein, M. (2004). Jerusalem without the East Jerusalemites: The Palestinian as the "other" in Jerusalem. *Journal of Israeli History, 23*(2), 174–199.

Kohlberg, L. (1976). Moral stages and moralization: The cognitive-development approach. In T. Lickona (Ed.), *Moral development and behavior: Theory, research and social issues* (pp. 31–53). New York: Holt, Rinehart & Winston.

Konefal, B. O. (2003). Defending the Pueblo: Indigenous identity and struggles for social justice in Guatemala, 1970 to 1980. *Social Justice, 30*(3), 32–47.

Lakin, M., Lomranz, J., & Lieberman, M. (1969). *Arabs and Jews in Israel: A case study in human relations training approach to conflict.* New York: American Academic Association for Peace in the Middle East.

Lamiell, J. T. (1981). Toward an idiothetic psychology of personality. *American Psychologist, 36*(3), 276–289.

Lamiell, J. T. (1998). "Nomothetic" and "idiographic": Contrasting Windelband's understanding with contemporary usage. *Theory & Psychology, 8*(1), 23–38.

Lamiell, J. T., Foss, M. A., Larsen, R. J., & Hempel, A. M. (1983). Studies in intuitive personology from an idiothetic point of view: Implications for personality theory. *Journal of Personality, 51*(3), 438–467.

Langhout, R. D. (2006). Where am I? Locating myself and its implications for collaborative research. *American Journal of Community Psychology, 37,* 267–274.

Larson, R. W. (2002). Globalization, societal change, and new technologies: What they mean for the future of adolescence. *Journal of Research on Adolescence, 12,* 1–30.

Lavee, Y., & Ben-David, A. (1993). Families under war: Stresses and strains of Israeli families during the Gulf War. *Journal of Traumatic Stress, 6*(2), 239–254.

Lavi, T., & Solomon, Z. (2005). Palestinian youth of the intifada: PTSD and future orientation. *Journal of the American Academy of Child and Adolescent Psychiatry, 44*(11), 1176–1183.

Lazarus, R. S., & Folkman, S. (1984). *Stress, appraisal, and coping.* New York: Springer.

Le Bon, G. (1969). *The crowd: A study of the popular mind.* New York: Ballantine. (Original work published 1895)

Leichtman, M. A. (2001). The differential construction of ethnicity: The case of Egyptian and Moroccan immigrants in Israel. *Identity: An International Journal of Theory and Research, 1*(3), 247–272.

Lemish, P. (2003). Civic and citizenship education in Israel. *Cambridge Journal of Education, 33*(1), 53–72.

Lévi-Strauss, C. (1962). *The savage mind.* Chicago: University of Chicago Press.

Lévi-Strauss, C. (1963). *Structural anthropology.* New York: Basic Books.

Lewin, K. (1946). Action research and minority problems. *Journal of Social Issues, 2*(4), 34–46.

Lewin, K. (1951). *Field theory in social science.* New York: Harper & Row.

Lieblich, A., Tuval-Mashiach, R., & Zilber, T. (1998). *Narrative research: Reading, analysis, and interpretation.* Thousand Oaks, CA: Sage.

Liebman, C., & Susser, B. (1998). Judaism and Jewishness in the Jewish state. *Annals of the American Academy of Political and Social Science, 555,* 15–25.

Lifton, R. J. (1993). *The protean self: Human resilience in an age of fragmentation.* Chicago: University of Chicago Press.

Litvak-Hirsch, T. L. (2006). The use of stories as a tool for intervention and research in the arena of peace education in conflict areas: The Israeli-Palestinian story. *Journal of Peace Education, 3*(2), 251–271.

Liu, J. H., & Hilton, D. J. (2005). How the past weighs on the present: Social representations of history and their role in identity politics. *British Journal of Social Psychology, 44*(4), 537–556.

Locke, J. (1998). *An essay concerning human understanding.* New York: Penguin. (Original work published 1690)

Lott, B., & Bullock, H. (2007). *Psychology and economic injustice: Personal, professional, and political intersections.* Washington, DC: American Psychological Association Press.

Louër, L. (2007). *To be an Arab in Israel* (J. King, Trans.). New York: Columbia University Press.

Lukács, G. (1971). *History and class consciousness: Studies in Marxist dialectics.* Cambridge, MA: MIT Press.

Lustick, I. (1980). *Arabs in the Jewish State: Israel's control of a national minority.* Austin, TX: University of Texas Press.

Lybarger, L. D. (2007). *Identity and religion in Palestine: The struggle between Islamism and secularism in the occupied territories.* Princeton, NJ: Princeton University Press.

Lynd, S., Bahour, S., & Lynd, A. (Eds.). (1994). *Homeland: Oral histories of Palestine and Palestinians.* New York: Olive Branch Press.

Maddy-Weitzman, E. (2005). *Waging peace in the holy land: A qualitative study of Seeds of Peace, 1993–2004.* Unpublished doctoral dissertation, Boston University.

Makdisi, S. (2008). *Palestine inside out: An everyday occupation.* New York: Norton.

Maoz, I. (2000a). Multiple conflicts and competing agendas: A framework for conceptualizing structured encounters between groups in conflict—The case of a coexistence project of Jews and Palestinians in Israel. *Peace and Conflict: Journal of Peace Psychology, 6*(2), 135–156.

Maoz, I. (2000b). Power relations in intergroup encounters: A case study of Jewish-Arab encounters in Israel. *International Journal of Intercultural Relations, 24,* 259–277.

Maoz, I. (2001). Participation, control, and dominance in communication between groups in conflict: Analysis of dialogues between Jews and Palestinians in Israel. *Social Justice Research, 14*(2), 189–208.

Maoz, I. (2004a). Coexistence is in the eye of the beholder: Evaluating intergroup encounter interventions between Jews and Arabs in Israel. *Journal of Social Issues,* 60(2), 437–452.

Maoz, I. (2004b). Peace building in violent conflict: Israeli-Palestinian post-Oslo people-to-people activities. *International Journal of Politics, Culture and Society,* 17(3), 563–574.

Maoz, I. (2006). Dialogue and social justice in workshops of Jews and Arabs in Israel. In M. Fitzduff & C. Stout (Eds.), *The psychology of resolving global conflicts: From war to peace* (Vol. 2, pp. 133–146). Westport, CT: Praeger Security International.

Maoz, I. (in press). Contact in protracted asymmetrical conflict: Twenty years of planned encounters between Israeli Jews and Palestinians. *Journal of Peace Research.*

Marcia, J. E. (1966). Development and validation of ego-identity status. *Journal of Personality and Social Psychology, 3*(5), 551–558.

Markus, H. R., & Kitayama, S. (1991). Culture and the self: Implications for cognition, emotion, and motivation. *Psychological Review, 98,* 224–253.

Marx, K. (1973). The material basis of society. In N. J. Smelser (Ed.), *Karl Marx on society and social change* (pp. 3–6). Chicago: University of Chicago Press. (Original work published 1846 and 1859)

Marx, K. (1978). Economic and philosophic manuscripts of 1844. In R. C. Tucker (Ed.), *The Marx-Engels reader* (2nd ed.). (pp. 66–125). New York: Norton. (Original work published 1844)

Marx, K. (1978). Theses on Feuerbach. In R. C. Tucker (Ed.), *The Marx-Engels reader* (2nd ed.). (pp. 143–145) New York: Norton. (Original work published 1888)

McAdam, D. (1982). *Political process and the development of Black insurgency, 1930–1970.* Chicago: University of Chicago Press.

McAdams, D. P. (1988). *Power, intimacy, and the life story: Personological inquiries into identity.* New York: Guilford.

McAdams, D. P. (1990). Unity and purpose in human lives: The emergence of identity as a life story. In A. I. Rabin, R. A. Zucker, R. A. Emmons, & S. Frank (Eds.), *Studying persons and lives* (pp. 148–200). New York: Springer.

McAdams, D. P. (1993). *The stories we live by: Personal myths and the making of the self.* New York: Guilford.

McAdams, D. P. (1995a). *The life story interview.* Evanston, IL: Northwestern University.

McAdams, D. P. (1995b). What do we know when we know a person? *Journal of Personality, 63*(3), 365–396.

McAdams, D. P. (1996). Personality, modernity, and the storied self: A contemporary framework for studying persons. *Psychological Inquiry, 7*(4), 295–321.

McAdams, D. P. (1997). The case for unity in the (post)modern self: A modest proposal. In R. D. Ashmore & L. Jussim (Eds.), *Self and identity: Fundamental issues* (pp. 46–80). New York: Oxford University Press.

McAdams, D. P. (2001). The psychology of life stories. *Review of General Psychology, 5,* 100–122.

McAdams, D. P. (2006). *The redemptive self: Stories Americans live by.* New York: Oxford University Press.

McAdams, D. P., & Pals, J. L. (2006). A new Big Five: Fundamental principles for an integrative science of personality. *American Psychologist, 61*(3), 204–217.

McDougall, W. (1921). *The group mind.* London: Cambridge University Press.

McKenry, P. C., & Price, S. J. (1995). Divorce: A comparative perspective. In B. B. Ingoldsby & S. Smith (Eds.), *Families in multicultural perspective* (pp. 187–212). New York: Guilford.

McLean, K. C. (2008). The emergence of narrative identity. *Social and Personality Psychology Compass, 2*(4), 1685–1702.

McLean, K. C., Pasupathi, M., & Pals, J.L. (2007). Selves creating stories creating selves: A process model of self-development. *Personality and Social Psychology Review, 11*(3), 262–278.

Mead, G. H. (1934). *Mind, self and society.* Chicago: University of Chicago Press.

Mead, M. (1928). *Coming of age in Samoa.* New York: Morrow.

Mead, M. (1970). *Culture and commitment.* New York: Anchor.

Memmi, A. (1965). *The colonizer and the colonized.* Boston: Beacon.

Memmi, A. (2000). What is racism? (S. Martinot, Trans.). In A. Memmi, *Racism* (pp. 183–196). Minneapolis, MN: University of Minnesota Press. (Original work published 1972)

Milgram, N. (1994). Israel and the Gulf War: The major events and selected studies. *Anxiety, Stress & Coping, 7*(3), 205–215.

Miller, N. (2002). Personalization and the promise of contact theory. *Journal of Social Issues, 58*(2), 387–410.

Mishal, S., & Sela, A. (2006). *The Palestinian Hamas: Vision, violence, and coexistence* (2nd ed.). New York: Columbia University Press.

Mishler, E. G. (1986). *Research interviewing: Context and narrative.* Cambridge, MA: Harvard University Press.

Mishler, E. G. (1996). Missing persons: Recovering developmental stories/histories. In R. Jessor, A. Colby, & R. A. Shweder (Eds.), *Ethnography and human development: Context and meaning in social inquiry* (pp. 73–100). Chicago: University of Chicago Press.

Mizrachi, N. (2004). "From badness to sickness": The role of ethnopsychology in shaping ethnic hierarchies in Israel. *Social Identities, 10*(2), 219–243.

Moghaddam, F. M. (1987). Psychology in the three worlds: As reflected by the crisis in social psychology and the move toward indigenous third-world psychology. *American Psychologist, 42*(10), 912–920.

Moghaddam, F. M. (2007). *Multiculturalism and intergroup relations: Psychological implications for democracy in global context.* Washington, DC: American Psychological Association Press.

Moghaddam, F., & Harré, R. (1982). Rethinking the laboratory experiment. *American Behavioral Scientist, 36*(1), 22–38.

Mohamad, H. (2001). Palestinian politics on the move: From revolution to peace and statehood. *Nationalism and Ethnic Politics, 7*(3), 46–76.

Mook, D. G. (1983). In defense of external invalidity. *American Psychologist, 38*(4), 379–387.

Morris, B. (1987). *The birth of the Palestinian refugee problem, 1947–1949.* Cambridge, England: Cambridge University Press.

Morris, B. (2001). *Righteous victims: A history of the Zionist-Arab conflict, 1881–2001.* New York: Vintage.

Moses, R., & Moses-Hrushovski, R. (1997). Some sociopsychological and political perspectives of the meaning of the Holocaust: A view from Israel. *Israeli Journal of Psychiatry and Related Sciences, 34*(1), 55–68.

Mosse, G. L. (1978). *Toward the final solution: A history of European racism.* New York: Howard Fertig.

Murray, H. A. (1938). *Explorations in personality.* New York: Oxford University Press.

Myerhoff, B., & Ruby, J. (1992). A crack in the mirror: Reflexive perspectives in anthropology. In M. Kaminsky (Ed.), *Remembered lives: The work of ritual, storytelling, and growing older* (pp. 307–340). Ann Arbor, MI: University of Michigan Press.

Naaman, D. (2007). Brides of Palestine/angels of death: Media, gender, and performance in the case of the Palestinian female suicide bombers. *Signs, 32*(4), 933–955.

Nadler, A. (2004). Intergroup conflict and its reduction: A social-psychological perspective (D. Reich, Trans.). In R. Halabi (Ed.), *Israeli and Palestinian identities in dialogue: The School for Peace approach* (pp. 13–30). New Brunswick, NJ: Rutgers University Press.

Nagel, J. (1998). Masculinity and nationalism: Gender and sexuality in the making of nations. *Ethnic and Racial Studies, 21*(2), 242–269.

Neiburg, F., & Goldman, M. (1998). Anthropology and politics in studies of national character. *Cultural Anthropology, 13*(1), 56–81.

Neslen, A. (2006). *Occupied minds: A journey through the Israeli psyche.* Ann Arbor, MI: Pluto.

Nelson, G., & Prilleltensky, I. (Eds.). (2005). *Community psychology: In pursuit of liberation and well-being.* New York: Palgrave Macmillan.

Nisbett, R. (2003). *The geography of thought: How Asians and Westerners think differently...and why.* New York: Free Press.

Nisbett, R., Peng, K., Choi, I., & Norenzayan, A. (2001). Culture and systems of thought: Holistic vs. analytic cognition. *Psychological Review, 108*(2), 291–310.

Okazaki, S., David, E. J. R., & Abelman, N. (2008). Colonialism and psychology of culture. *Social and Personality Psychology Compass, 2*(1), 90–106.

Opotow, S. (1990). Deterring moral exclusion. *Journal of Social Issues, 46*(1), 173–182.

Opotow, S. (2007). Moral exclusion and torture: The ticking bomb scenario and the slippery ethical slope. *Peace and Conflict: Journal of Peace Psychology, 13*(4), 457–461.

Oren, N., & Bar-Tal, D. (2007). The detrimental dynamics of delegitimization in intractable conflicts: The Israeli-Palestinian case. *International Journal of Intercultural Relations, 31,* 111–126.

Ostereicher, E. (1975). Praxis: The dialectical source of knowledge. *Dialectical Anthropology, 1*(3), 225–237.

Ouellette, S. C. (2008). Notes for a critical personality psychology: Making room under the critical psychology umbrella. *Social and Personality Psychology Compass, 2*(1), 1–20.

Palestine National Council (2001). The Palestinian National Charter. In W. Laqueur & B. Rubin (Eds.), *The Israel-Arab reader* (6th ed., pp. 117–121). New York: Penguin. (Original work published 1968)

Palestinian Central Bureau of Statistics (2005). Demographic statistics. Retrieved September 22, 2006, from http://www.xist.org/cntry/palestine.aspx

Pape, R. A. (2005). *Dying to win: The strategic logic of suicide terrorism.* New York: Random House.

Parekh, B. (2006). *Rethinking multiculturalism: Cultural diversity and political theory* (2nd ed.). New York: Palgrave Macmillan.

Parker, I. (2007). Critical psychology: What it is and what it is not. *Social and Personality Psychology Compass, 1*(1), 1–15.

Peacock, J. L., & Holland, D. C. (1993). The narrated self: Life stories in process. *Ethos, 21*(4), 367–383.

Peleg, I. (2004). Jewish-Palestinian relations in Israel: From hegemony to equality? *International Journal of Politics, Culture and Society, 17*(3), 415–437.

Peres, Y., & Yuval-Davis, N. (1969). Some observations of the national identity of the Israeli Arabs. *Human Relations, 22,* 219–223.

Peteet, J. (1994). Male gender and rituals of resistance in the Palestinian intifada: A cultural politics of violence. *American Ethnologist, 21*(1), 31–49.

Peters, J. (1984). *From time immemorial: The origins of the Arab-Jewish conflict over Palestine.* New York: Harper Collins.

Pettigrew, T. F. (1986). The intergroup contact hypothesis reconsidered. In M. Hewstone & R. Brown (Eds.), *Contact and conflict in intergroup encounters* (pp. 169–195). New York: Basil Blackwell.

Pettigrew, T. F. (1997). Generalized intergroup contact effects on prejudice. *Personality and Social Psychology Bulletin, 23*(2), 173–185.

Pettigrew, T. F. (1998). Intergroup contact theory. *Annual Review of Psychology, 49,* 65–85.

Pettigrew, T. F. (2003). Peoples under threat: Americans, Arabs, and Israelis. *Peace and Conflict: Journal of Peace Psychology, 9*(1), 69–90.

Pettigrew, T. F. (2008a). Future directions for intergroup contact theory and research. *International Journal of Intercultural Relations, 32*(3), 187–199.

Pettigrew, T. F. (2008b). The social science study of American race relations in the twentieth century. *Social and Personality Psychology Compass, 2*(1), 318–345.

Pettigrew, T. F., & Tropp, L. R. (2006). A meta-analytic test of intergroup contact theory. *Journal of Personality and Social Psychology, 90*(5), 751–783.

Phinney, J. S. (1989). Stages of ethnic identity development in minority group adolescents. *Journal of Early Adolescence, 9*, 34–49.

Phinney, J. S. (1990). Ethnic identity in adolescents and adults: Review of research. *Psychological Bulletin, 108*(3), 499–514.

Phinney, J. S. (1991). Ethnic identity and self-esteem: A review and integration. *Hispanic Journal of Behavioral Sciences, 13*(2), 193–208.

Piaget, J. (1932). *The moral judgment of the child* (M. Gabain, Trans.). Glencoe, IL: Free Press.

Pinsker, L. (1997). Auto-emancipation: An appeal to his people by a Russian Jew. In A. Hertzberg (Ed.), *The Zionist idea: A historical analysis and reader* (pp. 181–198). Philadelphia: Jewish Publication Society. (Original work published 1882)

Pinson, H. (2007). At the boundaries of citizenship: Palestinian Israeli citizens and the civic education curriculum. *Oxford Review of Education, 33*(3), 331–348.

Polkinghorne, D. E. (1988). *Narrative knowing and the human sciences.* Albany, NY: State University of New York Press.

Porter, T. M. (1986). *The rise of statistical thinking, 1820–1900.* Princeton, NJ: Princeton University Press.

Prilleltensky, I. (1989). Psychology and the status quo. *American Psychologist, 44*(5), 795–802.

Prilleltensky, I. (1994). *The morals and politics of psychology: Psychological discourse and the status quo.* Albany, NY: State University of New York Press.

Prilleltensky, I. (1997). Values, assumptions, and practices: Assessing the moral implications of psychological discourse and action. *American Psychologist, 52*(5), 517–535.

Punamäki, R. (1996). Can ideological commitment protect children's psychosocial well-being in situations of political violence? *Child Development, 67*, 55–69.

Punamäki, R., & Puhakka, T. (1997). Determinants and effectiveness of children's coping with political violence. *International Journal of Behavioral Development, 21*, 349–370.

Qouta, S., Punamäki, R., & El Sarraj, E. (2008). Child development and family mental health in war and military violence: The Palestinian experience. *International Journal of Behavioral Development, 32*, 310–321.

Qutb, S. (2000). *Social justice in Islam* (J. R. Hardie & H. Algar, Trans.). Oneonta, NY: Islamic Publications International. (Original work published 1953)

Qutb, S. (2006). *Milestones.* Cedar Rapids, IA: Mother Mosque Foundation. (Original work published 1964)

Qutb, S. (2006). *Basic principles of the Islamic worldview* (R. David, Trans.). North Haledon, NJ: Islamic Publications International. (Original work published 1960)

Rabinow, P., & Sullivan, W. M. (1987). The interpretive turn: A second look. In P. Rabinow & W. M. Sullivan (Eds.), *Interpretive social science: A second look* (pp. 1–30). Berkeley, CA: University of California Press.

Rabinowitz, D. (1992). Trust and the attribution of rationality: Inverted roles amongst Palestinian Arabs and Jews in Israel. *Man (N.S.), 27,* 517–537.

Rabinowitz, D. (2001a). Natives with jackets and degrees: Othering, objectification and the role of Palestinians in the co-existence field in Israel. *Social Anthropology, 9*(1), 65–80.

Rabinowitz, D. (2001b). The Palestinian citizens of Israel, the concept of trapped minority and the discourse of transnationalism in anthropology. *Ethnic and Racial Studies, 24*(1), 64–85.

Rabinowitz, D. (2002). Oriental othering and national identity: A review of early Israeli anthropological studies of Palestinians. *Identities: Global Studies in Culture and Power, 9,* 305–325.

Rabinowitz, D., & Abu-Baker, K. (2005). *Coffins on our shoulders: The experience of the Palestinian citizens of Israel.* Berkeley, CA: University of California Press.

Raviv, A., Raviv, A., Sadeh, A., & Silberstein, O. (1998). The reaction of youth in Israel to the assassination of Prime Minister Yitzhak Rabin. *Political Psychology, 19*(2), 255–278.

Raviv, A., Sadeh, A., Raviv, A., Silberstein, O., & Diver, O. (2000). Young Israelis' reactions to national trauma: The Rabin assassination and terror attacks. *Political Psychology, 21*(2), 299–322.

Reicher, S. (2004). The context of social identity: Domination, resistance, and change. *Political Psychology, 25*(6), 921–945.

Reicher, S., & Hopkins, N. (2001). Psychology and the end of history: A critique and proposal for the psychology of social categorization. *Political Psychology, 22*(2), 383–407.

Reuter, C. (2002). *My life is a weapon: A modern history of suicide bombing* (H. Ragg-Kirkby, Trans.). Princeton, NJ: Princeton University Press.

Ricoeur, P. (1992). *Oneself as another* (K. Blamey, Trans.). Chicago: University of Chicago Press.

Rodinson, M. (1973). *Israel: A colonial-settler state?* New York: Pathfinder.

Rogoff, B. (1990). *Apprenticeship in thinking: Cognitive development in social context.* New York: Oxford University Press.

Rogoff, B. (2003). *The cultural nature of human development.* New York: Oxford University Press.

Rogoff, B., & Angelillo, C. (2002). Investigating the coordinated functioning of multifaceted cultural practices in human development. *Human Development, 45,* 211–225.

Rogoff, B., Baker-Sennett, J., Lacasa, P., & Goldsmith, D. (1995). Development through participation in sociocultural activity. In J. Goodnow, P. Miller, & F. Kessel (Eds.), *Cultural practices as contexts for development* (pp. 45–65). San Francisco: Jossey-Bass.

Romann, M., & Weingrod, A. (1991). *Living together separately: Arabs and Jews in contemporary Jerusalem*. Princeton, NJ: Princeton University Press.

Rosler, N., Bar-Tal, D., Sharvit, K., Halperin, E., & Raviv, A. (2009). Moral aspects of prolonged occupation: Implications for an occupying society. In S. Scuzzarello, C. Kinnvall, & K. R. Monroe (Eds.), *On behalf of others: The psychology of care in a global world* (pp. 211–232). New York: Oxford University Press.

Rouhana, N. (1995a). The dynamics of joint thinking between adversaries in international conflict: Phases of the continuing problem-solving workshop. *Political Psychology, 16*, 321–345.

Rouhana, N. (1995b). Unofficial third party intervention in international conflict: Between legitimacy and disarray. *Negotiation Journal, 11*, 255–271.

Rouhana, N. N. (1997). *Palestinian citizens in an ethnic Jewish state: Identities in conflict*. New Haven, CT: Yale University Press.

Rouhana, N. N. (2004). Group identity and power asymmetry in reconciliation processes: The Israeli-Palestinian case. *Peace and Conflict: Journal of Peace Psychology, 10*(1), 33–52.

Rouhana, N. N. (2006). "Jewish and democratic"? The price of a national self-deception. *Journal of Palestine Studies, 35*(2), 64–74.

Rouhana, N. N., & Bar-Tal, D. (1998). Psychological dynamics of intractable ethnonational conflicts: The Israeli-Palestinian case. *American Psychologist, 53*, 761–770.

Rouhana, N., & Fiske, S. T. (1995). Perception of power, threat, and conflict intensity in asymmetric intergroup conflict: Arab and Jewish citizens of Israel. *Journal of Conflict Resolution, 39*(1), 49–81.

Rouhana, N., & Korper, S. H. (1996). Dealing with dilemmas posed by power asymmetry in intergroup conflict. *Negotiation Journal, 12*, 353–366.

Rouhana, N., & Korper, S. H. (1997). Power asymmetry and goals of unofficial third party intervention in protracted intergroup conflict. *Peace and Conflict: Journal of Peace Psychology, 3*, 1–17.

Rouhana, N. N., & Sultany, N. (2003). Redrawing the boundaries of citizenship: Israel's new hegemony. *Journal of Palestine Studies, 33*(1), 5–22.

Roy, S. (2004). The Palestinian-Israeli conflict and Palestinian socioeconomic decline: A place denied. *International Journal of Politics, Culture and Society, 17*(3), 365–403.

Rubinstein, D. (1991). *The people of nowhere: The Palestinian vision of home* (I. Friedman, Trans.). New York: Times Books.

Runyan, W. M. (1980). The Life Satisfaction Chart: Perceptions of the course of subjective experience. *International Journal of Aging & Human Development, 11*(1), 45–64.

Runyan, W. M. (1983). Idiographic goals and methods in the study of lives. *Journal of Personality, 51*(3), 413–437.

Sa'di, A. H. (2002). The peculiarities of Israel's democracy: Some theoretical and practical implications for Jewish-Arab relations. *International Journal of Intercultural Relations, 12*, 119–133.

Sa'di, A. H. (2004). Construction and reconstruction of racialised boundaries: Discourse, institutions and methods. *Social Identities, 10*(2), 135–149.

Sa'di, A. H., & Abu-Lughod, L. (Eds.). (2007). *Nakba: Palestine, 1948, and the claims of memory.* New York: Columbia University Press.

Sagiv, L., & Schwartz, S. H. (1995). Value priorities and readiness for out-group social contact. *Journal of Personality and Social Psychology, 69*(3), 437–448.

Sagy, S., Adwan, S., & Kaplan, A. (2002). Interpretations of the past and expectations for the future among Israeli and Palestinian youth. *American Journal of Orthopsychiatry, 72*(1), 26–38.

Said, E. W. (1978). *Orientalism.* New York: Vintage.

Said, E. W. (1979). *The question of Palestine.* New York: Vintage.

Said, E. W. (1994). *The politics of dispossession: The struggle for Palestinian self-determination, 1969–1994.* New York: Vintage.

Said, E. W. (2000). *The end of the peace process: Oslo and after.* New York: Vintage.

Said, E. W. (2003). *Culture and resistance.* Cambridge, MA: South End Press.

Salomon, G., & Nevo, B. (2001). The dilemmas of peace education in intractable conflicts. *Palestine-Israel Journal of Politics, Economics, and Culture, 8*(3), 64–77.

Sampson, E. E. (1993). Identity politics: Challenges to psychology's understanding. *American Psychologist, 48*(12), 1219–1230.

Sarbin, T. R. (Ed.). (1986). *Narrative psychology: The storied nature of human conduct.* New York: Praeger.

Sartre, J. (1948). *Anti-Semite and Jew: An exploration of the etiology of hate.* New York: Schocken.

Sasson-Levy, O. (2003). Military, masculinity, and citizenship: Tensions and contradictions in the experience of blue-collar soldiers. *Identities: Global Studies in Culture and Power, 10,* 319–345.

Savin-Williams, R. C. (2005). *The new gay teenager.* Cambridge, MA: Harvard University Press.

Schachter, E. P. (2004). Identity configurations: A new perspective on identity formation in contemporary society. *Journal of Personality, 72*(1), 167–200.

Schachter, E. P. (2005). Context and identity formation: A theoretical analysis and a case study. *Journal of Adolescent Research, 20*(3), 375–395.

Schiff, B. (2003). Talking about identity: Arab students at the Hebrew University of Jerusalem. *Ethos, 30,* 273–304.

Schwartz, S. J. (2001). The evolution of Eriksonian and neo-Eriksonian identity theory and research: A review and integration. *Identity: An International Journal of Theory and Research, 1*(1), 7–58.

Sears, D. O. (1986). College sophomores in the laboratory: Influences of a narrow data base on social psychology's view of human nature. *Journal of Personality and Social Psychology, 51*(3), 515–530.

Seeds of Peace (2010). Our mission. Retrieved from www.seedsofpeace.org/about/mission, May 15, 2010.

Seginer, R. (1999). Beyond the call of duty: The service of Israeli youth in military and civic contexts. In M. Yates & J. Youniss (Eds.), *Roots of civic identity: International perspectives on community service and activism in youth* (pp. 205–224). New York: Cambridge University Press.

Sen, A. (2006). *Identity and violence: The illusion of destiny.* New York: Norton.

Sen, A. (2008). Violence, identity and poverty. *Journal of Peace Research, 45*(1), 5–15.

Shafir, G., & Peled, Y. (1998). Citizenship and stratification in an ethnic democracy. *Ethnic and Racial Studies, 21*(3), 408–427.

Shafir, G., & Peled, Y. (2002). *Being Israeli: The dynamics of multiple citizenship.* New York: Cambridge University Press.

Shavit, Y. (1990). Segregation, tracking, and educational attainment of minorities: Arabs and Oriental Jews in Israel. *American Sociological Review, 55*(1), 115–126.

Sherif, M. (1958). Superordinate goals in the reduction of intergroup conflict. *American Journal of Sociology, 63*(4), 349–356.

Sherif, M., Harvey, O. J., White, B. J., Hood, W. R., & Sherif, C. (1961). *Intergroup conflict and cooperation: The Robbers' Cave experiment.* Norman, OK: Oklahoma Book Exchange.

Shlaim, A. (2001). *The iron wall: Israel and the Arab world.* New York: Norton.

Shweder, R. A. (1990). Cultural psychology—What is it? In J. W. Stigler, R. A. Shweder, & G. Herdt (Eds.), *Cultural psychology: Essays on comparative human development* (pp. 1–46). New York: Cambridge University Press.

Shweder, R. A. (1991). *Thinking through cultures: Expeditions in cultural psychology.* Cambridge, MA: Harvard University Press.

Shweder, R. A. (2003). *Why do men barbecue? Recipes for cultural psychology.* Cambridge, MA: Harvard University Press.

Shweder, R. A. (2004). George W. Bush and the missionary position. *Daedalus, 133*(3), 26–36.

Shweder, R. A., & Bourne, E. J. (1982). Does the concept of the person vary cross-culturally? In A. J. Marsella & G. White (Eds.), *Cultural conceptions of mental health and therapy* (pp. 97–137). Dordrecht, Holland: Reidel.

Shweder, R. A., & Sullivan, M. A. (1993). Cultural psychology: Who needs it? *Annual Review of Psychology, 44,* 497–523.

Silbereisen, R. K., Best, H., & Haase, C. M. (2007). Agency and human development in times of social change. *International Journal of Psychology, 42*(2), 73–76.

Silberstein, L. (Ed.). (2008). *Postzionism: A reader.* New Brunswick, NJ: Rutgers University Press.

Simmel, G. (1971). The stranger. In D. N. Levine (Ed.), *Georg Simmel: On individuality and social forms* (pp. 143–149). Chicago: University of Chicago Press. (Original work published 1908)

Sirin, S. R., Bikmen, N., Mir, M., Fine, M., Zaal, M., & Katsiaficas, D. (2008). Exploring dual identification among Muslim-American emerging adults: A mixed methods study. *Journal of Adolescence, 31*(2), 259–279.

Sirin, S. R., & Fine, M. (2007). Hyphenated selves: Muslim American youth negotiating identities on the fault lines of global conflict. *Applied Developmental Science, 11*(3), 151–163.

Sirin, S. R., & Fine, M. (2008). *Muslim American youth: Understanding hyphenated identities through multiple methods*. New York: New York University Press.

Slone, M. (2003). The Nazareth riots: Arab and Jewish Israeli adolescents pay a different psychological price for participation. *Journal of Conflict Resolution, 47*(6), 817–836.

Slone, M., Adiri, M., & Arian, A. (1998). Adverse political events and psychological adjustment: Two cross-cultural studies. *Journal of the American Academy of Child and Adolescent Psychiatry, 37*, 1058–1069.

Smith, C. D. (2001). *Palestine and the Arab-Israeli conflict*. Boston: Bedford/ St. Martin's.

Smith, M. B. (1969). *Social psychology and human values: Selected essays*. Chicago: Aldine.

Smith, M. B. (1994). Selfhood at risk: Postmodern perils and the perils of postmodernism. *American Psychologist, 49*(5), 405–411.

Smith, M. B. (2003). *For a significant social psychology: The collected writings of M. Brewster Smith*. New York: New York University Press.

Smooha, S. (1988). *Arabs and Jews in Israel* (Vol. 1). Boulder, CO: Westview Press.

Smooha, S. (1999). The advances and limits of the Israelization of Israel's Palestinian citizens. In K. Abdel-Malek & D. C. Jacobson (Eds.), *Israeli and Palestinian identities in history and literature* (pp. 9–33). New York: St. Martin's Press.

Smooha, S. (2002). The model of ethnic democracy: Israel as a Jewish state and democratic state. *Nations and Nationalism, 8*(4), 475–503.

Sofer, M., & Applebaum, L. (2006). The rural space in Israel in search of renewed identity: The case of the moshav. *Journal of Rural Studies, 22*(3), 323–336.

Spencer, H. (1969). *The man versus the state*. Baltimore, MD: Penguin. (Original work published 1884)

Spiro, M. E. (1956). *Kibbutz: Venture in utopia*. Cambridge, MA: Harvard University Press.

Spiro, M. E. (1975). *Children of the kibbutz: A study in child training and personality* (Rev. ed.). Cambridge, MA: Harvard University Press.

State of Israel (2001). Proclamation of Independence. In W. Laqueur & B. Rubin (Eds.), *The Israel-Arab reader* (6th Rev. ed., pp. 81–83). New York: Penguin. (Original work published 1948)

Stein, H. F. (1984). The Holocaust, the uncanny, and the Jewish sense of history. *Political Psychology, 5*(1), 5–35.

Steinberg, S., & Bar-On, D. (2002). An analysis of the group process in encounters between Jews and Palestinians using a typology for discourse classification. *International Journal of Intercultural Relations, 26*, 199–214.

Stetsenko, A. (2007). Agency and society: Lessons from the study of social change. *International Journal of Psychology, 42*(2), 110–112.

Stetsenko, A. (2008). From relational ontology to transformative activist stance on development and learning: Expanding Vygotsky's (CHAT) project. *Cultural Studies of Science Education, 3*(2), 471–491.

Stetsenko, A., & Arievitch, I. M. (2004). The self in cultural-historical activity theory: Reclaiming the unity of social and individual dimensions of human development. *Theory & Psychology, 14*(4), 475–503.

Strauss, A. L. (1997). *Mirrors and masks: The search for identity*. New Brunswick, NJ: Transaction. (Original work published 1959)

Suleiman, R. (2002a). Minority self-categorization: The case of the Palestinians in Israel. *Peace and Conflict: Journal of Peace Psychology, 8*(1), 31–46.

Suleiman, R. (2002b). Perception of the minority's collective identity and voting behavior: The case of the Palestinians in Israel. *Journal of Social Psychology, 142*(6), 753–766.

Suleiman, R. (2004a). Jewish-Palestinian relations in Israel: The planned encounter as a microcosm (D. Reich, Trans.). In R. Halabi (Ed.), *Israeli and Palestinian identities in dialogue: The School for Peace approach* (pp. 31–46). New Brunswick, NJ: Rutgers University Press.

Suleiman, R. (2004b). Planned encounters between Jewish and Palestinian Israelis: A social-psychological perspective. *Journal of Social Issues, 60*(2), 323–338.

Suleiman, R., & Beit-Hallahmi, B. (1997). National and civic identities of Palestinians in Israel. *Journal of Social Psychology, 137*, 219–228.

Sumner, W. G. (1906). *Folkways: A study of the sociological importance of usages, manners, customs, mores, and morals*. Boston: Ginn.

Suny, R. G. (2001). Constructing primordialism: Old histories for new nations. *Journal of Modern History, 73*, 862–896.

Tajfel, H. (Ed.). (1978). *Differentiation between social groups: Studies in the social psychology of intergroup relations*. New York: Academic Press.

Tajfel, H. (1981). *Human groups and social categories: Studies in social psychology*. Cambridge, England: Cambridge University Press.

Tajfel, H. (Ed.). (1982a). *Social identity and intergroup relations*. Cambridge, England: Cambridge University Press.

Tajfel, H. (1982b). Social psychology of intergroup relations. *Annual Review of Psychology, 33*, 1–39.

Tajfel, H., & Turner, J. (1979). An integrative theory of intergroup conflict. In W. G. Austin & S. Worchel (Eds.), *The social psychology of intergroup relations* (pp. 33–47). Monterey, CA: Brooks/Cole.

Tajfel, H., & Turner, J. (1986). The social identity theory of intergroup behavior. In S. Worchel & W. Austin (Eds.), *Psychology of intergroup relations* (pp. 7–24). Chicago: Nelson-Hall.

Talmon, J. L. (1970). *Israel among the nations: Reflections on Jewish statehood*. Jerusalem: World Zionist Organization.

Tamari, S. (1999). The local and the national in Palestinian identity. In K. Abdel-Malek & D. C. Jacobson (Eds.), *Israeli and Palestinian identities in history and literature* (pp. 3–8). New York: St. Martin's Press.

Tappan, M. B. (1997). Interpretive psychology: Stories, circles, and understanding lived experience. *Journal of Social Issues, 53*(4), 645–656.

Tappan, M. B. (2005). Domination, subordination and the dialogical self: Identity development and the politics of ideological becoming. *Culture & Psychology, 11*(1), 47–75.

Taylor, D. M., & Moghaddam, F. M. (1994). *Theories of intergroup relations: International social psychological perspectives* (2nd ed.). Westport, CT: Praeger.

Tedlock, B. (1991). From participant observation to the observation of participation: The emergence of narrative ethnography. *Journal of Anthropological Research, 47*(1), 69–94.

Teichman, Y. (2001). The development of Israeli children's images of Jews and Arabs and their expression in human figure drawings. *Developmental Psychology, 37*(6), 749–761.

Teichman, Y., & Bar-Tal, D. (2007). Acquisition and development of a shared psychological intergroup repertoire in a context of an intractable conflict. In S. M. Quintana & C. McKown (Eds.), *Handbook of race, racism, and the developing child* (pp. 452–482). New York: Wiley.

Tessler, M. (1994). *A history of the Israeli-Palestinian conflict.* Bloomington, IN: Indiana University Press.

Tessler, M., & Grant, A. K. (1998). Israel's Arab citizens: The continuing struggle. *Annals of the American Academy of Political and Social Science, 555,* 97–113.

Thabet, A. A. M., & Vostanis, P. (1999). Post-traumatic reactions in children of war. *Journal of Child Psychology and Psychiatry, 40,* 385–391.

Tilley, V. (2005). *The one-state solution: A breakthrough for peace in the Israeli-Palestinian deadlock.* Ann Arbor, MI: University of Michigan Press.

Tilly, C. (2004). *Social movements, 1768–2004.* Boulder, CO: Paradigm.

Triandis, H. C. (1989). The self and social behavior in differing cultural contexts. *Psychological Review, 96*(3), 506–520.

Turner, V. (1967). *The forest of symbols: Aspects of Ndembu ritual.* Ithaca, NY: Cornell University Press.

United Nations Development Program (2004). *Human Development Report 2004: Cultural liberty in today's diverse world.* New York: Oxford University Press.

Valsiner, J. (2001). Process structure of semiotic mediation in human development. *Human Development, 44,* 84–97.

van Gennep, A. (1960). *The rites of passage* (M. V. Vizedom & G. L. Caffe, Trans.). Chicago: University of Chicago Press.

Verkuyten, M. (2007). Social psychology and multiculturalism. *Social and Personality Psychology Compass, 1*(1), 280–297.

Vianna, E., & Stetsenko, A. (2006). Embracing history through transforming it: Contrasting Piagetian versus Vygotskian (activity) theories of learning and development to expand constructivism within a dialectical view of history. *Theory & Psychology, 16*(1), 81–108.

Vygotsky, L. S. (1978). *Mind in society: The development of higher psychological processes.* Cambridge, MA: Harvard University Press.

Vygotsky, L. S. (1986). *Thought and language* (A. Kozulin, Trans.). Cambridge, MA: MIT Press. (Original work published 1934)

Wallach, J. (2000). *The enemy has a face: The Seeds of Peace experience*. Washington, DC: United States Institute of Peace Press.

Wasserstein, B. (2001). *Divided Jerusalem: The struggle for the holy city*. New Haven, CT: Yale University Press.

Wasserstein, B. (2003). *Israelis and Palestinians: Why do they fight? Can they stop?* New Haven, CT: Yale University Press.

Wertsch, J. (1998). *Mind as action*. New York: Oxford University Press.

Wertsch, J. (2002). *Voices of collective remembering*. New York: Cambridge University Press.

Whyte, W. F. (1943). *Street corner society: The social structure of an Italian slum*. Chicago: University of Chicago Press.

Wright, S. C., Aron, A., McLaughlin-Volpe, T., & Ropp, S. A. (1997). The extended contact effect: Knowledge of cross-group friendships and prejudice. *Journal of Personality and Social Psychology, 73*(1), 73–90.

Wundt, W. M. (1916). *Elements of folk psychology: Outlines of a psychological history of the development of mankind* (E. L. Schaub, Trans.). New York: Macmillan.

Yiftachel, O. (2000). "Ethnocracy" and its discontents: Minorities, protests, and the Israeli polity. *Critical Inquiry, 26*, 725–756.

Zaal, M., Salah, T., & Fine, M. (2007). The weight of the hyphen: Freedom, fusion and responsibility embodied by young Muslim-American women during a time of surveillance. *Applied Developmental Science, 11*(3), 164–177.

Zajonc, R. B. (1968). Attitudinal effects of mere exposure. *Journal of Personality and Social Psychology, 9*(2, Suppl., Pt. 2), 1–27.

Zajonc, R. B. (2001). Mere exposure: A gateway to the subliminal. *Current Directions in Psychological Science, 10*(6), 224–228.

Zakrison, T. L., Shahen, A., Mortaja, S., & Hamel, P. A. (2004). The prevalence of psychological morbidity in West Bank Palestinian children. *Canadian Journal of Psychiatry, 49*(1), 60–63.

Zertal, I. (2005). *Israel's Holocaust and the politics of nationhood* (C. Galai, Trans.). New York: Cambridge University Press.

Zeruvabel, Y. (1995). *Recovered roots: Collective memory and the making of Israeli national tradition*. Chicago: University of Chicago Press.

Index